TANKS

TANKS

AN ILLUSTRATED HISTORY OF THEIR IMPACT

Spencer C. Tucker

A B C CLIO

Santa Barbara, California   Denver, Colorado   Oxford, England

Library of Congress Cataloging-in-Publication Data
Tucker, Spencer, 1937–
Tanks : an illustrated history of their impact / Spencer C. Tucker.
        p. cm. — (Weapons and warfare series)
Includes bibliographical references and index.
ISBN 1-57607-995-3 (hardcover : alk. paper)
ISBN 1-57607-996-1 (e-book)
1. Tank warfare. 2. Tanks (Military science) I. Title. II. Series.
                UE159.T83   2004
                623.7'4752—dc22

        04 05 06 07   10 9 8 7 6 5 4 3 2 1

This book is also available on the World Wide Web as an e-book.
Visit abc-clio.com for details.

ABC-CLIO, Inc.
130 Cremona Drive, P.O. Box 1911
Santa Barbara, California 93116-1911

This book is printed on acid-free paper.
Manufactured in the United States of America

CONTENTS

INTRODUCTION TO
WEAPONS AND WARFARE
SERIES

WEAPONS BOTH FASCINATE AND REPEL. They are used to kill and maim individuals and to destroy states and societies, and occasionally whole civilizations, and with these the greatest of man's cultural and artistic accomplishments. Throughout history tools of war have been the instruments of conquest, invasion, and enslavement, but they have also been used to check evil and to maintain peace.

Weapons have evolved over time to become both more lethal and more complex. For the greater part of man's existence, combat was fought at the length of an arm or at such short range as to represent no real difference; battle was fought within line of sight and seldom lasted more than the hours of daylight of a single day. Thus individual weapons that began with the rock and the club proceeded through the sling and boomerang, bow and arrow, sword and axe, to gunpowder weapons of the rifle and machine gun of the late nineteenth century. Study of the evolution of these weapons tell us much about human ingenuity, the technology of the time, and the societies that produced them. The greater part of technological development of weaponry has taken part in the last two centuries, especially the twentieth century. In this process, plowshares have been beaten into swords; the tank, for example, evolved from the agricultural caterpillar tractor. Occasionally, the process is reversed and military technology has impacted society in a positive way. Thus modern civilian medicine has greatly benefitted from advances to save soldiers' lives, and weapons technology has impacted such areas as civilian transportation or atomic power.

Weapons can have a profound impact on society. Gunpowder weapons, for example, were an important factor in ending the era of the armed knight and the Feudal Age. They installed a kind of rough democracy on the battlefield, making "all men alike tall." We can only wonder what effect weapons of mass destruction (WMD) might have on our own time and civilization.

This series will trace the evolution of a variety of key weapons systems, describe the major changes that occurred in each, and illustrate and identify the key types. Each volume begins with a description of the particular weapons system and traces its evolution, while discussing its historical, social, and political contexts. This is followed by a heavily illustrated section that is arranged more or less along chronological lines that provides more precise information on at least 80 key variants of that particular weapons system. Each volume contains a glossary of terms, a bibliography of leading books on that particular subject, and an index.

Individual volumes in the series, each written by a specialist in that particular area of expertise, are as follows:

Ancient Weapons
Medieval Weapons
Pistols
Rifles
Machine Guns
Artillery
Tanks
Battleships
Cruisers and Battle Cruisers
Aircraft Carriers
Submarines
Military Aircraft, Origins to 1918
Military Aircraft, 1919–1945
Military Aircraft in the Jet Age
Helicopters
Ballistic Missiles
Air Defense
Destroyers

We hope that this series will be of wide interest to specialists, researchers, and even general readers.

Spencer C. Tucker
Series Editor

PREFACE

And the Lord was with Judah;
and he drove out the inhabitants of the mountain;
but could not drive out the inhabitant of the valley,
because they had chariots of iron.

The Book of Judges 1:19

MENTION THE WORD "TANK" and most people think of an awe-somely powerful, seemingly unstoppable weapon. Tanks (often referred to loosely as "armor") may be defined as tracked, armored fighting vehicles armed with a high-velocity, flat-trajectory main gun designed for direct-fire engagement. This distinguishes them from artillery, which primarily employs indirect fire. Conceived in World War I as a means of ending the bloody stalemate of trench warfare on the Western Front, tanks were first employed by the British in September 1916 during the Battle of the Somme. Unfortunately for the British they were used in insufficient numbers and without sufficient thought or training in combined arms operations. The opportunity, if indeed it had existed, to win the war with this new weapons system was thus lost. By the end of the war, however, both the British and French were utilizing tanks in large numbers in their military operations.

Tanks reached their full potential only in World War II when, formed in entire divisions with infantry and artillery, they were the key element of the German blitzkrieg (literally, "lightning war") and early military triumphs against Poland and France and the Low Countries. Tanks were also immensely important on the flat plains of the Eastern Front. In the Soviet Union, however, the German blitzkrieg ground to a halt, because of the vast distances involved, the poor Soviet transportation system, and the breakdown in the superb German combined arms fighting combination. The Eastern Front was nonetheless the scene of the largest armor battles in world history. Tanks also proved vital in the fluid battles of North Africa and in the contest for France in 1944. They were less important when terrain and circumstance precluded their employment en masse, as in the mountainous terrain of Italy and in the jungle islands of the Pacific Theater.

Since World War II tanks have been a part of almost every major armed conflict. They helped secure victory for the State of Israel in the many Arab-Israeli wars. Indeed, these wars saw some of the largest tank battles. Tanks fought in the Korean War, in the wars between Pakistan and India, in the jungles of Vietnam, and in the long Iraq-Iran War of the 1980s, and they were a vital element of coalition victories in the 1991 Gulf War and the 2003 Iraq War.

There are many images of tanks at war. They include the ponderous, lozenge-shaped British machines of World War I trapped in the mud of the Western Front, German panzers on the plains of Russia, and the M4 Sherman medium tanks of Lieutenant General George S. Patton's Third Army racing across France. Most recently, there are the television images shown in real time of U.S. M1A1 and M1A2 Abrams tanks advancing across the flat terrain of southern Iraq.

Tanks are a powerful symbol of military force, but they are also an important sign of state power and authority. Thus in January 1996 the prime minister of India, P. V. Narasimha Rao, made a statement about India's progress as a military power by climbing into his nation's first indigenous-produced tank, the 56.5-ton Arjun. On occasion the reverse has been true, with the tank overwhelming the individual, as when the helmeted and smiling Democratic presidential candidate Michael Dukakis waved to photographers from an M1A1 Abrams tank. The Republicans seized on what was a rather unfortunate image and incorporated it into their campaign ads as somehow proof that Dukakis was soft on defense. Pundits cite this negative image as a factor in the 1988 presidential election.

There are abundant images of tanks as a powerful instrument of state power. Many of these are fixed in the mind, probably none more so than that of 5 June 1989, when nineteen-year-old Wang Weilin (first known to the West as "Tank Man") stepped in front of and temporarily blocked with his body the progress of a column of 40-ton People's Liberation Army NORINCO Type 69/59 main battle tanks moving down the Avenue of Perpetual Peace in Beijing to crush the student demonstrations at Tiananmen Square. The incident, its implications, and its use as a powerful symbol are discussed by Patrick Wright in *Tank: The Progress of a Monstrous War Machine* (New York: Viking, 2000), pp. 2–17.

There are many such moving images of individuals confronting this instrument of state authority: a young man hurling a rock at a Soviet T-34 tank during the 1953 East Berlin uprising; Soviet tanks crushing the 1956 Hungarian Revolution; students placing flowers in the barrels of Warsaw Pact tanks in Prague, Czechoslovakia, in 1968; and, more recently, Israeli Merkava tanks brushing aside private cars as if they were mere toys as the armored vehicles moved through Palestinian communities on the West Bank. Often tanks have been seen as symbols of awesome state power engaged in the repression of individual rights.

In warfare one of the constants is that superior doctrine and training may often compensate for shortcomings in both quality and quantity of equipment. This is most evident during the 1940 campaign for France. French tanks were more numerous than those of the Germans, and for the most part they had heavier guns and better armor. The French, however, persisted in thinking of their tanks in World War I terms as an infantry-support weapon, whereas the Germans concentrated their tanks in entire divisions. This truism of war was proven again in the 1960s and 1970s by Israel against the Arab states.

Another constant is that tanks, no matter how awesome they might appear, are, like any other weapons system, in constant danger of being overwhelmed by newer and more powerful weapons systems. This can be seen in the ever-increasing size of the main gun, from 37mm to 88mm and larger in the German tanks of World War II. These "landships" mirrored the constant race at sea between bigger guns and more effective armor protection. The small antitank missiles of today are only the latest in a number of threats to the tank.

One lesson of World War I, although it was not completely learned at the time, was that tanks were truly effective only when concentrated in large numbers in favorable terrain and with adequate logistics support. This truth was conclusively demonstrated in World War II. The German blitzkrieg worked well in the short distances of Poland and France, but it broke down completely in the great distances and formidable obstacles presented by a campaign in the Soviet Union. Also, Patton's Third Army had to halt in August 1944 when it could not be supplied with sufficient fuel, ammunition, and other supplies. Logistics arrested the Allied advance when the Germans could not.

Another key in armored warfare was the development of combined arms teams. The German panzers of World War II required infantry and artillery support, moving in trucks or tracked vehicles in order to keep up with the tanks. Air support was also vital. At least in open terrain, such as the deserts of North Africa or the Middle East, whichever side controlled the skies was in a position to wreak havoc on the ground troops and tanks below. The Germans controlled the skies in the Battle for France in 1940, and their accurate dive-bombing was an important factor in their victory there. The tables were turned in 1944. Not only did Adolf Hitler's panzers literally run out of gas in their December offensive in the Ardennes, but when the skies cleared Allied aircraft were able to devastate the German armor formations. The same was certainly true for the allied coalitions during the 1991 Gulf War and the 2003 Iraq War.

As with most modern weapons systems, tanks have also grown ever more complex and require specialized and highly trained personnel. The difficulty of utilizing poorly trained crews in inferior tanks was amply demonstrated in the 1991 Gulf War, when Coalition forces virtually wiped out the Iraqi armor at literally no cost to themselves.

This encyclopedia treats the development of modern tanks and armored warfare from their beginnings in World War I to the present. Unfortunately, even some 100,000 words do not permit a discussion of all tanks, and those of many nations have been excluded. The tanks included here are necessarily of the major military powers or those that had significant design influence. Although many more tanks are discussed in the text, the illustrated appendix provides information on 119 tanks. The criterion for inclusion in the latter is that these be significant either in design or in employment. I have also tried to include in the post–Cold War section the latest tanks of the major military powers that might be involved in armed conflict in the near future.

Weights of tanks are often confusing, as they might be expressed in British imperial tons (2,240 pounds), in U.S. short tons (2,000 pounds), or in metric tonne (2,205 pounds). For more modern tanks weights are usually expressed in kilograms (one kilogram equals 2.2046 pounds). In the text I have expressed weights as the nearest 100 pounds. In the statistical tables I have used exact weight expressed in pounds, although it must be pointed out that, even within the same type of tank, weights vary significantly. Speeds are assumed to be the maximum in optimum conditions for a paved surface, as opposed to speed over open ground.

The encyclopedia does not include armored fighting vehicles (AFVs) designed specifically to fight tanks (tank destroyers), self-propelled antitank guns, assault guns, or armored personnel carriers (APCs) and infantry fighting vehicles (IFVs). Most specialized vehicles, such as mine-clearing tanks, bridge-crossing tanks, flame-thrower tanks, and tank recovery vehicles, are also excluded, although I note these variants in major designs.

Although the focus in this encyclopedia is the tanks themselves, I have also tried to include some discussion of tactics and actual battles. Chapter 1 briefly discusses the history of armor in warfare and precedents to the tank. It then treats at length the British development of the tank and the employment of tanks in the war by the British, French, Americans, and Germans. Chapter 2 treats tank developments in the interwar period and also the principal theorists of armored warfare, including J. F. C. Fuller, Basil Liddell Hart, Charles de Gaulle, and Heinz Guderian. It also discusses how the various nations adopted or did not adopt the new ideas of armor deployment and how this was reflected in tank designs. Most especially it treats the German embrace of the tank and Germany's implementation of theories of high-speed mobile warfare. Chapter 3 traces tank development in World War II and the use of tanks in the conflict, especially on the Eastern Front, including some of the great tank battles. Chapter 4 addresses the employment of armor in the second half of the twentieth century, the period of the Cold War, including the Korean War, the Vietnam War, and the Arab-Israeli wars. Chapter 5 treats the post–Cold War period of contemporary tanks and discusses the world's major battle tanks and their employment in two wars with Iraq.

The section that lists the major tanks is an important part of this book. It includes statistical information and illustrations of major tank designs from World War I to the present. It lists such vital information as weight, speed, armor, armament, crew size, battle characteristics, and performance, and—if known—the number manufactured. Finally, I have included a glossary of terms and an annotated bibliography of leading works on tanks and tank warfare.

Fitting individual tank models within the chapter divisions presents some problems, as some span two different chronological periods. Thus the Soviet T-34 and the U.S. M4 are treated in both the chapter discussing tanks of World War II as well as that dealing with the Cold War. Also the Cadillac Gage Stingray, introduced at the end of the Cold War era, appears in that chapter, rather than in the chapter treating contemporary tanks.

I am most grateful for support for this project from the Virginia Military Institute and to the great help of two cadet assistants: now U.S. Army Second Lieutenant Alexander Haseley and Shelley Cox of the Illinois State Highway Patrol. Also I am most appreciative of the kind assistance of Major General Tom Tait, USA Rtd., former chief of cavalry and armor, U.S. Army; Brigadier General Philip Bolté, USA Rtd. and president of the U.S. Cavalry Association; and Jack Greene, who has written extensively about armored warfare in World War II. All three individuals have read the manuscript and have made many helpful suggestions. Any errors or omissions, however, are my own responsibility.

Spencer C. Tucker

TANKS

CHAPTER 1

Introduction of the Tank, 1914–1918

PRECURSORS TO THE TANK

Throughout the long history of warfare there is a constantly changing dynamic involving weapons, armor, and mobility. Combat vehicles are bound up in this. Vehicles have played a key part in war beginning in prehistoric times, when primitive man employed sledges to move heavy objects. In the ancient Middle East the armies of warring states utilized horse-drawn carts to transport weapons to the battlefield. Such carts then evolved into chariots, the elite striking force of ancient armies.

Chariots were in effect small carts, usually lightweight and two-wheeled, pulled by horses, which themselves often wore armor. Sometimes the chariots were armored. The chariots might also be fitted with sharp blades projecting from the whirling axles of their wheels that would act in the fashion of great scythes to mow down groups of infantry. Nobles and members of the royal family rode to battle in chariots, and at times they fought from them.

Apparently chariots were first introduced in Sumer in the Middle East about 2500 B.C. and were particularly dominant in warfare from about 1700 to 1200 B.C. The Egyptian chariot was a mobile firing platform for well-trained archers. The Hittites also fought from chariots, although with spearmen rather than archers. During the period 1100–670 B.C. the Assyrians developed chariot warfare to its greatest sophistication in Western Asia, with light chariots for archers and heavier chariots carrying as many as four spearmen. Chinese chariot warfare was similarly developed. Although chariots continued to be employed in battle for centuries thereafter, their effectiveness declined when they came up against well-organized cavalry as well as the dense phalanx formations of infantry developed by the Greeks and Romans.

Protective armor also developed. It was utilized by individual soldiers and by men working siege engines and battering rams against fortified enemy positions, especially castles. Siege engines might be protected by thick wooden boards on top and to the front and sides. Such armored siege engines might indeed be considered primitive precursors of the tank.

In the early Middle Ages mounted knights dominated the battlefields of Europe. Metallurgical improvements led to cheaper and stronger iron and lighter-weight steel armor. Because crossbow bolts and even longbow arrows could penetrate armor, the mounted soldiers demanded greater protection, and armor soon grew to the point where even a powerful warhorse, which was itself armored, could barely sustain the weight.

Firearms ended the era of the mounted knight. Gunpowder weapons, first introduced by the Chinese probably in the twelfth century, came to Europe in the fourteenth century. They were certainly employed by the English in the Battle of Crécy in 1346 during the Hundred Years' War. Firearms introduced a rough democracy on the battlefield, making "all men alike tall." Even the most unskilled foot soldier thus armed could slay an armored horse or its rider. The process whereby gunpowder weapons became dominant on the battlefield was a slow one, however, because early firearms were unwieldy, unreliable, and expensive.

The idea of marrying up firearms and some sort of armored vehicle found fruition in the early fifteenth century during the Hussite wars when Bohemian John Žižka, a follower of the Protestant revolutionary John Hus, modified ordinary four-wheeled, horse-drawn farm carts to carry small guns. Žižka's "battle-wagons" were the precursors of twentieth-century tanks and were employed with great success in the Hussite wars. Two types of carts evolved: the first an essentially defensive fighting vehicle with built-up sides to provide protection for up to 18 men, and a second type that mounted light cannon known as "snakes." The battle-wagons could be joined together end to end with extra protection in the form of heavy boards filling the meeting points between them, as well as the spaces underneath the carts between their wheels, in order to form a sort of mobile fort capable of being defended on all sides. Hundreds of these battle-wagons, capable of moving up to 25 miles in a day, were constructed, and they took part in perhaps fifty Hussite victories over a 14-year period.[1]

Many inventions have found application in warfare, and such was the case with windmills and gear trains, introduced into Europe in the early fourteenth century. These led to some early schemes for windmill-driven landships. Italian physician Guido da Vigevano designed such a machine in 1335, as did Robert Valturio in 1472. Leonardo da Vinci, a keen inventor as well as artist, in 1500 came up with a wheeled and armored "combat vehicle" that bristled with pikes and small cannon to be fired through slits and would be propelled by eight men working a hand-cranked transmission gear. Such a propulsion system was actually employed in the first submarines, the American *Turtle* (1775) during the War for American Independence and the Confederate *H. L. Hunley* (1863) during the U.S. Civil War.

The first practical railroad steam engine, invented by Englishman George Stephenson in 1825, provided a compact and more powerful power plant and led to a spate of suggestions for the production of armored, steam-powered land vehicles that could break through opposing infantry formations. But early steam engines were large, unreliable, and not very powerful. Despite this, a number of individuals saw the possibilities of an armored vehicle that could travel across country, span trenches and other natural obstacles, and at the same time mount guns and transport men. Kaiser Wilhelm II of Germany and futurist writer H. G. Wells were among those suggesting such a weapon.[2]

NEW TECHNOLOGIES

The real breakthrough in terms of a practical power plant was the internal combustion engine. Destined to revolutionize war, this small, reliable, efficient power plant utilized oil as a fuel. In 1882 German Gottlieb Daimler invented the first successful lightweight gasoline engine, and he deserves principal credit for the development of the automobile.

Another German, Rudolf Diesel, invented an engine in 1895 that helped to solve the fuel problem by using low-grade fuel oil. The diesel engine proved a tremendous boost to the submarine, which

needed an internal combustion engine that did not give off dangerous explosive fumes. These developments led armies to begin to experiment with motorized transport. In 1914, however, all armies still
relied on the horse to a considerable degree (as was indeed the case
for many armies, including the German, in World War II), and on
the battlefield most infantrymen moved on foot.

World War I, which began in August 1914, provided the first major test for military trucks and demonstrated the importance of motor transport in modern warfare. In 1914 General Joseph S. Galliéni
commandeered Parisian taxicabs to rush French troop reinforcements to the front during the September Battle of the Marne. Two
years later some 3,500 French trucks braved German artillery fire to
transport supplies along the 35-mile *Voie Sacrée* (Sacred Way) to the
French fortress of Verdun and carry out wounded. By war's end, the
major warring powers boasted a combined total of more than
200,000 trucks. The French were the most active truck-builders,
and by 1918 they had almost 70,000 trucks and steam tractors in
military service. The U.S. Army also experimented with truck transport. The 1916–1917 Punitive Expedition, commanded by Brigadier
General John J. Pershing, into northern Mexico in search of Pancho
Villa and his supporters established for army logisticians the superiority of supply by trucks as opposed to mules and horses.

Apart from motorcycles for communication and trucks for the
movement of men, it was inevitable that some sort of internal combustion engine–powered fighting machine would appear. In 1902
Englishman F. R. Simms demonstrated his fully armored Simms
Motor War Car armed with two machine guns and a 1-pounder. In
1906 no less than three designs appeared: from Daimler, from another German named Ehrhardt, and from the French firm Charron-
Girardot et Voigt. Each was a four-wheeled, light-armored truck
topped by a rotating turret. Indeed, Charron sold some of its armored cars to Russia that same year.

Virtually all warring nations experimented with armored cars. In
the United States Colonel R. P. Davidson invented a weapons carrier in 1898, but it elicited little interest from the army. Davidson
persisted, however. In 1915 he even led a column of eight Cadillac
combat vehicles from Chicago to San Francisco. These included the
first U.S. fully armored car. Capable of 70 mph, it sported a top-
mounted .30-caliber machine gun. The vehicles in Davidson's column included a kitchen car, a hospital car, a quartermaster car, and
a balloon-destroyer car mounting an upward-firing machine gun. Although the trip was a success and brought Cadillac considerable

publicity, the U.S. Army was not interested, and Davidson's efforts seem to have accomplished little more than elicit interest in improving the quality of the national road system.

The Italians were the first to use armored cars in war. Their Bianchi armored car saw service in the Italo-Turkish War of 1911–1912 and the Balkan Wars of 1912–1913. The Isotta Fraschini, another Italian armored car, was a large, boxlike vehicle with a revolving turret mounting a single machine gun.

The Belgians were the first to use armored cars in World War I. Lieutenant Charles Henkart armored two Minerva Tourers and employed them in the traditional cavalry roles of scouting and reconnaissance. Henkart's success encouraged the Belgians to armor other cars, but it was the British who led the way in the development of armored cars and, ultimately, the tank.

Because armor was as important as armament on a fighting vehicle, Commander Charles Samson of the Royal Navy partially armored two cars belonging to the Royal Navy Air Service. The two, a Mercedes and a Rolls-Royce, were the first armored cars to see action in the war. They lacked overhead protection, but each mounted a rearward-facing machine gun. The Rolls-Royce weighed in at 3.9 tons, had 8mm armor and a crew of three men, and was armed with a Vickers machine gun.

Such armored cars performed a variety of functions during the war, including reconnaissance, convoy protection, and mobile strongpoints. Armored cars were also used in limited situations to rescue downed fliers caught in no-man's land between the two opposing armies. Some, including a truck equipped with a 3-pounder gun, actually took part in infantry operations. The Germans also produced some armored cars. Despite the lack of encouragement from the German General Staff, Ehrhardt produced a turreted armored car in 1915, and Daimler built the Panzer Wagen, both of which saw action, principally on the Eastern Front. Italy also utilized them. But for a variety of reasons, chiefly their inability to cross torn-up ground and their light armament and armor, armored cars were not the answer to the battlefield impasse of trench warfare.[3]

Other new technologies were also transforming the battlefield, although the generals for the most part seem hardly to have noticed. Three developments particularly impacted land warfare at the beginning of World War I: improvements in the basic infantry rifle; the modern machine gun; and new, quick-firing artillery.

Bolt-action magazine rifles underwent dramatic improvement in the years prior to World War I. New smokeless powder and aerodynamically designed and downsized bullets (the Spitzer, or "boattail") led to higher muzzle velocity, longer range, and greater accuracy. These extended the battlefield, as well-trained defending infantry could break up charges by attacking infantry at far greater distances. The accurate long-range rifle fire of the British Expeditionary Force (BEF) was an important factor in the survival of the Allied forces in the West in the early weeks of World War I.

But it is the machine gun, more than any other weapon, that has been identified with World War I. American Hiram Maxim, working for the British firm Vickers, developed the first practical machine gun by the end of the 1880s. Early machine guns had used hand-cranking to fire the shell, extract the cartridge case, and then reload the gun. The Maxim used recoil energy in its functioning and was designed for utter reliability. It weighed only 100 pounds, was water-cooled, and had a five-man crew. Fighting against natives in Africa proved its awesome firepower. The impact of the machine gun in colonial warfare was well understood, but inexplicably its lessons for fighting in Europe were almost totally ignored, despite its proven devastating effectiveness in the conventional large land battles of the 1904–1905 Russo-Japanese War.

At 450–600 rounds per minute, one machine gun could equal the fire of 40–80 riflemen. It also had greater range than the rifle, enabling indirect fire in support of an attack. Light machine guns such as the excellent British Lewis Gun appeared later. Still, all armies in 1914 tended to regard the machine gun as a minor artillery weapon rather than one for infantry.

Important changes in artillery also occurred, the consequence of improved manufacturing techniques and tremendous advances in metallurgy, especially in steel alloys. New, slower-burning cannon powder produced more thrust against the shell and less pressure on the gun itself, allowing for lighter-weight artillery pieces.

The howitzer also increased in importance. This mid-trajectory, shorter-barreled weapon could fire at longer ranges than mortars. It came to be the preferred artillery piece in World War I because its high arc of fire allowed highly accurate plunging fire against enemy entrenchments. The Germans sensed the utility of the howitzer and augmented their corps artillery with batteries of it rather than field guns.

Steel guns appeared, machined to close tolerances. Then in 1891 both France and Germany developed systems in which the gun recoiled in a slide against springs that returned it to its original firing position. There were also new mechanical fuses, steel-coated projectiles, and high-explosive fillers. Such guns were quick-firing and accurate. The French 75mm gun was perhaps the best of its kind. Light, it could be managed with its ammunition caisson by four horses or even by two. Its mobility was matched by a superior rate of fire to its German rival, the Krupp 77. Its hydro-pneumatic recoil system meant a minimum of re-aiming. The French 75 could lob 20 shells a minute up to six miles. The French called it "The Father, Son, and Holy Ghost of Warfare," and they counted in 1914 on large numbers of these guns to support their offensive doctrine. The 75mm gun proved totally inadequate against German heavy field fortifications, however. World War I artillery in fact steadily increased in size. Larger, less mobile howitzers were more effective in smashing through heavy concrete defensive bunkers, an essential preliminary to any infantry assault.

Through the U.S. Civil War of 1861–1865 artillery was essentially a direct-fire antipersonnel weapon. Troops were usually safe from it if they were not in direct sight. An important change in artillery tactics occurred with aimed indirect fire. In 1882 Russian artillerist Carl Guk published a system for firing on an unseen target using a compass, aiming point, and forward observer; and by the 1890s most European armies had standardized the techniques of artillery fire, allowing for the massing of fire on remote targets. The Japanese refined this method, and in fighting against Russia they employed indirect fire with great success. Camouflage also came into use. During the 1899–1902 Boer War the Boers concealed their artillery pieces instead of exposing them in the open, as in British practice. New smokeless powders also meant that an artillery position would be more difficult to locate when the gun was fired. The machine gun notwithstanding, artillery was the great killer of World War I. Estimates claim artillery fire caused up to 70 percent of battlefield deaths.

THE BATTLEFIELD DEADLOCK

These technological developments changed modern war forever. By 1914 small numbers of machine weapons—particularly the machine gun—could destroy concentrations of men necessary to overwhelm a given number of enemy troops faster than the latter could be moved across the battlefield. In order for attacking infantry to advance, artillery first had to eliminate a defender's fieldworks, barbed wire, machine-gun nests, and artillery defenses.

The generals did not understand this, and the thinking of the general staffs of the major military powers tended to run in the old grooves. Most generals thought in terms of masses of men being thrown into battle armed principally with bolt-action magazine rifles and supported by light field artillery. Little thought was given to the implications for European warfare of the new technologies. The universal early expectation of a war of movement and rapid victory in 1914, almost realized by the Germans in August–September 1914, was followed by efforts on both sides to outflank the other (the so-called Race to the Sea). By the end of 1914, especially on the shorter Western Front, the war had settled down to the deadlock of trench warfare. Over time trench systems became highly sophisticated and were constructed in great depth, making it increasingly difficult for an attacker to smash through them. Tactical doctrine for the attack called for a prolonged preliminary artillery bombardment of enemy positions at a depth of 3,000 yards or so. For the first two years of the war the generals claimed that all that was necessary was a longer and more massive artillery bombardment in order to clear the way for the attacking infantry.

A heavy artillery preparation became the key offensive fire-support technique. The first large-scale preliminary bombardment of the war took place during the Battle of Neuve Chapelle, beginning on 10 March 1915. In the greatest artillery bombardment in military history to that point, 363 British guns fired on the German positions for 35 minutes. The attack failed, but the generals on both sides concluded that artillery needed to destroy everything in the infantry's path, and the more shells they could place on an objective, the easier the infantry's job would be.

In fact, long artillery preparations actually caused more problems for the attacker than advantages. They sacrificed surprise, alerting the defender as to exactly where the attack was coming. Often a defender could withdraw his front-line infantry entirely from the area being shelled, reinforce it, and then reinsert it once the preliminary bombardment came to an end.

The long artillery preparations failed to cut holes in the defender's barbed wire and indeed often made it worse for the infantry, tangling the wire further and forcing the attackers to bunch up at the few gaps. The shells also tore up the terrain, making it more difficult for the infantry with their heavy packs to cross no-man's land and impeding the movement of artillery forward to support the attack. The tearing up of the earth also prohibited the rapid forward movement of supplies essential to continue the assault. This in turn virtually guaranteed that attacks would falter as soon as the attacking infantry advanced beyond the range of their own stalled artillery.

By mid-1916 the war had degenerated into a dull, grinding struggle of attrition. The destruction by artillery doctrine reached its zenith (and finally demonstrated its own bankruptcy) during the great Western Front battles of 1916 and 1917. In February 1916 the Germans fired 100,000 shells an hour for more than 12 hours before their infantry attack at Verdun. The British Army began its July attack at the Somme with a seven-day-long artillery preparation, during which 1,537 guns fired 1,627,824 shells. When the British infantry began its assault on 1 July in straight linear formations, they had been assured that nothing could have survived the awesome shelling. Far from destroying the German barbed wire, as the generals had claimed would be the case, the artillery fire merely rearranged it and forced the attacking troops to bunch up in order to pass through. Sufficient numbers of German infantry survived the awesome bombardment; when it lifted they came out of their deep bunkers, set up machine guns in the new shell holes the British had just provided, and proceeded to mow down the attackers.

That day—1 July 1916—turned out to be the single bloodiest in British military history: almost half of the assaulting troops were casualties. The casualty rate for officers was a phenomenal 75 percent. In that single day the British sustained 57,470 casualties, 19,240 of whom were killed or died of their wounds. British losses that day exceeded their combined total for three wars: the Crimean War, the Boer War, and the Korean War. German losses were about 8,000 men, or one-seventh those of the British. The Battle of the Somme, which continued on into November, turned out to be the costliest of the war, claiming 1.2 million casualties.

Unfortunately for the British Tommies, their generals tried the same sort of thing at Passchendaele in July 1917. This time the artillery preparation was doubled. Over a 13-day span 3,168 guns of the Royal Artillery fired 4.3 million rounds at the German positions. The results were no better, and British losses for that five-month-long campaign ran to nearly 400,000 men.

Even if an enemy front were to be seriously cracked by these heavy blows, attackers could not take proper advantage of the situation because cavalry, the traditional exploiting arm, was vulnerable to massed long-range rifle fire, machine guns, and barbed wire. This did not prevent World War I armies from maintaining large numbers of cavalry for an anticipated breakthrough, although the numbers of horse cavalry, at least on the Western Front, diminished as the war wore on.

Although most ground commanders sought to break the deadlock by continuing the same tactics but with ever greater volume of fire and heavier guns, there were those on both sides who sought new methods. The Germans attempted new tactical doctrines with considerable success, whereas the Western powers chose to put their faith in new technology.

DEVELOPMENT OF THE TANK

It was logical that Britain and France would take the lead in new technology; after all, they were mounting the bulk of the attacks as they sought to drive the Germans from territory seized in Belgium and northeastern France. The Germans were for the most part content to remain on the defensive, hoping to win the war in the East while wearing down their antagonists in the West.

The armored car was not the answer to the impasse; its wheels made it impractical for navigating earth torn up by artillery fire and usually muddy from the high water table in northeastern France and the destruction of drainage systems by the shelling. A new weapon was required, one that could maneuver over the torn-up battlefield, break through masses of barbed-wire entanglements, and span trenches. The solution lay in an internal combustion engine–powered vehicle, but one that was tracked and armored as opposed to wheeled. Tracking was essential not only to allow navigation in battlefield conditions but also to distribute the heavy weight of the vehicle over a greater area.

In 1915 both Britain and France began development of armored and tracked fighting vehicles. Neither coordinated with the other, and the result was a profusion of different types and no clear doctrine governing their employment. Other nations—Italy, Russia, Japan, Sweden, Czechoslovakia, Spain, Poland, and the United States—produced tanks either during or immediately after World War I and during the 1920s, but only Great Britain, France, and Germany manufactured tanks that actually saw combat service in World War I, and Germany produced only a few.

The Royal Navy took the lead. This was the consequence of the Admiralty having been assigned the task of defending Britain from

German air attack, which in turn led to the stationing of British naval air squadrons at Dunkerque (Dunkirk) in northeastern France to attack German Zeppelin sheds and airplane bases in Belgium. These air bases required perimeter defense, and the new armored car squadrons provided it. To prevent these vehicles from moving about, the Germans cut gaps in the roads, and First Lord of the Admiralty Winston Churchill immediately called "for means of bridging those gaps." Throughout his long public life, Churchill remained immensely interested in military gadgetry and innovation. He was, in fact, quite proud of his role in the development of the tank.[4]

As the British increased both the numbers and efficiency of their armored cars in late 1914, trench lines on both sides reached the English Channel and it was no longer possible to outflank enemy positions. Now it would be necessary to go through these lines.

Even before the war, Churchill had opened discussions with retired Rear Admiral Reginald Bacon, who had been director of Naval Ordnance in 1909 but had retired to become general manager of the Coventry Ordnance Works. Shortly after the beginning of the war Bacon discussed with Churchill a plan for a 15-inch howitzer to be transported by road. Bacon believed that even the largest fortresses could not withstand bombardment from such powerful siege artillery. This was borne out a few weeks later in the German destruction of Belgian forts, most notably those at Liège. Churchill then entered into more talks with Bacon and proposed to the War Office that it contract with him to build 10 such guns. Secretary of State for War Field Marshal Horatio Kitchener supported the idea, and the guns were completed in time to take part in the aforementioned Battle of Neuve Chapelle in March 1915. Each of these great howitzers, along with its firing platform and ammunition, was moved in sections by eight enormous field tractors.

When in October 1914 Bacon showed Churchill photographs of the tractors, Churchill sensed the possibilities and asked him whether the tractors could be made to span trenches and carry guns and infantry, or whether another such vehicle could be constructed to perform these tasks. Bacon then produced a design for a "caterpillar tractor" able to cross over a trench by means of a portable bridge, which it would lay beforehand and then retrieve afterward. Early in November Churchill ordered Bacon to manufacture an experimental model. This showed sufficient promise that in February 1915 Churchill ordered Bacon to manufacture 30 of them.

The War Office tested the first of Bacon's machines in May 1915 but rejected it because it proved unable to meet certain conditions, including climbing a 4-foot bank or going through 3 feet of water, a feat not achieved by any tank to the end of the war. Churchill's order for 30 of the machines had already been canceled by the time of the first test because a better design had appeared, advanced by Lieutenant Colonel of Engineers Ernest D. Swinton.

At the beginning of the war Swinton was serving as deputy director of railway transport, but Kitchener made him a semiofficial war correspondent for British forces in France following public opposition to a ban on war correspondents in the war zone imposed by the French army commander, General Joseph Joffre. Swinton wrote his articles under the pen name "Eyewitness."

In traveling the front Swinton realized the deadlock imposed by trench warfare and above all by the machine gun. He envisioned "a self-propelled climbing block-house or rifle bullet-proof cupola." But on the evening of 19 October 1914, while driving by car to Calais, Swinton recalled a report on the California Holt tractor. Swinton believed the new war machine would have to have such a caterpillar track. Although Swinton claimed to have originated the idea, others were already experimenting independently with caterpillar tracks at the beginning of 1915.

Whether he originated the idea or not, Swinton certainly was the key figure in British tank development. Completing his assignment as a war correspondent, he returned to Britain to serve as assistant secretary for the Committee of Imperial Defence, known since the beginning of the war as the Dardanelles Committee of the Cabinet. Later in October Swinton met with the secretary of the committee, Lieutenant Colonel Maurice Hankey, and suggested to him the conversion into fighting machines of Holt gasoline engine–powered caterpillar tractors used for repositioning artillery. The process for converting the idea of a fighting "landship" into a practical machine had begun. It would be a case of plowshares being beaten into swords.

Well before the war, in Britain and especially in the United States, steam-powered tracked vehicles had been developed for agricultural purposes. As such tractors would have to move over plowed terrain, there was also considerable experimentation with both suspension and track linkage systems. Yet there was little enthusiasm for such machines for military use in the years before World War I. When a representative of the Holt Company of Britain tried to interest the German Army in a military tractor, for example, he was told, "No importance for military purposes."[5]

In December Hankey produced a paper supporting the idea of a military vehicle based on the farm tractor, which he then circulated among members of the War Cabinet. Churchill, who was already at work on the same concept with Bacon, supported it in a lengthy memorandum to Prime Minister Herbert H. Asquith on 5 January 1915, in which he urged the manufacture of

> a number of steam tractors with small armoured shelters, in which men and machine guns could be placed, which would be bullet proof. Used at night they would not be affected by artillery fire to any extent. The caterpillar system would enable trenches to be crossed quite easily, and the weight of the machine would destroy all wire entanglements. Forty or fifty of these engines prepared secretly and brought into position at nightfall could advance quite certainly into the enemy's trenches, smashing away all the obstructions and sweeping the trenches with their machine-gun fire and with grenades thrown out of the top. They would then make so many *points d'appui* for the British supporting infantry to rush forward and rally on them.[6]

Churchill proposed that a committee of "engineering officers and other experts" meet at the War Office to examine the possibility. Never patient where a new military idea was concerned, Churchill opined that something should have been done in this regard months before. He urged speed as well as the manufacture of different patterns. "The worst that can happen," he wrote, "is that a comparatively small sum of money is wasted."[7]

Prime Minister Asquith agreed and urged Kitchener, who supported the plan, to proceed. But the effort then bogged down in the War Department bureaucracy. Churchill continued to give some attention to the plan, and in late January he directed that experiments be undertaken with steam rollers that might be used to smash in enemy trench systems. This scheme proved unsuccessful. Then on 17 February 1915, Churchill met with some officers of the armored car squadrons and the conversation turned to discussion of the creation of "land battleships."

Three days later, on 20 February, Churchill ordered the formation of the Landships Committee at the Admiralty. By late March it had come up with two possible designs, one moving on large wheels and the other by tracks. On 26 March, on his own responsibility and at a cost of about £70,000, Churchill ordered manufacture of 18 landships: six wheeled and 12 tracked. A variety of designs now came forward, each registering improvements.

The failure of the Allied Powers to achieve a breakthrough on the

Western Front produced more support for the armored fighting vehicle concept, and that June Swinton drafted a memorandum for a means of overcoming the German machine guns. He also provided specific details of capabilities for such "armored machine-gun destroyers." Swinton called for the weapon to weigh about 8 tons, have a crew of 10 men, and mount two machine guns and a quick-firing 6-pounder gun capable of firing high-explosive shells. It was to have a 20-mile radius of action, 10mm thick armor, a top speed of not less than 4 mph on flat ground, a capability of traveling in reverse, the ability to carry out a sharp turn at top speed, a trench-spanning capability of 8 feet, and the ability to climb a 5-foot earthen parapet.

Arthur Balfour, who followed Churchill at the Admiralty on the latter's resignation in May over the failure of the Dardanelles/Gallipoli campaign, was sympathetic to the project, as was Minister of Munitions David Lloyd George. Under pressure from Field Marshal Sir John French, the BEF commander in France who demanded that the War Office research Swinton's ideas, the Landships Committee at the Admiralty became a joint army-navy group with the War Office director of fortifications as its chair.

Balfour approved construction of one experimental machine. The contract went to William Foster and Co., a manufacturer of agricultural machinery in Lincoln. William Tritton, managing director of Foster, had already designed a 105-hp trench-spanning machine as well as models of other armored vehicles and howitzer tractors. The prototype for the British government contract became known as "Little Willie." Designed by Tritton and Major William Wilson, who was assigned as a special adviser for the project, it ran for the first time on 3 December 1915.

Little Willie, the first tracked, potentially armored vehicle, bears a remarkable resemblance to its tank successors, or at least to APCs, into the twenty-first century. It weighed some 40,300 pounds, had a 105-hp gasoline engine, a road speed of 1.8 mph, and 6mm steel plating. Its set of trailing wheels, designed to provide stability in steering, proved unsuccessful, however. Although Little Willie was never armed, the top of the hull sported a ring with the intention that it would mount a mock-up turret. Little Willie went on to serve as a training vehicle for tank drivers.

As Little Willie was making its appearance, Foster was completing work on a battlefield version. Because the chief requirements for the vehicle were that it be able to cross open ground as well as wide trenches, Tritton and Wilson came up with a lozenge-shaped design with a long, upward-sloping, tall hull and all-around tracks on either

Little Willie. *Courtesy of Art-Tech/Aerospace/M.A.R.S/TRH/Navy Historical.*

side that carried over its top. These maximized the vehicle's trench-crossing ability. Because a turret would have made the machine too high, its designers mounted the guns in sponsons, one on either side of the hull. As it turned out, this was not a satisfactory arrangement. The resulting machine was first known as "Centipede," then "Big Willie," and finally "Mother."

Mother first moved under its own power on 12 January 1916. Thirty-two feet long and weighing some 69,400 pounds, it debuted on 29 January 1916 in Hatfield Park, within a mile of Lincoln Cathedral and under extremely tight security. A second demonstration on 2 February took place in front of British military and political leaders, including cabinet members. In Swinton's words,

> it was a striking scene when the signal was given and a species of gigantic cubist steel slug slid out of its lair and proceeded to rear its grey hulk over the bright-yellow clay of the enemy parapet, before the assemblage of Cabinet Ministers and highly placed sailors and soldiers collected under the trees.[8]

Although Mother met the expectations placed on it, even crossing a 9-foot trench with ease, Kitchener was unimpressed. He held to

Big Willie. *Image courtesy of Art-Tech/Aerospace/M.A.R.S/TRH/Navy Historical.*

his already stated belief that the new weapon was little more than "a pretty mechanical toy." But Kitchener was in the minority. Most of those in attendance were quite persuaded as to the new weapon's potential. The enthusiasts included Chief of the Imperial General Staff Sir William Robertson, Prime Minister Balfour, and Lloyd George. Balfour was even given a ride. Churchill was certainly correct when he wrote in his memoirs that Mother was "the parent and in principle the prototype of all the heavy tanks that fought in the Great War."

Another trial was held on 8 February before King George V. Three days later the BEF in France requested the new weapon be sent there, and shortly thereafter the government ordered 100 units (later increased to 150), with production to be overseen by a new committee.

Unfortunately, the perceived need to rush the new weapon into production meant that design flaws remained largely uncorrected. For one thing Mother was woefully underpowered. The 28-ton vehicle was propelled by a 105-hp Daimler engine, the only one available. This translated into only 3.7 horsepower per 1 ton of weight. Half of Mother's eight-man crew was engaged simply in driving it: one as commander, another to change the main gear, and two "gearsmen," or "brakemen," who controlled the tracks; the remaining four men manned two 6-pounders (57mm/2.25-inch) and two machine guns. The new machine was also insufficiently armored. Its 10mm protection could not keep out German armor-piercing bullets at close range, and a direct hit by a high-explosive artillery round would most likely be fatal.

The production model, known as the Mark I, was almost identical to Mother. It weighed some 62,700 pounds and had a top speed of only 3.7 mph—over rough ground only half that—and it had a range of some 23 miles. Its principal parts were a simple, steel box–type armored hull, two continuous caterpillar tracks, a 105-hp Daimler gasoline engine, and armament of cannon and/or machine guns. A two-wheeled trailing unit assisted with steering, but this was soon discarded as ineffective over rough ground and vulnerable to enemy fire. The clutch-and-brake method was then employed on the tracks but required four crewmen. And though it could span a 10-foot trench, the Mark I was only lightly armored in the mistaken belief that this would be sufficient to protect against rifle and machine-gun fire. Armor varied in thickness from 6mm to 12mm.

Turning the tanks was a time-consuming, difficult process. One British participant in the Battle of Cambrai recalled that rounds

were striking the sides of the tank. Each of our six pounders required a gun layer and a gun loader, and while these four men blazed away, the rest of the perspiring crew kept the tank zig-zagging to upset the enemy's aim. . . . It required four of the crew to work the levers, and they took their orders by signals. First of all the tank had to stop. A knock on the right side would attract the attention of the right gearsmen. The driver would hold out a clenched fist, which was the signal to put the track into neutral. The gearsmen would repeat the signal to show it was done. The officer, who controlled two brake levers, would pull on the right one, which held the right track. The driver would accelerate and the tank would slew round slowly on the stationary right track while the left track went into motion. As soon as the tank had turned sufficiently, the procedure was reversed.

In between pulls on his brakes the rank commander fired the machine gun.[9]

The Mark I came in two types. Half of them mounted two 6-pounder/.40-caliber naval guns in sponsons, or half-turrets, on the sides that provided a considerable arc of fire, with four machine guns; these were known as the "male" version. The "female" version mounted six machine guns and was intended to operate primarily against opposing infantry.

The name "tank," by which these armored fighting vehicles became universally known, was intended to disguise the contents of the large crates containing the vehicles when they were shipped to France. The curious would draw the conclusion that the crates held water tanks. The French made no such effort at name deception; they called their new weapon the *char* (chariot).

The Mark I was the mainstay of tank fighting in 1916 and early 1917, but it had notable defects. The stabilizer tail proved worthless; its fuel tanks were in a vulnerable position; the exhaust outlet on the top emitted telltale sparks and flame; and there was no way for a "ditched" tank to retrieve itself. Some of these deficiencies were addressed in the Marks II and III. These tanks appeared alongside the Mark I in early 1917.

The Foster Company manufactured 50 Mark II and 50 Mark III tanks. Produced in the same male and female versions and almost identical to the Mark I, they differed only in details. The Mark II, for example, had wider track plates fitted at each sixth link that distributed its weight over a larger area, preventing it from becoming as easily bogged down. The Mark III had improved armor. Superseded by the Mark IV, many Mark IIs and IIIs were converted into supply and specialist vehicles.

The Mark IV, also produced by the Foster Company, had the same general appearance as Marks I–III but incorporated further refinements. The most visible change with the Mark IV was in its smaller sponsons. These were swung inward rather than having to be removed for transport by rail. Armor protection was also increased because the armor of the Marks I–III proved incapable of keeping out German armor-piercing bullets. The Mark IV made much more extensive use of 12mm armor, which was sufficient to defeat an armor-piercing bullet and thus would leave artillery as the primary means of stopping the tank. The Mark IV also had an improved fuel-line system, silenced exhaust, and better ventilation. The Mark IV also employed the short version of the 6-pounder main gun, and .303-caliber Lewis machine guns replaced the Hotchkiss and Vickers machine guns of the earlier tanks. The female version mounted six machine guns. The air-cooled Lewis gun did not prove satisfactory as a tank weapon, however, and the Hotchkiss was reinstalled.

Ditching had proven a major problem with the earlier British tanks, and each Mark IV was equipped with a large wooden beam. It could be attached to the tracks by a chain, so that the tracks could pull the beam under the tank, enabling the tank to free itself. The Mark IV was also equipped to carry fascines (bound bundles of brushwood), which the tank could then drop into a trench as an aid in crossing it. More Mark IVs were produced than any other British tank of the war—1,015, of which 420 were males and 595 females.

The Mark IV was also the most numerous German tank of the war. Captured and repaired Mark IVs equipped four German tank companies and were known as the *Beutepanzerkampfwagen* IV (Captured Tank IV).

The Mark IV first appeared in the Battle of Messines in June 1917, but its greatest impact came in the Battle of Cambrai that September. Variants of the Mark IV also appeared, the most important of which was an unarmed tank tender, with a 125-hp Daimler engine, used to bring tank supplies forward.

The Mark V first saw action on the battlefields of France in May 1918 during the German Spring (Ludendorff) Offensive. Of the same appearance as its predecessor and the same crew size of eight men, it nonetheless incorporated important design changes, most notably a new transmission in the epicyclic gearbox, designed by Wilson. This was a dramatic technological leap forward, as it did away with the need for gearsmen; for the first time the tank could now be driven by one man. It also had a more powerful 150-hp, six-cylinder Ricardo engine, capable of propelling the 66,100-pound tank at a maximum speed of 4.6 mph with a range of 25 miles. All of its machine guns were of the Hotchkiss type. Viability was also improved, but the Mark V was not well ventilated. By the end of the war the Foster Company and the Metropolitan Carriage Wagon and Finance Company had built 400 Mark Vs (200 males and 200 females). Sixty Mark Vs saw action at Hamel on 4 July 1918, and 288 saw service at Amiens on 8 August 1918.

The final version of the basic Mother design was the Mark V*. Various manufacturers produced a total of 642 of this model. It differed from the basic Mark V tank by the adding of another machine gun (male with five, female with seven), and it was also heavier (73,900 pounds male and 71,700 pounds female). The Mark V* was 6 feet longer and could span a 14-foot-wide trench. It had a range of 40 miles. The Mark V* tank participated in the Tank Corps's final engagements of the war.

The Mark I through Mark V* were all heavy tanks. With the relative success of the first tanks, however, the British set out to develop lighter vehicles. Based on the prototype Tritton "Chaser," it became the Medium A tank, known as the "Whippet." Making its appearance in 1917, the Whippet was what became known as a "cavalry tank," an attempt to replace horse cavalry with an armored vehicle capable of exploiting a breakthrough of an enemy position. Foster produced 200 Whippets. The new tank weighed some 31,400 pounds, was powered by two 45-hp engines, and had a crew of three men. Armed with four machine guns, it had maximum armor protection of 12mm. With a maximum speed of 8 mph, it was twice as fast as the heavy tanks. Its range of 40 miles was also greater.

This first British light tank had serious disadvantages. The driver had the difficult task of combining the speeds of two separate engines to maneuver. Between them the commander and gunner had to man four separate machine guns that, while covering an arc of 360 degrees, were fired from a fixed cupola at the top of the tank rather than a rotating turret. Spare gasoline was carried outside the tank, which could prove to be disastrous in combat. Whippets saw service beginning during the Germans' Spring Offensive of 1918 through the end of the war that November.

The British also experimented with a truly heavy tank that would actually be protected against shell fire and might have been decisive. Designed by Tritton in 1916 and named the "Flying Elephant," this behemoth weighed in at some 222,600 pounds (111 tons) and was powered by two 120-hp Daimler six-cylinder engines. The engines drove both outer and inner tracks, the latter located near the center line of the hull to prevent "bellying," whereby the tank would become caught on higher ground between the two outer tracks. The Flying Elephant was 10 feet high, nearly as wide, and 29.5 feet long. It had 2-inch side and 3-inch frontal armor protection, a crew of eight men, and was armed with a 57mm forward-firing gun and six machine guns firing to the sides and rear.

This promising design never saw service in the war. Ready for testing in January 1917, it was abandoned because of its high cost, the demonstrated success of the Mark I, and the promise of the Whippet. Truly heavy tanks that would be capable of withstanding shell fire were left to the next war.

Even before the first tanks had gone into action the British were at work on more specialized tracked vehicles, one of which was a gun carrier. An adaptation of the Mark I, it was designed to carry a 6-inch howitzer through the initial German defensive zone in order to provide artillery support to advancing troops. Other tanks were modified to serve as troop carriers, supply tanks, and even signal vehicles.

FRANCE

Although the British built the first tanks, the French actually built many more of them (4,800 French tanks to 2,818 for the British). The French first became interested in a tracked vehicle in 1915, as a means to flatten barbed wire. Then, that December, a French artillery colonel, Jean E. Estienne, wrote General Joffre suggesting that the French build caterpillar-type vehicles similar to the Holt tractors he observed in use by the British to move about their artillery. Estienne, who stressed the need for speed in development, proposed an armored box that would mount a quick-firing gun.

In February 1916, following an investigation of the possibilities, Joffre ordered 400 of these from the Schneider Company and, shortly thereafter, another 400 from the Compagnie des Forges d'Honecourt at Saint Chamond. The first Schneider CA1 was delivered to the French Army on 8 September 1816. It was not an innovative design. It basically consisted of an armored box hull mounted on a Holt tractor chassis. The chief changes from the original design were that the Schneider had a crew of six men rather than four and mounted a short 75mm gun instead of a 37mm main gun. The Schneider weighed some 32,200 pounds and had a vertical coil suspension system. Double doors at the rear provided access for the crew, and there was a ventilator attached to the top. The 75mm main gun was mounted on the right-hand side facing forward; the Schneider also had two machine guns, one to each side. Maximum armor thickness was 11.5mm and its 70-hp liquid-cooled engine could drive the tank at a maximum speed of 3.7 mph.

The St. Chamond was far bigger than the Schneider. It weighed 50,700 pounds and had a 90-hp engine that produced a maximum speed of 5.3 mph. Dual controls allowed the tank to be driven from either end, but it had poor cross-country maneuverability. Its crew of nine men manned a 75mm main gun and four machine guns. Its 75mm, unlike that on the Schneider, was a normal rather than short-barreled gun. Unlike the British, the French did not place great emphasis on trench-spanning or cross-terrain capability in their armored vehicles and thus their types were inferior to those of their ally in cross-terrain capability. The Schneider could only span a trench of 70 inches, a major shortcoming. The St. Chamond could span an 8-foot trench. As with all the early tanks, the St. Chamond was mechanically unreliable; and with the moving parts of the engine exposed inside the tank, the tank interior was a dangerous place for the crew. The St. Chamond seemed superior on paper to

St. Chamond tanks moving to the trenches for the attack at Moyenville, Oise.
Courtesy of Art-Tech/Aerospace/M.A.R.S/TRH/Navy Historical.

the Schneider because of its superior main gun, longer track, and an electrical as opposed to mechanical transmission, which made driving it far easier. But its greater weight made it less maneuverable over soft ground, and the front of its hull projected well over the tracks, greatly reducing its trench-spanning ability. It also was far less reliable mechanically than the Schneider.

In 1916 the French army made the decision to refocus tank production on light, rather than medium, tanks. In July 1916, at the suggestion of Estienne, the French ordered an armored machine-gun carrier from Renault, to weigh 6 tons and be capable of accompanying assaulting French infantry. The result was the Renault FT-17, the prototype of which appeared at the end of 1916. Following trials in early 1917, the government placed an initial order for 1,000; later orders raised the total to some 4,000 of what would be the least expensive and simplest tank of the war.

The two-man Renault was powered by a four-cylinder, 39-hp gasoline engine and could attain a speed of 5 mph. This was not deemed a problem as it was designed to move at the pace of advancing infantry. Its armor was a maximum thickness of 22mm, which could be penetrated by a high-powered rifle with armor-piercing ammunition. The Renault was of simple design, constructed of flat steel armored plates. It had a fully rotating turret, the world's first. It mounted an 8mm Hotchkiss machine gun, later changed to a short 37mm (1.46-inch) Modèle 1916 "Trench Cannon" served by the tank commander in the turret. The second crew member was the driver. The tank had no chassis, the armored hull bearing the weight. The Renault's rear "tail" assisted in trench-crossing.

The little Renault could span a 6.5-foot-wide trench and had a 24-mile cruising range. From the spring of 1918 a new battalion of the Renaults joined the French field forces each week thereafter. The FT-17 first went into action at Ploisy-Chazelle on 31 May 1918. Throughout the remainder of the war the tiny Renault became the commonplace image of the World War I tank. The Americans began production of a Renault clone, the 1917 "6-Ton" in 1918, but none was delivered in time to see action. Other countries also produced variants, and it was exported after the war to Brazil, Canada, and China. The most numerous tank of World War I, the Renault was also the most common armored fighting vehicle between the two world wars. The French used it in colonial warfare, and it participated in virtually all armed conflicts of the period, including the Spanish Civil War of 1936–1939. In World War II the French army had eight front-line battalions of Renaults armed with 7.5mm machine guns. The Germans employed captured FT-17s in a variety of roles, including policing, and as tractors or mobile command posts. Renault FT-17s used by the Germans saw action as late as 1944.

UNITED STATES

The United States entered World War I in April 1917 and employed French and British tanks, aircraft, and artillery. This was because the Western powers' need for American soldiers was far more pressing than for military equipment. No American-made tank saw combat in the war. The U.S. Tank Corps, created in December 1917, for the most part employed the Renault FT-17 light tank, which was well suited to U.S. theories of mobile warfare. U.S. tank units, which made their first appearance in the September 1918 St. Mihiel Offensive, utilized both the Renault and the Schneider CA1 tanks. Another U.S. tank unit, the 301st Heavy Tank Battalion, served with the British army and was equipped with British Mark V and Mark

U.S. troops of the 27th Division training near Beauquesne on the Somme Front
with Renault FT-17 tanks, September 13, 1918.
Courtesy of Art-Tech/Aerospace/M.A.R.S/TRH/Navy Historical.

V* tanks. In 1918 the Americans began production of a Renault
clone, the 1917 6-Ton, but none was delivered in time to see action.

GERMANY

During World War I the Germans were not much interested in
tanks. After they recovered from the initial shock of the first tank
deployment, the Germans dismissed the tanks on the basis of their
September 1916 experience on the Somme and April 1917 performance against the Chemin des Dames as both unreliable and a
waste of effort; indeed, development of German tank warfare was
left to the next generation. The only German-built tank of the war,
the A7V, first went into action on 21 March 1918. This was the
opening day of Germany's great Spring Offensive, its all-out effort to
win the war on the Western Front before U.S. troops could arrive in
sufficient numbers to tip the balance in favor of the Western powers. On that day nine German A7V tanks saw action at St. Quentin.

German *Sturmpanzerwagen* going into action outside a French village, June 1918.
Courtesy of Art-Tech/Aerospace/M.A.R.S/TRH/Navy Historical.

The A7V *Sturmpanzerwagen* took its designation from the section of the General Staff responsible for its development and deployment. The A7V tank, which was to have been ready by November 1916, was not produced in wooden mockup until January 1917. Shortly thereafter the army ordered 100 of them. Appearing in prototype in October, the A7V was an armored box on top of a Holt-type chassis. A huge vehicle, it seemed to take its inspiration from Kaiser Wilhelm's fantasy battle machine of a decade earlier. Only 20 of them were ever built.

Weighing in at some 65,900 pounds and thoroughly unwieldy, the A7V was more than 26 feet long and nearly 11 feet high. Built by the Daimler Motor Company near Berlin beginning in the spring of 1917, the A7V was powered by two 100-hp Mercedes-Daimler engines. Capable of a speed of 8 mph on level, firm ground, and crewed by 18 men, the A7V sported poor-quality 30mm plate armor. The tank could span a 6-foot trench but only climb an 18-inch vertical wall.

The A7V was armed with one 57mm main gun at the bow and six machine guns, two on each side and to the rear. The hull overhung the suspension system and tracks, resulting in poor trench-crossing and cross-country capabilities. Each track could be powered separately, forward or backward, so the tank could almost "neutral steer," providing the short-radius turning normally associated with the modern cross-drive transmission found in later tanks.

The Germans were impressed with the new Whippet tanks and sought to counter them with a light tank of their own, the LK II ("LK" for *Leichte Kampfwagen*). Largely a copy of the Whippet in exterior form, the LK II, at 19,600 pounds, was considerably lighter than the Whippet and was actually better-powered with a 55-hp engine. One version mounted a 57mm gun and another sported two machine guns. The Germans planned to produce 580 of them, but the war ended before the LK II could appear on the battlefield. Sweden used it as the foundation for its Strv M-21 of 1921, the basis of that nation's tank technology.

EMPLOYMENT OF TANKS ON THE BATTLEFIELD

Early prophets of the new weapon thought of tanks in ambitious terms. Colonel Swinton, for example, believed they could be decisive in war. Rather than reveal them prematurely, Swinton wanted to build a large number of tanks and then employ them without the warning of a preliminary bombardment. As he put it in his highly perceptive January 1916 "Notes on the Employment of Tanks":

> Since the chance of success of an attack by tanks lies almost entirely in its novelty and in the element of surprise, it is obvious that no repetition of it will have the same opportunity of succeeding as the first unexpected effort. It follows, therefore, that these machines *should not be used in driblets* (for instance, as they may be produced), but the fact of their existence should be kept as secret as possible until the whole are ready to be launched, together with the infantry assault, in one great combined operation.[10]

Swinton understood what many generals did not, even well into World War II: that the success of the tank would hinge on the tanks working in conjunction with artillery and infantry in combined arms teams. Infantry would work closely with tanks, following closely as they crushed the barbed wire, crossed over enemy trenches, and destroyed opposing machine-gun nests. They could then exploit the breakthrough while artillery performed counterbattery work against enemy guns. Swinton also understood the need for the tanks to be able to communicate with each other and with their supporting arms by means of telephone or radio. Although this concept seems reasonable today, it was thought ridiculous at the time. At the same time, Swinton could not conceive of tanks operating independently. Tanks were merely a supporting arm to advancing infantry.

By the summer of 1916 the British and French were producing numbers of tanks, but unfortunately for the Allied side, there was no design coordination or joint plan for their use. The British, who had the lead in their production, were also the first to employ tanks in battle.

BATTLE OF THE SOMME

On 1 July 1916, as noted, the British began a massive offensive against German positions along the Somme. Field Marshal Sir Douglas Haig unleashed this offensive prematurely, in large part to respond to a desperate appeal by the French for a diversion to draw off German forces from Verdun. The Battle of the Somme developed into the deadliest engagement of the entire war. In fighting from July to November it claimed some 1.2 million men on both sides.

Despite the horrific casualties of the first day on the Somme, Haig continued the offensive in the belief that his men could indeed break through the German lines and end the war. Desperate for anything that might tip the balance, Haig called on the tanks, even though but few were available. Swinton opposed their deployment before they were available in sufficient numbers and the crews could be properly trained. But he was promptly overruled and replaced, not the last of the tank pioneers to be thus treated.

The men of the new force operated under the cover of the Armored Car Section of the Motor Machine-Gun Service. Many of those who were recruited to operate the new machines had little knowledge of soldiering. Training in driving (first with Little Willie), gunnery, and rudimentary tactics went forward, but one tank commander who took part in the subsequent attack on the Somme later wrote:

I and my crew did not have a tank of our own the whole time we were in England. Ours went wrong the day it arrived. We had no reconnaissance or map reading . . . no practices or lectures on the compass . . . we had no signalling . . . and no practice in considering orders. We had no knowledge of where to look for information that would be necessary for us as Tank Commanders, nor did we know what information we should be likely to require.[11]

Some of the men and their machines were then shipped to France. As a consequence of the feverish efforts to prepare for action, many of the crewmen were completely exhausted before they even got into battle. On the night of 13 September, the drivers, guided by white tape on the ground, with the tanks creating considerable amazement for those who watched them, moved into their assembly areas.

Shortly after first light on 15 September 1916, a new chapter in warfare opened when the tanks went into action. Of 150 Mark I tanks, only 59 were in France when Haig made the decision to employ them, and of these only 49 actually reached the front. Plagued by mechanical problems abetted by nervous crewmen, only 35 tanks reached the line of departure; 31 crossed the German trenches, and only nine surmounted all problems and pushed on ahead of the infantry.

The tanks were thus far from impressive in their debut, mostly because they were too widely dispersed and not used according to any plan. Their crews were also not well trained, and there was the spate of breakdowns. Regardless, the few tanks that did get into action had a profound impact on Haig; five days after the attack he urgently requested 1,000 more. Haig also demanded the establishment of a new central office charged with improving their fighting ability. Even before the end of the Battle of the Somme, Haig had created the Tank Corps Headquarters.

For the most part the Germans were not impressed. They saw the tank as simply a psychological weapon designed to affect the defenders' morale. Destruction of the tanks would be left to the artillery.

Astonishingly, the French and British worked on the new war weapons quite independently. As with the British, the French endeavored to keep their work secret; but unlike their ally, the French resisted the temptation to use the new weapon before they thought they had sufficient numbers. One can thus imagine the chagrin of the French to learn that the British had employed their tanks first. The French did not deploy their tanks until seven months later, during the April 1917 Nivelle Offensive on the Western Front.

In July 1916 Colonel Estienne had been reassigned from his artillery command at Verdun and attached to Joffre's headquarters in order to organize and command the French tank units, what became known as the *"Artillerie d'assault."* Estienne organized the tanks into groups (*groupes*) of 16 tanks each, each of which was organized as the artillery into four batteries of four tanks. Organization of the *Artillerie d'assault* began in August 1916 at Marly near Paris (the first group was organized that October). Later the French established a training center at Cercottes near Orléans. Estienne also established his headquarters at Champlieu, where a tank camp was also located. By the end of March Estienne had assembled there 13 groups of Schneiders and two of St. Chamonds. The crews were drawn from the army and even the navy, but for the most part they came from the cavalry, which was steadily being reduced in numbers during the course of the war. As with the first British tank units, the crews for the most part lacked any technical expertise whatsoever, although the French assumed that two to three months' training would be sufficient.

Much to Estienne's profound disappointment, the British employment of tanks at the Somme the previous September ended the possibility of a surprise mass attack and caused the Germans to widen their trenches. His original plan had been for a surprise mass attack against the German trenches in which the tanks would precede the infantry. Upon crossing the first trench line, half of the tanks were to pin down the German defenders with fire, allowing the infantry to flow through the gaps opened and secure the German trenches.

Estienne now scaled down his ambitions and developed new tactics. Under these, the tanks were assigned the more modest role of serving as a form of "portable artillery" operating in support of infantry. Their task was to accompany the infantry and reduce those pockets of resistance not wiped out in the preliminary bombardment. This became stated French armor doctrine into World War II.

Estienne's general order of January 1917 called for tank assaults to be mounted in early morning and in fog, if possible. Attacks were to be continuous with the tanks to be capable of moving at 2 mph for up to six hours to be followed by carriers transporting fuel and supplies. Estienne also stressed the need for thorough coordination beforehand with infantry, artillery, and aircraft. Infantry operating with the tanks were to be specially trained and would assist the tanks in crossing obstacles. Tanks were, however, free to move ahead of the infantry if unimpeded.

Although all 400 tanks ordered from the Schneider Works were to have been delivered by 25 November 1916, only eight were in army hands by that date. These were also of lighter construction, being built for training purposes. By mid-January 1917 there were only 32 training tanks. By April 1917, when their first tanks saw action, the French had 200 Schneiders ready, four times the number the British had used on the Somme. There were only 16 Chamonds available by that date, and the only ones to accompany the Schneiders were four unarmed vehicles used to carry supplies.

NIVELLE OFFENSIVE

At 6:00 A.M. on 16 April 1917, following a 14-day bombardment by 5,544 guns, the French army commander, General Robert Nivelle, launched a massive offensive against the Germans in the Champagne area of the Western Front. Touted by Nivelle as a means to break the deadlock on the Western Front, the offensive is known as the Second Battle of the Aisne and Third Battle of Champagne and also the Nivelle (or Spring) Offensive. Unfortunately the plans had been so widely discussed as to be an open secret; the Germans even captured a copy of the French operations order in a trench raid before the attack. The Germans had built a defense-in-depth and pulled back most of their front-line troops, which meant that the effect of the preliminary French bombardment was largely wasted against a lightly held German forward defensive zone. On 16 April General Joseph Alfred Micheler's 1.2 million–man Reserve Army Group attacked along a 40-mile section of front between Soissons and Reims, his objective the wooded ridges paralleling the front known as the Chemin des Dames. The brunt of the attack was borne by General Charles Mangin's Sixth Army and General Olivier Mazel's Fifth Army.

In the attack Mazel's Fifth Army deployed 128 Schneider tanks. Although they went into action the first day, they contributed little to the outcome of the battle, their crews finding it difficult to negotiate the rough terrain. St. Chamonds first saw action several weeks later at Laffaux Mill on 5 May 1917, but they experienced similar problems and indeed did not perform as well as the Schneiders. Many broke down during the long approach march and did not even make it to the battlefield. From the group of 16, only 12 made it to the line of departure. Several more were unable to advance, and three were destroyed in action.

The Schneiders and St. Chamonds had little impact on the outcome of the offensive, which the French called off on 9 May with only minimal gains. Far from winning the war, the Nivelle Offensive turned into near-disaster for the French army, as it led to widespread mutinies among the French front-line divisions. New French army commander, General Henri Philippe Pétain, charged with restoring the army, sought to improve conditions for the men and address their concerns. He told them he would not spend their lives needlessly and that he would remain on the defensive until such time as a true war-winning offensive was possible. "I am waiting for the Americans and the tanks," he declared.[12]

The British again used tanks in the April 1917 Battle of Arras. On 9 April 1917, the British began a diversionary attack along a 14-mile front to draw off German reserves from the Aisne. Haig's plan called for General Henry S. Horne's British First Army and General Sir Edmund Allenby's British Third Army to attack positions held by General Baron Ludwig von Falkenhausen's German Sixth Army. If these were successful, Haig planned to insert General Hubert Gough's British Fifth Army and exploit any breakthrough with cavalry. More than 2,800 guns supported the six-day attack. Haig also had 48 tanks, but in the Battle of Arras these were again distributed along the entire line, rather than used en masse, and they had virtually no effect in the battle, which was a British setback.

BATTLE OF CAMBRAI

Despite major battles along the Western Front in 1917 and attendant wastages of manpower and military equipment, the Western powers continued to build up their tank strength. Training and tactics also improved. By late November the British army had taken delivery of 1,000 Mark IVs, although fewer than half were ready for action. By that date also, the French had some 500 Schneiders and St. Chamonds.

The British also reorganized their tank forces. To head the now-renamed Tanks Corps, Haig selected Colonel Hugh Elles. In January 1916 Haig, informed of the tanks by Churchill, had sent Elles of his headquarters staff to England to investigate the new weapon, and Elles had provided a favorable report. Elles, a sapper by training, was soon joined by a skeptical infantry officer, Major J. F. C. Fuller, who became one of the most influential champions of armored warfare. Together the two men, and those working for them, gathered all possible technical information on the tanks and worked to develop new tactics for their employment. The men of the Tank Corps were also now thoroughly trained. Although the crews were most enthusiastic about their mission, the tradition-bound senior army leadership proved far more difficult.

Tanks first revealed their potential in the 20 November–5 December 1917 Battle of Cambrai. On the British side it involved 19 divisions and three tank brigades of General Julian Byng's Third Army. The Germans initially countered the British with six divisions of General Georg von der Marwitz's Second Army; later they committed 20 divisions.

From their first use of tanks in 1916, the British had deployed them in small packets. At Cambrai, however, they had more than 400 tanks under their own commander, Elles, now a brigadier general. These included 376 of the latest Mark IV model, the slightly more powerful but better-armored version of the Mark I. For the first time as well, tanks were the key element of the British plan and this time were used en masse.

Haig aimed his main attack at German-held Cambrai, about 35 miles south of Lille. This area had the advantages of firm, dry ground (essential for tanks), sufficient cover to assemble a large attacking force in secrecy, and a thinly held enemy line. The German defenses there consisted of a series of outposts in front of three well-constructed lines: the main Hindenburg Line and two secondary lines located about 1–4 miles farther back. A 13-mile-long tunnel, 35 feet below ground, allowed German reserves to wait and rest in safety.

Lieutenant Colonel Fuller, Elles's deputy, developed the initial attack plan, envisioning it as the first in a series of tank raids leading to a decisive battle in 1918. Haig and Byng, however, expanded Fuller's plan into a full-blown offensive designed to smash a 6-mile-wide gap in the German lines and capture Bourlon Ridge 4 miles west of Cambrai. As soon as that was achieved, Haig planned to launch five cavalry divisions through the gap between the Canal du Nord and the Canal de l'Escaut to disrupt the German rear areas.

The plan was overly ambitious for World War I conditions: success depended on complete surprise and the securing of Bourlon Ridge before the Germans could deploy their reserves. For their attack the British used low-flying aircraft to mask the noise of the arriving tanks. They also brought up 600 additional artillery pieces to provide supporting fire, without, however, benefit of registration.

The assault by nine tank battalions (374 tanks) followed by five

United Kingdom Mark V heavy tank with crib, disabled at the Hindenburg Line. *Courtesy of Art-Tech/Aerospace/M.A.R.S/TRH/Navy Historical.*

infantry divisions began at 6:20 A.M. on the dry but foggy morning of 20 November. Instead of a long and counterproductive preliminary bombardment, 1,003 British guns laid down a short but intense barrage on the German front line, then shifted their fire rearward to disrupt the movement of reserves and blind German direct-fire artillery with smoke. The tanks led, with each transporting at its front a large fascine, a large bundle of wood longer than the width of the tank and bound tightly into a round shape by chains or wire. This would enable them to cross the antitank ditches, some up to 13 feet wide, that the Germans had constructed along the length of the Hindenburg Line.

Fuller had worked out the details of the attack carefully. Closely followed by the infantry, the British tanks advanced in small groups in open order rather than in the usual extended line assault formation. They worked in teams of three, with each having a well-defined task. The first would crush a gap in the wire and, without crossing the enemy trench, turn left to work down the near side of the front trench and sweep it with machine-gun fire. The second would drop its fascine into the German trench and use it to cross over the trench before turning left to work down the far side. The third then would move to the support trench, drop its fascine to cross, and also turn left. With their fascines, each team of tanks would be able to cross three obstacles. The plan was that the infantry would then mop up survivors, secure the captured trenches against any German counterattack, and prepare for the next move forward by the tanks.

On the first day the attack went largely according to plan. The tanks easily breached the German wire, pressing it flat and leaving a clear path for the following infantry. Most German infantry simply panicked and fled. At Masnières, however, the Germans blew a bridge while a tank was crossing the canal there, forcing the British infantry to fight without tank support and impeding its progress. The chief obstacle was at Flesquières, where a British infantry division came under withering German fire. More than a dozen tanks were knocked out in succession by German guns firing from behind well-sited and camouflaged concrete bunkers. One of the myths of the battle is that here one German defender knocked out up to 16 tanks with a single field gun.

The engagement at Flesquières unhinged the infantry-tank team. Had the British infantry been able to operate with the tanks, the German artillery pieces might have been destroyed. The lesson of the fighting at Flesquières was clear: In order to be successful, tanks, infantry, and artillery all had to work in tandem.

By nightfall the British had penetrated the Hindenburg Line up to 5 miles in depth. In Britain church bells rang out in celebration, but it was premature. The Germans held at Bourlon Ridge, and Bavarian Crown Prince Rupprecht rushed up reserves to plug the gap. Because of their heavy losses in the Battle of Passchendaele (Third Ypres) during 31 July–10 November, the British lacked sufficient infantry reserves to counter them. They also did not have tank reserves; too many tanks had been deployed in the first two waves and were either knocked out by German field guns or, more often, suffered mechanical breakdowns. In the first day 65 tanks were lost to enemy action, 71 broke down, and 43 were stuck. The great tank armada no longer existed. The next day, when the British resumed their attack, cooperative action between tanks and infantry largely ended and the battle reverted to the typical World War I pattern.

Although they gained a foothold, the British never completely captured Bourlon Ridge. In the week that followed, virtually no more gains were made. Reinforced to 20 divisions, the Germans mounted a counterattack beginning on 29 November. Utilizing new infiltration assault techniques, they also made effective use of ground-attack aircraft.

On 3 December Haig ordered a partial withdrawal. When the battle finally ended two days later, the Germans had retaken 75 percent of the territory lost on the first day and even made inroads into the original British positions in the extreme south. In the battle the British lost about 44,000 men, 166 guns, and 300 tanks; German casualties were equally heavy: more than 41,000 men and 142 guns.

Despite the failure to realize Haig's hopes, the Battle of Cambrai restored surprise as an attack element on the Western Front. It also showed that the tank and infiltration tactics could restore battlefield fluidity, which would be a hallmark of fighting on the Western Front in 1918.

Meanwhile revolution gripped Russia. The Bolsheviks seized power in early November 1917 and shortly thereafter took Russia out of the war. This enabled the Germans to shift substantial resources west. By the third week in March 1918 all was ready, and the Germans launched their great Spring Offensive, a final supreme effort to win the war. On 31 March 1918, the Germans put five captured British Mark IV tanks into action at St. Quentin.

German tank tactics consisted merely of "mopping up strongpoints," and there was no appreciation of the need for tanks to cooperate with other fighting arms. German tank units were organized into sections (*Abteilungen*) of five vehicles each. The German Tank Corps consisted of four sections of A7V tanks and five of captured British tanks. At no time during the war did German tank strength exceed 40: 15 AFVs and 25 captured British models. The Germans also never employed more than 25 at any one time. Tank crews came from three different army branches. Artillerymen had charge of the main gun, infantry manned the machine guns, and mechanics drove and maintained the tank itself. This policy did not make for a cohesive team effort, and German Tank Corps morale tended to be poor, no doubt also because the crews knew their tanks were ineffective.

On 24 April 1918, during part of the Spring Offensive, dubbed Operation GEORGETTE, the Germans attacked toward Amiens from Villers-Bretonneux. This battle is notable in that it featured the first tank-versus-tank engagement in history. In their advance the Germans employed 13 A7V tanks, moving them forward in three groups in thick mist. The presence of the German tanks drew British tanks, of which there were 20 in the vicinity: 13 Mark IVs and seven Whippets. One British participant recalled,

Opening a loophole, I looked out. There, some 300 yards away, a round, squat-looking monster was advancing: behind it came waves of infantry, and further away to the left and right crawled two more of these armoured tortoises. So we had met our rivals at last![13]

At a range of about 200 yards the center group of six German tanks exchanged fire with a section of three British Mark IV tanks and hit both females with shells that opened large holes in their sides, rendering them defenseless and forcing them to retire. As the infantry in the trenches looked on, the duel continued. The German tanks came under 6-pounder cannon fire from the male Mark IV; one was knocked out and the other driven back. Some 6-pounder canister shot broke up the German infantry assault. The British male Mark IV was soon disabled by a direct hit from a German artillery shell, forcing its crew members to seek refuge in an infantry trench.

Later one of the German tanks in the southernmost group knocked out one of the British Whippets. This first tank-to-tank battle in history underscored the need for tanks to have an antitank capability. That night the British launched a counterattack and drove the Germans back.

On 28 May Schneider tanks supported the U.S. 1st Division in its attack on the village of Cantigny. Following the battle, Lieutenant Colonel George S. Patton interviewed the French tank leaders in order to capitalize on the lessons for the American Light Tank School at Langres.

The last great German offensive effort came during the Second Battle of the Marne in mid-July 1918. Here the strategic initiative passed to the Entente powers. Even as the struggle to control the city of Reims raged, Allied Supreme Commander General Ferdinand Foch husbanded a reserve of 20 divisions—two American and 18 French—and 350 tanks. On 18 July Foch launched a counteroffensive with the Tenth Army and Sixth Army to its right. The American Expeditionary Forces (AEF) 1st and 2nd Divisions spearheaded the Tenth's attack, which fell on the right side of the Reims Salient about 5 miles south of German-held Soissons.

Although casualties were heavy for the Allies (the 1st Division sustained 7,200 men killed and wounded that day and the 2nd Division nearly 5,000), the attack succeeded brilliantly. The 1st Division captured 3,800 prisoners and 70 guns from the seven German divisions it encountered; the 2nd Division took 3,000 prisoners and 75 guns. In all, the Allies captured 12,000 prisoners and 250 guns from 11 German divisions. The Second Battle of the Marne ended the threat to Paris, and from this point on the Allies were advancing and the Germans were on the defensive. On 20 July Ludendorff called off his planned Flanders drive to concentrate on holding the area to the south, but he rejected sound advice that the army retire to the Hindenburg Line.

A week later Allied commanders met in Paris, where Foch, promoted by Premier Georges Clemenceau to marshal of France on 6 August, informed them of his plans for a series of attacks from Flanders to the Marne that would allow the Germans no respite. The first of these was known as the Amiens Offensive. Lasting from 8 August to 4 September and aimed at reducing the second German salient south of the Somme, Foch entrusted it to Haig, whose ideas dominated the remainder of the 1918 campaign.

Haig's Allied army group consisted of the Fourth British Army and the First French Army. Fourth Army had been considerably enlarged to 14 infantry and three cavalry divisions of British, Canadian, and Australian troops and two U.S. regiments. It also had 2,070 artillery pieces (684 of them heavy), 430 tanks (including 324 Mark Vs and a number of new Whippet tanks that acted as cavalry), 12 armored cars, and 800 aircraft. The French First Army had seven divisions, 1,066 guns (826 heavy), 90 tanks, and 1,104 aircraft. Opposing them was Marwitz's German Second Army of 14 divisions (four of which were in reserve), 749 guns (289 heavy), and 365 aircraft.

The Allies made every effort to ensure secrecy and employ combined arms concepts. This included the use of not only tanks but also armored cars operating in the place of cavalry as an exploitation arm. The day of 8 August was one of the most important of the war. Early that morning, protected by heavy ground fog, the tanks rumbled forward. Simultaneously, Allied artillery opened up in heavy barrage, and the infantry "went over the top." The main blow, delivered by the Canadians and Australians, came south of the Somme. The day really belonged to the tanks; only north of the river, where the British had few tanks, was there significant German resistance. Once they had pried open the front, the British introduced armored cars. These ranged freely in the German rear areas, disrupting German troop concentrations, impeding the arrival of reinforcements, forcing the Germans to evacuate their headquarters at Famerville, and even destroying a German train.

By the end of the first day, at little cost to themselves, the British had advanced up to 6 miles along a 12-mile front. They had also inflicted nearly 28,000 casualties (almost 16,000 prisoners) and taken 400 guns. Ludendorff wrote in his memoirs that "August the 8th was the black day of the German Army in the history of this war."[14]

Ludendorff's assessment was not for the ground lost but the large number of Germans who surrendered after at most token resistance. The three-day total was some 75,000 German casualties (30,000 prisoners) and 500 guns with Allied losses of approximately 45,000 men. By 9 September the Allies had retaken all the territory lost to the Germans in the Spring Offensive. The Amiens Offensive revealed the collapse of German fighting ability following the spring offensives and paralleled war weariness in Germany. By September the British tanks, now equipped with "cribs," a new cylindrical frame that could be lowered in a trench in front of the tank to ease its passage, had smashed their way through the Hindenburg Line.

Tanks were now an accepted and integral part of any battlefield offensive. On 8 October Haig initiated the Second Battle of Cambrai. Launched along an 18-mile front, it involved Byng's Third Army and General Sir Henry Rawlinson's Fourth Army and 82 tanks, all that the Tank Corps had available after the heavy losses sustained in the early August attack at Amiens.

The battle was noteworthy in that it saw a rare counterattack by German tanks and was only the second tank-versus-tank battle of the war. The Germans employed captured Mark IVs in groups of four or five near Awoing. The British knocked out two of the German tanks, one with a 6-pounder shell from a British tank and the other apparently by a shell fired by a captured German artillery piece laid by a British tank section commander.

With the German armies crumbling before the advancing Allies on the Western Front and Austria-Hungary fast breaking up, the German military trotted out the political leaders to secure an armistice. Later this enabled the same German generals to proclaim the lie that the army had not been defeated in the field but rather "stabbed in the back" by the "November criminals." The armistice went into effect on 11 November 1918, and the guns at last fell silent. Tanks and airplanes were now an established part of the battlefield.

ENDNOTES

1. Kenneth Macksey and John H. Batchelor, *Tank: A History of the Armoured Fighting Vehicle.* New York: Charles Scribner's Sons, 1970, p. 6.

2. Ibid., pp. 6–9.

3. Ibid., pp. 9–10, 17; Stephen M. Cullen, "Armored Cars," in *The European Powers in the First World War: An Encyclopedia,* edited by Spencer C. Tucker. New York: Garland, 1996, pp. 65–66.

4. Winston S. Churchill, *The World Crisis, 1914–1918*, vol. 2. New York: Charles Scribner's Sons, 1923, p. 61.

5. Macksey and Batchelor, *Tank: A History*, p. 20.

6. Ibid., p. 94.

7. Ibid., p. 65.

8. Patrick Wright, *Tank: The Progress of a Monstrous War Machine*. New York: Viking, 2000, p. 29.

9. David Fletcher, ed., *Tanks and Trenches: First Hand Accounts of the Tank Warfare in the First World War*. Stroud, UK: Sutton, 1994, p. 87.

10. Quoted in Spencer C. Tucker, *The Great War*. Bloomington: Indiana University Press, 1998, p. 115.

11. Kenneth Macksey, "The Tank Story," in *Tanks & Weapons of World War I*, edited by Bernard Fitzsimons. London: Phoebus, 1973, p. 94.

12. Stephen Ryan, *Pétain the Soldier*. Cranbury, NJ: A. S. Barnes, 1969, p. 136.

13. Bryan Perrett, *Iron Fist: Classic Armored Warfare Case Studies*. London: Arms and Armour, 1995, p. 57.

14. Quoted in D. J. Goodspeed, *Ludendorff: Genius of World War I*. Boston: Houghton Mifflin, 1966, p. 259; Cullen, "Armored Cars," p. 66.

CHAPTER 2

The Interwar Years, 1918–1939

Tanks, which had become a permanent fixture on the battlefield during the course of World War I, did not realize their full potential in that conflict. Although the utility of this new armored fighting vehicle (AFV) had been demonstrated by the end of the war, it had not proven decisive in battle. The period after World War I leading up to World War II was the most important period in the development of this new weapon.

Even those who supported the use of tanks were divided on their employment, and this led to sharp disagreements as to the most desirable types of AFV. Some advocates favored lighter, more mobile vehicles operating much like cavalry had for screening and reconnaissance. Others wanted heavier tanks with greater firepower and armor protection that would accompany infantry in the attack. Speed would not be a factor for such "infantry tanks," as they came to be called, for they would have only to move at the slow pace of foot soldiers. As it worked out, most tanks fell between the two to the satisfaction of neither school. In any case, emphasis in tank development after World War I centered not so much on armament and armor as on improved drive, braking, and suspension systems.

In the period immediately after the war armies pared down or did away with their tank corps entirely. Under the terms of the Treaty of Versailles with Germany, that nation was prohibited any tanks whatsoever. In the United States the National Defense Act of 1920 downsized the army to 280,000 officers and men. Amendments to that act abolished the Tank Corps and relegated tanks and their development to the infantry. In most nations, tank advocates found themselves marginalized; career officers interested in armor were encouraged to go elsewhere. Thus Lieutenant Colonel Dwight D. Eisenhower and Major George S. Patton Jr., disparaging of a future with tanks, reluctantly transferred to other military branches. Not until 1931 did the U.S. Army cavalry, which still employed horses, receive light "tankettes," known as "combat cars."

Such tankettes, which were built by all the major armies, were small, largely unsophisticated, easily manufactured, and inexpensive AFVs. These lightly armed and armored tanks manned by two-man crews became the basis for subsequent weapons carriers and light tanks. One of these, the British Vickers 6-Ton series, led to the Polish 7 TP of 1932 and the Soviet T-26A tank of World War II. It also influenced design of the U.S. Light Tank T1, the prototype for the M1–M3 light tank series.

Poland and Italy, in particular, turned out hundreds of small, low-cost AFVs. For the tankers, such vehicles were better than nothing, and they at least enabled crews to practice maneuvers, develop procedures, and establish tactics that would be useful when the demands of war would bring to the fore more satisfactory vehicles.

Many changes occurred in the basic tank design in the period. Efforts were made to reduce tank silhouettes, the central turret with improved lateral vision came into common use, main gun sizes increased, and engine performance greatly improved. Crew arrangements were made more efficient, there were major changes in suspension systems, and the radio came into more general use. Everything centered on the turreted main tank gun. The larger the gun, the larger and heavier the turret, and thus the heavier the vehicle and the greater the power plant necessary to propel it.

There was a close ratio between guns, armor, and performance. Increasing the armor thickness to keep out shells as well as bullets adversely affected other capabilities, such as speed and the size of the main gun that could be carried. Military planners were constantly having to choose between more thinly skinned, and hence lighter and faster, AFVs for reconnaissance and independent action, versus the heavily armored, and slower, tanks that would operate closely with infantry.

Tank armor also underwent change, and not only in thickness. Armor plate had to be of high quality, without impurities; if it were not, the plate might fail when struck by an enemy shell. But such armor was hard to work in the manufacturing process, leading to high construction costs and time-consuming manufacturing methods.

Initial armor was of steel boiler plate, easy to secure and riveted in place. This early boiler-plate armor was not of high quality and would not block shells, or even some bullets. Rivet-and-bolt construction was unsatisfactory, even dangerous to the crews, as bolts could pop free during battle and become lethal projectiles inside the tank.

The general construction procedure called for armor plate to be drilled and then hardened, after which it was attached to the tank frame by means of rivets. The seams where the plates came together were points of weakness, and a shell striking there could produce molten metal, known as "spall," or "splash," which would then act against anything inside the tank, including personnel and ammunition. Experience led to better joining, which helped reduce the problem of splash.

Hardening armor plate was more difficult and often led to cracking. The same process was occurring in ship armor during this period. The armor was carbonized by heating the plate and then playing coal gas across its face. This injected deposits of carbon into the armor to form a hard skin. All the world's armor manufacturers experimented with different processes, each of which brought its own problems, using various combinations of nickel, carbon, chromium, and manganese to produce the strongest steel.

Electric welding also came into extensive use. It produced greater strength and simplified construction procedures. British manufacturers were slow to move in this direction, but all German tanks after 1934 were of welded construction.

GREAT BRITAIN

The French had large numbers of their small Renault tank and no particular desire to add others of that type. At the same time, the United States did away with its Tank Corps altogether, and the Treaty of Versailles prevented Germany from having tanks. For these reasons, by default the British took the lead in tank development. Indeed, in Britain the deemphasis on tanks was less pronounced compared to most other major military powers. Britain had pride of place; the nation was the first to field a tank on the battlefield, and it also had the most outspoken advocates of tank development. These men were quick to point out that superior technology might help offset Britain's glaring population disadvantage vis-à-vis the other Great Powers. For these reasons, then, Great Britain continued to lead the world in tank development in the years immediately after the war.

In the 1920s most available British tank development funds went into designs for tankettes and light tanks, but some advances also occurred in other AFVs. The medium Whippet of World War I lacked the range and the speed to execute the deep envelopments that J. F. C. Fuller imagined, and the Whippet's successor, the Medium B, was also unsatisfactory; but in late 1917 a follow-on, the Medium C, appeared. Although slightly faster and with greater range, the Medium C was insufficiently armed and armored. Fuller wanted a tank that could reach 20 mph, and the Medium D more fully met his demands. With a weight of some 44,800 pounds, a crew of four, and powered by a 240-hp engine, it was capable of 25 mph across level ground. The Medium D, however, had only 10mm maximum armor thickness. It mounted a 57mm main gun and three machine guns.

None of these tanks saw service in World War I, but the Medium D influenced tank design afterward. It incorporated superior steering and suspension systems, and its flexible track also could be bowed to permit the tank to change direction, thus saving the power lost in having to brake a track and ensuring a smoother ride for the crew.

The immediate postwar economic boom in Britain, largely the result of the release of pent-up wartime savings, soon gave way to a deep and prolonged recession. Given the economic hard times in 1923, the government closed the Department of Tank Design, ending further development on the Medium D and leaving only the firm of Vickers in tank development and production. Vickers in the 1920s remained the world's preeminent tank manufacturer. Vickers relied on British government orders, but was also drawn to tank manufacture by the prospect of export sales.

In 1921 the War Department asked Vickers to produce an inexpensive, reliable medium tank to compete with the official versions then in service. The result was the Vickers No. 1. Weighing some 19,600 pounds, it was less than half the weight of the Medium D. Powered by a 90-hp engine and carrying a four-man crew, the No. 1 boasted only 8mm armor but could reach 30 mph. It mounted a 47mm main gun, not in sponsons as was past practice, but in a rotating turret, and it also had two machine guns. The Vickers No. 1 also did away with the previous complicated suspension systems and incorporated a simple plate track operating around coil-sprung bogies. This revolutionary new tank, which Vickers created at least in part for export sales, marked an important step forward in tank design.

Vickers Mark 1. *Courtesy of Art-Tech/Aerospace/M.A.R.S/TRH/Navy Historical.*

In 1922 the firm came up with the Vickers Medium, the final version of which was the Mark II series (Mk II, IIA, and II*). The Medium II followed the Vickers No. 1 as being relatively inexpensive, a fact that greatly enhanced its sales potential. Crewed by five men (commander, driver, radio operator, and two gunners) and weighing some 29,600 pounds, the Medium II was powered by an Armstrong Siddeley 90-hp engine that drove it a maximum speed of 18 mph.

In order to achieve its relatively high speed, the Medium II sacrificed armor, which was initially a maximum of only 6mm (hardly sufficient to keep out even small-arms bullets); later the armor thickness was increased to 8mm, still inadequate. Compounding the danger of thin armor was the positioning of the Medium II's gasoline fuel tank inside the crew compartment. In addition, the Medium II was undergunned, with a 3-pounder (47mm) main gun and 3 x .303-caliber machine guns.

The Medium Tank Mark II, delivered to the British Army during 1923–1928, remained the standard Tank Corps tank until 1938. During World War II it served as a training vehicle in Britain. Some in Egypt at the start of hostilities were pressed into a combat role against the Italian Army during 1940–1941, seeing service in the Battles of Mersa Matruh and Tobruk. The Medium II did have an important impact on subsequent designs. Apart from its relatively inexpensive cost, its chief advantages were its speed and reliability.

British Mark II tanks of the 2nd Battalion Royal Tank Corps participating in
maneuvers on Salisbury Plain, England.
Courtesy of Art-Tech/Aerospace/M.A.R.S/TRH/Navy Historical.

It also boasted a specially designed power plant in the air-cooled
Armstrong Siddeley engine and a sprung bogie suspension that provided a smoother cross-country ride. Its redesigned crew compartment layout enhanced cooperation among crew members, and the
Medium II could easily be modified for other roles. For example, removing the turret allowed it to become an artillery tractor, command
vehicle, or bridge-layer. The Medium II also was the tank utilized by
the British Army in developing theories about the future employment of tanks in battle.

A follow-on to the Medium II—the Type C, developed in 1928—
was a commercial variant of the Medium Mark I. It had a taller hull
superstructure with a steeply sloped glacis over the driver's position
and a turret face swept back to reflect shot. It was subsequently exported to Japan, where it influenced development of the Japanese
Type 89, and to Eire (Ireland).

In 1928 Vickers developed a new light tank for the British Army,
known as the Six-Ton. Actually weighing in at more than 7 English
tons (some 15,700 pounds), the Six-Ton had a three-man crew, an
80-hp engine, a top speed of 22 mph, and maximum 13mm armor

protection. The Type A had a curious twin turret design; each turret mounted a .303-caliber Vickers machine gun. Known for its great reliability, it incorporated a new Armstrong Siddeley engine, an improved suspension system, and a new manganese steel track that allowed 3,000 miles of travel without replacement. It was subsequently upgunned to a slightly heavier single-turret two-man Type B. Weighing some 17,600 pounds, it had a crew of three men, maximum 17mm armor, and mounted a 3-pounder (47mm) main gun and a coaxial .303-caliber machine gun.

The Vickers Six-Ton was Vickers's greatest commercial tank success in the pre–World War II years. Widely sold abroad beginning in 1929, the Vickers Type B was exported to the Soviet Union (where it became the T-26 and served into World War II) as well as Bolivia, Bulgaria, Finland, Greece, Poland, Portugal, and Thailand. The Americans copied many of its features in their Light Tank T1, the prototype for the M1–M3 series of light tanks. Although the British army never did order this tank, at the start of World War II it requisitioned those being built for other countries, removed their armament, and used them as training vehicles for the remainder of the conflict.

That same year, 1928, Vickers also introduced a new medium tank, the A6, known as the "16-Tonner." The A6 weighed some 39,100 pounds, had a 180-hp engine, a crew of six, maximum 14mm armor protection, and a top speed of 30 mph. It mounted a 3-pounder (47mm) main gun and three machine guns. Vickers intended the A6 as the successor vehicle to the Medium. Unfortunately, it came at the wrong time. The Medium still had a number of years of usable service, and the 1925 Locarno Pacts, by which Germany guaranteed its western borders as final and promised not to resort to war with its neighbors, seemed to presage a period of prolonged peace and thus military retrenchment. Nonetheless, the A6 served as a useful test bed for advanced ideas, the most important of which came in the form of the A6E3, with its 180-hp Ricardo diesel engine and experimental Wilson epicyclic gearbox. Diesel engines offered a number of advantages in tanks, including increased range, reduced risk of fire, and greater mechanical reliability. The advantages helped offset the disadvantage of the clouds of telltale smoke the engine emitted when started up, and the Wilson gearbox helped compensate for the engine's loss of power when steering. The chief drawback to the A6 was its scant (14mm) armor protection and relatively light (47mm) main armament. The A6E3 (and also the German PzKpfw V [*Panzerkampfwagen*, or "tank"]), however, represented considerable improvements over their predecessor medium tank designs. Well organized for crew efficiency, their more centrally located and rapidly traversed turrets also provided excellent range of vision and fields of fire.

In the early 1930s Vickers came up with the Mark II Light Tank. Ultimately produced in Marks II through VI, the original Mark II weighed some 9,250 pounds, had a crew of two, was powered with a 66-hp engine, and was capable of 30 mph. It had maximum 10mm armor and armament consisted of one .303-caliber machine gun. This reconnaissance tank was successful in a policing role throughout the British Empire in the 1930s, but it was totally obsolete for the World War II battlefield. Under battlefield exigencies the British did employ a few Mark IIs in a combat role, in North Africa and in the 1941 Abyssinian campaign.

The Mark II then went through a series of modifications, including an improved suspension in the Mark IV, which entered service in 1934, and the Mark V, which appeared in 1935. The Mark V was the first light tank with a three-man crew, two of whom were in the turret. The Mark VI series, produced from 1936 to 1940, had a slightly heavier weight of 10,800 pounds, which actually improved handling characteristics; a crew of three; an 88-hp engine for a top speed of 35 mph; maximum 14mm armor; and armament of .50-caliber and .303-caliber machine guns (a 15mm and a 7.92mm in the VIE). Whereas the Mark VI was still totally inadequate for a combat role in World War II, its mechanical reliability nonetheless made it popular in difficult conditions. The Mark VI was by far the most numerous British tank in France in 1940 as well as in the Western Desert. The British were often forced to use their Mark VIs in a "cruiser" rather than reconnaissance role, which often proved disastrous for the crews. Mark VIs were used to reequip British armored divisions following the Dunkirk evacuation and remained in service until 1942, when they were relegated to a training role.

Introduced in 1925, the Mark II Medium Tank remained for 15 years the standard British medium. Both the A6 ("16-Tonner" Mark III) and the "Independent" had in the early 1930s been abandoned for financial reasons, and the same thing happened to the prototype A7 and A8 designs by Woolwich Arsenal. In 1934, however, Sir John Carden of Vickers-Armstrong came up with a new medium tank, designated the Cruiser Tank Mark I (A9).

In 1936 the War Office had designated two types of tanks for future development: the cruiser tank (essentially the old medium) and the infantry tank (essentially the old heavy tank, equipped with a large gun as well as machine guns for its own defense and heavily armored, able to engage enemy weapons). Although speed was an important element in the cruiser design, it was not so with the infantry model, which would be expected only to keep pace with infantry advancing on foot. Thus the A9 was officially designated the Cruiser Tank Mark I.

Incorporating the best features of the Mark III, this design was made much lighter so that it might be produced more cheaply in being powered by a commercial gasoline engine. A prototype underwent testing beginning in 1936, and the new tank went into production the next year. A total of 125 A9s were produced during 1937–1938. The production model turned out to weigh some 26,900 pounds, heavier than the designed 10-ton weight. This forced the substitution of a more powerful 150-hp bus engine as its power plant.

The A9 had a speed of 25 mph, a crew of six men, and thin 14mm, unsatisfactory riveted armor. It mounted a 2-pounder (40mm/1.57-inch) main gun and three machine guns. Its close-support (CS) model substituted a 3.7-inch howitzer for the main ordnance, along with three .303-caliber machine guns. The A9 incorporated important innovations, including the first hydraulic turret traverse system, a small auxiliary engine powering a fan for crew compartment ventilation, and battery charging facilities for its radio. Its boat-shaped hull provided no external vertical surfaces. Combat experience in the 1940 Battle for France revealed its major shortcomings of inadequate armor and insufficient speed for a cruiser role. It also had a poor suspension system, the tracks tended to come off, and there was insufficient interior space for its crew of six. Nonetheless, the A9 rendered useful service in the North African desert in 1941.

The follow-on to the A9, the A10, was also designed by Carden. Designated a "heavy cruiser" tank and put into production in July 1938, it very much resembled the A9 externally. It also had the hydraulic turret traverse but improved on the A9 in that it had heavier 30mm armor; indeed, it was the first British tank with composite armor construction and the first armed with the Besa machine gun. The A10 weighed 31,700 pounds but had the same 150-hp engine of the A9 and thus a slower speed (15 mph). The A10 had a crew of five men and mounted a 40mm gun and two machine guns. Some of this model also appeared with a short 94mm howitzer in place of the 40mm gun, for mobile close artillery support. A total of 175 Mark IIs (Mk II, Mk IIA, and Mk IIA CS) were produced by September

1940. The A10 served in the Battle for France and later in North Africa and Greece.

Orders for the A9 and A10 were restricted, based on the British Army decision to produce a more advanced and faster cruiser tank that would incorporate the Christie suspension system (designed by American J. Walter Christie) and have improved armor. In late 1936 Lieutenant Colonel G. Le Q. Martel, a pioneer in British tank design, became assistant director of mechanization at the War Office. Having traveled to the Soviet Union earlier that year, Martel was much impressed with the Soviets' Christie-influenced designs. He now pushed adoption of a new tank that would utilize the Christie suspension system and follow Christie's practice of employing as power plant a lightweight aircraft engine, such as the American Liberty. The British government then authorized purchase and licensing of a Christie design through Morris Commercial Cars Ltd.

The Christie vehicle delivered was designated a "tractor" and was without turret. It became the basis of the important Cruiser Tank A13 design, the first in a long series of Christie-suspension British cruiser tanks during World War II. Although the A13 utilized the Christie vehicle system of large-diameter road wheels and spring suspension, the British decided that the option of running the tank without tracks was unnecessary. The A13 also had a slightly larger chassis for a turret capable of mounting a 2-pounder gun. It incorporated the same Liberty engine, now built under license. Following testing of two prototypes, the A13 was ordered into production as the Cruiser Tank Mark III (A13). A total of 65 were manufactured. The Mark III weighed some 31,400 pounds, had a crew of four, a 340-hp engine producing a vehicle speed of 30 mph, and was armed with a 2-pounder main gun and one machine gun. It had maximum 14mm armor protection.

Although by 1936 Germany's three panzer divisions were a matter of public record, and Chancellor Adolf Hitler had brought Europe to the brink of war that March when he ordered the army to remilitarize the Rhineland, in the process abrogating both the Treaty of Versailles and the Locarno Pacts, Britain was slow to rearm. Only in 1937–1938, at the eleventh hour, did the British government accelerate armaments production. Even then priority in rearmament went to the Royal Air Force and Royal Navy, considered as vital counterparts to what was perceived by most observers to be the powerful French Army. Still, the government did produce a total of 665 Mark IVs, beginning in 1938.

The Cruiser Tank Mark IV (A13 Mk II) was an uparmored version of the Mark III. It added more than 1,200 pounds of additional armor, chiefly on the nose, glacis, and turret front, for a total weight of 33,040 pounds. The addition of V-shaped armor on the Mark IV's turret side, later utilized in German designs, was the chief difference in its appearance from the Mark III. Because of its high-performance 340-hp engine there was no loss of speed. It mounted a 2-pounder (40mm) main gun and one machine gun.

Although the British did little with heavy tank design, they did not abandon it altogether. If nothing else, large tanks conveyed prestige, much like battleships at sea. In 1924 the General Staff of the British Army ordered a heavy tank prototype, which became known as the Independent. Only one was produced. Weighing some 70,500 pounds, the Independent had a crew of eight men (the commander communicated with his crew by means of an intercom system), a 398-hp engine, a top speed of 20 mph, maximum 29mm armor protection, and an armament of 1 x 47mm main gun and four machine guns. The Independent also incorporated a new hydraulic braking system. Its weight and speed were such that the manufacturers of braking gear had to develop this new system. Some believe that the tank was never put into production because of its great cost, but undoubtedly trials revealed the dubious notion of deploying a tank with such a large crew.

In the late 1930s British Army armored doctrine still favored World War I–style infantry divisions supported by heavily armored tanks with limited firepower. The one British Mobile (later Armored) Division was relegated to the specialist role of exploiting a possible breakthrough by conventional forces. Thus it is not surprising that in the years immediately before the war the British concentrated on developing a heavily armored infantry support tank rather than cruiser-type tanks that might operate independently.

The resulting AFV was something of an anachronism. Designed by Sir John Carden and designated Infantry Tank Mark I (A11), the first prototype was delivered to the army to undergo trials in September 1936. In order to keep costs low, it was of simple design and utilized a standard Ford commercial V-8 engine and transmission as well as components adapted from the Vickers light tanks. The army ordered 60 of the new tank in April 1937. This was later increased, and by the time production ceased in August 1940 a total of 140 had been produced, including the pilot vehicle.

Major General Sir Hugh Elles, head of army ordnance and responsible for tank procurement, named the A11 "Matilda" because of its small size and ducklike appearance and gait. The Matilda I

Infantry Tank Mark I, nicknamed "Matilda."
Courtesy of Art-Tech/Aerospace/M.A.R.S/TRH/Navy Historical.

had a battle weight of some 24,700 pounds and a two-man crew. Powered by a standard Ford V-8 70-hp engine, it had a speed of only 8 mph. With maximum 60mm armor, the Matilda I was initially armed with only one .303-caliber machine gun, which meant it would have no chance to knock out an enemy tank. Later models sported a .50-caliber machine gun, which, though somewhat of an improvement, was difficult to work in the tank's very confined turret space. Nonetheless, the A11 formed the chief armament of the 1st Army Tank Brigade of the British Expeditionary Force (BEF) in France in 1940. And though it proved virtually immune to German antitank gunfire, its machine-gun armament rendered it obsolete on the battlefield; it was withdrawn from production after the British evacuation at Dunkirk.

The Matilda II resulted from the need to rectify the lack of firepower of the Matilda I. Because limitations made it impossible simply to upgun the Matilda I, an entirely new tank was necessary. Design work on the new tank began in November 1936. "Matilda Senior," as it was first known, was later officially designated the A12 Infantry Tank Mark II. Weighing some 54,400 pounds, it had two 87-hp diesel engines and was capable of 15 mph. Crewed by four men, the Matilda II had impressive 78mm maximum armor protection and mounted a 2-pounder (40mm) main gun and one machine gun.

With withdrawal of the Matilda I (A11), the Matilda II simply became known as the Matilda. The Matilda II performed well early in the war. Although only two were in service at the outbreak of war in September 1939, a number subsequently equipped the 7th Tank Regiment with the BEF in France, where they performed well in the 1940 Battle for France. The Matilda is best remembered, however, for its service in North Africa. There its heavy armor provided excellent protection against the light Italian antitank guns, and its 40mm gun proved sufficient to defeat the Italian tanks. More powerful Axis antitank guns, especially the superb 88mm, and the arrival of larger Axis tanks in mid-1941 reversed the situation, however.

The last employment of the Matildas as gun tanks occurred in the Battle of El Alamein. From that point forward Matildas served only in secondary roles. They were soon adapted to mine-clearing operations with the addition of a chain or flail device used to beat the ground in front of a slow-moving tank and explode mines. The British also employed the Matilda II in the Eritrea campaign, and the Australian army utilized them against the Japanese in New Guinea. The Matilda enjoys the distinction of being the only British tank to serve for the duration of the war. Some remained in Australian army reserve units after the war.

The last British infantry tank to enter production before World War II was the Infantry Tank Mark III "Valentine." It took its name from the fact that Vickers submitted the design to the War Office just prior to St. Valentine's Day in February 1938. The chief objection to the new design was the small turret, with space for only two men. In June 1939, however, as war loomed, the government placed an order for 275 Valentines without even a prototype. The first tank was delivered in May 1940. Because of a shortage of cruiser tanks, Valentines served in that role in British armored divisions. They entered the fighting in North Africa in June 1941 and were a staple of fighting thereafter. The Mark I Valentine weighed some 39,000 pounds, had a crew of three, a 135-hp engine, and top speed of 15 mph. It was armed with a 2-pounder main gun and coaxial machine gun and had maximum 65mm armor protection.

The Valentine was a stable gun platform and mechanically reliable. It underwent constant upgrades during the war, including up-gunning to a 6-pounder, a more powerful engine, and the addition of long-range fuel tanks. The Valentine was one of the most important British tanks of World War II. A total of 8,275 were built through early 1944, 1,420 of which were manufactured in Canada (all but 30 of these were shipped to the Soviet Union). Valentines also appeared in a wide variety of special purpose AFVs.

FRANCE

French tank development lagged after World War I, simply because of the large numbers of Renault tanks still on hand. The General Staff of the French Army also persisted in thinking of tanks in World War I terms as can openers for accompanying infantry. Thus there was little emphasis on improving tank speed, and most design innovation went into heavier guns and thicker armor, although the French did achieve improvements in suspension systems and in rubber tracks.

These changes were seen in the NC-27 light tank, which offered improved cross-country performance at moderate speed. The NC-27 had a crew of two and weighed some 19,000 pounds. Driven by a 60-hp engine and capable of 12 mph, it had maximum 34mm armor and mounted a 37mm (1.46-inch) main gun and one machine gun. The French subsequently sold some of these tanks to Japan, where they were known as the NC-31.

Not until 1930 did the French decide to build a new tank to replace its World War I Renault M-17s. The resulting Renault Char D-1 series was envisioned as providing for the needs of both the cavalry and the infantry. As a result it satisfied neither role, being too lightly armored for the infantry and too high in silhouette to suit the cavalry. The D-1 weighed some 30,900 pounds and had a three-man crew. It had a one-man turret for the commander, who had the impossible task of both directing the tank's operations and manning its main gun and one machine gun. The other two crewmen were positioned in the hull. The second crew member was the driver, and the third manned the radio and the second machine gun. The D-1 had a 64-hp engine and a top speed of 11 mph. It had maximum 30mm armor protection and was armed with a 37mm main gun and two machine guns.

The D-2, which appeared in 1932, was heavier than and an improvement over the D-1. It had the same crew size but weighed 44,800 pounds and had a much more powerful 150-hp engine and speed of 14 mph, 40mm maximum armor thickness, and a heavier 47mm main gun along with two machine guns.

In 1934 the French began experiments with purely armored formations in creation of their first *Division légère mécanique* (DLM, Light Mechanized Division). Essentially a cavalry formation, maneuvers involving the DLM revealed the need for heavier armament. This led to the Renault R-35 and the Hotchkiss H-35 tanks, basically downsized D-2s. These two were the most numerous French tanks in World War II. Both had two-man crews, but the R-35 weighed about 22,000 pounds and had an 82-hp engine, speed of 12–13 mph, maximum 40mm armor thickness, and armament of one short-barreled 37mm main gun and one machine gun. The French built about 2,000 R-35s and exported them to Poland, Turkey, Romania, and Yugoslavia. The Germans later captured and modified a number of these for their own use and also converted some to artillery tractors and gave others to Italy.

The Hotchkiss H-35 had identical armament but was heavier, some 23,400 pounds. It had a 75-hp engine, top speed of 17 mph, and maximum 40mm armor protection. An improved model appeared in 1938. The H-38 was basically the H-35 with a more powerful, 120-hp engine and a higher rear deck to accommodate the engine and its cooling system.

These French tanks incorporated cast turrets and hulls. Although more expensive, they were not as resistant to shot as homogenous armor plate. They also incorporated Cletrac steering, which minimized power loss and improved cross-country performance. Instead of braking one track to turn, the system transferred power to the other tread by means of a differential and gear box.

The last French light tank before the war was the Hotchkiss H-39, officially the Char léger Hotchkiss, modèle 1939-H. The follow-on to the H-35, it mounted a long-barreled 37mm gun and one machine gun and had a more powerful, 120-hp engine. It weighed some 26,700 pounds, had a two-man crew, and was capable of 22 mph.

The Germans later utilized a number of these captured light tanks in the occupation of France, throughout the Mediterranean Theater, and in the initial invasion of the Soviet Union. They were also used by Vichy French and Free French forces in the Middle East, where some continued in Israeli service until 1956.

The H-35, R-35, H-38, and H-39 were all of high quality compared to the German tanks at that time. The chief drawback in the French tanks was probably their one-man turret. All three symbolized the French embrace of the doctrine of light tanks operating in support of infantry, a concept seriously open to question; French tankers deserved better.

French Char B-1 tanks. *Courtesy of Art-Tech/Aerospace/M.A.R.S/TRH/Navy Historical.*

France also had an excellent medium tank at the beginning of World War II. SOMUA (the Société d'Outillage de Méchanique et d'Usinage d'Artillerie at St. Oeun, Seine) was responsible for the design and construction of an outstanding tank, probably the best all-around French or Allied tank at the time of the German invasion in May 1940. Well-armed and mobile, the SOMUA S-35 also had armor superior to any other comparable tank of the time. Produced beginning in 1935, the S-35 weighed about 43,000 pounds, had a three-man crew, a 190-hp engine, and top speed of 25 mph. The S-35 had the same cast turret of the Char B-1 bis (*bis* meaning "improved") heavy tank (the SOMUA was the first tank ever with a cast hull and a cast turret).

Armed with a 47mm gun and one machine gun, the S-35 statistically compared most favorably against the PzKpfw III, backbone of the German panzer divisions. The S-35 had 55mm armor protection as compared to only 30mm for the PzKpfw IIID. Their top speeds were about the same, but the French tank had a 47mm gun versus only a 37mm for the German. The S-35 also had electric turret traverse and radio as standard. It did suffer from the problem endemic to French tanks of the period in that the commander was isolated in the turret and forced to fire the main gun as well as direct the vehicle in battle. In contrast, the PzKpfw III crew was grouped together in the turret to form an effective fighting unit—a key factor in battle.

Unfortunately for the French Army, too few S-35s were available. France had produced about 430 by the time of its defeat in 1940, and only about half of those reached front-line units. Negotiations were under way to open a second factory in the United States to manufacture many more (there was talk of building 20,000 S-35s), but nothing had come of this by the time France was defeated.

The Germans pressed into service many captured S-35s, gave some to the Italians, and placed others in storage. Some S-35s also served with the Free French in North Africa, and following the 1944 Allied invasion of France any that could be found were added to Free French units. A number of S-35s served in the French Army well after the war.

France had fought World War I without a heavy tank. In July 1918, at the very end of that conflict, it began development of such a machine. Manufactured by FCM (Forges et Chantiers de la Méditerranée, Le Seyne, Toulon), the Char 2C was intended as a breakthrough tank or "Fortress Tank" (Char de forteresse), intended to lead the great Allied offensives that were planned for the spring of 1919. France planned to produce 300, but only 10 were ever built. This monster had a crew of 12, weighed some 152,100 pounds, and was powered by two Maybach or Daimler Benz 250-hp gasoline engines. It had a speed of 7.5 mph. The Char 2C had maximum 45mm armor and was armed with a turreted 75mm gun (later a 155mm) and four machine guns.

The French heavy tank in World War II was the Char B series. The first of these was produced beginning in 1929. Char B development included three pilot tanks built by Renault and FCM in cooperation. The tank featured a deep hull with all-around tracks and a small turret. It weighed some 56,000 pounds, had a crew of four, a 180-hp engine, a top speed of 12 mph, and 40mm maximum armor protection. The Char B mounted a short 75mm main gun in the hull front, along with four machine guns—two in the hull front and the other in the turret.

The production model, the Char B-1, appeared beginning in 1931. The chief changes from the Char B were that the turret was now a cast unit and it mounted a 47mm gun, along with a coaxial machine gun. The hull still mounted the short 75mm gun, along with one machine gun. The tank tracks still reached the hull top, but the ends were lowered in order to improve driver visibility. It also weighed more than the prototype, some 67,200 pounds. No more than 35 of these were produced by 1935, when production went over to the Char B-1 bis.

The French Army's main battle tank in 1940, the Char B-1 bis was unchanged in external appearance from the B-1. The principal changes were heavier armor, a more powerful engine, and a new turret with a more powerful gun. The Char B-1 bis offered an excellent mix of cross-country ability, armor protection, and firepower. It weighed some 71,600 pounds and had a crew of four. The Char B-1 bis had a 300-hp engine that gave it a speed of 17 mph. It had unusually thick 60mm maximum armor and was also heavily armed. It had both the hull-mounted, forward-firing short 75mm (2.95-inch) main gun on the right side, the 47mm high-velocity gun in its small one-man turret with a commander/gunner cupola on its top, and two 7.5mm (.29 cal) machine guns. The Char B-1 bis, excellent in some areas, suffered from major flaws. The chief problem was its poor internal design. The commander, alone in the turret, had to direct the tank, search for enemy targets, communicate with the crew and with other tanks, and fire the 47mm turret gun unaided. Also its short 75mm main gun, though it could be elevated and depressed, was fixed laterally and could be traversed only by turning the entire vehicle. A later version, the Char B-1 ter (third version), had a limited traverse hull gun, but very few of these were built. The 60mm armor of the Char B series did present a real problem for German gunners in the 1940 Battle for France. In any case, France had only about 365 of the Char B-1 bis tanks when it was defeated in June 1940. The French Army compounded the error of small numbers of Char B-1 bis tanks by dispersing them into small groups rather than massing them in decisive numbers in large armored formations.

POLAND

France's chief ally in the East—a poor substitute for Russia in terms of sheer power—was the new state of Poland. Poland reemerged as an independent nation as a consequence of World War I. It was formed largely of territory expropriated at the end of the eighteenth century by Prussia, Russia, and Austria. Save for the Baltic Sea, Poland after World War I lacked natural frontiers. Poland also claimed considerably more territory than was awarded it in the Treaty of Versailles at the end of the war, and Polish leaders went to war to achieve it. This included the seizure of Upper Silesia from Germany, Vilna from Lithuania, Eastern Galicia from Ukraine, part of Teschen from Czechoslovakia, and a considerable stretch of territory secured from Russia as a result of war with that country during 1919–1920. This expansionist policy, however, meant that some 90 percent of Poland's borders had to be considered as menaced by hostile neighbors.

This fact, of course, gave Poland a strong interest in maintaining a powerful army, and its chief ally, France, tried to assist the Poles in that effort. As early as 1919 and Poland's war with Russia, France supplied Renault FT-17 tanks. After that conflict the Poles reorganized their tanks along French lines, assigning them to the infantry.

At first the Poles set out to improve the Renault FT-17, including a new flexible track, which enhanced the tank's speed. Some FTs also received a new turret that mounted a 37mm gun and coaxial machine gun. From late 1924 there was considerable pressure for a domestically produced heavy tank capable of infantry support, but the prototypes advanced by several firms proved unsuccessful and the project was dropped.

In the late 1920s the Poles acquired the Vickers tankette and used that to produce their own version, the 3,900-pound, two-man TK.1 and, subsequently, the TK.2 and TK.3. The latter was the first tank produced in quantity in Poland. A total of 300 were produced during 1931–1932. The TK.3 tankette weighed 5,500 pounds, had a crew of two, and had a 40-hp Ford Model A engine that drove the tank at 29 mph. It was armed with one 7.92mm machine gun and had maximum 8mm armor. Surprisingly, Poland continued to produce other tankettes up to the time of its defeat by Germany in September 1939.

The need for a more powerful armored vehicle was increasingly obvious, because the TK.3 was not capable of an actual combat role. Poland then copied the British Vickers 6-Ton. The Polish version, produced by the state-run PZI Institute, was the 7 TP light tank. It weighed 21,000 pounds, had a crew of three, and had heavier (maximum 17mm) armor than the Vickers. Its Swiss-patented Saurer six-cylinder 110 diesel engine (produced under license in Poland) made it the first mass-production diesel-powered tank. It was capable of 20 mph. The first version of the 7 TP followed experiments by other nations in multiturret tanks, the idea being that gunners could thus simultaneously engage multiple targets. The 7 TP had twin turrets with a machine gun in each. A second version, introduced beginning in 1937, had heavier armor and a single turret with a 37mm gun and one machine gun. A third version had an enlarged turret with overhang in the rear and still heavier armor. Produced during 1934–1939, a total of 169 7 TPs were in service at the time of the September 1939 German invasion.

Polish 7 TP tanks in Warsaw, 1939.
Courtesy of Art-Tech/Aerospace/M.A.R.S/TRH/Navy Historical.

During the mid-1930s there was considerable debate in Poland over whether the nation, with its limited manufacturing resources, should attempt to produce its own tanks or follow the more economical approach of purchasing what it required abroad. Although it defaulted on purchase of two of J. Walter Christie's tanks, in 1938 Poland did copy the Christie suspension system in its 10 TP fast tank. Weighing some 28,700 pounds, it had a crew of four, was powered by an American La France V-12 gasoline engine, and was capable of 31 mph on tracks and 47 mph on wheels. It mounted a 37mm main gun and two 2.79mm machine guns and had maximum 20mm armor protection. The Polish army envisioned the 10 TP as the mainstay for four mechanized cavalry brigades planned under the 1936–1937 army modernization plan, but the 10 TP arrived too late; the prototype was still in testing at the time of the German invasion.

On 1 September 1939, Poland had 339 tanks: 169 7 TPs, 50 Vickers 6-Tons, 53 Renault R-35s, and 67 Renault FTs. It also had 693 TK and TS tankettes and 100 armored cars. For Poland it was a case of too little, too late.

UNITED STATES

The United States produced few tanks during the interwar years. Those developed were intended for infantry support, because the National Defense Act of 1920 had made tanks an infantry responsibility. The U.S. Army General Staff had decreed that the role of the tank in war was "to facilitate the uninterrupted advance of riflemen in the attack."[1]

Tanks were to be of two types: light and medium. Light tanks were to weigh no more than 5 tons so that they could be transported by truck; the mediums were to be no more than 15 tons to meet bridging requirements. Tank development in the United States was severely hampered by budgets in the 1920s, which allowed production of only two experimental models per year.

Influenced by the British, in 1927 the General Staff set up the small experimental Mechanized Force of light tanks, but in 1931 Chief of Staff General Douglas MacArthur decreed that tanks would have an exploitation role apart from infantry support, and the cavalry took over the Mechanized Force. In order to get around the National Defense Act, cavalry tanks were designated as "combat cars."

The Light Tank T1E1 of 1929 was an unsuccessful design, although its sprocket drive and rear engine were both adapted in later models. Then in 1931 the United States purchased a Vickers 6-Ton Model B and used it as the basis for the four-man T1E4 of the same date. At some 17,200 pounds, the T1E4 had a 150-hp engine, a top speed of 20 mph, and maximum 16mm armor protection. It was armed with a 37mm main gun and single machine gun. It also had the two features (a rear engine and sprocket drive) adopted in subsequent U.S. light tanks.

The United States did not lack capable tank designers, and the most brilliant of these was certainly John Walter Christie of Hoboken, New Jersey. Christie produced a large number of revolutionary prototypes that had worldwide impact. During World War I he had designed several tracked gun carriers, one of which was a wheel-and-track carriage for an 8-inch gun. This experience led Christie to design the first U.S. postwar tank, the three-man, 30,200-pound Medium Tank M1919. Manufactured by Christie's Front Drive Motor Company, and popularly known as the Christie M1919, the new tank resembled the Renault light tank in external appearance but incorporated important new design features, including sloped armor.

The steel track links of the early tanks soon destroyed less durable roads, so Christie's M1919 was designed to run on interchangeable tracks or wheels. It featured sloped armor and center bogies that could be raised to allow the tank to run on its wheels. The tank crew could remove the track in about 15 minutes and store it around the tank hull during road operations. It also had the same speed in either forward or reverse and a superior power plant and suspension system. Christie's design immediately increased power, speed, and range, but it was also plagued by mechanical problems. The Christie M1919 had a 120-hp engine, a top speed of 7 mph, a three-man crew, and maximum 25mm armor. It was armed with a 57mm main gun and one machine gun.

Christie had no shortage of designs. His Amphibious Gun of 1921 was a 75mm gun carrier that had its sides packed with cork to increase flotation. It led to the first amphibious tank. Another had sets of wheels to the front and rear of the tank hull that could be lowered to permit it to run without the treads.

In 1928 Christie introduced his "National Defense Machine," the M1928, often referred to as the M1940, because it was regarded a decade in advance as far as tank technology was concerned. The M1928 was indeed a breakthrough in tank design. Powered by a Liberty aircraft engine, it incorporated a practical drive system with chain link from sprocket wheel to rear bogie. It also had a revolutionary suspension system of large weight-bearing wheels on torsion bars. Each solid rubber–tired bogie wheel was located at the end of a crank, pivoted in the hull and sprung by a vertical coiled spring. This enhanced the tank's stability as a firing platform as well as its speed, potentially increasing the tactical and operational mobility of armored fighting vehicles in general. Army Chief of Staff General Charles Summerall, who supported the development of light tanks, was so impressed with the M1928 that he circumvented the Ordnance Board and ordered the Infantry Tank Board to test it.

Christie continued to modify the M1928 chassis even as it underwent testing. In August 1929 the Infantry Tank Board recommended that the M1928 be included in the army's tank production program. The chief of infantry recommended that the army purchase five tanks for tactical experimentation and one for mechanical and performance tests. Almost immediately disputes developed between the Tank School, the chief of cavalry, and the Ordnance Department. In March 1929 the Ordnance Department's technical staff cited problems with Christie's past work, including poor design and workmanship, and recalled recommendations of 1924 that it terminate all contact with Christie's projects.

Disappointed with his reception in the United States, Christie opened contacts with foreign governments to sell his tanks abroad, notably to the Soviet Union and Poland. The Red Army acquired several M1928s, and these became the basis for their BT-series tanks. The Soviets' T-34 tank, which may have been the best all-around single tank of World War II, utilized a Christie suspension system.

Christie's M1928 weighed some 19,300 pounds, had a three-man crew, and, thanks to its 338-hp engine, was capable of record speeds of 26 mph on tracks and 50 mph on wheels. Its chief drawbacks were its light armor (13mm) and armament (two machine guns). Although the U.S. Army did purchase six M1928s, some criticisms of the tank were certainly justified. The armament was totally inadequate, and the tank itself was mechanically unreliable. It took 30 minutes to discard the tracks in favor of the wheels, and the higher pressure and narrowness of the rubber tires meant that the tank could run only on hard-surface roads in wheel mode. The tracks were also not satisfactory and tended to come off or break.

Christie was well aware of the limitations of the M1928 and soon introduced a new model, the M1931. It was easily the most successful of his tanks in numbers built and influence abroad, with sales to the Soviet Union, Britain, and Poland. The U.S. Army purchased three M1931s, designating it the T3. Christie sold two others to the Soviet Union. The M1931 weighed some 23,500 pounds, had a 338-hp engine, a crew of three men, 16mm armor, and top speeds of 25 mph on tracks and 50 mph on wheels. It mounted a 37mm gun and a .30-caliber machine gun.

Christie next sought to introduce a tank capable of being transported by air. His M1932 made use of lightweight materials. One of the most unusual tanks ever built, it had a forward-facing propeller that enabled it to be dropped from low-flying aircraft, whereupon it could fly down and hit the ground running! Powered by a 750-hp Hispano-Suiza engine, the M1932 could make road speeds of 36 mph on tracks and 65 mph on wheels and could leap a 20-foot gap from a 45-degree ramp. There was thought of giving the M1932 a helicopter rotor, but this was abandoned in favor of attaching conventional airfoils to the hull and working out a system whereby power would be transferred from tracks to propeller at the critical moment and allow the tank to take off. This tank was also sold to the Russians. The M1932 had a crew of three, weighed 11,000 pounds, with maximum 13mm armor, and mounted a 37mm gun and one machine gun.

The T5 Combat Car. *Courtesy of the Patton Museum.*

Christie's M1936 weighed 13,400 pounds, had a two-man crew, and was capable of cross-country speeds of up to 60 mph. In Britain it evolved into the first cruiser tank. Christie did other defense work as well. He designed the first U.S. standard turret track for battleships as well as gun mounts and carriages.

While Christie continued to develop original designs, the United States had no armored force, and its tank development was limited to light models. The cavalry and the infantry could not reach agreement on the type of machines required. Finally they settled on an Ordnance Department design along Christie lines, the Combat Car T4E1 of 1931. The cavalry wanted a fast, cross-country vehicle, and the T4E1 met these needs. It weighed some 30,400 pounds, had a powerful 168-hp engine, a crew of four, a top speed of 25 mph, and 15mm armor. Armament consisted of two machine guns. It also incorporated the rear engine and front sprocket drive that became characteristic of subsequent U.S. light tanks.

Meanwhile, other designers were at work. By 1922 Rock Island Arsenal had produced three experimental light tanks: the T2, T2E1, and T2E2. The T2 drew heavily from the Vickers Armstrong 6-Ton, including its leaf-spring suspension system. Because of budget constraints, Rock Island Arsenal came up with a similar vehicle for cavalry use. Known as the T5 Combat Car, it entered service with the cavalry in 1937 as the M1 Combat Car and became the Light Tank M1A1 in July 1940.

The M1A1 light tank weighed some 19,600 pounds and had a four-man crew. Powered by a 250-hp gasoline engine, it was capable of 45 mph. Protected by a maximum of 16mm armor, its armament consisted of three machine guns: one .50-caliber and one .30-caliber in the turret and a .30-caliber in the hull front. The M1A1 had a rugged suspension system, rubber tracks, and a Cletrac transmission to reduce power loss during steering. The improved M2A1 incorporated a trailing idler for better traction and improved ride. The M2A1 had the same armament as the M1; the M2A2 and M2A3 of 1936–1938 had twin turrets (with a 270-degree arc of fire), each mounting a single machine gun.

With the demonstrated combat effectiveness of the full-traverse single turret, Rock Island Arsenal came up with the M2A4 tank. Heavier (23,000 pounds) than its predecessors, it had a single turret mounting a 37mm gun, three hull machine guns, and thicker (maximum of 25mm) armor. Built by American Car & Foundry, the first M2A4s came off the assembly line in April 1940. Experiments were also carried out on some Model M2s with diesel engines and electric transmissions.

The establishment of the Armored Force in 1940 abolished the distinction between infantry and cavalry tank units. The M1 and M2 Combat Cars then became the M1A1 and M1A2 light tanks. Declared obsolete in 1940, they did not see combat in World War II but were utilized extensively as training vehicles and as the basis for subsequent light tank designs. There was also an M2 light tank. It differed from the M1 only in having 25mm armor, a top speed of 45 mph, and three machine guns mounted in twin tandem turrets. When World War II began in Europe the United States had only these inadequate light tanks.

In 1938 the Rock Island Arsenal came up with a design for a medium tank. It did away with Christie's convertible wheel/narrow track concept. Designated the T5, the new tank was based on the M2 light tank. Its designers sought to make use of as many parts as possible, both for economy and standardization. Thus the T5 employed the M2 radial air-cooled Continental 250-hp engine, transmission, and suspension system. The T5 weighed some 30,400 pounds, had 25mm armor, and was armed with a 37mm main gun in a central turret and six .30-caliber machine guns, sited to provide all-around fire. Tests with the T5 showed it to be underpowered, leading to the substitution of a Wright nine-cylinder, 350-hp radial engine. In June 1939, upon completion of tests, the tank was redesignated the Medium Tank M2. It weighed some 38,000 pounds. Production of 15 M2s at the Rock Island Arsenal began in August 1939, a month before the outbreak of war in Europe.

SOVIET UNION

The Soviet Union produced a large number of tank designs in the period between the two world wars. Early Russian experiments with AFVs in World War I had been limited to armored cars, such as the Austin Putilov. Based on a British chassis, it had entered service early in World War I. Lacking the industrial base of the other major military powers, the Russians concentrated in the postwar period on light tanks of simple design. Their first tanks were a few British and French models captured by the Bolshevik forces (known as the Reds) from their opponents (the Whites) during the Russian Civil War. The first Russian-built tank appeared in August 1920. It weighed some 15,700 pounds and had armor up to 16mm thick.

With no tank design experience of their own, the Russians came to rely on the Germans in this regard. The new Bolshevik government of Russia and Weimar Germany found themselves at odds with the Western powers after World War I, and in 1922 at Rapallo the two governments normalized relations. Following this the two states undertook a clandestine military collaboration that included a German-Soviet tank-testing facility at Kazan in the Soviet Union. This gave the Germans an opportunity to carry out tank development in violation of the Versailles treaty, and the Soviets gained access to German technological and design developments.

Although its designers had their own plans, the Soviet Union, in order to take advantage of new developments abroad, purchased a number of prototype tanks from other countries, including the Vickers tanks from Britain and Christie designs from the United States. The Vickers 6-Ton was the license-built Soviet T-26A. The T-26 of 1931 appeared in A and B versions. The A version, designed for infantry support, had twin turrets. The first production model mounted one 7.62mm machine gun in each turret. A follow-on mounted first a 27mm gun and then a 37mm gun in the right turret. The T-26A weighed some 19,000 pounds and had a crew of three. Powered by an 88-hp gasoline engine, it had a maximum speed of 22 mph. It had maximum 15mm armor protection.

The single-turret T-26B version was intended as a mechanized cavalry AFV and mounted a high-velocity gun. The initial model mounted a single 37mm gun; follow-on models mounted a 45mm main gun. Despite their obsolescence, Soviet T-26 tanks fought in the early battles on the Eastern Front during World War II.

The Soviet Union also purchased the light Vickers/Carden-Loyd tankette that the British abandoned. The Soviets enlarged it and put it into production in 1934. Some 1,200 were made as the T-37 light amphibious reconnaissance tank. The T-37 employed the Vickers hull and suspension married to a turret of Soviet design. A small propeller at the rear of the tank pushed it through water. Weighing some 7,100 pounds and capable of being air-lifted beneath a bomber, it had a 40-hp engine and could reach 21 mph on the road. It mounted a single 7.62mm machine gun and had only 10mm armor.

An improved T-37 appeared in the T-38, produced beginning in 1936. Basically the T-37 in terms of armament and armor, it had an improved engine, transmission, and suspension. The T-38 remained in service until 1942.

The final tank in this immediate series of light amphibians was the T-40. Quite different in appearance from its predecessors, the T-40's hull incorporated buoyancy tanks and had an upswept bow front similar to the later PT-76. It also had a small, sloped turret and was propelled in water by means of a small propeller. The T-40S version was simply a light tank without the amphibian feature. The T-40 weighed some 12,300 pounds and had a two-man crew. It was armed with two machine guns, or a 20mm cannon and one machine gun. It had an 85-hp engine and was capable of 38 mph. The T-40 influenced the later T-60 and T-70 light tanks, the latter serving into the Cold War.

The U.S. Christie designs and French tanks introduced a sprung bogie suspension system in place of a rigid system. This enabled increased speed without sacrificing armor or requiring an increase in the size of the power plant. This appealed to Soviet designers, and they copied the Christie M-1931 in their BT series of fast tanks ("BT" standing for *bystrochodny tankovy*, literally "fast tank"). The Soviet BT-1 was an exact reproduction of the Christie. The BT-1 weighed some 20,000 pounds, had a crew of three, and had top speeds of 65 mph on wheels and 40 mph on tracks. It mounted two machine guns and had maximum 13mm armor protection.

Soon the Soviet Union was producing large numbers of BT tanks. The follow-on BT-2 was essentially the same hull as the BT-1 but with a new turret and a 37mm main gun and one machine gun. It was still in service in World War II. The BT-3, introduced in 1934, was essentially the BT-2 but with solid-disk road wheels instead of spoked wheels and a 45mm main gun instead of the 37mm.

The BT-5 incorporated a number of improvements, chiefly in its lightweight 350-hp gasoline engine, originally an aircraft design. Entering production in 1935, the tank itself weighed some 25,300 pounds, had a crew of three, maximum 13mm armor, and could reach 40 mph on tracks. The BT-5 was armed with a 45mm main gun and one machine gun. It formed the basis of Soviet armored formations of the late 1930s. It was in fact superior in almost all performance characteristics to the German PzKpfw I, which mounted only two machine guns. The two tanks came up against one another in the Spanish Civil War of 1936–1939.

The follow-on BT-7 of 1937 was essentially an improved BT-5 incorporating sloped armor. The BT-7 was heavier and slower than the BT-5, reflecting the race between guns and armor and increasing concern about the lethality of antitank guns. Weighing some 30,600 pounds and crewed by three men, it utilized a new engine and had increased fuel capacity. Its two-man turret continued the 45mm main-gun armament. Armor thickness was a maximum 22mm.

Following experience gained in the Spanish Civil War, the BT-7's armor was increased, and it received a new engine. The resulting BT-7M medium tank, also known as the BT-8, was produced only in limited numbers. The hull was modified and included a new full-width, well-sloped front glacis plate instead of the faired nose of the earlier BT series. The BT-7M also mounted a 76mm gun and two machine guns.

BT-7 tanks played a key role in the Soviet victory against the Japanese in the Battle of Nomonhan/Khalkhin Gol during May–September 1939. BT variants included command tanks, bridge-laying tanks, and a few flamethrower tanks. The BT-7 was certainly the most important Soviet tank in September 1939.

The final BT-series tank, the BT-1S, appeared in prototype only. Employing sloping side armor and glacis, the BT-1S also had removable side skirts. The first Soviet tank with all-sloping armor, it was an important step forward to the T-34.

The first indigenous Soviet medium tank design, the T-28, incorporated multiple turrets and was intended for an independent breakthrough role. Inspired by the Vickers A6 (its suspension was a clear copy) and German *Grosstraktor* designs, it grew out of the 1932 Red Army mechanization plan and was first produced by the

Leningrad Kirov Plant. Intended for an attack role, the T-28 had a central main gun turret and two machine-gun turrets in front and to either side. The T-28 weighed 28,560 pounds, had a six-man crew, and was powered by a 500-hp engine and had a road speed of 23 mph. It had only 30mm maximum armor protection. The prototype mounted a 45mm gun, but production vehicles had a 76.2mm low-velocity main gun and two machine guns. Combat experience with the T-28 led to changes. Armor was increased on the C version to 80mm for the hull front and turret. Some T-28s substituted a low-velocity 45mm gun in the right front turret for the machine gun normally carried there. The T-28 had a poor combat record, however.

The Soviets also came up with a number of heavy tanks. Indeed, from the early 1930s Soviet heavy tank design was dominated by multiturret "land battleships," many of which saw service in the 1939–1940 Winter War with Finland and even into the June 1941 German invasion of the Soviet Union. Among these was the T-28 heavy tank with five turrets. Weighing some 110,200 pounds, the T-35 had a crew of 11 and was powered by a 500-hp engine that gave it a speed of nearly 19 mph. It had only maximum 30mm armor protection, however. The T-35 mounted a 76mm gun, two 45mm guns, and six machine guns.

The Soviet experimental SMK (Sergius Mironovitch Kirov) heavy tank (with two turrets, one superimposed), which never went into production, was even larger. Weighing 58 tons, it had a 500-hp engine, a crew of seven, and 60mm armor, double that of the T-35. It was capable of 15 mph. Armament consisted of a 76mm gun, a 45mm gun, and three machine guns. Although these huge machines proved no match for the more nimble German tanks and artillery in 1941, the turrets, guns, and suspension systems developed for them did find their way into the KV series of heavy tanks.

Ultimately the strain on their production facilities forced the Soviets to decide between a few monster tanks or more numerous smaller ones. They opted for continuation of the BT series and one heavy tank, the KV-1 (described in Chapter 3). The Soviets and the Germans recognized what the British and Americans did not: at least some of the tanks in a nation's armor inventory needed to mount heavier guns capable of firing shells in order to engage and destroy enemy tanks. Both Germany and the Soviet Union settled on the 75mm (2.9-inch) gun or 76mm (3-inch) gun as their chief heavy weapon; the biggest tank gun in most other national armies was a 47mm (1.85-inch) gun or smaller.

The Italian Fiat-Ansaldo Light in an exercise on the Bridge of V'idor on the Veneto, 1937. *Courtesy of Art-Tech/Aerospace/M.A.R.S/TRH/Navy Historical.*

ITALY

Italy also was involved in tank development. In 1923 Fiat came up with its 3000 light tank. Basically a copy of the World War I French light two-man M-17 Renault, it was in fact a significant improvement. Weighing some 12,100 pounds, with a crew of two, and powered by a 65-hp engine that delivered a maximum speed of 15 mph, the Fiat 3000 was lighter, faster, and more heavily armed than the Renault, although speed was achieved at high cost to crew comfort and the vehicle itself. The 3000 at first mounted two machine guns in the turret, but one of these was later replaced with a long 37mm gun, which led to worldwide interest in higher-velocity main guns with armor-piercing capability. With an improved engine and suspension, the Fiat 3000 was the backbone of Italian AFVs for most of the 1930s, and a few even survived to 1943.

The Fiat-Ansaldo was another Italian light tank of the period, introduced beginning in 1930 and based on the British Carden-Loyd tankette. Its suspension system was by double-wheel bogies sprung by torsion bars. Weighing some 10,600 pounds (it was also known as the 5-Ton) with a crew of two and a 45-hp engine that delivered a road speed of 20 mph, the prototype Fiat-Ansaldo had a 37mm gun in a fixed mount; the second model carried a turret with a machine gun and saw service in the invasion of Ethiopia. The third and final model mounted a 37mm gun in the turret and two machine guns in the hull. The Fiat-Ansaldo was the basic model for the most numerous Italian light tank of World War II, the Model L6/40.

JAPAN

The Japanese purchased some French NC-27 light tanks, redesignated as the NC-31. As modified by the Japanese, the NC-31 was somewhat heavier (21,300 pounds) and had a more powerful engine (75 hp). It retained the same two-man crew, maximum 34mm armor protection, top speed of 12 mph, and armament of one 37mm gun and one machine gun. The Japanese preferred the Vickers products, however, probably because of a mix of technology and better terms.

Although the Japanese began construction of a heavy tank, they encountered so many problems that they decided to purchase French and British tanks to assist indigenous designers. The Vickers Medium C tank of 1926, a direct descendent of the Medium II, was in fact developed in response to a Japanese order. Crewed by five men, the Type C weighed in at 11.6 tons, had a 165-hp engine and speed of 20 mph, very light 6.5mm armor, and a 57mm main gun and four machine guns. The Japanese modified the Type C, leading in 1929 to their Type 89A built by Mitsubishi Heavy Industries. It would see extensive service in fighting in China in the 1930s. Their Type 89A had a four-man crew, weighed 12.7 tons, had a 118-hp engine, speed of 15 mph, maximum 17mm maximum armor, and a main 57mm gun with two machine guns.

Japanese vehicle nomenclature dating from the 1920s through 1945 needs some explanation. The type number was derived from the last two digits of the Japanese calendar year in which the tank was adopted. Happily, the last digit is the same for the Western calendar. Thus, the Type 89 dates from 1929, the Type 94 from 1934, and the Type 0 from 1940. (Since the 1960s Japanese fighting vehicles have utilized the Western calendar for their model numbers.)

Because of the severe cold weather of Manchuria, the Japanese also adopted diesel power for their new medium tank, the Type 89B.

It was in fact the world's first production tank powered by a diesel engine, the type of power plant that would become standard for most tanks. The Type 89B weighed about 25,300 pounds, had a six-cylinder, 120-hp diesel engine, and was armed with a 57mm main gun and two machine guns. But it was also too slow (15 mph) and lightly armored (maximum 17mm) to be anything but an infantry support AFV, as the Japanese soon discovered when they deployed it to Manchuria.

The Type 95 Ha-Go light tank, produced beginning in 1935, was intended as a companion to the Type 89 medium tank in the newly formed Japanese mechanized brigade in Manchuria. Essentially a larger version of the Type 94, the Ha-Go utilized an advanced, air-cooled, six-cylinder, 120-hp diesel engine and had a speed of 40 mph. It was armed with a 37mm main gun (later models had a 45mm) and two machine guns (one in the hull front and the other in the turret rear). Production began in 1935, but only 100 had been manufactured by 1939. A total of 1,161 were built by the time production ended in 1942. It had a one-man turret, slightly offset to the left of the hull. One of the best Japanese tanks of the Pacific War, it was popular with its crews but suffered from many problems, including thin (12mm maximum) armor protection, vision slits that let in bullets and shell fragments, and a gap between the hull and turret; in combat an opposing infantryman who could approach the tank from one of its blind spots could jam the turret with a bayonet or even a knife. Certainly the Type 95 light tank was outclassed by comparable Allied tanks.

The army laid down specifications for a new medium tank to replace the Type 89. Design specifications called for a weight of 15 tons, top speed of 22 mph, and a 47mm main gun. Mitsubishi Heavy Industries and the Osaka Army Arsenal submitted designs. The Mitsubishi tank fully met the specifications; the Osaka version emerged as a lighter 10-ton tank with a speed of only 17 mph. Both tanks featured low, sloped designs.

With the resumption of fighting with China in 1937, the Japanese decided to put the larger Mitsubishi tank into production that same year as the Type 97 Chi-Ha medium. Essentially a scaled-up Type 95 light tank with a two-man right-offset turret, the Type 97 weighed some 33,100 pounds and ran on six double rubber-tired wheels per side. It saved weight by employing a bell-crank suspension with helical springs. There were no shock absorbers. Steering was by means of clutch and brake. The commander in the turret communicated internally by 12 pushbuttons connected to 12 light panels and a buzzer in the driver's compartment. The Chi-Ha had a 170-hp engine, a maximum speed of 24 mph, a crew of four, 8–25mm armor protection, and was armed with a 57mm main gun and two machine guns. Probably the best Japanese tank design of the period, it became the most widely used Japanese medium tank of World War II. It was also no match for comparable Allied tanks.

The main drawback in Japanese tanks remained the commander's position within the vehicle turret, where he was responsible for commanding the tank as well as loading and firing the main gun and turret machine gun. This rendered it almost impossible for fighting. In doctrine as well, the Japanese remained frozen in World War I tactics. Thus they did not think of tanks operating independently as an arm of decision. Even during World War II the Japanese considered tanks to be essentially infantry support vehicles to engage weaker opponents.

Japanese tanks of the 1920s and 1930s and even through World War II remained relatively thin-skinned and undergunned infantry-support vehicles. Because their opponents, the Chinese, possessed few advanced weapons, the light Japanese tanks were largely effective in the fighting of the 1930s. When the incentive to change appeared in the form of superior U.S. and British tanks, it was too late.

GERMANY

Despite the popular image of masses of panzers advancing across the Russian steppe early in Operation BARBAROSSA, Hitler's invasion of the Soviet Union, Germany was in fact slow to develop tanks. As has been noted, it produced only a handful in World War I, and the Treaty of Versailles imposed by the victors in June 1919 prohibited Germany from possessing tanks, as well as heavy artillery, military aviation, and submarines.

Despite the Treaty of Versailles, which all Germans regardless of political affiliation saw as a vengeful *diktat* to keep their country in permanent subjugation, the German General Staff (forbidden by the peace treaty but operating under the cover of the Truppenamt [Troop Office]) was determined to learn from its mistakes in World War I. It undertook a thorough study of the military reasons behind the defeat of 1918. In defiance of the Versailles restrictions, Germany also conducted military development programs in a number of other countries, including the Netherlands, Switzerland, Sweden, and the Soviet Union, looking to the day when the nation might again openly rearm.

By far the most important of the clandestine German rearmament programs was with the Soviet Union after 1922. Even before 1935, when Hitler openly defied the Treaty of Versailles by announcing his nation's rearmament, Germany operated an air training facility at Lipetsk, a gas warfare school at Torski, and a tank school at Kazan. In the case of tank design and development, the Germans learned as much or more from the Soviets as they passed along to them.

Germany's first post–World War I tanks were built in great secrecy and tested in the Soviet Union. One of these, the *Leichttraktor* of 1928, weighed some 21,300 pounds and mounted a 37mm main gun and one 7.92mm machine gun. It closely resembled the Vickers Medium. Another, the *Grosstraktor* heavy tank of 1929, was produced only in prototypes. Weighing some 17.5–20 tons, it was a partial copy of the Vickers Independent but also drew on the prototype A7U, which in turn was modeled on the World War I A7V. Powered by a 300-hp engine, crewed by six men, and mounting a 75mm (2.95-inch) gun or 105mm (4.13-inch) howitzer and three 7.92mm machine guns, it had very thin (14mm maximum) armor protection.

German tank designers followed some of the same Soviet dead ends in armor design, including multiturret heavy tanks. Although the Germans did abandon these, they and the Soviets understood that some tanks should mount the heaviest guns in order to be able to destroy enemy tanks. The main thrust of German tank design was not in heavy AFVs but toward lighter, more maneuverable, and faster machines that would carry almost the same armament as heavier counterparts. Despite ample evidence to the contrary, a myth of German superiority in tank design persists. In point of fact, through much of World War II the Germans played catch-up in tank capabilities.

At first the Germans had to develop their home-grown designs in secret. Krupp won an initial design competition with the prototype introduced in 1933. An adaptation of a Carden-Loyd vehicle, it was disguised as the "Agricultural Tractor." This Krupp design for a tank became the PzKpfw I, Germany's first mass-produced post–World War I AFV.

The PzKpfw I light tank was essentially a tankette/training vehicle and was never really intended for fighting. The PzKpfw I Ausf. (variation) A model was a two-man tank weighing 12,100 pounds with maximum 13mm armor protection. Its air-cooled 57-hp Krupp engine was located in the rear and provided a maximum speed of 24 mph and range of 90 miles. Its armament consisted only of two

German PzKpfw I light tanks on parade.
Courtesy of Art-Tech/Aerospace/M.A.R.S/TRH/Navy Historical.

coaxial 7.62mm machine guns. The progenitor of all German tanks to follow, the PzKpfw I saw action during the Spanish Civil War and actually spearheaded the panzer divisions that invaded Poland in September 1939 and France in May 1940. Despite highly inferior armament, it managed to spread panic among defending troops. It remained in service until 1943, and surplus hulls were converted to a variety of uses. The PzKpfw I B model was slightly longer than its predecessor but, more significantly, was fitted with a Maybach 100-hp engine and sported an improved transmission, allowing a top speed of 25 mph and a greater power-to-weight ratio. It was introduced in 1935.

The first real trials of the PzKpfw I came during the 1936–1939 Spanish Civil War. The Germans did not hesitate to introduce their latest tanks, aircraft, and artillery into Spain to test their effectiveness in combat and to allow development of sound tactical doctrine; both the A and B variations saw service there. In late 1936 the Germans sent two battalions of 16 PzKpfws manned by 10 officers and 225 men under Major (later General) Wilhelm von Thoma to Spain.

They fought in the Battle of Pozuelo in early 1937. German combined arms tactics worked well, although the PzKpfw I suffered in comparison to the superior firepower of Soviet tanks in the hands of Republican forces.

The next German tank was the PzKpfw Mark II light tank of 1935. Weighing some 22,000 pounds, it had a 140-hp engine, crew of three, up to 35mm armor, and a top speed of 34 mph. Employed chiefly for reconnaissance purposes, its armor was insufficient to keep out anything but small-arms fire, and its gun was not large enough to penetrate the armor of most opposing tanks, even at close range. It was armed with a 20mm cannon and one machine gun. Despite its shortcomings, the PzKpfw II formed the bulk of the panzer divisions that overran Poland in 1939 and France and the Low Countries in 1940.

The main hitting power of Germany's new panzer divisions came from the PzKpfw III medium, introduced in 1937 to meet a German army requirement for a light medium tank design. Weighing 30,800 pounds in its Ausf. A version, it was powered by a 300-hp engine that gave a top speed of nearly 25 mph. It had maximum 30mm armor protection. It mounted a 37mm gun and three machine guns, whereas the PzKpfw II had only a 20mm main gun and one machine gun.

Unlike the PzKpfw IV, the PzKpfw III would have to close to very short range for its 37mm gun to be effective against an enemy tank, and this in turn would make it vulnerable to enemy antitank guns. Subsequent modifications to the PzKpfw III (discussed in Chapter 3), however, made it almost the equal in battle of the PzKpfw IV. Later versions utilized the excellent Porsche torsion-bar suspension system. The bar was attached to the tank hull and flexed according to the movement up and down of the wheel. But perhaps the chief advantage of the German tanks was in their crew organization. Unlike the French tanks that isolated the tank commander in the turret, the German fighting vehicles had an excellent crew compartment design that produced an effective fighting unit in battle.

The largest tank in the German Army's pre–World War II arsenal was the PzKpfw IV. Developed in response to a 1934 request from the Weapons Department of the German Army for a medium infantry support tank, its hull was formed of welded plates with a bolted superstructure on top holding the turret ring. The turret was also welded and large enough to accommodate three crew members and permit mounting of larger guns.

Krupp-Gruson began production of the PzKpfw IV in October 1937 and by August 1939 had produced 211 in models Ausf. A through C. The PzKpfw IV was the backbone of Germany's new panzer divisions. Weighing some 40,600 pounds in its Ausf. A version, it had a 250-hp engine, a speed of 24 mph, a crew of five men, and maximum 15mm armor protection. Subsequent models had a larger 300-hp engine and steadily thicker armor protection (up to 80mm). The PzKpfw IV mounted a short-barreled low-velocity 75mm (2.95-inch) cannon designed for close support, as well as two machine guns. Among the chief advantages of the PzKpfw IV was its 16-wheel suspension system, sprung by elliptic springs, which proved particularly reliable.

The PzKpfw IV offered nothing revolutionary or of special advantage. Its relatively thin armor offered little protection for the crew, and the gun was not especially powerful. Yet this tank more than held its own against all comers through 1941 because it had the right combination of speed, armor, and armament and because its crews understood how to exploit these to the best advantage.

The Germans also benefited greatly from Czechoslovak tanks secured just before World War II in the German absorption of Bohemia and Moravia in March 1939. These were the PzKpfw 35(t) and 38(t). The PzKpfw 35(t) was originally the Czech S-2a and LT-35 ("LT" standing for *lehky tank,* or "light tank"), the main battle tank of Czechoslovakia in the years immediately before the German occupation. A fine design for its time, the LT-35 was initially unreliable mechanically. These defects were overcome, and the Czechs produced 424 of them. The Germans utilized 219 of them, and the newly designated PzKpfw 35(t) tanks saw service in the September 1939 invasion of Poland. Virtually all were destroyed by late 1941 in the subsequent invasion of the Soviet Union.

The PzKpfw 38(t) was originally the Czech LT Vz 38, which had not yet entered service when the Germans occupied Bohemia and Moravia. The PzKpfw 38(t) light tank went through eight different models. The Ausf. E and F weighed 23,500 pounds, had a crew of four, mounted a 37mm gun and two 7.92mm machine guns, and had maximum 30mm armor. The PzKpfw 38(t) saw service in Poland and in Norway, indeed in most theaters of the war in Europe, although it did not go to North Africa. Production continued into June 1942.

FORMATION OF TANK DOCTRINE: THE ADVOCATES

The lack of adequate machines in the period immediately after World War I did not preclude armor advocates from presenting their case. Ironically, in view of Germany's success in World War II with the blitzkrieg and armor warfare, the chief tank advocates and theorists before that conflict came from the former allied powers of Britain and France, the two nations that had taken the lead in tank warfare. The individuals were J. F. C. Fuller and Basil Liddell Hart in Britain, and Charles de Gaulle in France.

Fuller saw the tank as a war-winning weapon. As chief of staff of the British Tanks Corps at the end of World War I, Colonel Fuller had drawn up Plan 1919 during the winter of 1917–1918. Designed to be implemented if the war extended into another year, it in fact laid the foundation for the employment of tanks to the present.

Fuller believed that the key to defeating an enemy army lay in the destruction of its command centers. Such headquarters were, however, sufficiently removed from the front lines as to be immune from attacks by horse cavalry and infantry. And though they were well within the range of aircraft, Fuller believed that enemy command centers and lines of communications could not be destroyed by bombers, and that this in fact was a task for tanks. In something that would hold true through the 2003 Iraq War, Fuller argued in 1917 for a surprise mass attack by tanks acting in concert with aircraft that would break down enemy command and control centers, create panic and confusion, and achieve victory.

Fuller called for the offensive to be mounted along a 90-mile front. He would make no effort to disguise the forthcoming offensive preparations so as to encourage the enemy to reinforce to a strength of four to five armies. This part of Fuller's plan was revolutionary, for he hoped that "fixing" enemy units in place might lead to them being cut off and destroyed in an encircling attack, much as the Germans would do in their *Kesselschlacht* (encircling battle) of World War II.

Fuller referred to his plan as a "morcellated attack." While large numbers of friendly aircraft struck enemy command centers behind the front and disrupted lines of communication and supply, masses of medium tanks would slice through enemy front lines and move at top speed in wide, enveloping movements against the rear headquarters. Neutralizing these would, Fuller believed, create "strategic paralysis": enemy front-line units would become confused, lose their cohesiveness, and begin to panic. At that point friendly tank, infantry, and artillery attacks would drive through the front lines at numerous points and carry out more shallow envelopments of about 10,000 yards. Enemy units could then be attacked from the rear or flanks and smashed there with heavy tanks.

The war ended before Fuller's Plan 1919 could be put into effect, but the idea of armor operating in great envelopments played out during World War II. This is precisely how the Germans employed their panzers in 1939 in Poland, in 1940 in France, and in 1941 in the initial invasion of the Soviet Union.

The generals who had won World War I had little interest in Fuller's schemes. Most of them continued to think along old lines and did not understand the implications or significance of the new weapon. A scarcity of development and research funds in the period after the war contributed to this mind-set, as did the fact that there were few revolutionary developments in either tank design or tactical employment during the 1920s and 1930s.

In late 1926 Fuller was chosen to command the new Experimental Force (or Tank Brigade)—the pinnacle of his military career. Fuller called for nothing short of a military revolution: a general staff coordinated by a single commander in chief to lead a totally mechanized army operating in conjunction with aircraft. He also stressed tank offensives that would penetrate deep behind enemy lines.

Fuller succeeded in putting together a motley collection of tanks, gun carriers, armored cars, and mechanized infantry and artillery and conclusively demonstrated, even in peacetime maneuvers, what they could accomplish against a horse-drawn and foot army. Fuller failed to secure what he wanted and resigned the command, which was disastrous for both him and the immediate future of mechanization in the British Army. Ironically, his successor got all that Fuller had asked for, thanks largely to an article by Liddell Hart in the *Daily Telegraph*.

Fuller was his own worst enemy. His sharp tongue, vanity, and intolerance of those who disagreed with him led to consignment to the military wilderness for the next six years, although he advanced to major general before his retirement in 1933. Fuller then began a new career as a journalist and historian, and he also embraced fascism.

Liddell Hart, who had fought in World War I, was gassed, and then was invalided out of the army in 1924, retired as a captain in 1927 and took up a new career as a military analyst and prolific writer on defense topics. Liddell Hart agreed with Fuller, but he also advocated motorized infantry to accompany the tanks and a flexible approach to strategy. He was the chief advocate of the "indirect approach" that emphasized maneuver rather than attrition warfare and quality over quantity. As with Fuller, Liddell Hart's influence was diluted because of the same personality traits, including egocentrism and dismissiveness of critics. Acerbic comments by the two men regarding World War I commanders did not sit well with the former assistants who were now running the army.

The problem of controlling large numbers of tanks in battle, hardly achieved by flag signals, was solved by the introduction in the early 1930s of crystal radio sets. By this point, however, there were many in senior positions in the British Army who believed that what the tank advocates really sought was an all-tank army. Thus when the British Tank Brigade was permanently established, at the end of 1933, it attracted as much suspicion as interest.

In September 1934 the British Army brought together the elements of what was then called the "Mobile Division" under Major General George Lindsey. Centered on Brigadier General Percy Hobart's Tank Brigade, it also brought together the 7th Infantry Brigade and a motorized field artillery brigade. The infantry moved in wheeled vehicles and some tracked carriers. The maneuvers on Salisbury Plain, the so-called Battle of Hungerford, saw the mobile force pitted in mock battle against a larger conventional force. Tank advocates claimed, with considerable justification, that the maneuvers were rigged so that the mobile force, which had embarrassed the conventional forces in previous maneuvers, would fail. The mobile force was required to start from 70 miles away, to advance in broad daylight, and to cross the River Severn. With only one satisfactory route to the objective, the attack had to be canalized, making it considerably easier for the defenders. The maneuvers did reveal serious problems, including a lack of bridging equipment to cross rivers and too few aircraft to supplement information provided by scout cars and light tanks, but to the careful observer it established what might be accomplished by armored divisions against an outmoded force.

In France the problem was not so much equipment as tactical doctrines governing its use. As victors in World War I, French military leaders did not feel the need to change doctrines in the way that the Germans did. Senior French commanders of the 1920s and 1930s had learned their trade in World War I and did not understand the implication of changes in military technology for tactics and strategy. The French high command rejected outright the new theories of armor warfare and continued to view tanks in World War I terms as mere can openers in support of infantry. Besides, the French hoped to offset inferior numbers (in 1939, 40 million Frenchmen to 60 million Germans) by putting their faith in the defensive and artillery, as exemplified by the expression "stingy with blood, extravagant with steel."

The French high command also rejected the notion of entire divisions of tanks. Some forward-thinking French officers, most notably Lieutenant Colonel Charles de Gaulle, argued for change. De Gaulle, who had been several times wounded and then captured, had spent much of the war in German prisoner-of-war camps, which perhaps helped allow him the reflection and detachment that others lacked. De Gaulle advocated a larger professional force formed on speed and maneuverability centered on armor divisions with organic artillery, motorized infantry, and air support. There is no indication that anyone on the French Army Council showed more than a passing interest in de Gaulle's important book on armored warfare, *Vers l'armée de metier* (1934, translated into English as *The Army of the Future*). In all three of World War I's victor states—Britain, France, and the United States—military nonconformity was discouraged. The U.S. Army's two-division Armored Force was created only in July 1940, after the defeat of France.

In the 1930s the Soviet Union possessed more tanks than any other nation, but Soviet authorities lacked the Germans' visionary approach to the employment of armor formations. The vast flat expanse of the western Soviet Union lent itself to high-speed armor warfare, and the Soviets did experiment with a number of 100-tank brigades. These were grouped with infantry and artillery elements into what became known as the "Mechanized Corps." However, Soviet tactical doctrine called for the employment of the tanks in a cavalry role, which may explain Moscow's interest in the Christie tank designs.

In war, victors tend to rest on their laurels, whereas it is the defeated powers that seem chiefly interested in military innovation. Germany, a loser in 1918, had the incentive to change and integrate unorthodox doctrines with lessons learned in the last months of World War I. But even losing generals tend to be bound by tradition, and most are not known for innovative thinking. Indeed, the bulk of the German military leadership mirrored the defense establishments of the other major military powers in that it was essentially conservative and traditional in its approach to weapons and their employment.

German military reformers pushed for a new concept of high-speed warfare. In this they gained the support of Adolf Hitler, who came to power in Germany in January 1933. Hitler's ambitious foreign policy demanded a powerful military establishment, and he immediately began a massive rearmament program. When he openly announced his defiance of the peace settlement, and the signatories to the Versailles treaty took no action against Germany, it further emboldened him. Hitler planned to build the world's most powerful military. He accomplished this only as far as the air force (Luftwaffe) was concerned; the general European war of September 1939 came a half-decade too early for the German navy (Kriegsmarine), which was projecting a powerful balanced fleet. The situation was also mixed as far as the German army (Wehrmacht) was concerned.

Fortunately for German military reformers, Hitler embraced tanks. After all, these and his new Luftwaffe were the means by which he might intimidate his neighbors into securing concessions short of war. In the event of armed conflict, they also held the promise of quick, decisive victory, the only war that Germany could hope to win. Hitler's support was crucial, and he extended it to Colonel Heinz Guderian, the principal armor theorist in the German Army and father of its World War II panzer divisions.

One of the key reasons that Germany had failed to win a quick victory in 1914, and hence lost World War I, was that the army had been essentially a slow, foot-bound force that had been unable to interfere with French mobilization and the ability to bring up reserves via the railroad. As a member of the *Truppenamt* after the war, Guderian in 1922 was charged with studying ways in which a German Army bereft of tanks might rectify that situation. Working with the scant resources of the 7th (Bavarian) Motorized Transport Battalion, Guderian became an authority on mechanized warfare, particularly tanks.

At first Guderian's ideas were largely theoretical, as the only tanks available were those secretly produced. But Guderian also read widely and studied theories propounded by Fuller, Liddell Hart, and de Gaulle. He followed with keen interest the British military maneuvers and experiments, especially with massed tank formations controlled by radio. War games orchestrated by Guderian in 1929 with mockup tanks confirmed the British theories. Others were also important in promoting mechanization in the German Army, including the army commander, General Hans von Seeckt, and Guderian's superior, Major General Oswald Lutz, but Guderian was clearly the most forceful figure in the development of German armored warfare doctrine.

Guderian also developed his own concept of *Stosskraft* (dynamic punch) that saw tanks as being the chief shock force in future war. The tanks would not achieve victory on their own, however. The key to success in future wars, Guderian believed, lay in combined arms, an effort in which airpower would also play an important role along with adequate logistics support. Commanders would lead their tank-dominated formations, what became the explosive panzer divisions of World War II, from the front rather than in the rear as in World War I, and they would control them through radio that would connect all the vehicles. In many ways Guderian's theories were the logical extension of the so-called stormtroop (or Hutier) tactics that had evolved in 1918, combined with new technology.

Guderian made little progress in convincing his tradition-minded superiors. That changed with Hitler at the helm. Observing the maneuvers of motorized troops at Kummersdorf in January 1934, Hitler exclaimed, "That's what I need! That's what I want to have!"[2]

Hitler's support was crucial, although he certainly did not see what might really be possible with the new panzer units. Their power was not revealed until the invasion of Poland in September 1939, what came to be known in the West as the blitzkrieg (literally, "lightning war"). Hitler's support did not mean that he was won over entirely by the concept of an all-motorized and armored German Army. Guderian had to work hard to wring changes in the traditional force structure from Hitler and the senior army generals, and he made many enemies in the process.

Yet Guderian was a true visionary. As early as 1933 he envisioned panzer divisions operating independently of slower-moving forces and carrying out surprise thrusts against the enemy flank and rear. In 1935 Guderian virtually on his own secured approval for the formation of three tank divisions, the world's first, although as yet Germany had few tanks.

At first, with their separate tank and infantry brigades, these new divisions looked like the British Mobile Division. But then Guderian added a reconnaissance unit of scout cars and motorcycles as well as field artillery and mobile antitank guns, in addition to some half-tracked armored carriers in place of unarmored trucks. In effect a new military formation was born, capable of entirely independent action and lacking only aircraft for the purposes of reconnaissance and close air support.

In 1937 Guderian published his book *Achtung! Panzer!*, essentially a propaganda document for his theories of high-speed tank warfare. Although the British and French would develop tank formations roughly paralleling those of Germany, they lagged behind the Germans in their concept of tactical employment. Guderian saw the panzer divisions operating independently, much like the divisions de Gaulle envisioned as the spearpoint to the shaft of the foot-bound force. The tank brigade, which was to smash through the enemy formations and make possible deep penetrations, was its key.

Guderian's first tank brigades had a large number of tanks: 560 PzKpfw Is. What they lacked in hitting power they would make up for in shock value. The number of tanks per German division declined throughout World War II, however.

The British and the Germans envisioned tanks and infantry working together. The difference was that the British held that infantry and artillery, assisted by heavy tanks, must first smash a hole in the enemy defensive front. Only when this had been accomplished would the Mobile Division rush through the gap at high speed into the enemy rear areas to disrupt command centers and lines of communication, breaking down the front-line units. The German plan called for reconnaissance units to probe the enemy front, locating the weakest points. A panzer regiment (equivalent to the British tank brigade) moving independently and well in front of its supporting infantry would then carry out a flanking attack against the enemy front without benefit of preliminary bombardment. The supporting infantry would be as much as a mile or two behind the panzers, moving forward in trucks, their flank protected by antitank guns. Behind these came towed artillery pieces, which could fire on enemy positions whenever the attacking tanks and infantry encountered a point of resistance.

From the beginning the Germans managed to get the correct mix of speed, armor protection, and firepower. Guderian and his supporters realized the need for the right combination of fighting and support vehicles and that it was simply impossible to build all the desired capabilities into a single type of machine. In their calculations the Germans initially rejected a heavy armored tank; they counted on massed numbers of light and medium thinly armored vehicles to provide the protection. The whole idea was to keep moving at the highest possible speed.

Tactical airpower formed a key element of the German battle plan. Reconnaissance aircraft patrolled over the advancing columns, ready to call back to a Luftwaffe representative at divisional headquarters, who was authorized to order out dive-bombers to conduct precision attacks against any bottlenecks. Essential to the early German success was its "flying artillery" in the form of the Junkers 87 Stuka. Developed in 1935, this superb single-engine dive-bomber later proved vulnerable to antiaircraft guns and high-performance fighters, but it was also a highly mobile and accurate artillery platform; and as long as Germany controlled the skies, the Stuka could operate with relative impunity.

By September 1939 the German Army fielded a small number of new-type divisions: six armored, four mechanized ("light"), and four motorized infantry. These 14 new-type divisions were only a small proportion of the whole German Army of 98 divisions, but in the first nine months of the war they were worth more than the others put together. In his history of World War II, Liddell Hart concluded that "the German Army achieved its amazing run of victories, not because it was overwhelming in strength or thoroughly modern in form, but because it was a few degrees more advanced than its opponents."[3] It was truly a case of the sum being greater than its parts.

ENDNOTES

1. Peter Chamberlain and Chris Ellis, *British and American Tanks of World War Two: The Complete Illustrated History of British, American, and Commonwealth Tanks, 1933–1945.* London: Cassell, 2000, p. 84.

2. Kenneth Macksey, "Guderian," in *Hitler's Generals,* edited by Correlli Barnett. New York: Grove Weidenfeld, 1989, pp. 244–245.

3. Basil H. Liddell Hart, *History of the Second World War.* New York: G. P. Putnam's Sons, 1970, p. 22.

CHAPTER 3

World War II,
1939–1945

Tanks came into their own during World War II. Although tanks proved to be a vital component of the armed forces in that conflict, masses of tanks alone would not ensure battlefield success. That rested on tactics that combined tanks, infantry, artillery, and supporting aviation in one integrated effort.

In 1939 there was simply no one universal tank that could meet all requirements placed upon it, although designers had struggled to come up with such a tank during the preceding two decades. Different classes of light, medium, and heavy tanks emerged. At the risk of generalizing, light tanks at that time were essentially those of up to about 10 tons; fast and thin-skinned, they tended to be armed with machine guns. Medium tanks weighed up to about 20 tons each; capable of performing a variety of roles, they were slower and mounted a main gun and one or two machine guns. Heavy tanks weighed up to about 30 tons; they were slow and heavily armored to enable them to defend against up to 37mm high-velocity guns, and they mounted a large main gun to enable them to defeat other tanks. Indeed, the chief lesson learned in the war was that the gun rather than the tank itself was the key to tank development. Once the superior gun had been selected, then the tank could be designed around it. Everything else, including armor, was subordinate to that single consideration.

Initially the British and French armies had light, medium, and heavy tanks, and the Germans had only light and medium models.

The German PzKpfw III mounted a 37mm (1.46-inch) gun, and the PzKpfw IV had a 75mm (2.9-inch) gun. The German tanks generally had only up to 30mm armor protection compared to as much as twice that for their opponents. The Soviet Union had all three classes of tanks. The Japanese and Italians, meanwhile, concentrated on infantry-support vehicles, which on the battlefield proved to be inferior in all major respects to the tanks of the other major combatants.

World War I had shown the dominance of machines on the modern battlefield and the subsequent importance in modern war of a nation's industrial capacity. Those powers with significantly greater industrial production, such as the United States and the Soviet Union, would have a decided advantage if a conflict could be sufficiently protracted for that capacity to be translated into actual weapons. The following figures show how industrial production translated into numbers of tanks produced:[1]

	1939	1940	1941	1942	1943	1944	1945
UK	969	1,399	4,841	8,611	7,476	5,000	—
USA	—	c.400	4,052	24,997	29,497	17,565	11,968
USSR	2,950	2,794	6,590	24,446	24,089	28,963	15,400
Germany	c.1,300	2,200	5,200	9,200	17,300	22,100	—
Japan	—	1,023	1,024	1,191	790	401	142

Although these figures exclude Italy (which produced no more than 1,800 tanks and self-propelled guns a year) on the Axis side and France on the Allied side, they nonetheless reveal an Allied advantage in tanks produced of nearly 4:1. Japan's total tank production of 4,571 units is minuscule next to the 105,232 manufactured by the Soviet Union, the largest producer of tanks of the war. Soviet tank production, which was not that far ahead of the United States, was twice that of Germany with its 57,300 units. Such production usually translated into advantage in individual battles and campaigns (Poland in 1939 being a notable exception), when the Allies generally enjoyed superiority in at least numbers of equipment.

The Germans hoped that they might be able to make up for this deficit by superior tanks and tactics, countering increasing Allied armored fighting vehicle (AFV) production with their own PzKpfw Mark V Panther and PzKpfw Mark VI Tiger tanks. They also manufactured increasing numbers of assault antitank guns and *jagdpanzers,* self-propelled guns that mounted the heaviest possible limited-traverse antitank gun on a tank chassis. Although these enjoyed success against the British and Americans, who lacked a heavy tank until late in the war, they were less successful against the Soviet Union's later T-34 medium tank with an 85mm gun, and especially the 46-ton IS-1 (JS-1) heavy tank mounting a 100mm (3.9-inch) or 122mm (4.7-inch) gun. The U.S. decision until late in the war to postpone bringing a new heavy tank on line in favor of increasing the numbers of existing and improved medium M4 Shermans proved unfortunate, although the tardy arrival of the U.S. heavy tank, the 90mm-gun M26 Pershing, in early 1945 helped redress the balance.

One of the myths of World War II is that the Germans enjoyed superiority in numbers as well as quality of tanks. This is simply untrue. What the Germans possessed was a better mix of vehicles for the circumstances, a superior tactical doctrine for their employment, and more effective leadership. In the end better Allied equipment and, above all, superior numbers simply overwhelmed the German forces.

GREAT BRITAIN

The obsolete reconnaissance Mark VIB Light Tank discussed in Chapter 2 comprised the bulk of British tank strength in France and in the Western Desert in May 1940. Thinly armored (maximum 14mm) and mounting only two machine guns, this tank was occasionally forced by circumstances into a cruiser role, for which it was totally inadequate. Its follow-on design was the Mark VII Tetrarch Light Tank (A17). Developed by Vickers beginning in 1937, the Tetrarch's designers intended it to overcome the significant handicap of only machine-gun armament on the Mark II to Mark VIs. Weighing some 16,800 pounds, crewed by three men, powered by a 165-hp engine, and having a speed of 40 mph, the Mark VII mounted a 2-pounder (40mm/1.57-inch) main gun and one machine gun. It had maximum 14mm armor protection.

The Mark VII incorporated a modified Christie suspension based on four large wheels to each track; the front wheels could be steered, thus bending the tracks for gentle turns. This had the advantage of preventing the loss of power by steering a tank by skidding the tracks on the ground. For sharper turns, the controls automatically braked one track to allow a conventional skid turn.

Beginning in 1938 the War Office tested the Mark VII as a light cruiser tank and by the end of the year ordered 120 of them, later doubled to 240. To free Vickers for other work, the War Office arranged transfer of production to Metropolitan-Cammell. Production was delayed as a consequence of this transfer, the decision that followed the spring 1940 Dunkirk evacuation to concentrate on infantry and cruiser tanks, and German bombing of the tank factory. Ultimately only 177 Mark VIIs were produced. Its inadequate cooling system precluded sending the new tank to the Western Desert, although some were shipped to the Soviet Union under Lend-Lease. The Mark VII first saw combat when a squadron participated in the British invasion of Madagascar in May 1942.

The Mark VII was officially named the "Tetrarch" in 1943 when the British Army decided to utilize it for airborne use. The large Hamilcar glider was specifically developed to carry one of these tanks into battle. A squadron of Tetrarchs in the 6th Airborne Division landed in Hamilcars on 6 June 1944, the first day of the Normandy invasion. Some Tetrarchs continued in service until 1949, when the British abandoned airborne gliders.

Apart from light tanks for reconnaissance, the British had cruiser (the former mediums) and infantry (essentially former heavy) tanks. The 125 Mark I Cruiser Tanks, armed with either a 2-pounder (40mm) gun or 3.7-inch howitzer main armament (the latter tank designated the Mk ICS, for close support), served with the 1st Armored Division in France in 1940 and in the Western Desert until late 1941, as did 175 follow-on Mark II Cruiser Tanks, 65 Mark IIIs, and 665 Mark IVs.

Britain's first cruiser design actually introduced during World War II was the Mark V Cruiser Tank (A13 Mk III), designated in 1940 as the Covenanter (thus beginning the British practice of naming tanks). The A13 originated in a 1936 trip to the Soviet Union by Lieutenant Colonel G. Le Q. Martel, assistant director of mechanization, and his inspection there of the T-28 Soviet tank, itself influenced by the British Vickers 16-Tonner of 1929.

The A13 was intended as a high-speed and heavier armored AFV able to operate in an independent role. Three designs of this medium or heavy cruiser were developed, but the A13 Mark III was the one selected. To speed production it was to utilize as many A12 parts as possible, but the new tank would have 30mm armor protection and be of lower height. This latter requirement necessitated a new engine, the Fiat-12, an enlarged version of the engine employed in the Tetrarch light tank and located in the front of the vehicle to the driver's left. The Covenanter weighed some 40,300 pounds, had a crew of four, a 280-hp engine, and a top speed of 31 mph. It mounted a 2-pounder (40mm/1.57-inch) main gun and one machine gun and had maximum 40mm armor protection. Delivery of Covenanters began in early 1940. The new tank suffered from a number of problems, chiefly frequent breakdowns caused by a faulty cooling system that led to overheating. This deficiency was never completely solved, and the 1,771 Covenanters ended up as training tanks through 1943.

The A15, which became the Mark VI Crusader, stemmed from the same requirement for a medium cruiser tank for independent action. Essentially an enlarged A13 Mark III, it was adopted over contending designs in large part because it included many elements of the A13 series, including the modified Christie suspension, and thus could be put into production faster. Its greater length (one additional bogie wheel on each side) offered improved trench-spanning capability. Ultimately nine firms produced the tank, designated the Crusader.

Produced in Marks I–III, the Mark I version weighed 42,560 pounds, had a crew of three men, a 340-hp engine for a speed of 27 mph (often exceeded), and was armed with a 2-pounder main gun and one machine gun. It carried maximum 40mm armor. Marks II and III carried heavier armor and also did not have the small front auxiliary machine gun turret, which proved of limited value. Its removal allowed greater ammunition storage. The Mark III also substituted a 6-pounder (57mm/2.24-inch) gun.

The Crusader first saw action in North Africa in June 1941. With a total of 5,300 produced by nine different firms, the Crusader was from 1941 the principal British-designed tank of the war. Fast and maneuverable, it was nonetheless insufficiently armored and outmatched by the German PzKpfw III's 50mm main gun. It also fell victim to German 50mm, 75mm, and 88mm antitank guns. As soon as possible the British Army replaced the Crusader with the U.S. M3 and M4 mediums. Although obsolete as a medium tank, the Crusader was subsequently modified and served in a variety of roles until the end of the war, as an antiaircraft tank, tank recovery vehicle, antimine tank, combat engineer tank, and artillery tractor for the 17-pounder (76.2mm) gun.

The deficiencies of the Covenanter and Crusader medium cruiser tanks, demonstrated in the Battle for France and early fighting in North Africa, led to a crash British effort to develop a heavy cruiser tank capable of taking on and defeating the German Panzer PzKpfw III. Among specifications sought for the new tank were heavier armor (65mm on the hull front and 75mm on the turret), larger (60-inch) turret ring, more powerful engine, heavier (6-pounder) gun, weight of not more than 24 tons, speed of at least 24 mph, and above all greater mechanical reliability.

Vauxhall offered a scaled-down Churchill infantry tank, designated the A23, while Nuffield Mechanization and Aero, already producing the Crusader, offered the A24 design based on it, which had the advantage of retaining its Christie suspension, Liberty engine, and Wilson epicyclic gearbox. The Tank Board selected the A24 as an interim design and ordered 500 without prototype or testing. The first A24, designated the Cavalier, was produced in January 1942.

The Cavalier turned out to be an unsatisfactory design. It did not meet the desired specifications, and its far greater weight of some 59,400 pounds led to inferior performance and short engine life. The Cavalier was also subject to frequent mechanical breakdowns. Production vehicles were utilized for training as gun tanks until 1943, when about half of them were converted into mobile observation posts and provided to the artillery regiments of British armored divisions, in which capacity they saw service in the fighting in Europe during 1944–1945. Other Cavaliers became tank recovery vehicles.

At the time of the competition for the tank that became the Cavalier, Leyland Motors had suggested a design that would use a chassis similar to the Crusader but employ the more powerful Rolls-Royce Merlin aero engine and the new Merritt-Brown gearbox introduced in the Churchill heavy tank. The essential element of this A27 design was the Merlin engine, designated the Meteor in its tank version. But all Merlin/Meteor engine production was then required for aircraft, so the new design was held in abeyance and the Cavalier placed into production.

Nonetheless, work went forward on the A27. Pending the availability of the Meteor engine, Leyland was asked to come up with a design that would utilize the Liberty engine of the Crusader, yet could be modified to take the Meteor when it became available. The design was known as the A27L (for Liberty). The first production models, designated the Mark VIII Centaur Cruiser Tank (A27L), began coming off the assembly lines in late 1942. Some 950 Centaurs were manufactured, including 80 that substituted a 95mm howitzer as the main gun for purposes of close infantry support. The Centaur weighed 63,500 pounds, had a five-man crew, was powered by a 395-hp Liberty engine that drove it at 27 mph, and was armed with a 6-pounder (57mm) main gun and one machine gun. It had maximum 76mm armor protection.

The Royal Marines Armored Support Group employed Centaurs in the Allied invasion of Normandy on 6 June 1944, using them to provide covering fire from LCTs (landing craft tank) and then fire over the beaches. Centaurs saw extensive service throughout the remainder of the war in the fighting in northern Europe. Some were later converted to Cromwells by the substitution of the new Meteor engine. Others, fitted with a dummy main gun and extra radio equipment, became artillery observation post (OP) tanks, and others were modified as antiaircraft tanks, engineer tanks, and armored recovery vehicles. A few became armored personnel carriers (APCs) and were known as Centaur Kangaroos.

The Cromwell was the A27 with the powerful 600-hp Meteor and designated the A27M. The new engine drove it at up to 40 mph. Originally designated the Cromwell III, it entered production in January 1943 as the Cruiser Tank, Mark VIII, Cromwell (A27M). Fighting in North Africa led to a demand for a gun that could fire both high-explosive (HE) and armor-piercing (AP) shells, and the result was a British version of the U.S. 75mm gun, essentially a bored-up 6-pounder that could fire U.S.-made 75mm ammunition. Problems with the new gun were not completely corrected until May 1944.

Numerically, the Cromwell was the most important British heavy cruiser tank of the war; it and the U.S.-built M4 Sherman were the principal AFVs of the British armored divisions that fought across northern Europe in 1944–1945. The Cromwell's 75mm gun, however, made it inferior to the German PzKpfw V and even late model PzKpfw IVs. Its narrow hull, however, precluded upgunning. It and the Centaur had the same boxlike turret construction.

The Cromwell appeared in a wide variety of models (Mks I through VIII). Later models saw the introduction of all-welded construction in place of riveting. The Cromwell continued in service with the British Army after World War II, and after 1950 a number of them were given a new turret and a 20-pounder gun.

The Centaur/Cromwell tanks seem to have solved the major problem for the British—unreliability—but the British Army wanted a tank that mounted a gun sufficiently powerful to destroy the largest German tanks. This led to a contract with the Birmingham Carriage & Wagon Company, a manufacturer of train rolling stock, to utilize the basic Cromwell chassis design and same Meteor engine but with a new turret that would mount a more powerful 17-pounder gun.

The result was the Cruiser Tank, Challenger (A-30). It utilized a lengthened Cromwell chassis, adding an additional road wheel (for a total of six) to each side. The center hull was also widened to accommodate the new turret. The completely redesigned turret was also taller. The Challenger was rushed into service before teething problems were completely overcome in order to counter the German PzKpfw IV and its long 75mm gun.

The Challenger's height, more than 9 feet, 1 foot higher than the Cromwell, made it a prominent target for enemy fire. Although it had a maximum 101mm armor, its far heavier battle weight of 72,800 pounds—5.5 tons more than the Cromwell—meant some reduction in capabilities. It had a top speed of 31 mph and only one machine gun, the hull machine gun being eliminated to save space for main gun ammunition.

The Challenger was utilized chiefly in a tank destroyer role. Distributed to British tank divisions in similar proportion to antiaircraft and close-support tanks, it provided the capability of taking on and defeating the largest German tanks, even those mounting the 88mm gun. Ongoing problems with the Challenger, however, caused the British to concurrently upgrade the 75mm gun on their U.S.-built M4 Shermans with the same 17-pounder gun (becoming known as the Firefly). Ultimately the Firefly proved superior to the Challenger as a tank destroyer.

The first Challengers were not ready until May 1944. They did not take part in the Normandy invasion, because no provision had been made for them to be able to get ashore in deep water from the LCTs. Late in 1944, however, they were issued to British armored divisions and fought in the campaign across northern Europe.

The follow-on design to the Challenger was the Comet Cruiser Tank (A34). Developed by Leyland, it was based on the A27 design. In order to avoid having to widen the hull, the designer incorporated a new compact Vickers-Armstrong 17-pounder gun. Later known as the 77mm, this lighter-weight gun had a shorter barrel and breech. Although the designers had hoped to utilize the A27 turret, a larger version proved necessary. Ultimately the Comet utilized only about 40 percent of the A27 design. The 78,800-pound Comet was powered by the Rolls-Royce Meteor 600-hp engine and capable of 29 mph. It had a five-man crew and maximum 101mm armor protection. The Comet also incorporated a stronger suspension system with the addition of track return rollers, and it boasted all-welded construction. Production began in September 1944, and although a few Comets were issued earlier, most went to the 11th Armored Division beginning in March 1945.

A fast and reliable tank, the Comet was the first British tank to approximate the German Panther in main armament and performance. It appeared too late in the war to have a major impact, although it remained in service with the British Army into the early 1960s.

Among British infantry tanks, the Matilda I and II tanks, discussed in Chapter 2, played an important role in the early desert campaigns. The most successful tank in the 1940 fighting in North Africa, the Matilda's armor rendered it impregnable to any Italian tank or antitank gun until the Germans began employing their 88mm antiaircraft gun in an antitank role in mid-1941. In June 1941 the Matildas were joined by the excellent Valentine infantry tank, which was pressed into service in North Africa in a cruiser role.

In September 1939 at the beginning of the war the British War Office still believed that ground fighting would resemble that of the Western Front in World War I. It therefore sought a heavy infantry tank with sufficient armor to protect it from enemy antitank guns, as well as excellent cross-country and trench-spanning capabilities. Woolwich Arsenal drew up specifications for this new AFV, designated the A20, and the government contracted with the firm of Harland and Wolff to build a test model. Specifications for the A20 called for it to have a speed of 15 mph, a seven-man crew, 80mm maximum armor protection, and ability to climb a 5-foot parapet. A variety of main armaments were considered, with two 2-pounders being selected: one in the turret and another in the nose. In early 1940 four pilot models were ordered, but the A20 was still undergoing testing and was found to have gearbox problems by the time of the Dunkirk evacuation that summer.

The evacuation at Dunkirk forced the British Expeditionary Force (BEF) to abandon virtually all its heavy equipment in France. Fewer than 100 tanks were left for the defense of Britain. Vauxhall Motors was charged with continuing development of the A20, slightly reducing its size, and bringing it into production as rapidly as possible. By November 1940 Vauxhall had a new version ready, the Mark IV Churchill Infantry Tank (A22). Because of the speed of the process, however, the A22 suffered from a host of teething problems, leading to considerable modifications, even to the point of sending Vauxhall engineers to the units that were using the tank. Not until 1943 were these problems entirely overcome.

The Churchill Mark IV continued the outdated concept of a light high-velocity gun in a small turret with a large low-velocity forward-firing support gun carried in the hull between the tracks. The first

Churchills weighed 87,360 pounds, had a 350-hp engine and top speed of 15 mph, a crew of five, maximum 102mm armor thickness, and a hull-mounted 76mm (3-inch) gun and a turret-mounted 2-pounder and one machine gun. The original plans to outfit the new heavy infantry tank with a heavier gun were scrapped in the aftermath of the Dunkirk evacuation when priority had to be given to weapons systems already in production.

The Churchill incorporated the Merritt-Brown regenerative-steering system that saved much of the power lost during steering. The turning circle could also be reduced depending on the gear engaged; a lower gear enabled a tighter turning radius, and in neutral the tank could be pivoted on its axis. The Churchill utilized hydraulics in the steering and clutch controls, which reduced driver fatigue. Its 22 bogie wheels gave a somewhat rough ride, but a number of them could be shot off and the remainder could continue to support the tread. Its roomy interior allowed it to carry 58 rounds of ammunition for the 76mm gun and 150 for the 40mm. The Churchill Mark III, which mounted the 6-pounder (57mm) gun, first saw action in the August 1942 Dieppe Raid, where it gave an indifferent performance. From that point on Churchills were in almost constant action.

Early mechanical problems were overcome, and the Churchill turned out to be a reliable AFV. Changing tactical requirements led to changes in armament and upgrades in armor. The Mark III was the first Churchill to mount a 6-pounder gun in the turret, necessitating a new, welded turret; the Marks V and VIII, intended for a close-support role, mounted a 95mm howitzer. About 10 percent of the 5,640 total Churchills produced throughout the war mounted the 95mm howitzer. Produced in Marks I through XI and in many specialist versions, Churchills continued in service with the British Army into the 1960s.

Other heavy infantry tanks were under development toward the end of the war, including the Black Prince (A43) of 112,000 pounds, mounting a 17-pounder on a widened Cromwell chassis, and the Valiant Infantry Tank (A38), weighing 60,400 pounds and mounting a 75mm gun, but these did not go into production. There were also heavy assault tank designs—the 100,800-pound A33 with a 75mm gun and the 174,720-pound Tortoise (A39). The A39 was prompted by the appearance of the Germans' King Tiger; the Tortoise mounted a 32-pounder, the largest gun for any British AFV design of the war. Neither the A33 nor the A39 reached production status before the end of the war.

CANADA

Canada developed its own tanks during the war. Cut off from the supply of British tanks due to the hostilities, the Canadian government decided to produce its own. The Canadians adapted the major components of the U.S. M3 but removed its sponson-mounted 75mm main gun in favor of a turret-mounted 40mm gun. Production of this tank, dubbed the Mark I Ram Cruiser Tank, began at the end of 1941. It weighed some 57,100 pounds and had a 400-hp engine producing a speed of 25 mph. The Ram had a crew of five. It was armed with a 2-pounder (40mm) gun and two coaxial 7.62mm machine guns. It had maximum 89mm armor.

Following production of the first 50 tanks, the Ram design was modified to enable the tank to mount a 6-pounder main gun. This changeover was easily accomplished because the turret had been designed from the beginning with the 6-pounder in mind. It also made use of a gyro-stabilizer for control of gun elevation. By the end of production in September 1943, a total of 1,899 Ram IIs had been manufactured. Most Rams were shipped overseas.

By the time the Ram began to reach the European Theater in quantity, the United States had introduced the M4 Sherman. The Canadians then withdrew the Ram II from service and adopted the M4 as their standard tank throughout the war. The Canadian-built version of the Sherman was known as the Grizzly. Its few modifications included the installation in the turret of a 2-inch smoke mortar. The changeover from Ram to Grizzly was complete by the invasion of France in June 1944, although Canada continued to produce the Ram chassis and hull for the Sexton self-propelled gun.

AUSTRALIA

Australia had purchased four medium Vickers Mark IIA tanks in 1928, but beginning in the summer of 1940, as war with Japan seemed ever more likely, and with Britain unable to supply AFVs to Australia, the Ministry of Munitions undertook at some expense and effort to build an entirely indigenous tank. In November the General Staff produced a list of specifications and estimated that it would need about 2,000 new tanks.

The Australian government asked the British to send out a tank-design expert, and Colonel Watson traveled to Australia by way of the United States in December 1940. There Watson reviewed the latest designs for the U.S. M3. On his arrival in Australia, Watson was appointed director of design. Impressed by what he had seen of its mechanical features while in the United States, Watson proposed to utilize a copy of the M3's final drive and gearbox manufactured in Australia. Although Watson would have preferred a diesel engine, the ready availability of truck engines, first the Ford and later the more powerful Cadillac, led to their adoption instead.

A wooden mockup of the new tank was ready in early 1941. The tank was to have cast or rolled armor from alloys available in Australia. Although difficulties were encountered in producing the final drive with machinery then available in country, a simplified final drive was adopted with components that could be manufactured in Australia. The first prototype, the Sentinel Cruiser Tank (AC I), was produced in January 1942. Its cast hull and turret were landmarks, as nothing this complicated had been attempted by Australian industry. Following trials, the first production model was completed in August 1942 by the Challuna Tank Assembly Shops in New South Wales, built expressly for this purpose.

Only 66 Sentinels were built when all orders were canceled and production ceased in July 1943. By that date the supply situation had changed, with the United States able to provide all AFVs required to equip the 1st Australian Armored Division, which had then formed. As a consequence, the AC I was used only for training and never saw combat service. Despite this, it was an excellent design. Weighing 62,720 pounds with a one-piece cast hull, the AC I was powered by three Cadillac V-8, 117-hp engines and was capable of 30 mph. It had maximum 65mm armor protection and was armed with a 2-pounder main gun and two machine guns. Despite the fact that it did not see combat service, the Sentinel was an extraordinary achievement for a nation with limited heavy industrial resources.

GERMANY

Surprisingly, given the great success of German armored warfare doctrine early in World War II, most of the tanks that Germany took to war were second-rate. Although at the outbreak of World War II the German Army had some 2,900 tanks of its own manufacture, the overwhelming majority of these were PzKpfw I and PzKpfw IIs. Germany had some 1,400 PzKpfw Is, 1,200 PzKpfw IIs, 98 PzKpfw

IIIs, and 211 PzKpfw IVs. The PzKpfw I was basically a tankette, and the PzKpfw II mounted only a 20mm gun.[2]

Fighting in Poland proved that the PzKpfw I's light armor and firepower were insufficient. Although they were obsolescent, 523 PzKpfw Is were employed in the invasion of France. During World War II the PzKpfw I was also modified to fill a number of roles. In 1939 the body of the tank was fitted with an antitank gun, which proved effective in North Africa. Others were modified to become armored supply vehicles or command vehicles. An unusual experiment involved using the chassis of a PzKpfw I in an attempt to create radio-controlled tanks and explosive charge–layers. These were known as the *Ladungsleger* I, but they never got beyond the experimental stage. By late 1941 the PzKpfw I had clearly outlasted its usefulness. It was replaced by faster tanks with more armor protection and higher-caliber weapons, capable of competing with Allied technology.

The PzKpfw II, although basically a light reconnaissance vehicle, often was pressed into service with the panzer divisions in a light combat tank role. Experience gained in Poland and France led to a series of upgrades (Ausf. B–G), most of which were additional armor protection. The tank remained in production until late 1942, and it continued as variants until 1944, including the *Flammpanzer* (flamethrower) tanks on the Ausf. D chassis. They were also converted into antitank guns (including the 105mm gun) and a river-crossing variant that was employed on the Eastern Front.

The PzKpfw III medium tank was the chief tank of the German panzer divisions from 1940 onward. As with the PzKpfw II, it received a series of modifications. The Ausf. E and F received additional armor protection and improved suspension. The Ausf. H was the first production model to receive a 50mm (1.97-inch) main gun in place of the original 37mm; the Ausf. N mounted a 75mm (2.9-inch). PzKpfw hulls were adapted to virtually every possible role. It proved such an adaptable design that the PzKpfw III was still in production at war's end.

The PzKpfw IV also underwent significant change during the war. Ausf. A–C were produced before the war; seven other models would follow and production continued virtually to the end of the war. The PzKpfw IV became the backbone of the Wehrmacht's armor, especially in the Soviet Union. The basic chassis remained the same but armor was tremendously increased, from a maximum of 15mm in the A model to 80mm in the H and J versions. The caliber of the main gun, 75mm, remained the same but velocity was increased.

Life for tank crew members was not necessarily easy. Although riding in a tank was preferable to marching on foot, the tanks were also ready targets. Of necessity, tank crews bonded into tight-knit units, but they faced their own particular problems. One German tanker describes his experience in these words:

The need to have the tank working without fault meant that the crew were always together within a vehicle. The crew became a family and the tank a home where one was secure and rested. Rested because of track vibration, aching feet, sore back, pulled muscle were all gone after half an hour on the road. And each tank had its own smell; a combination of the odours of hot oil, petrol, steel and earth.

There was also the other side of being a crewman. I have had to drive in freezing rain, the wind coming through the tank, and I could have cried because I was so cold. On these occasions there was only one way to thaw out—take it in turns to go outside on to the back of the tank, lie flat on your back on the engine planes and let the heat come through your tank-suit. Spread-eagled, one was perfectly safe and none of us ever fell off while moving along the roads.

For the enemy, the tank with its steady, fast pace and covered in dust and earth looks unstoppable. There was little sound from the silenced engines, but the noise made by the metal tracks on cobblestones or the steel-squeal on the roads was unlike anything previously heard and was very frightening.[3]

While they enjoyed relatively easy success with their tanks against Poland in 1939 and France in 1940, the Germans discovered that in the case of the Soviet Union in 1941–1942 they had nothing to counter the Soviet T-34 and even more powerful heavy KV-1 tank. Part of the solution was to upgun their prewar tanks, and it is a testament to the effectiveness of their basic designs that the Germans were able to do this. This stop-gap measure proved insufficient, and even at Stalingrad in the winter of 1942–1943 the Germans had inferior armor. One German soldier, a gun-loader on a self-propelled tank hunter, recalled years later, "The veterans who marched on Stalingrad said to us, 'Hopefully we'll get better tanks now.' They had marched on Stalingrad and they were still primarily equipped with tanks that had the 50mm [main gun]—the 'door knocker' we called it. We were inferior to the Russians as far as tanks were concerned. They had the legendary T-34, a completely different type of tank weapon."[4]

General Guderian came up with the novel solution that the Germans should simply copy the Soviet T-34. Hitler rejected this idea

The German Panther V heavy medium tank.
Courtesy of Art-Tech/Aerospace/M.A.R.S/TRH/Navy Historical.

outright, leading to two entirely new tank designs: the PzKpfw V
Panther and the PzKpfw VI Tiger.

After the Germans carefully studied the T-34, Hitler ordered production of a new tank of similar 30-ton class. The result was the
PzKpfw Panther, one of the top tanks of World War II. MAN and
Daimler-Benz each received orders to develop its chassis, and the turret was designed by Rheinmetall-Borsig. When the MAN chassis was
discovered to be superior, Hitler ordered it into production. He
wanted the new tank ready in time to take part in the 1943 campaign.

The PzKpfw V was instantly recognizable by its more elongated,
low-silhouette turret. Indeed, the design heavily influenced the design of countless turrets to come in the tanks of many nations. Similar in size to the Soviet T-34 and introduced in early 1943, the
PzKpfw V Ausf. D Panther weighed some 94,800 pounds. Crewed
by five men, it had a 700-hp engine and was capable of 28 mph. It
had maximum 100mm armor protection, enhanced by the use of
sloped surfaces in the turret and hull and sheet steel side skirts. The
Panther mounted a long, high-velocity (L/70, or 70 calibers of the
bore in length) 75mm gun and also had three machine guns (one
each of hull, turret, and antiaircraft).

Some observers rate the Panther as the best all-around tank of the war. It represented an excellent combination of armament, protection, and mobility. The Panther's high-velocity main gun had great striking power and could engage and knock out at long range all but the most powerful Allied tanks.

Panther production was set at 600 units a month, but such a figure was never realized despite the consortium of manufacturers. The Panther remained expensive and difficult to manufacture, and production was plagued by continued Allied bombing. Only 850 Ausf. D Panthers, the first production model, were manufactured between January and September 1943. Hitler insisted that the new tank go into action immediately, and without proper testing it experienced a series of teething problems, especially mechanical. Panthers fought in the greatest tank battle in history, the Battle of Kursk in July and August 1943. Two subsequent Panther upgrades, Ausf. A and Ausf. G, featured thicker armor protection, strengthened road wheels, and changes to the hull to ease production. Panther variants included 347 armored recovery vehicles.

Easily the most feared German tank during the war was the PzKpfw VI Tiger. It resulted from an Ordnance Department order in 1937 from Henschel for a heavy breakthrough tank that would be 50 percent heavier than the PzKpfw IV and protected by 50mm armor. First manufactured in March 1941, the Tiger went through several prototypes before production began in earnest on the Ausf. E in July 1942. The PzKpfw VI Tiger weighed some 125,700 pounds (making it the world's heaviest tank), had a crew of five, a 700-hp engine that produced a maximum speed of 24 mph, and was armed with a powerful 88mm (3.46-inch) gun. It had 100mm hull front armor and 120mm armor on the gun mantlet, the movable piece of armor surrounding the main gun.

Although the Tiger was not especially nimble and was in fact better suited to defense than offense, its gun could destroy any other tank in the world. It in turn could be destroyed only by the heaviest Allied antitank guns, and then only at much shorter ranges than that of the Tiger's main gun. Guderian had urged the Tigers be held back until sufficient numbers were available to enable them to effect a major victory, but Hitler insisted on trying out the tanks that September in the Leningrad sector, where they fell prey to well-sited Soviet antitank guns. Guderian noted that the result was "heavy, unnecessary casualties, but also the loss of secrecy and of the element of surprise for future operations."[5]

The Tiger was a complicated AFV and thus difficult to manufac-

The German PzKpfw VI Tiger.
Courtesy of Art-Tech/Aerospace/M.A.R.S/TRH/Navy Historical.

ture and maintain. It also had an overlapping wheel suspension that tended to clog in muddy conditions or freeze up in cold weather, immobilizing the tank. Nonetheless, its superb 88mm high-velocity main gun took a heavy toll of Allied tanks through the end of the war. The Soviets learned through the hard experience of tank-on-tank combat that the only way to nullify the Tiger's longer-range 88mm gun was to close the distance before firing. In the close-quarters fighting of Stalingrad, for example, distances hardly mattered.

The final German tank of the war was the PzKpfw Tiger II, Königstiger (King Tiger). With a weight of some 149,900 pounds, it had a hull design similar to the Panther series and the same engine. Its frontal armor was well sloped to increase its effectiveness. Its far heavier armor (up to 180mm in the turret), however, rendered it slow (21 mph) and hard to maneuver. The King Tiger mounted the superb 88mm gun and two machine guns. Issued to training units beginning in February 1944, it did not begin to arrive in combat units until that June, five months after production had begun. In the fighting at Normandy, the Tiger II proved more than a match for any Allied tank. Although it could withstand most Allied antitank weapons, there were insufficient numbers of King Tigers either to employ them in mass formations or to erase the great deficit in numbers of Allied tanks. It also suffered from mechanical unreliability, and its considerable bulk was difficult to conceal from Allied aircraft, which by this time enjoyed complete air superiority over the battlefield.

One other German tank deserves mention here: the PzKpfw Maus (Mouse) super-heavy tank. A wildly impractical design, it was more suited as a mobile fort (no river bridge existing at the time could take its weight). Produced only as a prototype, the Maus owed its development to Adolf Hitler's love of the grandiose; he ordered it from Porsche in 1942. Weighing some 421,000 pounds, the Maus was quite simply the heaviest tank in history. It had a 200mm armored carapace over the front hull and mounted a 128mm (5-inch) main gun as well as a coaxial 75mm gun and one 7.62mm machine gun. The intention was that the production version would mount a 160mm (5.9-inch) or even 170mm (6.7-inch) main gun. Although 150 of these monsters were ordered in 1943, the Maus program was plagued by problems, not the least of which was developing an engine capable of moving the immense weight. Only two prototypes were ever produced, one of which survives in a museum near Moscow.

ITALY

The basic Italian light tank of the war was the Fiat Carro Armato L6/40, the descendent of the 5-ton Fiat-Ansaldo light tank of the 1930s. Somewhat equivalent to the German PzKpfw II, the L6/40 weighed approximately 15,000 pounds, had a 70-hp engine, and was capable of 26 mph. It mounted a 20mm (.79-inch) main gun and one machine gun and had maximum 40mm armor protection. Unsuitable for front-line service because of its light armament, the L6/40 was utilized in the fighting in North Africa in cavalry and reconnaissance roles. It also was sent to the Eastern Front in fighting against the Soviet Union, and it served in Italy. Variants included command tanks and flamethrower tanks, and the L6/40 was also utilized in the *Semovente* 47/32 self-propelled assault vehicle mounting a 47mm antitank gun.

In 1940 the Italians decided to build a new tank, the Fiat M13/40, which was to be the basis of future Italian armor formations. It became the principal Italian medium tank and mainstay of Italy's armor force in North Africa. Broadly based on the M11/39, which was obsolete by the time it was introduced, the 30,900-pound

M13/40 had a crew of four. The new tank incorporated the basic hull design of its predecessor but was larger and carried a new high-velocity 47mm gun in the turret, with secondary armament of four machine guns in the hull, the reverse of its predecessor. It had improved but still inadequate (maximum 42mm) riveted armor protection. It was unreliable mechanically and, at 125 hp and 30,900 pounds, underpowered. The M13/40 also had a tall silhouette (nearly 8 feet).

The M14/40 first entered action in December 1940 in Libya and was used extensively in North Africa against British forces. Its deficiencies, including mechanical problems, soon became apparent. Although a practical design, it was no match for heavy British infantry tanks such as the Matilda. The M13/40 was also cramped and tended to catch fire easily when hit by antitank rounds. The Germans dubbed them *Der Rollende Saerge* (the Rolling Coffins). Given the shortage of British tanks in the early fighting in North Africa, Commonwealth forces did press a number of captured M13/40s into temporary service.

The M13/40 gave rise to the successful *Semovente* 75/18 self-propelled assault gun. This utilized the M13/40 chassis but replaced the turret with a boxlike superstructure mounting slightly right of center a limited-traverse 75mm Model 75/18 howitzer. It had a low silhouette(6 feet), a great advantage for an assault gun. The 75/18 saw extensive service during the war in North Africa as well as in Italy with both German and Italian forces. It also appeared as a command vehicle. The same M13/40 chassis was used in the *Semovente* 90/53, one of the most powerful antitank guns of the entire war. Similar to the German 88mm in that it was a converted antiaircraft gun, it was mounted, because of its size, in the open on the rear end of an M14/40 chassis. Only 24 were made, and all were destroyed in the 1943 Sicily campaign.

In mid-1942 Italy considered building the successful German PzKpfw III under license. The idea was rejected outright in early 1942, probably because of pressure from Fiat and Ansaldo, which controlled Italian tank construction.

JAPAN

For the European powers the Spanish Civil War of 1936–1939 had shown the ineffectiveness of light tankettes on the modern battlefield, but the Japanese had learned no such lesson from fighting in China, and they continued to build light-skinned vehicles that could be penetrated even by small-arms fire. As the principal Japanese opponents of the 1930s, the Chinese, had no tanks, the Japanese lacked the incentive to change.

In 1938–1939, however, the Japanese fought several large-scale battles against the Soviets in an undeclared border war in the Soviet Far East and Manchuria. This fighting was quite different, especially the Battle of Nomonhan/Khalkhin Gol in Mongolia in March–September 1939. Here the Japanese were rebuffed by General Georgi K. Zhukov's massed heavy armor formations. Although Tokyo then considered the formation of separate tank divisions, nothing came of it at the time.

Throughout World War II, Japanese tanks remained relatively thin-skinned and undergunned infantry-support vehicles, clearly outgunned by U.S. tanks. Most formations in the Imperial Japanese Army were basically light infantry, and the army leadership regarded tanks as little more than armored personnel carriers or infantry support vehicles. Not until the summer of 1942 did the Japanese activate their first two tank divisions, but production and shipping difficulties forced abandonment of the armored force the next year. The army was also sadly deficient in numbers and types of artillery. The failure of the Japanese to develop a satisfactory machine gun between the wars is more surprising, given their reliance during the war on infantry charges. The principal Japanese rifle, the Arisaka M-38, was 35 years old and a clumsy weapon, particularly in the jungle. Actually too big for the average Japanese soldier, it had been adopted as a good example of a Western weapon.

Fighting the heavier-gunned Soviet tanks in Mongolia in 1939 revealed to the Japanese the inadequacy of the 47mm gun on their basic Japanese medium tank, the Type 97 Chi-Ha. The Japanese then designed a new turret for the Type 97, replacing its low-velocity 6-pounder (57mm/2.24-inch) main gun with a longer, high-velocity 47mm (1.85-inch). Designated the Type 97 Shinhoto (new turret) Chi-Ha, the 35,400-pound tank had a number of desirable features, including monocoque construction, a diesel engine, and sloped armor, but it had only 25mm maximum armor and a 47mm main gun and was far outclassed by the more powerful U.S. M3s and M4s it encountered. The Type 97 was the most widely used Japanese medium tank of World War II. It also appeared in engineer and command tank versions.

The Japanese produced yet another Type 97 tank in the Type I

Chi-He. Slightly longer and taller than the Type 97 Chi-Ha, it mounted the new high-velocity 47mm and two machine guns and had a new turret, thicker (60mm) welded armor, and a more powerful 240-hp diesel engine that produced a speed of 27 mph. The Chi-He weighed some 38,100 pounds and had a crew of five (as opposed to four for the Chi-Ha).

For too long Japanese leaders continued to believe in *bushido* and the spirit of the *samurai*. No one would dispute that their soldiers were highly motivated and ready to die to the last man, as they often did. But that misses the point. Their leaders believed that human will could triumph over machines, an astonishing conclusion in modern war. By way of comparison, every U.S. field soldier fighting in the Pacific was supported by 4 tons of equipment, whereas every Japanese soldier was supported by 2 pounds.[6] By the time the Japanese had realized their error and discovered the need for a heavier tank to seek out and destroy enemy fighting vehicles, they lacked the means to mass-produce it.

SOVIET UNION

In the late 1930s the Soviet Union, not Germany, was the nation most interested in massive armor formations. It also possessed by far the largest number of armored fighting vehicles of any nation. In June 1941 the Soviet Union had 23,140 tanks (10,394 in the West), whereas the invading Germans had only about 6,000. Besides the advantage in numbers, the Soviets also had some of the best tanks in the world. During the war the Soviet Union built more tanks than any other power; these included a wide range of AFVs, from light to heavy tanks.

At the beginning of World War II the Soviets possessed a large number of their medium BT-series tanks, chiefly BT-5s and BT-7s. These and the Soviet T-26s were superior in armor, firepower, and maneuverability to the German light PzKpfw Marks III and IV and could destroy any German tank. The Russian T-34 medium introduced in 1941 and KV-1 heavy tank introduced in 1940 both mounted the 76.2mm (3-inch) gun and were superior to the PzKpfws III and IV and every other German tank in 1941.

Generally speaking, the Soviets followed a gradual approach in tank design, modifying a proven design rather than starting from scratch. This was certainly the case with light tanks, the early types chiefly being the T-60 and T-70. The T-60 was the follow-on to the T-40 series of light amphibious tanks, and it led to the T-70. The T-40 suffered from very light armor, which was necessary for its amphibious capability. The T-60, which entered production in July 1941 and replaced all other Soviet light tanks, was designed from the start to be nonamphibious. Although based on the T-40 chassis and with a similar suspension system, the T-60 weighed some 11,400 pounds, had a two-man crew, and mounted a 20mm gun and heavier (25mm) armor. Through 1943, when production ceased, the Soviets produced 6,292 T-60s.

The follow-on T-70 was the last Soviet light tank built in quantity. Designed to rectify the problems of light armament and armor of the T-60 and to be mass-produced by the automotive industry, the T-70 was produced in even greater numbers: a total of 8,226 were built. It was intended as a stop-gap measure for infantry support until Soviet factories could mass-produce the new T-34 medium and heavier Soviet tanks.

The T-70 was much heavier (21,900 pounds) than the T-60. It had a crew of two and greater power than the T-60, with two 70-hp engines giving a road speed of up to 31 mph. The T-70 mounted a 45mm main gun and one machine gun, and it had maximum 60mm armor.

The last Soviet light tank was the T-80. Closely modeled on the T-70, it had virtually the same dimensions and capabilities with the exception of additional welded-on armor and a cupola. Few T-80s were built, however. The Soviets discontinued light tanks altogether in 1944, their role being taken by U.S. Lend-Lease half-tracks.

Among medium tanks in September 1939, the Soviets had a large number of their BT series, chiefly BT-5s and BT-7s. These tanks were popular with crews and combined an excellent mix of firepower, maneuverability, and reliability. Their chief shortcoming, revealed in the Soviet invasion of Finland in November 1939, was inadequate armor protection; the BT-7 had only a maximum of 22mm. The last Soviet BT-series tank, the BT-IS, produced only in prototype, had heavier (30mm) armor. It was an important step forward toward the T-34. The first Soviet tank with all-sloped armor, the BT-IS had an enlarged turret that permitted mounting of a 76mm gun, but it had a 45mm. The tank weighed some 36,600 pounds.

Based on the experiences of Soviet armor in the Spanish Civil War, General Dimitri Pavlov ordered the design of a new medium tank, the A-20. It weighed some 44,400 pounds. Produced in prototype only, the A-20 featured a Christie suspension with track- and wheel-running capabilities. It had the BT-IS fully sloped hull on the basic BT-7M chassis. With a crew of four, a 450-hp engine, and a maximum speed of 40 mph, it mounted a 45mm gun and two machine guns. It had maximum armor protection of 60mm. The A-20 also featured a widened track. The A-20 was then further modified as the A-30 medium. Also only a prototype and basically the same design, the A-30 was heavier (some 46,000 pounds) and mounted the 76.2mm (3-inch) gun in place of the 45mm.

Building on test experience with the A-20 and A-30, the Soviet Union introduced the T-32 (A-32) medium in 1939. It weighed some 41,800 pounds and had a crew of four. Its 450-hp diesel engine drove it at a maximum speed of 38 mph. In addition to the main 76.2mm gun, the T-32 mounted two 7.62mm machine guns and had maximum 60mm armor protection. It retained the Christie suspension system and the excellent sloped armor protection of its predecessors. Combat experience in Mongolia against the Japanese, and then in Finland, led the Soviet Defense Committee to order an upgunned and heavier-armored T-32 into production in December 1939.

At the same time, however, Soviet designers were at work on a redesign of the T-32. This resulted in the T-34 medium, the most widely produced Soviet tank of the war and perhaps the single most important weapons system in the Soviet arsenal on the Eastern Front. The first T-34 test models were ready in 1940, with the production model entering service in 1941.

Simple in design and easy to mass-produce, the T-34 had heavier armor than the T-32. Low in silhouette, it retained the basic Christie suspension system with five large road wheels per side, and wide (18.7-inch) tracks for improved traction in mud or snow. The initial T-34A model weighed 58,900 pounds, had a crew of four, a 500-hp diesel engine, a top speed of 33 mph, and a 76.2mm main gun and two or three machine guns. It also had maximum 45mm sloped armor protection. Its diesel engine was safer than the gasoline engine on the German tanks, and its frontal armor could be penetrated only by 50mm antitank rounds at under 500 meters. The 76.2mm gun T-34 became known as the T-34/76.

The upgunned T-34/85 weighed some 70,500 pounds, had a five-man crew (as opposed to four on the T-34/76), the same 500-hp engine as the T-34/76, a top speed of 31 mph, maximum 90mm armor, and mounted in a larger turret an 85mm (3.3-inch) main gun adapted from the prewar 85mm Model 1939 antiaircraft gun. Effective up to a range of 1,000 meters (914 yards), it could penetrate the

The Soviet T-34/85 Medium tank.
Courtesy of Art-Tech/Aerospace/M.A.R.S/TRH/Navy Historical.

frontal armor of the German Panther and Tiger. The T-34/85 also utilized a new, five-speed gearbox. Apart from this, the chassis was much the same as for the T-34/76. The addition of a loader to the crew reduced demands on the commander and gunner and significantly enhanced the tank's combat efficiency. The T-34/85 entered service with the First Guards Tank Army in early 1944 and gradually replaced the T-34/76, although not completely. Able to hold its own against the most powerful German tanks, especially at close range, it may have been the best all-around tank of World War II.

The Soviets produced some 53,000 T-34s of all types, along with 5,000 T-34 chassis for assault guns. Between 1943 and May 1945 alone, Soviet factories turned out 35,000 T-34s. During the same period the Germans manufactured only slightly more than 5,000 PzKpfw V Panthers, the only real rival to the T-34. Although the Panther had a slight edge in capabilities, it could not overcome the significantly greater numbers of T-34s.

In 1944 the Soviets began a redesign of the T-34. Designated the T-44, it appeared in prototype form that summer. A somewhat more streamlined T-34, with a larger turret and thicker turret and hull armor, it also had a torsion-bar suspension system in place of the Christie system on the T-34. The T-44 weighed some 76,100 pounds.

Powered by a 512-hp engine, the T-44 was the first tank to mount its engine transversely. Crewed by only four men (instead of five as in the T-34), it dispensed with the hull gunner and utilized that space for additional ammunition storage. Initially the T-44 mounted the 85mm gun of the T-34, but later this was replaced with a 100mm gun. The T-44 also had two 7.62mm machine guns.

The T-44 entered limited production in 1945, and a few saw service against the Germans at the end of the war. Although it was perhaps the most sophisticated tank design of the war, the T-44 proved to be mechanically unreliable. As with the British Centurion, the T-44 marked the end of the distinction between heavy and medium tanks and the beginning of the all-purpose main battle tank (MBT). This highly influential design was the basis for the postwar Soviet T-54, T-55, and T-62 tanks.

In heavy tanks, the Soviets began the war with the KV-1. Design work began in 1938, trials were held in September 1939, and it was fully accepted for service in December 1940. Wholly a Russian design, the KV was the successor to the T-35 heavy and named for Defense Commissar Klimenti Voroshilov. Initially the KV-1 had a 550-hp diesel engine. This was upgraded to 600 hp in the KV-1B. The KV-1B weighed nearly 95,000 pounds, had a five-man crew, torsion-bar suspension, and a maximum speed of 22 mph. The KV-1 mounted the powerful 76.2mm gun and three machine guns. It had maximum 100mm armor protection that would defeat shells from the 88mm gun and anything else the Germans might throw against it, except for heavy artillery, as the Germans discovered early in their invasion of the Soviet Union. Certainly the KV-1 disproved the myth of Soviet technological backwardness.

The KV-1 had an excellent balance of speed, armor, and armament; its chief drawbacks lay in its lack of maneuverability and mechanical problems. Nonetheless, the Soviets used the KV-1 effectively to exploit breakthroughs and spearhead advances. The KV-85, produced beginning in 1943 in limited quantities, featured the basic KV-1 design but mounted an 85mm (3.34-inch) gun in a larger cast turret.

Fighting in Finland in the Winter War of 1939–1940 against the Mannerheim Line had shown the need for a "bunker-busting" tank, and this resulted in the KV-2. It utilized the KV-1 hull, chassis, and suspension but had a large, tall turret that mounted a powerful 153mm (5.9-inch) howitzer, the shell of which could penetrate 72mm steel armor at 1,500 meters. The KV-2 also fired a special shell to penetrate concrete pillboxes. Although it proved virtually im-

penetrable to most heavy German weaponry, the KV-2 was hopelessly outclassed in the rapid warfare that marked the German invasion of the Soviet Union. The Germans learned to shoot off its
tracks, leaving the immobilized KV-2 to be finished off by following
infantry and/or engineers.

The same process of gradual improvements led to the evolution of
the KV-1 into the IS-1 through IS-3, the final Soviet heavy tanks of
the war and the most powerful tanks in the world for a decade thereafter. IS (or JS) stood for Soviet dictator Iosef (Joseph) Stalin. The
IS-1 was produced beginning in 1944 to counter the new, more
powerful German tanks. Although based on the KV-1 design, the IS-
1 had improved transmission and suspension systems as well as a re-
designed hull and a new, larger turret mounted well forward.

The IS-1 weighed nearly 99,000 pounds and had a crew of four.
Powered by a 600-hp diesel engine, it was capable of 23 mph. The
first IS-1 tanks mounted the 85mm gun, but shortly thereafter it
had a 100mm gun. Some IS-1s even mounted the 122mm gun fitted
with a muzzle brake and placed in a larger turret. In addition, it had
four machine guns. The IS-1 was followed by the IS-2. It featured
an improved hull shape to reduce shell traps and streamlining
throughout. Some 2,250 were built.

The IS-3 was a complete redesign of the IS-1 and IS-2 series,
based on the experience of the first two tank types in combat. The
IS-3 had a lower silhouette and ballistically shaped hull and the
new, "inverted frying pan" low-profile turret shape to provide maximum deflection against incoming shells. It weighed nearly 102,000
pounds and mounted an improved 122mm gun and two machine
guns. The IS-3 entered service in January 1945 and participated in
the spring 1945 Battle for Berlin. Although never available in large
numbers, it was for a decade the most powerful tank in the world
and a major influence on subsequent tank designs. After the war the
IS-3 was supplied to the Soviet bloc countries of Czechoslovakia,
the German Democratic Republic (DDR, East Germany), and
Poland; it was also exported to Egypt, Libya, and Syria.

UNITED STATES

The German employment of armor divisions in the September 1939
German invasion of Poland, and especially in the May–June 1940
defeat of France, dramatically changed U.S. Army attitudes toward

tanks and their role. In April 1940 an improvised U.S. armored division, formed from the 7th Cavalry Brigade (Mechanized) from Fort Knox, Kentucky, and the Provisional Tank Brigade from Fort Benning, Georgia, dominated the army's Louisiana maneuvers. Then, in July 1940 the army created the U.S. Armored Force, led by Brigadier General Adna Romanaza Chaffee Jr., to test the feasibility of tank divisions. In July 1943 the Armored Force was redesignated the Armored Command, and in February 1944 it became the Armored Center, ending the hopes of some that the Armored Force would become a new branch of the army.

The first U.S. light tank introduced after the start of the war in Europe was the M3 series of light tanks. Based on the M2A3, the M3 was designed at Rock Island Arsenal in the spring of 1940 and incorporated lessons learned in the early European fighting. Approved in July 1940, the M3 entered production in March 1941. The M3 saw extensive service in North Africa with the British (who called it the General Stuart) and then the Americans.

The M3 went through three different models, eventually incorporating a gyro-stabilizer for the main gun, a diesel engine, and an all-welded turret and hull (the first being riveted). It also received two jettisonable 25-gallon fuel tanks to increase its range in the desert. The problem with its riveted armor was that even a glancing shot to the hull by an enemy shell could sheer the heads off rivets and send the remainder flying around the inside of the tank, causing serious personnel injuries and/or igniting ammunition or damaging the engine.

The M3 weighed some 27,400 pounds, had a crew of four, maximum 51mm armor, and was armed with a 37mm gun in the turret and 3 x .30-caliber machine guns. The M3A1 version of 1942 eliminated the turret cupola to reduce overall height and also did away with the two sponsoned machine guns, fired remotely by the driver. These had proved of limited use, and doing away with them reduced the tank's weight and increased its internal storage.

The final version M3A3 entered production in early 1943. Weighing some 31,800 pounds, it had a new all-welded hull that was enlarged by extending the sponsons and increasing the driver's compartment forward and upward. This extra room allowed for additional ammunition storage and fuel tanks.

Although the M3 in its various models performed well in its primary reconnaissance role, the tank was both undergunned and underpowered. The M3 proved a welcome addition to British armor assets in North Africa in 1941–1942, and its crews there thought highly enough of the reliable M3 to refer to it as "Honey." The U.S. Army declared the M3 obsolete in July 1943; it remained in the service of other nations through the end of the war and beyond.

The follow-on to the M3 was the M5 series, also designated the General Stuart. The same basic design as the M3, it had twin Cadillac automobile engines as well as the commercial Cadillac hydro-matic transmission used in automobiles. Officials of the Cadillac Division of General Motors Corporation suggested this change to the Ordnance Department, which converted a standard M3 in the fall of 1941. Subsequent tests proved satisfactory.

Originally to be the Light Tank M4, the new tank was designated the M5 to avoid confusion with the M4 medium Sherman tank then entering production. Recognizable by its stepped-up rear deck to accommodate its new power plant, the M5 had the same hull as its predecessor, save for a sloping glacis. The M5 had a crew of four, weighed some 33,000 pounds with maximum 67mm armor, and had armament of one 37mm gun and two .30-caliber machine guns.

Superior to the M3, the M5 was not produced in large numbers because of the appearance of its successor, the heavier M24. The U.S. Army declared the M5 to be "substitute standard" in July 1944. In British service both the M5 and M5A1 were known as the Stuart VI.

In May 1941, following consultation with the Armored Force and the Army Air Corps, the Ordnance Department called for the manufacture of an airborne tank of 8 tons, about half the weight of an M5, with carriage dimensions so that it would be transportable either inside or under the belly of a cargo aircraft. Christie, General Motors, and Marmon-Herrington all submitted designs. The Marmon-Herrington design was judged to be best, and the government ordered a test model, designated the T9. Following initial testing, Marmon-Herrington built two other pilot models.

The production model, the M22 Locust, had a rolled plate hull and a cast turret. Four hull brackets facilitated slinging the hull under an aircraft. It also featured an easily removable turret to facilitate air transport. The Locust could also be transported in the hold of a British Hamilcar glider. The M22 was of conventional, although compact, design, but its thin armor gave it limited tactical application. It had a battle weight of 16,400 pounds, a crew of three, a 162-hp engine, a maximum speed of 40 mph, maximum 25mm armor, and mounted a 37mm main gun and one .30-caliber machine gun.

The M22 was a specialized, limited production tank. The follow-on U.S. tank to the M5 was the M24 Chaffee. Based in large part on observations of British experience in the Western Desert with the M3 series of light tanks, the U.S. Army determined that its light tanks should mount a 75mm gun. The M5 series could carry the larger 75mm, but only with sharply restricted interior storage space; this forced the design of a new tank.

In April 1943 the U.S. Army Ordnance Department and Cadillac, which had produced the successful M5, began work on a new design that was to make use of the best aspects of the M5, such as the twin Cadillac engines and hydromatic transmission, while incorporating changes based on combat experience. The new design incorporated angled hull surfaces for maximum crew protection, and road wheels on torsion arms provided a smoother ride.

The first of two pilot models, delivered in October 1943, proved so successful that the Ordnance Department immediately ordered production, first for 1,000 vehicles, and then 5,000. At first designated the T24, the new tank was delivered to U.S. units late in 1944, replacing the M5. It was designated the M24 in May 1944.

The all-welded, 40,500-pound M24 had a crew of five, two 110-hp engines that delivered a maximum speed of 35 mph, maximum 25mm armor protection, and mounted a 75mm gun and three machine guns: two .30-caliber (one coaxial with the main gun) and one .50-caliber for antiaircraft protection. This highly successful tank combined a rugged design with high speed, simplicity, reliability, and heavy armament for its size. The M24 was also employed by the British Army, and it continued in U.S. service well after the war. It appeared in a variety of guises, all of which had the same engine, power train, and suspension system. These included howitzer and mortar motor carriages. The M24 could also be easily fitted with a dozer blade when necessary.

The United States also developed medium tanks, the need for which was clearly revealed in the 1940 Battle for France. Although U.S. observers during the Spanish Civil War had reported that a low silhouette, a 360-degree traverse turret, and a powerful engine were more important features than armor protection, the earliest U.S. medium tanks hardly met these criteria. The M2 medium tank with its 37mm gun entered limited production in August 1939. An improved model, the M2A1, was introduced the next year. Weighing some 47,000 pounds, it differed chiefly from the original in having a wider turret, increased maximum armor thickness of 32mm (from 25mm), wider tracks, and a supercharger that delivered 400 hp.

Mass production of the new tank was already under way by American Car & Foundry, and a contract had been signed to produce 1,000 of them at a new Chrysler factory to be built in Michigan (known as the Detroit Tank Arsenal) when the M2 was rendered obsolete by the demonstrated superiority of the heavier-gunned (75mm) German PzKpfw IV in the Battle for France. In August the commander of the Armored Force, Brigadier General Chaffee, met with Ordnance Department representatives at Aberdeen Proving Ground, Maryland, where a consensus emerged in favor of a 75mm gun for the army's medium tanks. As there was insufficient room in the M2's small turret for such a large main gun, the army decided in favor of developing an interim AFV that would incorporate the hull, general layout, and mechanical arrangements of the M2 yet mount a limited-traverse 75mm gun on the right side of the hull sponson. At the same time, work would proceed on a new medium tank with a 75mm gun in a turret capable of full traverse. In August the government contract with Chrysler for the M2A1 was canceled and rolled over to the new as-yet undesigned AFV, designated the M3. Only 94 M2s were actually built, and they were used only for training purposes.

The M3 was designed, tested, and rushed into mass production probably faster than any other tank in history. Critical in the large numbers produced was construction of the Detroit Tank Arsenal at Center Line, Michigan, conceived to mass-produce the M2. Following the defeat of France, the United States adopted a new national munitions program that included large numbers of medium tanks. William S. Knudson, president of General Motors and a member of the National Defense Advisory Commission responsible for coordinating U.S. industry with national defense requirements, believed that heavy engineering firms would not be capable of turning out the large volume of tanks required and that this could be met only by the automobile manufacturers. Knudson suggested that a new tank-manufacturing facility be built to employ the mass-production assembly lines used in the automobile industry and arranged for Chrysler to build and operate the plant for the U.S. government. Work commenced on the huge new Detroit Tank Arsenal (1,380 feet by 500 feet) in September 1940 and was completed in only six months.

At the same time, Rock Island Arsenal was working with Chrysler engineers to design the M3. Rock Island consulted with the firms that would build the new tank, as well as with members of the British Tank Commission who had been sent to the United States in June 1940 to acquire U.S.-built tanks for the British Army. The British provided useful input based on actual combat experience against the Germans in the fighting for France.

Beginning in April 1941 three firms produced M3 pilot models, and by August full production was under way at American Locomotive, Baldwin, and Detroit Arsenal. Outclassed when it was built, the M3 was conceived as an interim design. Nonetheless, a total of 6,258 M3s were produced through December 1942 in a half-dozen different models.

The 30-ton Medium Tank M3 was similar in dimensions to the M2A1 it replaced and had the same engine and suspension system. The M3 had a 10-foot, 3-inch silhouette and was powered by a Wright radial 340-hp engine that produced a maximum speed of 26 mph. It had a crew of six, maximum 37mm armor, and mounted a 75mm gun in the right sponson with secondary armament of a turreted 37mm gun and three or four .30-caliber machine guns. The 75mm gun had only a 34-degree traverse, but the 37mm gun in the left-offset turret had full 360-degree traverse. The turret and sponson were cast, but the hull initially was of riveted armor. The M3 also had side doors in the hull.

The M3 underwent a half-dozen modifications, the most important of which was the introduction of gyro-stabilizers on both heavy guns, permitting accurate fire while under way. Both guns were fitted with periscope sights, and the turret could be traversed by power or by hand. The British used the standard M3 version in North Africa, naming it the "Lee" for U.S. Civil War Confederate General Robert E. Lee. Beginning with the M3A3, the "rivet popping" during battle that plagued the Lee in fighting in North Africa was eliminated with the introduction of an all-welded hull. At the same time, the side doors were either welded up or eliminated.

The British placed special orders for M3s from U.S. manufacturers under the "Cash and Carry" arrangement, a U.S. program whereby the United States would sell war materials to belligerents provided they could pay cash for the purchase and transport the materials in their own vessels. The M3s had slightly longer cast turrets, did away with the cupola, and had other modifications. These M3s saw extensive service in North Africa. The British knew this version of the M3 as the Grant after U.S. Grant, the Union general of the U.S. Civil War and 18th president of the United States. Some 200 of these Grants arrived in the Middle East early in 1942, and for the first time in the war the British had a tank superior in firepower to any Axis tank. They gave the British a quantitative as well as qualitative edge. The M3's main gun could outrange the German tanks and fire AP shells against enemy tanks and HE shells in an infantry close-support role. A total of 167 Grants constituted the bulk of AFVs in the British

4th Armored Brigade in the important Battle of Gazala beginning in late May 1942. Two authorities have described the M3 as "at that time, the most important new addition to the British armoury."[7]

The passage by Congress of Lend-Lease legislation in March 1941 made U.S. weapons and war supplies of all kinds available on a lease/loan basis to countries fighting the Axis powers. This allowed the British to obtain the standard M3 version for service in North Africa. By June an additional 250 M3 tanks had arrived for Eighth Army in Egypt, and by the time of the Battle of El Alamein at the end of October, a total of 600 M3s had been delivered under both "Cash and Carry" and Lend-Lease. By June 1942 U.S. personnel were stationed at a maintenance facility near Cairo to assist the training of their British counterparts in the M3 and then the M4. Although most M3s were shipped to the Middle East, some were also sent to Britain for training and special conversions. When M4s began to replace M3s in North Africa, the remaining M3s were sent on to Burma to replace obsolete Matildas, Stuarts, and Valentines. The M3 appeared in a variety of variants, and its chassis was used in the development of gun motor carriages, including the M12, which mounted a 155mm gun. The U.S. Army employed it as a heavy bombardment weapon in European fighting in late 1944 and early 1945, including the taking of Köln (Cologne).

In October 1941, when the M4 Sherman became the U.S. standard medium tank, the army reclassified the M3 as "substitute standard." In April 1943, when the M4 came into full service, the M3 became "limited standard," and in April 1944 it was declared obsolete.

Even while design work was being carried out on the M3 tank, the Armored Force Board drew up specifications for its successor. These called for a 75mm gun, but unlike the M3, the new medium would carry the heavier gun in a full-traverse turret. In April 1941 the Armored Force Board decided to employ the straightforward approach of utilizing the M3 medium chassis, power plant, transmission, suspension, and other parts where possible while introducing a new cast or welded hull top and new central turret. A pilot model, designated T6 and employing the same hull side doors as the M3, underwent testing at Aberdeen Proving Ground in September 1941. The next month the T6 was redesignated Medium Tank M4.

Meanwhile, following the German invasion of the Soviet Union that June, President Franklin D. Roosevelt personally ordered a sharp increase in U.S. tank production, increasing mediums from 1,000 to 2,000 per month. This led to additional manufacturing facilities being brought on line for the M3 and plans to begin production of the M4 at 11 different plants in 1942. To facilitate this schedule, the government ordered construction of a second tank production facility, the Grand Blanc Tank Arsenal, also in Michigan. Work on it began in January 1942, and it started tank production in July. By then, three factories had already begun producing the M4, which differed from the test Model T6 in eliminating the hull side doors.

The M4 medium, known by its British name of "German Sherman" (more often simply "Sherman") after William T. Sherman, the Union Army Civil War general and later commanding general of the U.S. Army, was the most important Allied tank of the war. Although not the best Allied tank qualitatively (it was inferior in armor and armament to the best German and Soviet tanks), it was nonetheless the most widely produced and utilized Allied tank of the war. During 1942–1946 U.S. factories turned out more than 40,000 M4 series tanks and modified chassis AFVs.

The M4A1 weighed 66,500 pounds, had a crew of five, and maximum 51mm armor. It mounted a 75mm main gun and had a .50-caliber antiaircraft and two .30-caliber machine guns. The Sherman had two great advantages over the German tanks: its powered turret enabled crews to react and fire more quickly, and it offered greater mechanical reliability and repairability. Rugged, simple in design, easy to maintain, and highly maneuverable, the M4 was consistently upgraded in main gun and armor during the course of the war. The M4A1 had a cast iron hull; the M4A2, used only by the Marine Corps, had two General Motors diesel engines to overcome the shortage of Continental gasoline engines; the M4A4 and M4A6 had longer hulls and tracks. Some variants also employed improved appliqué armor.

Sherman variants performed a wide variety of roles, including but not limited to tank recovery, flamethrowers, mine-clearing, and bridging. The Sherman chassis also provided the basis for the M7B1 howitzer motor carriage, which superseded the M7 based on the M3 medium tank. Both mounted a 105mm howitzer as its principal armament and were standard equipment for artillery battalions in U.S. armored divisions. The M4 chassis was also utilized in the M10 and M10A tank destroyers, essentially a gun motor carriage mounting a 3-inch gun, as well as the more satisfactory M36 series mounting a 90mm gun.

The M4 entered combat for the first time with the British Eighth Army in the October 1942 Battle of El Alamein. Indeed, Shermans

M4 Sherman medium tanks and infantry of the Third U.S. Army moving
toward Metz, the last German stronghold in France, 1944.
Courtesy of Art-Tech/Aerospace/M.A.R.S/TRH/Navy Historical.

and M3 Grants made up almost half of the 1,100 British tanks committed to that pivotal battle. The M4 saw service on virtually every
fighting front of the war and had a long life thereafter. Indeed, it remained in service until only recently in the armies of some nations.

In part because comparable British tanks, the Cromwell IV and VII, were not available until the end of 1943 and not in wide use until the spring of 1944, the Sherman has been called "the most important tank in British service and more widely used than any of the British designed or British produced types from 1943–1945."[8]

Initially the Sherman was a poor match for the most numerous German tank, the PzKpfw Mark IV Panther. At a range of 1,000 yards the Sherman's 75mm gun stood little chance of knocking out a Panther, while at that range the Panther's high-velocity 75mm could knock out the Sherman. In such an encounter, U.S. tankers could only hope that they could use their powered turret to good advantage in order to lay the main gun quickly and get off several rounds before the Panther could fire.

German tanks had thicker frontal armor and a much higher velocity gun. The Tiger's 88mm and the same caliber *Panzerschreck* antitank weapon could easily knock out the Shermans, whereas the U.S. 2.36-inch bazooka (copied from the *Panzerschreck*) was effective only against German side armor. Also, the Sherman's track width was only 14 inches, whereas German tanks had a track 30–36 inches wide and thus were not as easily bogged down. Indeed, U.S. tanker crews often added extensions to their tank tracks in order to rectify this situation.

Although the British utilized all models of the M4, the most numerous was the M4A4 type, of which more than 1,600 were supplied to Eighth Army in Italy in 1943. The major British innovation regarding the Sherman was to replace its 75mm main gun with a 17-pounder (76.2mm). This upgunned M4, known as the Sherman Firefly, was the most powerfully armed British tank of the entire war. Conversion began as a fallback position should the new Challenger tank encounter problems in testing. The Challenger indeed experienced difficulties, and in February 1944 conversion of the Shermans received priority. Because of delays in the Challenger program, that tank was not available for participation in the Normandy landings, and the Firefly was the only British tank capable of taking on and defeating the German Tigers and Panthers. Owing to a shortage in 17-pounder guns for tank use, the Firefly was initially supplied one per cavalry troop. Not until early 1945 was the upgunned Firefly available in large numbers.

The British also developed many Sherman variants. These included the Adder, Salamander, Crocodile, and Badger flamethrower tanks; fascine carrier; Twaby Ark, Octopus, and Plymouth bridging vehicles; rocket launchers; and the Scorpion, Lobster, and Crab flail antimine tanks. In April 1943 the British also began experiments with a duplex drive (DD) on the Sherman. The DD had proven successful with their Valentine tank, which by that date was obsolete. Sherman DD tanks were waterproofed and fitted with a collapsible canvas screen around the hull to provide flotation. Struts, erected by means of rubber tubing filled by compressed air, held the canvas in place. Two small propellers, folded away while on land, pushed the Sherman through the water at a speed of about 4 knots. Sherman DD tanks constituted an entire brigade of the 79th Armored Division in the Normandy landings and were the first British tanks to land, "swimming" ashore from LCTs. DD tanks, however, were easily swamped and required careful handling and the right conditions in which to operate.

The Sherman's great disadvantages were its engine and main gun. Its gasoline (versus diesel) engine led GIs to nickname it the "Ronson" after the Ronson cigarette lighter (sold with the slogan "lights first time, every time"). The Sherman was also consistently outgunned by the larger German tanks against which it had to fight. Its 75mm gun was relatively ineffective, but the replacement 76mm (17-pounder) gun with much higher muzzle velocity proved successful. After the British began mounting the 76mm on their Shermans, the Americans followed suit in February 1944. These appeared in the M4A1 through M4A3 models.

One of the major problems for the U.S. Army in the European Theater was its lack of a heavy tank to confront the German tanks with their thicker frontal armor and higher-velocity guns. In the course of 1944–1945 the 3rd Armored Division alone lost 648 Sherman tanks completely destroyed in combat and another 700 knocked out, repaired, and put back into operation. This represented a loss rate of 580 percent. In fact, the United States lost 6,000 tanks in Europe during World War II. The Germans never had more than half that total.[9]

The answer to the German tanks was a heavy tank. The United States had developed the T26 medium tank with a 90mm gun, but the head of Army Ground Forces, General Lesley J. McNair, did not consider the 90mm gun suitable for a medium tank because it would encourage tank crews to hunt other tanks, a role that army doctrine had assigned to tank destroyers. In June 1944, meanwhile, the T26 was reclassified as the T26E1 Heavy Tank. Following extensive trials with 10 prototype T26E1s and modifications that included an improved transmission, better engine access, and increased ammunition storage, the Ordnance Department recommended in August 1944 that the T26 be placed in production. The Army Ground Forces went so far as to request that the T26E1 be re-designed to mount the 76mm gun, an idea rejected by the Ordnance Department.

Opposition from the user arms, however, imposed delay. This stemmed in large part from Third Army commander Lieutenant General George S. Patton's insistence that the army concentrate on increasing production of M4 Shermans. Patton expected to use his Shermans en masse to tear huge holes through enemy defenses, through which armored infantry might pass as the tanks continued on into the enemy rear areas. Patton agreed with McNair that protection of U.S. tanks and destruction of their enemy counterparts should be left to antitank guns and tank destroyers. Tanks should not fight other tanks, at least not when an inexpensive gun could do the same job. But the U.S. M10 Wolverine tank destroyer of 1942 mounted only a 76mm gun. The M36 Jackson, introduced in 1944, did have a 90mm gun, but the latter's 2,850 foot-per-second muzzle velocity made it less powerful than the German PzKpfw VIb King Tiger's 88mm; and the M36's shell could not penetrate the Tiger's 6-inch frontal armor. The M36 in turn had only 1.5 inches of frontal armor and only 1 inch of side armor. Its gun was also mounted in an open-top turret, making it vulnerable to artillery airbursts. Both the M10 and M36 used the Sherman chassis.

The T26E1 was placed into limited production only in November 1944. The Ordnance Board recommended early in December that a number be shipped to Europe for testing in combat, but the Army Ground Forces opposed this plan as well, demanding that the new tanks be first assigned to the Armored Force for testing there. The Battle of the Bulge (December 1944–January 1945) changed this thinking, again revealing the weakness of the M4 medium against heavy German tanks.

The General Staff then intervened, and the first 20 T26E3s were sent to Europe, although they did not arrive until January 1945, too late for the Battle of the Bulge. Assigned to the 3rd and 9th Armored Divisions, the new tank soon proved its worth, and commanders demanded more of them. Ordered into full production in January 1945, the T26E3 was redesignated that June as the Heavy Tank M26 General Pershing. Some Pershings saw action in the Pacific Theater later in the war in the Battle of Okinawa.

Weighing 92,000 pounds, the M26 had a crew of five, a 500-hp gasoline engine providing a speed of 20 mph, maximum 102mm (4-inch) armor, and a 90mm main gun, along with one .50-caliber and

The M-26 Pershing heavy tank.
Courtesy of Art-Tech/Aerospace/M.A.R.S/TRH/Navy Historical.

two .30-caliber machine guns. The muzzle velocity of its main gun did not match the 88mm German tank guns, but the M26 was almost a match for the fearsome Tiger in firepower, and it surpassed its German counterpart in reliability and mobility.

ARMORED WARFARE DURING WORLD WAR II

The great tank battles of World War II occurred in North Africa and in Europe. Tanks were less effective in mountainous terrain, such as Italy, and were of only limited use in the jungle fighting typical of the Pacific Theater.

Probably there was no time as favorable for Adolf Hitler to initiate a war than September 1939. Although his own nation's rearmament was far from complete, Hitler was afraid to wait any longer because his enemies were now fully alarmed and rearming as fast as possible in an effort to redress the military imbalance. Germany's enemies had the potential of being more powerful, and they would have newer equipment.

In September 1939 the Allied powers of Britain, France, and Poland appeared to have the advantage militarily, at least on paper. Their naval assets were far greater, and they outnumbered the Germans 3:2 in ground forces. France alone had 3,200 tanks, more than the German total of some 2,900; the French tanks were also generally of better quality. Only in numbers of aircraft and antiaircraft guns were the Allies at a significant disadvantage.

The German Army was not totally prepared for high-speed warfare. As noted, the bulk of its divisions were based on the World War I pattern and were horse-drawn. In 1939 a single German infantry division required 4,077–6,033 horses for movement; even the vaunted panzer divisions utilized them. This reliance on horses continued throughout the war; indeed, as late as 1944 85 percent of German Army divisions were horse-drawn, with few vehicles. Nonetheless, the Germans were a few vital degrees better than their opponents, and as it turned out, that made all the difference.[10]

Germany did enjoy the considerable advantage of having already established tank and motorized/light divisions along with a doctrine governing their use. These new-style divisions were, however, only a small minority of the total. Of Germany's 98 divisions (40 of which were still forming) in September 1939, 14 were new-style: six panzer divisions (1st, 2nd, 3rd, 4th, 5th, and 10th) and eight motorized/light divisions (two of the latter being SS). The original plan was to equip the panzer divisions with 570 tanks apiece, but production failed to keep up with the expansion of the German armored force, so tanks were in short supply at the beginning of the war.

This shortage of tanks forced a reorganization of the panzer divisions, the nucleus of which was a panzer brigade of two regiments. Each regiment had two battalions (*Abteilungen*) and each of these usually had two light companies of the PzKpfw I and II and one medium company with the PzKpfw III and IV. In addition, each panzer division had a reconnaissance battalion, a motorized infantry regiment, an engineer battalion, and a signals squadron. Each battalion had 71–74 tanks, of which five were command tanks, and this meant that a regiment would have 150–156 tanks, 12 of them command tanks. Thus during the Polish campaign the panzer divisions had only about 300 tanks each.

The number of tanks per division continued to decline during the war. In 1940 few panzer divisions had as many as 150 tanks, and in 1944 panzer divisions were down to only slightly more than 100 tanks apiece. Each panzer division was also to have its own reconnaissance, infantry, artillery, transport, communications, medical, and service components, but the composition varied sharply depending on the division. The motorized/light divisions of 1939 became the mechanized Panzergrenadier divisions, which by 1940 each were to have 28 tanks. In 1944 these divisions had 48 tanks each.

By way of contrast, at the beginning of the war the French Army had no tank divisions whatsoever and the British only one. As has been stressed here, German tanks were not always superior to those they faced and were often markedly inferior. The key to German success on the battlefield was in the tactical doctrine governing their use, as well as in training and leadership.

The Germans were successful in their initial campaigns because they worked out a flexible system that combined infantry, artillery, tanks, and supporting aviation in one integrated military effort. Unit commanders had great flexibility, and they could concentrate forces quickly to exploit any situation that might develop. Command and control between units and even individual tanks was facilitated by the efficient use of radio.

The French, regarded by many observers as having the most powerful army in Europe, in fact lacked the ability to employ their military strength promptly and to good advantage. It was primarily a failure of doctrine rather than any equipment shortcomings that did in the French. The French Army divided control of its tanks between the infantry and cavalry. Infantry commanders saw the tanks solely as a means of infantry support; the cavalry regarded them chiefly in a reconnaissance role. Another consequence of this division was a multiplicity of designs.

Following the declaration of war, the French were slow to mobilize, and in the two weeks it required them to call up reservists and bring artillery from storage, it became clear that Poland was already collapsing. Even so, a vigorous French thrust would have carried to the Rhine with tremendous consequences for the course of the war, as the German strategic plan committed the vast bulk of German strength, some 60 divisions, to Poland and left only a weak force to hold the Rhineland. The latter numbered only 40 divisions (36 of which were untrained), with no tanks, little artillery, and few aircraft. The French moved belatedly and timidly and, after securing a few villages, withdrew the few divisions committed to the effort. Senior French and British commanders had rejected the new theories of high-speed armor warfare. They persisted in viewing tanks as operating in support of infantry, to be spread over the front in small packets rather than being massed in entire divisions.

The Polish campaign of September 1939 revealed the errors in Allied thought concerning armor. In their invasion the Germans pressed into service all available tanks, hoping that sheer numbers and their employment en masse would make up for any equipment and armament shortcomings. As noted earlier, in all they had some 2,900 tanks, most of them PzKpfw Is and IIs.

The success of the German blitzkrieg lay not in numbers of tanks but in the formation of combined arms teams. The problem in World War I had been the inability of an attacker's reserve formations to close quickly once a breech had been created in an enemy's lines; the attacker's artillery would also have to be repositioned to support a further advance. The new German theory of high-speed warfare called on mechanized reserves and artillery to move at the speed of the tanks, all supported by aircraft, greatly compressing the time line in favor of the attackers.

General Heinz Guderian, who developed the blitzkrieg, saw the need to use the tanks en masse in divisions for breakthrough shock power rather than dispersing them. German forces were to locate weak points in the enemy battle line, then build up strength at these points, holding them with infantry and antitank guns, hoping to lure enemy tanks into attacking and running into the more powerful antitank guns. Such tactics would save the German tanks for the exploitation role.

These reinforced points would serve as pivots, from which the tanks would achieve fast, sudden breakthroughs without warning or the benefit of preliminary bombardment. Infantry would move with the tanks in a column of tracked vehicles and trucks. The whole idea was to keep moving and to stage deep penetrations and encirclements of enemy forces. The attacking forces would be largely self-contained for a matter of three to four days. Vital to German success was control of the air, ensured by having the world's most powerful air force. The Luftwaffe was basically a tactical air force, developed for close ground support, and the key to this was the "flying artillery" provided by the Ju 87 Stuka dive-bomber. Although it later proved vulnerable to antiaircraft guns and high-performance fighters, the Stuka's early opponents had few of those types of equipment, and it proved to be a highly mobile and accurate artillery platform that greatly aided the advance of the tanks below.

During the Polish campaign, enemy dispositions played into the Germans' hands. Polish forces were still in the process of mobilization, thanks to the British insistence that the Poles provide no excuse for the Germans to invade. Also, Polish Army leaders placed the bulk of their forces far forward. They were unwilling to yield territory to the Germans (indeed, they expected to carry the war into Germany themselves), but in such forward positions they were more easily cut off, surrounded, and destroyed. Poland was also at sharp geographical disadvantage. Attacked by German forces on three sides, it in fact had little chance. With France slow to move, and then only with a small force, and with the Soviet Union invading

Poland from the east two weeks after the initial German invasion (in accordance with a secret arrangement with Germany), Poland succumbed after one month.

Airpower played such an important role in the German success in Poland that the German Army then assigned each panzer division its own air force element. The Germans also learned from the Polish campaign that it was difficult for truck-mounted infantry to keep up with the tanks and that it was impossible for them to move across open country. Trucks were vulnerable even to enemy rifles and machine guns. Accompanying infantry required cross-country mobility and some armor protection, and this meant increasing reliance on armored personnel carriers and other tracked vehicles.

One often overlooked factor in the German success in Poland, as well as in the May–June 1940 campaign against the Low Countries and France, was the short distances involved and thus the assurance of adequate resupply of fuel and ammunition. The blitzkrieg functioned well in the dry, flat terrain and the relatively short distances of Poland and the well-developed road network of France in 1940. It broke down completely in the vast distances and poor transportation system of the Soviet Union in 1941.

When the German Army invaded the Soviet Union in June 1941 it found itself heavily outnumbered in terms of numbers of men and equipment of all kinds. Eventually superior Soviet numbers, the distances involved, the poor transportation network, difficult weather conditions, and improving Soviet armor doctrine all took a toll on the attacking Germans.

The Italians had a well-developed armor doctrine that closely paralleled the Germans' blitzkrieg. They planned to utilize medium tanks to punch holes in enemy lines while light tanks served as the exploiting arm. Early on, especially in the fighting in North Africa, the Italians lacked mobile artillery, although their later self-propelled guns, the *Semovente,* helped make up for this. The Italian artillery doctrine of *fuoco da manovra* (fire and maneuver) called for artillery and antitank guns to be located close to the front line supported by infantry.

The chief deficiency in Italian armored doctrine was the lack of tactical air support, the consequence of Italy's embrace of Guilio Douhet's doctrine of strategic bombing. Other handicaps included a lack of radio equipment in the tanks. As with the French, Italian tank crews communicated in battle primarily with flags. Italian forces were also not as well trained as the Germans. As two scholars have summed up, "Italy had developed the concepts but lacked the materiel to implement them."[11]

The Allies understood the important role tanks could play in stiffening the resolve of infantry. They also introduced some numbers, albeit insufficient, of assault guns and self-propelled antitank guns working with the infantry. Such weapons came to play a key role in armored warfare, as did development of larger high-velocity guns to defeat improved armor protection.

Following its 3 September 1939 declaration of war against Germany, Britain deployed only a single tank brigade to France with the BEF. In the experience of the defeat of France and the subsequent Italian invasion of Egypt, British leaders at last realized the necessity of building a large armored force. Prime Minister Winston Churchill called for the creation of 10 armored divisions by the end of 1941, and the government launched a crash program to build the tanks required to equip them. Much might have been saved had this decision been taken earlier.

The Allies' problem was that they did not fully understand or appreciate the use of combined arms, especially the concept of tanks and antitank guns working in concert. It took the 1940 Battle for France and serious reversals in the North African desert for the British to understand this. British armor doctrine provided that infantry tanks, armed basically with machine guns, would operate in support of infantry that would punch a hole through enemy lines. Cruiser tanks would then push through the gap, operating independently of infantry and other arms in a cavalry-type role. For example, in Operation CRUSADER in North Africa during November 1941, the British 7th Armored Division operated essentially alone, without infantry or supporting artillery. In the early fighting in North Africa the British incorrectly assumed that the Germans used tanks to destroy other tanks, whereas German armored doctrine assigned that task to antitank guns while the tanks were to destroy infantry.

Major General Eric Dorman-Smith summed up early British generalship in North Africa with these words:

> In the Middle East Command, during the autumn of 1941, there arose the tactical heresy which propounded that armour alone counted in the Desert battle, therefore British armour should discover and destroy the enemy's equivalent armour, after which decision the unarmoured infantry divisions would enter the arena to clear up what remained and hold the ground gained.[12]

Only through the crucible of experience did the British Eighth Army learn how to conduct mobile warfare effectively. In North Africa, both sides learned to keep their tanks waiting in cover, rarely firing on the move. The commander of Germany's Afrika Korps, General Erwin Rommel, employed his antitank guns and field artillery in an offensive role, pushing them as far to the front as possible, where they could be employed against British tanks and strongpoints. When on the move, the Germans dispersed their antitank guns among the length of the march column so they could be quickly deployed.

During the attack Germans invariably opened up first with artillery and antitank guns. The tanks would then advance as quickly as possible until within range of enemy positions. The leading tanks were accompanied by 105mm howitzers and field guns operating in a direct support role as highly trained infantry worked in close concert to reduce enemy antitank defenses. If Commonwealth forces counterattacked with tanks, the German antitank guns, infantry, and artillery were in position to work in concert to destroy them. These tactics were amply demonstrated during British reversals at the hands of Axis forces in North Africa in 1941–1942.

Although the Germans perfected this system, they could not overcome the Allies' overwhelming superiority in numbers of tanks at the start of the Battle of El Alamein in late October 1942. Also, the British generals, who initially failed to comprehend the concept of mobile mechanized warfare, corrected their earlier tactics with new equipment. Not until after Alam Halfa did the British have widely available in Eighth Army the new 6-pounder antitank gun, a weapon that could stop the German panzers. Major General William H. Gott, commander of 7th Armoured Division in Eighth Army, was largely responsible for the belated British policy of breaking down the traditional, rigid British organizations into combined all-arms groups, a process that became standard in the British Army. General Bernard L. Montgomery summed up the importance of combined arms in tank warfare with these words: "I cannot emphasize too strongly that victory in battle depends not on armoured action alone, but on the intimate cooperation of all arms; the tank by itself can achieve little."[13] The Americans would have to learn the same lesson for themselves in 1943.

During the course of the war, guns and antitank guns also steadily increased in caliber and lethality. In 1940 the Germans provided their infantry with an improved 50mm antitank gun. The British, meanwhile, increased main-gun armament on their tanks to 57mm and also improved the armor protection on the newest medium tanks to 80mm. By the end of the war, as has been noted, main-gun armament had gone to 88mm and more.

Tanks proved critical in fighting in flat and relatively open terrain and even in the hilly and forested Ardennes in 1940. They were especially important in the later fighting in the vast spaces of the Soviet Union and North Africa. Distances in these latter two theaters were such that static defenses might easily be outflanked. But armor was also effective in the 1941 Balkan campaign and in the 1944 struggle for France. Throughout, armored formations enjoyed their greatest success against weaker opponents; they diminished against forces of relative equality.

The Soviet Union had led the world in the employment of tanks in mass formations, but in 1939 Soviet dictator Joseph Stalin had decided to disband the five Soviet tank corps. With the benefit of the German campaigns against Poland and the Low Countries and their own near-disastrous invasion of Finland, the Soviets reversed field: they stopped considering tanks solely for infantry support and began a rapid buildup of armored and mechanized units based on the German pattern. On 6 July 1940, closely following the defeat of France, Stalin ordered the creation of nine new mechanized corps, and in February and March 1941 additional decrees led to the establishment of 20 more.

The Poles can hardly be blamed for not understanding the blitzkrieg. The French Army had far less excuse (its senior generals regarded Poland as a special case, not likely to be repeated). The Soviets, with the benefit of these earlier campaigns, had no excuse whatsoever. This did not prevent Stalin from committing a series of major blunders early in the German invasion of his country, including placing the bulk of defending units too far forward and commanding major formations to remain in place rather than authorizing them to withdraw when necessary; the latter led to their encirclement and destruction by the rapidly moving German armored columns.

Based simply on sheer numbers, Stalin had every reason for confidence should the Germans choose to attack his country. The disparity in military hardware in June 1941 was telling. For its invasion of the Soviet Union, Germany assembled 6,000 tanks, the Russians 24,000 (11,000 in the West). Germany had 2,000 aircraft, the Russians 13,211 combat-ready aircraft (8,723 in the West). It was only inept Soviet tactics that allowed the Germans' dominance.[14]

Despite the fact that even in 1941 the Soviets had some of the best tanks of the war and held a tremendous advantage in terms of numbers of AFVs, in the second half of 1941 the Germans destroyed at least 17,000 Soviet tanks, most of them lighter models.

The unintended result of the destruction of many light tanks, how-ever, was that in 1942 the most numerous Russian tank in action was the formidable T-34.

The Soviets learned from bitter experience that if a German ar-mored spearhead broke through, the defenders should try to close on both flanks in order to attempt to halt the flow of the German advance. Meanwhile, other units would take up defensive positions to the rear. And large reserve armored units would then be brought up to drive against the German flanks. The Soviets also employed large numbers of antitank guns and minefields along the expected axes of German advance.

Where possible, Soviet infantry rode on the tanks while supplies were transported forward in trucks. The Soviets benefited tremen-dously from prodigious quantities of U.S. Lend-Lease trucks, some 375,000 in the course of the war. These made possible the great en-circling movements carried out by Soviet forces in 1943–1945. Stalin, who during the course of the war soaked up specialist military knowledge and came to be a competent strategist, placed great re-liance on artillery and insisted that it be able to keep up with the ad-vancing tanks. This led to the development of self-propelled artillery units and assault guns, especially in the last campaigns of the war.

Another factor in the Allied success was certainly the Luftwaffe's dwindling resources. In the Soviet Union by 1943 and in the West-ern Theater in 1944 the superb Luftwaffe-panzer combination that had once proved so lethal no longer existed. Allied air superiority by the end of the war made massed German panzer formations impos-sible. This was clear during the last big German offensive effort of the war, the Battle of the Bulge in December 1944–January 1945. Once the weather cleared, Allied airpower and artillery was able to devastate German armor.

On occasion German tactics played into Soviet hands, as at Stal-ingrad in the winter of 1942–1943, when Hitler threw away the German advantage in mobile warfare and played to the Soviet ad-vantage of tenacious resolve in set-piece defense. The same was evi-dent at Kursk in July 1943, the largest tank battle in history. There Hitler delayed the German offensive to bring up new Panther and Tiger tanks, and he also expanded the offensive well beyond the spoiling attack envisioned by Field Marshal Erich von Manstein. The delay allowed the Soviets, who knew the outlines of the Ger-man plan, to prepare defenses up to 2 and 3 miles deep in places, with their secondary and tertiary defenses reaching back up to 25 miles. The Soviets brought in more than 1 million men and studded the area with strongpoints and bunkers, supported by massive amounts of artillery, antitank guns, and more than 1 million mines. They also deployed 5,128 tanks and self-propelled guns.

The Germans deployed 780,900 men and 2,980 tanks and assault guns, but these numbers proved insufficient; the German offensive of July 5–17 was beaten back. If one considers the wider struggle that lasted some 50 days, it involved 3.5 million men, 12,000 aircraft, and 10,600 tanks in the largest armored battle in history. Although the Germans registered substantial gains in the early going, they were unable to break through the deep Soviet defenses. Soviet aircraft were invaluable, just as the Stukas had been earlier to the Germans. This time it was the Il-2 Shturmovik ground-attack aircraft that proved lethal to the Germans. Flying at low altitude and firing rockets, Il-2s knocked out large numbers of German Tigers. The Germans called the Il-2 *Der Schwartz Tod* (the Black Death).

The extended Battle of Kursk took a heavy toll on both sides. It cost the Soviets more than 863,000 casualties out of some 2.5 million engaged and 6,064 tanks out of 7,360. Exact German losses, although believed to have been lower than the Soviet totals, are unknown.

Kursk was the biggest battle of the entire war and the turning point on the Eastern Front; from that point forward the Soviets held the operational initiative. In the last year of the war the Soviet Army also proved its mastery of the strategic offensive, with vast operations employing great resources that won comparable gains, such as the destruction of German Army Group Center.

As German armor began to erode and encountered increasing numbers of Allied tanks, the Germans developed effective countermeasures to include counterattacks keyed to man-made obstacles, and they laid great minefields to delay tanks and to channel them into killing zones, which were manned with antitank guns and artillery. The extensive German use of minefields forced the Allies to develop at last effective combined arms teams as well as specialized AFVs, especially flail antimine tanks that could breach minefields and, in the Normandy countryside in 1944, dozer tanks to deal with the thick and nearly impervious hedgerows. Increasingly, at least in the European Theater, attrition warfare dominated, the Allies trying to wear down the German defenses until the point that they could launch their own armored thrusts.

U.S. armor doctrine built on the experiences gained by the other belligerents earlier in the war. As noted, the U.S. Armored Force came into being only in July 1940, but it was hindered by the commander of Army Ground Forces, General McNair, who saw infantry and artillery, rather than tanks, as the key to success on the battle-field.

The U.S. armored division was the basic element of the Armored Force. In 1941 the U.S. Army postulated that to win a war against Germany and Japan it would be necessary to raise 215 maneuver divisions, of which 61 were to be armored. The army ended the war fielding only 89 divisions, of which a far smaller percentage—only 16 divisions—were armored. As it turned out, this smaller number of divisions was sufficient to bring victory. The U.S. divisions were the most heavily armed, mechanized, and maneuverable to that point in history. In addition to purely armored divisions, each army corps also had a group of tank battalions for infantry division support.

The U.S. armored division was designed to be a self-sufficient combined arms organization, capable of rapid movement and penetration deep into an enemy's rear areas. The old heavy foot-bound four-brigade divisions of World War I gave way in November 1940 to a triangular system centered on an armored brigade of 368 tanks organized into three armored regiments: two light and one heavy. The division also contained a field artillery regiment and reconnaissance element consisting of a ground reconnaissance battalion and attached aviation observation squadron. Support elements included an armored infantry regiment, a field artillery battalion, and an engineer battalion. Division service units included quartermaster, ordnance, and medical battalions, along with a signal company. The total authorized strength of the division was 12,697 men.

The U.S. Army triangular concept continued down through the unit of one maneuver element to hold an enemy in place, another maneuver element to turn its flank, and a third maneuver element in reserve.

In March 1942 the army introduced the "heavy" armored division, and the 1st through 3rd Armored Divisions went into combat under this organization. These divisions were organized around two armored regiments with two light and four medium tank battalions of three companies each. The single brigade was replaced with two combat commands (Combat Command A [CCA] and Combat Command B [CCB]). The divisional artillery was reorganized as three regiments, which thereafter became standard. Under the 1942 reorganization the division had 390 tanks (232 medium and 158 light) and 14,620 personnel.

In September 1943 another U.S. Army reorganization was applied to all armored divisions, save for the 2nd and 3rd. These became "light" armored divisions. The two armored regiments were replaced with three tank battalions, with each comprising four tank companies: three medium and one light. A Reserve Combat Command (CCR) was added to the CCA and CCB. The number of authorized tanks per division was reduced to only 263 (186 medium and 77 light), and personnel strength was 10,937 men.

The U.S. Army also operated separate tank battalions. In December 1944 it had 65 separate tank battalions as compared to 66 infantry divisions. Standard operating procedure called for attaching a tank battalion to each front-line division.

Classic examples of armored warfare in World War II include the British Eighth Army's defeat of Axis forces in the Second Battle of El Alamein in North Africa; the Soviet double envelopment of Axis forces at Stalingrad in Operation URANUS; and the Allied breakout from Normandy in Operation COBRA and Patton's dash across France with Third Army in the summer of 1944. These operations were stopped not so much by German opposition as by logistical shortcomings that forced the advancing units to halt and resupply, allowing the German defenders time to reinforce and consolidate.

There were no great armored battles in the Pacific, in part because of the limiting factors of terrain and jungle. The Japanese did not activate their first tank divisions until summer 1942, and by the next year production and shipping problems at home caused them to abandon their plan for an armored army. All too aware of their weakness in tanks, the Japanese employed them in twos and threes in support of infantry, utilized them as mobile pillboxes, or simply dug them in as defensive artillery. Not until near the end of the war in China in 1944 did the Japanese utilize tanks in massed formations. Small numbers of tanks could often make a considerable difference, however, as in Burma.

The Japanese failure to appreciate the extent to which their opponents would employ tanks and be able to utilize them in areas where the Japanese assumed they could not operate also led the Japanese to ignore the development of antitank weapons. Their hasty improvisations included suicide bombers with explosive devices, crouched in small holes in routes over which Allied tanks would have to pass. This was hardly a successful answer to Allied armor. Throughout the war—in the Philippines, Burma, and on the Pacific Islands—the Japanese repeatedly found themselves engaging far greater numbers of superior Allied tanks.

In the Pacific Theater the Allies' specialist tanks were of immense help, especially flamethrower tanks to ferret out Japanese defenders in caves or hidden defenses. Dozer tanks saw wide use. The Allies also employed increasing numbers of amphibious AFVs in the Central Pacific campaigns.

World War II also saw the development of small antitank weapons. These included antitank rifles and antitank rockets, such as the German *Panzerfaust* and *Panzerschreck* and the U.S. bazooka. Such weapons were the forerunners of today's effective antitank missiles and missile-firing antitank helicopters, and they introduced a new element into armored warfare and reflected the continued contest between increasingly powerful weapons and improved armor protection.

ENDNOTES

1. I. C. B. Dear and M. R. D. Foot, eds., *The Oxford Companion to World War II*. Oxford, UK: Oxford University Press, 1995, p. 1060.

2. Figures vary from some 2,500 to 2,900. The higher figure, used here, is from Bob Carruthers, *German Tanks at War*. London: Cassell, 2000, p. 15.

3. Quoted in Len Deighton, *Blitzkrieg: From the Rise of Hitler to the Fall of Dunkirk*. New York: Alfred A. Knopf, 1980, p. 137.

4. Ibid., p. 130.

5. Heinz Guderian, *Panzer Leader*, translated by Constantine Fitzgibbon. London: Harborough, 1957, pp. 280–281.

6. Meirion Harries and Susie Harries, *Soldiers of the Sun: The Rise and Fall of the Imperial Japanese Army*. New York: Random House, 1991, pp. 348–352.

7. Peter Chamberlain and Chris Ellis, *The Complete Illustrated History of British, American, and Commonwealth Tanks, 1933–1945*. London: Cassell, 2000, p. 112.

8. Ibid., p. 130.

9. See Belton Y. Cooper, *Death Traps: The Survival of an American Armored Division in World War II*. Novato, CA: Presidio, 1998.

10. Dear and Foot, *The Oxford Companion to World War II*, p. 38.

11. Jack Greene and Alessandro Massignani, *Rommel's North African Campaign, September 1940–November 1942*. Conshohocken, PA: Combined, 1999, p. 236.

12. Jeremy Black, *Warfare in the Western World, 1882–1975*. Bloomington, IN: Indiana University Press, 2002, p. 112.

13. Ibid., p. 113.

14. David M. Glantz, *Stumbling Colossus: The Red Army on the Eve of World War*. Lawrence: University Press of Kansas, pp. 21, 116–117, 155.

CHAPTER 4

Tanks of the Cold War, 1945–1989

DESPITE MANY WHO BELIEVED that atomic weapons had rendered conventional weapons such as tanks obsolete, armored fighting vehicles (AFVs) continued to see wide service in the world's armies after World War II. Tanks had come of age in that conflict, and all powers, especially the Soviet Union, placed great credence in large numbers of them. The Soviet Union saw AFVs as an essential element of forces that would engage and defeat an enemy on the great plains of Central and Eastern Europe. Tanks proved a key element in the many wars of the period in the Middle East, and they also saw extensive use, but with less effectiveness because of terrain limitations and other conditions, in both Korea and Vietnam. Tanks were also used by governments as a means to repress their own peoples.

The day of the heavy tank also came to an end in the 1950s. Technological advances allowed the functions usually fulfilled by heavy tanks to be performed by the lighter, more maneuverable, and less expensive main battle tanks (MBTs). The new, most powerful tanks on the battlefield, MBTs in essence combined the old medium and heavy tanks of World War II.

One lesson of World War II was the need in the future for all military components in a military force to be as mobile as the tanks. This led to the introduction in all armies of armored personnel carriers (APCs) to transport infantry as well as field artillery, antiaircraft weapons, rockets, and mortars. The Soviets, whose armies benefited tremendously toward the end of World War II from substantial numbers of U.S. Lend-Lease trucks, took the lead in this. They developed a considerable number of APCs to transport men and to mount antiaircraft weapons, rockets, and mortars. Ultimately, Soviet APCs did far more than merely transport infantry to the battlefield. Their BMP series (*Boevaia Mashina Pekhoti,* or Combat Vehicle Infantry) was the first infantry fighting vehicle (IFV) in the world. Infantry could now fight from within the vehicle, and some BMPs mounted a powerful gun and carried antitank missiles, enabling them to provide effective close infantry support.

During the period of the Cold War, systems were also developed to provide some protection for tank crews against the new threats of nuclear, biological, and chemical (NBC) attack. In addition, new sights, night-vision equipment, improved aiming systems, and more powerful guns and projectiles came into widespread use. All these served to increase the tanks' lethality as well as their battlefield survivability.

GREAT BRITAIN

In Europe the main concern for the Western democracies was a westerly offensive and invasion of the Republic of Germany (West Germany) by Soviet forces that would necessarily include large numbers of tanks. In the post–World War II period the United Kingdom had a number of tanks from that conflict still available, and these saw extended postwar service. They included Comet and Centurion cruiser tanks, as well as the Churchill infantry tank.

Introduced in late 1944 and described in Chapter 3, the Comet (A34) mounted a 77mm main gun. It fought in the Korean War and remained in the British inventory until the early 1960s. The last British cruiser tank developed in World War II, the Centurion (A47), entered service too late to see combat in that conflict. Developed in response to the British experience of fighting in North Africa, it was designed as a heavy cruiser tank meeting the need for an all-purpose AFV capable of engaging other tanks and performing a variety of infantry support roles. The army called for the new tank to mount a main gun capable of firing both armor-piercing (AP) and high-explosive (HE) rounds.

The first six Centurion tanks (designated Centurion I) were rushed to Europe in May 1945 for testing in combat with the 22nd Armoured Brigade, but they did not arrive by the end of the war. Its uparmored version, designated the Centurion II, was the production model.

The Centurion II remained the principal British MBT during the first decades of the Cold War. It went through 13 basic models, with a number of variants. The Centurion Mark VII had a battle weight of more than 114,000 pounds and a crew of four. It had a 650-hp engine producing a speed of 21 mph or more and mounted a 105mm main gun and two machine guns. It had maximum 152mm armor protection.

Of 4,423 Centurions built until production ended in 1962, 2,500 were exported. The Centurion saw widespread combat service during the Cold War in Korea, the Middle East, southern Africa, Pakistan, and Vietnam. It remained in British service until 1969. The Centurion Royal Engineer Armored Vehicle (known by the acronym "AVRE") continued in service thereafter. The British Army utilized it in Northern Ireland to clear roadblocks, in the Falklands War as an armored recovery vehicle, and in the 1991 Gulf War. It mounted a 165mm (6.5-inch) demolition gun.

The heavy Churchill Infantry Tank (A22), which had first seen combat in August 1942, also fought in Korea. Most of those so employed were the Mark IIIs. Variants included those mounting a 95mm howitzer, a flamethrower tank, a bridge-layer, and a recovery vehicle.

The threat posed by Soviet heavy tanks in Europe led the British to develop the Conqueror heavy tank, introduced in 1956. It mounted a 120mm (4.72-inch) gun based on the U.S. 119mm (4.7-inch) antiaircraft gun. The U.S. gun utilized a brass cartridge case, necessitating a large turret that also contained a rangefinder and fire-control equipment. The turret also had a device that, when it was working, automatically ejected the spent cartridge case through a hatch in the turret side. The Conqueror weighed nearly 146,000 pounds, had a crew of four, a 810-hp engine, top speed of 21 mph, a 120mm main gun, and two machine guns. It had maximum 178mm armor protection. Some 200 of these tanks were built between 1955 and 1958, but all were replaced by 1963 by the Centurion.

In 1956 Leyland Motors, the design source for the Centurion Mark VII, produced three prototypes of an MBT, designated the FV4202. Leyland built another half-dozen prototypes during 1961–1962. A year later, in May 1963, the British Army accepted the new tank, officially designated the Chieftain Mark V MBT. It remained in front-line British service until 1996. The Chieftain weighed some 121,000 pounds, had a four-man crew, a 750-hp engine, a speed of

30 mph, and mounted a 120mm main gun and three machine guns. Armor protection is classified. The Chieftain went through 12 different marks, along with additional submarks. Modifications included a new power train and engine, improved fire-control systems, and NBC packs. The Chieftain mounted an infrared/white light searchlight that remained online with the gun for target illumination. Later models utilized laser ranging as well as the Thermal Observation and Gunnery Sight, also on the Challenger I MBT.

British Army Chieftains, except the Mark I, also were retrofitted for the Improved Fire-Control System, which utilized a digital computer to automatically calculate the ballistic solution and proper laying offset for each target and automatically laid the gun in readiness to fire. The gunner and commander each had a firing switch for the main gun, with the commander having override. Of 900 Chieftains manufactured, some 450 were exported to Iran, Kuwait, Jordan, and Oman.

During the post–World War II period, the British continued their long-standing practice of building tanks for export, in this case to meet the needs of nations not able to afford the more expensive NATO-standard MBTs. Three such tanks in the 1960s and 1980s were the Vickers Mark I MBT, Vickers Mark III MBT, and the Khalid MBT. The Vickers Mark I utilized the steering and fire-control systems of the Chieftain and the 105mm gun in the later versions of the Centurion. These were mounted in a new light-weight hull and chassis. Options included an NBC system, night-vision equipment, and a flotation screen that could be secured within a half-hour to the hull. Produced beginning in 1964, the Vickers Mark I chiefly went to India, which contracted for 2,200 built in Britain; it was also produced under license in India beginning in 1965 at the government's tank factory at Avadi near Madras. Production ended there in the mid-1980s. In Indian service the Mark I is known as the Vijayanta (Victory). Vickers also built 70 Mark I tanks for Kuwait, but these were lost in the 1990 Iraqi invasion.

The Mark I weighed approximately 85,000 pounds, had a four-man crew, and a 650-hp engine capable of 30 mph. It was armed with the 105mm main gun and three machine guns, including a 12.7mm (.50-caliber) for main-gun ranging and two 7.62mm, one of which was coaxial. It had maximum 80mm armor protection.

The Vickers Mark II was never built. The Mark III, produced beginning in 1977, was essentially the Mark I with a new engine and new turret with cast front. Somewhat lighter, at 82,650 pounds, than the Mark I, the Mark III was also powered by a 720-hp diesel engine. The Mark III had an all-welded, rolled steel hull divided into driver compartment, engine and transmission compartment, and fighting compartment. It retained the same 105mm main gun and the 12.7mm (.50-caliber) machine gun for fire against thin-skinned vehicles and for ranging purposes if the laser rangefinder or fire-control computer failed. It also mounted two 7.63mm machine guns, one coaxial and the other on the commander's cupola. Optional equipment includes an NBC kit, passive night-vision equipment, a deep wading and flotation kit, and automatic fire detection and suppression equipment.

Kenya ordered 83 Mark IIIs (seven of them armored recovery vehicles), and Nigeria ordered 94 (six of them armored recovery vehicles and 12 of them armored vehicle bridge-layers). A modified version of the Mark III, developed for Malaysia, incorporated explosive reactive armor (ERA) over the front of the hull, turret, and side skirts. It also had a Global Positioning System (GPS) and a laser warning system connected to a bank of eight 76mm smoke-grenade launchers.

The third export MBT was the Khalid. Combining features of the Chieftain and the Challenger, this tank was built by the Royal Ordnance Factory Leeds on a 1974 order from the government of the shah of Iran for 1,350 MBTs, designated the Shir (125 Shir Is and 1,125 slightly modified Shir IIs). The new Islamic government of Iran cancelled the order, although production had already begun. In 1974 Jordan then took delivery of 274 slightly modified Shirs (with improved sights and fire-control system), which was then renamed the Khalid. The Khalid was essentially a later version of the Chieftain with a modified fire-control system and the power system of the Challenger MBT used by the British Army. The Khalid weighed 127,832 pounds and had a four-man crew. It had a 1,200-hp engine capable of driving the tank at 30 mph. The Khalid mounted a 120mm main gun and two 7.62mm machine guns, one of which was coaxial. Armor is classified but was of steel.

The chief British MBT of the 1980s was the Challenger. The first in the series, Challenger I, proved an excellent design. It was derived from the Shir 2 MBT developed for Iran. In late 1978 the British Ministry of Defence ordered 243 Challenger I tanks, sufficient to equip four British armored regiments. Delivered to the army beginning in March 1983, it was built by the Royal Ordnance Factory Leeds, which had been acquired by Vickers in 1986. Challenger I weighed about 137,000 pounds, had a crew of four, and had a 1,200-hp engine that provided a maximum speed of 35 mph. It mounted the same 120mm rifled gun as the Chieftain and also had two machine guns. Exact specifications are classified, but the Chieftain utilized Chobham armor in both its hull and turret. Chobham armor consisted of multiple layers of steel interspersed with ceramic-based light alloys; this provided excellent protection against both kinetic and chemical energy rounds. The Challenger also had an improved fire-control system with a laser rangefinder and thermal imaging system, all of which is known as the Bar and Stroud Thermal Observation and Gunnery System.

The Challenger I performed well in the 1991 Gulf War, when it served with the 5th and 7th Armored Brigades. For that war it received extra armor skirts and ERA on the glacis plate. The 120mm gun worked well, although Challenger crews experienced problems with the thermal imaging sight, which did not always function properly.

FRANCE

In the immediate post–World War II period France relied extensively on World War II equipment. The French could make use not only of substantial quantities of U.S. tanks supplied to the French Army at the end of the war but also stocks of captured German tanks, most notably the Panther, which the French operated into the late 1940s.

This was not a satisfactory situation, and immediately after the war the French government decided to reequip the army with French-built AFVs. The most successful of these was the excellent, lightweight, air-transportable AMX-13, which is still in service in some countries. Development began in 1948, with production commencing in 1952 and continuing into the 1980s. Initial manufacture was by the Atelier de Construction Roanne, although by the 1960s production had switched to Mécanique Creusot-Loire. Among the innovations was an automatic loader in the turret bustle with two revolver-type magazines, each holding six rounds. This feature allowed the gunner to get off a dozen quick rounds. After that the loading was accomplished manually. The turret was mounted somewhat to the rear of the vehicle and was of oscillating type: the gun was fixed in the turret's upper part, which then pivoted on trunnions against the lower portion.

The AMX was used as the foundation for a number of armored

vehicles, including self-propelled guns, armored recovery vehicles, engineer vehicles, armored bridge layers, and IFVs. The AMX-13 weighed only 33,000 pounds, had a crew of three (the problem in the pre–World War II French tanks of poor crew placement was avoided with both the commander and gunner located in the turret and the driver in the hull), and was propelled by a 250-hp engine at a maximum speed of 37 mph. At first the AMX-13 mounted a long-barreled 75mm main gun developed by the Germans at the end of World War II, but this was subsequently upgraded to a 90mm gun, and in 1987 Creusot-Loire had introduced the option of a low-recoil 105mm gun. There was also one machine gun. The AMX-13 had maximum 40mm armor protection.

The French sold the AMX-13 widely abroad, including to Israel. Although developed primarily for airborne warfare, the AMX-13 was mostly used as a general-purpose light tank. Its low height (7 feet, 7 inches) made it useful as a tank destroyer. A number of nations developed upgrade packages for the AMX-13 to prolong its service life.

Initial French efforts after the war to develop an MBT concentrated on the Char AMX-50. Heavily influenced by the German World War II Panthers and Tigers, the AMX-50 resembled the Panther in its armored hull, and its suspension was similar to that of the Tiger. It mounted a 120mm (4.72-inch) high-velocity gun, a caliber well in advance of its time. Its most innovative aspect, however, was the oscillating turret, similar to that of the AMX-13 described above. The AMX-50 weighed nearly 131,000 pounds, had a five-man crew, and sported maximum 120mm armor. The tank was judged to be too large and too heavy, and it remained in prototype only. The French decided to concentrate their interest in developing an MBT in what became the AMX-30.

Until the mid-1950s both France and the Federal Republic of Germany relied chiefly on the U.S. M47 Patton as their MBT. Both these nations and Italy then decided to develop a lighter and more powerful MBT for common use. As is so often the case, however, each nation then decided to proceed with its own design. The Germans produced the Leopard, whereas the French developed the AMX-30.

Ordered by the French Army in 1963, the AMX-30 entered production in 1966. Designed by the Atelier de Construction d'Issy-les-Moulineaux, it weighed some 79,000 pounds, had a crew of four, a 720-hp engine capable of 40 mph, and mounted a powerful (105mm) main gun, along with a coaxial 20mm cannon and one machine gun for antiaircraft protection.

The AMX-30 underwent numerous upgrades, including in the B2 model of 1979 with a more modern fire-control system, night-vision equipment, and NBC protection. Although supplemented by the more powerful Leclerc, the AMX-30 remains in French Army service, having been upgraded with ERA and a more powerful engine. A large number of AMX-30s were sold abroad and remain in service there as well, including in Spain, where they have been produced under license.

In 1975 the French began production of the AMX-32, essentially an AMX-30 entirely for export with a 120mm gun; but the AMX-32 failed to attract purchasers and was dropped in favor of a brand new design, the AMX-40 MBT. It appeared in 1983. Weighing more than 96,300 pounds, it mounted a 120mm gun. Although it was tested by several nations in the Middle East, none was sufficiently impressed to buy it, and it did not progress beyond the prototype stage.

WEST GERMANY

As World War II drew to a close in Europe, Germany was developing a whole new line of tanks. The E-series ranged from light to super-heavy types and had considerable promise. None, however, reached beyond the prototype stage.

During World War II the Allies had expressed their resolve to disarm Germany completely after its defeat, but this changed with the Cold War between East and West. Another consequence of this tension was the division of Germany into two separate states, East Germany and West Germany. The Federal Republic of Germany (West Germany), established in September 1949 from the U.S., British, and French occupation zones, was initially barred from having an army, let alone heavy weaponry such as tanks. Intensifying confrontation with the Soviet Union and the shooting war in Korea, the first of the Cold War, changed the entire picture. The situation in divided Korea, in which the communist Democratic People's Republic of Korea (DPRK, North Korea) had attacked the Western-allied Republic of Korea (ROK, South Korea), seemed an ominous portent for divided Germany, and it shocked many West Germans into a change of attitude. At the same time, with much of the French military fighting in Indochina, the North Atlantic Treaty Organization (NATO) was starved for manpower. In these circumstances the United States pushed for German rearmament. With the blessing of NATO (France most reluctantly), West Germany was permitted to rearm beginning in 1955.

Initially West Germany employed the U.S. M47 Patton as its MBT. As noted, France and West Germany hoped to develop a common MBT, but each nation then decided to go its own way, with the Germans developing the Leopard. First appearing in 1963, the Leopard MBT entered production in 1965. A total of 2,347 Leopards (later the Leopard 1) were built for the German Army by Krauss-Maffei (later Krauss-Maffei-Wegmann) during 1965–1984, and the tank remained in service until 1999. The Leopard was also built under license in Italy.

The Leopard 1 resembled the French AMX-30 in that it sacrificed armor protection for speed and maneuverability. It went through a variety of marks and submarks during the period it was in service, the final versions including computerized fire-control and thermal night-vision systems. Its 105mm main gun allowed use of the full-range of standard NATO ammunition.

This reliable, effective MBT attracted a number of foreign purchasers, and Germany exported the Leopard 1 to a number of other nations, including Australia, Brazil, Canada, Chile, Greece, and Norway. Withdrawn from service in Germany (which had since re-united following the collapse of the Soviet Union) in 1999, the Leopard 1 has undergone upgrades and remains in service with the armies of half a dozen states.

SOVIET UNION

The Soviet Union ended World War II with a large inventory of AFVs. The excellent T-34/85 remained in production until the late 1940s. In 1947 the Soviets introduced an upgraded model, the T-34/85 II, which remained the principal Soviet MBT into the 1950s. Produced under license in Poland and Czechoslovakia in the 1950s, it was exported widely, and production did not cease until 1964.

The T-34/85 II saw extensive service in the Korean War. The Korean People's Army (the North Korean Army) had 150 T-34/85 tanks at the beginning of the Korean War. The tank also fought in the succession of conflicts in the Middle East and Africa and saw combat as recently as the 1990s in conflict in the former Yugoslavia.

The Soviets led post–World War II development of armored personnel carriers. Although APCs are excluded from this volume, the Soviet Union developed a whole series and modified them to carry a variety of weapons. These were gradually replaced by the BTR (*Bronirovanniy Transportnaya Rozposnania*, Armored Wheeled

Transporter) series of eight-wheeled APCs through missile-armed BRDM (*Boevaya Razvedyvatnaya Descent Mashina*, Airborne Combat Reconnaissance Vehicle) scout cars and the BMP series of personnel carriers. The BMPs mounted a large gun capable of providing effective support to dismounted infantry. They also carried antitank missiles and were constructed to allow infantry to fight from inside the vehicle, which distinguished this IFV from the less capable APCs.

Along these lines the Soviets developed the PT-76 light tank. It had no equivalent in the NATO armies. As large as an MBT, the PT-76 was, however, thinly armored and was developed chiefly to lead amphibious assaults and conduct reconnaissance. Easily identifiable by its pointed nose and low, round turret with sloped sides and flat roof, the PT-76 was designed to be an amphibian without any preparation. Its powerful engine was adequate for both land and water propulsion, with movement through water accomplished by means of water jets from the rear of the hull. The PT-76 weighed about 32,000 pounds, had a crew of three, a 140-hp engine that produced a maximum speed of 28 mph, and was armed with a 76.2mm (3-inch) main gun and one machine gun.

The PT-76 entered service with the Soviet Army and Naval Infantry reconnaissance units in 1955 (three to five per company) and continued in service until 1967. It saw wide use in the armies of Soviet bloc countries and also was utilized by Afghanistan, Benin, Cambodia, Congo, Croatia, Cuba, Guinea, Guinea-Bissau, Indonesia, Iraq, Laos, Madagascar, Nicaragua, North Korea, North Vietnam, Uganda, Yugoslavia, and Zambia. South Vietnamese and U.S. forces encountered the PT-76 during the Vietnam War. It also fought in the 1964 India-Pakistan War and in various conflicts in Africa. Popular because it offers excellent characteristics, reliability, and low cost, the PT-76 continues in wide service today.

The IS-3 (described in Chapter 3) remained the principal Soviet heavy tank in the period immediately after World War II. The first postwar Soviet MBT, introduced in 1948, was the formidable T-54, itself a refinement of the T-44, the short-lived redesign of the T-34/85 at the end of World War II. The T-54 had improved mechanical ability, especially in its torsion-bar suspension and transmission. It had five road wheels per side, with a noticeable gap between the first and second road wheels. There were no return rollers. The original turret design tended to deflect rounds downward into the turret ring and was replaced by a more hemispherical "frying pan" shape with internal mantlet.

The T-54 had a longer hull than the T-44, as well as a larger and better-shaped turret. It also had improved tracks, a torsion-bar suspension system, and a transverse-mount engine at the hull rear. The T-54 weighed some 79,300 pounds, had a crew of four, and a 520-hp diesel engine giving a maximum road speed of 30 mph. It mounted a 100mm main gun and three machine guns. The bow machine gun, done away with on the T-44, resurfaced in the T-54, but without return of the crewman for it; manning the bow gun was now the responsibility of the driver. The T-54 had maximum 203mm armor protection.

In the mid-1950s the T-54 received a bore evacuator near the muzzle of the main gun, which was also stabilized for elevation. The T-54B of 1957–1958 introduced a stabilized gun for both elevation and traverse. It also had infrared driving lights and snorkel equipment enabling it to cross rivers while submerged.

The T-55 appeared beginning in 1958. The chief difference between it and the T-54 was in the latter's more powerful V-55 580-hp diesel engine. It also had a slightly modified turret, an improved 100mm main gun, a better transmission, a revolving turret floor (meaning that the crew did not have to shift position as the turret rotated), and increased ammunition storage. In 1963 the T-55 received an NBC system. The bow machine gun was also eliminated. In the late 1980s the T-55s received new supercharged engines, improved fire-control and laser-range finding systems, and appliqué and explosive armor.

The T-54/T-55 had a very long service life. Production continued until 1981, with a phenomenal 95,000 tanks manufactured, more than any other tank in history. Both the Chinese and Romanians have produced copies. Even at the end of the Cold War the T-54/T-55 constituted some 38 percent of overall Soviet tank strength and as much as 86 percent of non-Soviet Warsaw Pact armor. Reliable and relatively inexpensive, the T-54/T-55 was exported to more than 35 other nations (outside of the Warsaw Pact these included Egypt, Finland, India, Iraq, Libya, and Syria). Although obsolescent, these tanks nonetheless remain in service today. Egypt has upgraded its T-55s with U.S. engines, guns, and fire-control systems. Israel captured a number of T-54/T-55s from Egypt and Syria and proceeded to upgrade them with General Motors engines and 105mm M68 guns.

The T-54/T-55s have had a mixed combat record. Although sufficient to crush the Hungarian Revolution of 1956, they were not successful against Western-supplied Israeli armor in the 1967 Six

Day War. They continued as the mainstay of Egyptian as well as Syrian armor in the 1973 Yom Kippur War, and although these tanks inflicted losses on Israeli tanks in that conflict, the Arab armies were again defeated. This was more a failure of doctrine and training than of equipment, however. The T-55 continued to serve in Africa, Asia, Afghanistan, and in Iraq. They were easily outclassed by the Coalition's armor in the 1991 Gulf War.

In 1953 the Soviets introduced their last heavy tank, the T-10 Lenin. The successor to the KV/IS series of World War II heavy tanks, the T-10 was basically an enlarged IS with a heavier gun and more powerful engine. It had a stretched hull with a total of seven road wheels. The Lenin weighed some 114,600 pounds, had a 690-hp engine that provided a maximum speed of 26 mph, and had a crew of four. It mounted a 122mm main gun and three machine guns, with maximum 270mm armor protection. Expensive to build, heavy, and difficult to maintain logistically, the T-10 was phased out in the mid-1960s in favor of the T-62. It equipped a number of Warsaw Pact armies and was exported to both Egypt and Syria.

The Soviets solicited designs from two different design groups for a tank to succeed the T-54/T-55. The first of these designs to appear was the T-62. Entering service in 1961, it remained in first-line Soviet service for two decades. Of similar layout and appearance to the T-55, the T-62 nonetheless introduced a number of improvements. Wider and slightly longer than the T-55, it had a more rounded turret, lower in the front. The T-62 had five road wheels, with no return wheels, and its drive sprocket was at the rear and the idler at the front. Instead of a wider gap between the first and second road wheels, it had between three/four and four/five.

The T-62 weighed some 88,200 pounds, had a crew of four, a 580-hp engine, and a maximum speed of 31 mph. It mounted the larger, new 115mm (4.53-inch) smoothbore main gun—the first smoothbore tank gun in the world—with a longer and thicker barrel than that on the T-55 and a bore evacuator. Its gun enabled the T-62 to fire AP fin-stabilized discarding sabot rounds that could destroy any tank at ranges of under 1,500 meters. It also had two machine guns and heavier (maximum 242mm) armor protection.

Although its engine provided excellent cross-country performance, the T-62's suspension system provided a rough off-road ride. The main gun, though a highly effective antitank weapon under 1,500 meters, could fire only four rounds per minute, and its automatic spent-case ejection system was a danger to the crew in that it led to buildups of carbon monoxide in the crew compartment. It was also a potential crew hazard in the event of misalignment caused by rough ride, which would cause cartridge cases to bounce off the turret wall. The Afghanistan War revealed the weakness of the T-62 to antitank weapons and led to the addition of appliqué armor to the glacis plate and horseshoe armor to the turret front, as well the addition of extra antimine belly armor. Other modifications included improved fire-control systems, new sights, laser rangefinders, ERA, and more powerful engines.

The Soviets built some 20,000 T-62s, and it was the principal Soviet MBT of the 1960s and much of the 1970s. It constituted 24 percent of overall Soviet tank strength at the end of the Cold War. T-62s were also built in large number by the People's Republic of China, Czechoslovakia, and North Korea.

The T-62 had a checkered combat record. Many were exported to the Middle East, and though the Israeli Army respected the T-62s for their slight silhouette and powerful main gun, these tanks proved vulnerable to hostile fire. The turret crew was also in line on the left side of the tank, and the Israelis learned that a kinetic round on that side of the tank would usually kill them all. In Afghanistan many T-62s were lost to portable antitank weapons such as the RPG7.

Although the T-62 was simply an improvement of the T-55, the next Soviet MBT, the T-64, was a completely new design that represented a considerable advance in firepower, armor protection, and speed. The latter was a major priority as the T-54/T-55 and T-62 series tanks had difficulty keeping up with the new BMP-1 IFV. Entering production in 1966 and designed to replace both the T-54/T-55 series and T-62, the T-64 nonetheless suffered from automotive and suspension problems.

The T-64, which somewhat resembled the T-62 in its turret area, weighed some 92,600 pounds. An autoloader eliminated the need for the loader, reducing crew size to only three. Powered by a 750-hp engine, it had a maximum road speed of 47 mph. Initially the T-64 was armed with a 115mm gun, but Soviet designers decided that the tank was undergunned against the U.S. M60A1, and they upgraded the definitive version T-64A to a more powerful 125mm smoothbore. The T-64B version could fire the 4,000 meter–range Songster antitank guided missile. The T-64 also mounted two machine guns and had maximum 200mm armor protection.

The T-64 had a new suspension system. Rather than large road wheels alone, as was the case on the T-55 and T-62, its suspension utilized six small road wheels and four return rollers. Skirting plates

The Soviet T-72 MBT tanks. *Courtesy of the Patton Museum.*

provided some protection to the return rollers. This new system provided excellent cross-country performance. Uncharacteristically for Soviet tanks, the new engine had serious reliability problems, as did the transmission, fire-control system, and loader. As a consequence, although the Soviets produced some 14,000 T-64s and reequipped their own forces with them, the tank was never exported. Instead the Soviets exported the follow-on, somewhat less-capable T-72.

The second of the two MBT designs to replace the T-62, the T-72 was developed by the Uralvagon design team at Nizhni Tagil. Slower in entering production, it nonetheless proved to be both more reliable and far cheaper to produce. Manufactured at Nizhni Tagil beginning in 1971, the T-72 is quite similar in appearance to the T-64, and both utilize the same gun, suspension, and track. The road wheels on the T-72 are closer together, however.

The T-72 weighs about 100,000 pounds and has a crew of three. It is powered by a transverse-mount 840-hp engine capable of producing a maximum speed of 40 mph. Although its enormous 125mm smoothbore main gun allows the T-72 to fire projectiles with great destructive capability, ammunition flaws mean that the gun has a reputation for inaccuracy beyond about 1,500 meters. The gun is stabilized, allowing it to fire on the move, but it is only truly effective at short ranges, and most crews halt the tank before firing. This puts the T-72 at an enormous disadvantage with Western tanks, which have far superior gun stabilization systems. The T-72 has an automatic carousel-type loader developed by Uralvagon with charges above and projectiles below. The turret, though quite low, is cramped.

In the late 1980s the Soviets introduced the 9K120 Svir laser-guided antitank projectile. It extends the range of the main gun out to 5,000 meters (about 3 miles). Reputedly the Svir can penetrate 700mm of armor. Four to six Svirs are carried per tank.

A number of T-72 variants have appeared, offering an improved diesel engine, thicker armor, and better sights. Explosive reactive armor was introduced in 1984. The T-72 equips the Russian Army and the former Warsaw Pact armies, and it has been widely employed to the Middle East and Africa. Manufactured mostly in the Soviet Union, it has also been produced under license in Czechoslovakia, India, Iran, Iraq, Poland, and the former Yugoslavia. It is in fact the world's most widely deployed tank.

Despite its many sales, the T-72 has not fared well in battle. The Israeli Defense Forces (IDF) encountered Syrian T-72s during the Israeli invasion of Lebanon in 1982. The 105mm guns on the Israeli Merkavas, Centurions, and M60s penetrated the armor on the T-72s at a range of up to 4,000 meters (2.5 miles); the Syrian T-72s had much less success.

Both Iran and Iraq employed T-72s during the eight-year Iran-Iraq War during the 1980s, but there is little information about their effectiveness. Iraq counted some 1,000 T-72s in its inventory during the 1991 Gulf War, but they were easily defeated by the U.S. M1A1 Abrams, which was able to take on the T-72 and destroy it at twice the effective range of the T-72's main gun. No M1A1s were destroyed by Iraqi tank fire. More often than not penetration hits by Coalition tanks during that war set off ammunition stored inside the T-72s and killed their crews, the result of the failure to compartmentalize the ammunition.

Despite these failings, it should be remembered that the T-72 was not designed to defeat Western armor—that was to be left to the T-64s and T-80s. Rather, it was intended as a relatively inexpensive MBT that would be both reliable and easy to maintain and could be widely exported. It met these criteria quite well.

The T-80 was the MBT designed to take on and destroy U.S. and other Western tanks. The last Soviet Union MBT, it appeared in prototype in 1976 but did not enter production until 1980. The T-80 was not a new design but basically the follow-on to the T-64 with the flaws corrected. It included many aspects of both the T-64 and T-72 MBTs. The chief difference over its predecessors was that it had a new engine and a new suspension system. The engine was the GTD-1000 gas-turbine, the first gas-turbine engine in Soviet tank service. It both runs quieter and provides a higher speed. The suspension was actually a return to the torsion-bar system instead of the unreliable hydro-pneumatic suspension of the T-64. The T-80 also has the ability to fire the Songster AT-8 antitank guided missile from its 125mm main smoothbore gun. It also has an automatic loader.

The T-80 weighs nearly 93,700 pounds, has a crew of three, and an 1,100-hp engine capable of producing a speed of nearly 44 mph. It is armed with the 125mm smoothbore gun and two machine guns and is protected by composite explosive-reactive armor. The T-80 has systems comparable to Western tanks and was the first Soviet production tank with a ballistics computer and laser rangefinder. The T-80 continues in production both in Russia and Ukraine. It has gone through upgrades and has been sold to the People's Republic of China, Pakistan, and South Korea. It is uncertain how the T-80 would perform against Western tanks.

UNITED STATES

The United States Army developed several new tanks following World War II. The M24 Chaffee light tank continued in service well after the conflict and was the main U.S. light tank until 1953. Employed by reconnaissance units in the U.S. Army, it was the only tank available to the occupying U.S. divisions in Japan at the start of the Korean War in June 1950. All were in what were supposed to be the divisional heavy tank battalions, with each division deploying 15–17 M24s. No match for the more powerful T-34 mediums of the Korean People's Army (KPA, i.e., the North Korean Army), the Chaffee was gradually replaced by M41s and M47s.

The Chaffee saw wide service abroad in other armies and remained in service with some into the 1990s. Taiwan equipped its M24s with a 90mm main gun. France also used the M24 extensively in Indochina.

Before the end of World War II the U.S. Army was at work on a new light tank to replace the Chaffee. This was the M41 Walker

Bulldog, named for Lieutenant General Walton Walker, commander of the U.S. Eighth Army in the Korean War who was killed in a jeep accident there in December 1950. The M41 was designed to be highly maneuverable while packing heavier firepower than the Chaffee to enable it to engage and defeat Soviet tanks.

The army hoped to develop an entire family of AFVs on the same chassis, including a light tank, an antiaircraft tank, and an armored personnel carrier. The M41 was also one of the first U.S. tanks to be designed around a suitable engine, rather than designing the tank first and then trying to find an engine to suit. Three different prototypes were produced, all with different turrets and 76mm guns. The second proved the most promising, and in 1949 it was designated the T41 and then the M41. Weighing nearly 52,000 pounds, the M41 would have been classified during World War II as a medium tank.

The M41 had a crew of four. It was powered by a 500-hp engine and was capable of 45 mph. The M41 mounted a 76mm main gun and two machine guns and was protected by maximum 32mm armor.

The M41 saw extensive and long service in the armies of Brazil, Chile, Denmark, the Dominican Republic, Guatemala, Taiwan, Thailand, and Uruguay. Indeed, it remains in service in most of these armies today. Bernardini of Brazil has rebuilt more than 400 M41s for that country's army and marines. Among modifications are improved engines and better armor, as well as a bored-out 90mm main gun. These tanks were designated the M41/B and M41/C. The Danes also rebuilt their M41s and fitted them with a new engine, an NBC system, skirts, and thermal sights. Some of Uruguay's M41s mount the 90mm Cockerill Mark IV gun.

In the 1960s the U.S. Army tried to counter the growing weight of tanks with the M551 Armored Reconnaissance/Airborne Assault Vehicle (AR/AAV) Sheridan, a lightweight, air-transportable armored vehicle with a heavy gun capable of knocking out any known tank. Amphibious and weighing nearly 35,000 pounds, the Sheridan had a crew of four, a 300-hp engine, and a maximum speed of 43 mph. The Sheridan mounted a 152mm (5.98-inch) gun, designed to fire the Shillelagh high-explosive antitank (HEAT) missile or combustible cartridge case conventional projectiles, and two machine guns. Weight reduction was achieved through the use of aluminum armor.

The Sheridan experienced numerous problems that took years to correct, including difficulty with the combustible cartridge case in the conventional round for its main gun and the transmission. First

The U.S. M551 Sheridan tank. *Courtesy of the Patton Museum.*

deliveries of the tank were in 1966, but problems forced their rebuilding; the Sheridan did not enter service until 1968.

Strictly speaking not a tank, the M551 was nonetheless used as one, although it had only limited armor protection. It replaced the M48 in regimental and divisional cavalry squadrons. The M551 also provided some antiarmor protection to the 3rd Battalion, 73rd Armor of the 82d Airborne Division. The Sheridan experienced numerous problems that took years to correct, including difficulty with the combustible cartridge case in the conventional round for its main gun and the tank's transmission. The fire-control systems were also hard to maintain. In Vietnam the crews rewired the fire controls to disable the missile system, useless in the fighting there. First deliveries of the tank were in 1966, but problems forced their rebuilding, and the Sheridan did not enter service until 1968.

The Sheridan saw service in the Vietnam War, although its crews preferred the M48 for its superior armor protection against mines and rocket-propelled grenades (RPGs). A number of Sheridans were completely destroyed by mines, leading many crew members to ride on top of the tank, rather than inside, when not under enemy fire. But the Sheridan could be devastatingly effective firing a new "beehive" canister round against dismounted troops. Dramatic temperature changes and high humidity in Vietnam also played havoc with the M551's all-electronic fire-control system. The shock of firing the main gun also lifted the tank off the ground, damaging its radio mount, and on the early Sheridans there was no protection for the tank commander when he was firing the cupola-mounted .50-caliber machine gun. Despite problems, the Sheridan remained in service with the 82d Airborne Division into the 1990s and saw service in Panama in 1989 and in the Gulf War in 1991. Some remain in service with the National Training Center in California disguised as a variety of possible enemy tanks.

The final U.S.-produced light tank of the Cold War era was the Cadillac Gage Stingray. A private venture and first introduced as a prototype in 1984, the Stingray was designed by Textron Marine & Land Systems (previously Cadillac Gage Textron). A total of 106 Stingrays were produced during 1988–1990 and purchased by Thailand. The Stingray weighs nearly 42,000 pounds, has a four-man crew, and has a 535-hp diesel engine for a maximum speed of 43 mph. With its 105mm rifled gun and two machine guns, it has the armament of an MBT and is thus an inexpensive alternative to the MBT.

In order to lower costs in the Stingray, Textron utilized as many proven systems as possible. The Stingray also incorporates a gun stabilizer and laser rangefinder for first-hit capability, and it has NBC protection. The Stingray's chief drawback is its light armor, exact information on which remains classified. Given the lethality of modern HEAT ammunition, however, that may make little difference.

The United States also developed heavier tanks. The Sherman M4A3 and M4A3E8 medium tanks, the mainstay of U.S. armored forces at the end of World War II, continued in active service with the U.S. Army for a number of years after the war and fought with the United Nations Command (UNC) forces in Korea. As noted, there were many models and variants of the basic design, including dozers, 105mm howitzers, rocket launchers, tank retrievers, and flamethrowers. The M4A3E8 (76mm), the last production model of World War II, mounted a small metal box affixed to the right rear, containing an EE-8 sound-powered telephone, enabling an infantryman to communicate with the tank commander.

A great many Shermans were exported to other countries after World War II. Israeli Shermans, which were kept in operation for decades from a wide variety of sources, were also armed with an equally wide panoply of weapons, including antiradiation missiles. The French upgraded a number of the Israeli Shermans with 75mm

The U.S. M46 Patton medium tank.
Courtesy of Art-Tech/Aerospace/M.A.R.S/TRH/Navy Historical.

and 105mm main guns. Known as M50 and M51 Super Shermans, these fought modified M4 Egyptian Army Shermans in the 1973 Yom Kippur War.

The M26 Pershing, which entered service only in the last few months of the war in Europe, also fought with the U.S. Army and Marines in Korea. Also seeing service in Korea was the M45 medium, essentially the M26 Pershing mounting a 105mm howitzer in place of the 90mm main gun. Only a limited number of M45s were produced, however.

Pending introduction of a new medium tank, World War II M26 Pershings were converted into the M46 medium. The Ordnance Corps had decided to utilize a standard engine and transmission for its future tanks and settled on the Continental V-12 engine and Allison cross-drive transmission. As the M26s came in for overhaul beginning in 1947, they became the first of many U.S. AFVs of the 1950s and 1960s to utilize the Continental engine and Allison transmission.

The M46 was unofficially known as the "Patton," the name later officially bestowed on the M47. Intended as a short-term solution, the M46 remained in service for a longer period because of the Korean War. It and the M26 bore the brunt of UNC armor combat there. The M46 had many of the same basic characteristics as the M26. It weighed nearly 97,000 pounds, had a five-man crew, and was powered by a 704-hp engine. Capable of 30 mph, it mounted a 90mm main gun and three machine guns (one antiaircraft) and had maximum 102mm armor protection.

The Korean War caught the U.S. Army in the midst of development of a new medium tank. The T42 design was not ready, but its turret and new gun were. As a stopgap measure, these were then adapted to the M46 hull, in effect the old World War II M26 with a new engine and other upgrades. This marriage of convenience became the M47 Patton. To the surprise of many, the M47 was a successful design. The turret was well contoured and had a prominent bustle for radio equipment.

The Patton was among the first tanks to mount a gun equipped with a blast deflector and bore evacuator fume extractor. It also had an optical rangefinder in the turret roof, and some later production vehicles had an early ballistic computer. The M47 had a five-man crew. It weighed nearly 102,000 pounds, had an 810-hp engine, and was capable of 37 mph. It was armed with a 90mm gun and three machine guns and had maximum 100mm armor protection.

First produced in 1951, the M47 experienced difficulties that the army demanded be corrected before the tank was formally accepted into service in 1952. The first M47s were converted from M46s; a total of 8,676 M47s were produced pursuant to the emergency tank production program during the Truman administration. Although it did not see service in the Korean War, the Patton had an extensive service life in the U.S. Army and abroad. Replaced in U.S. front-line service by the M48, the M47 was then transferred to the National Guard. A number were also supplied to other countries under the Mutual Defense Aid Program. West Germany was the first foreign country to receive the M47s, and it modified them to eliminate one crew member in order to store to 105mm main-gun rounds internally. This change was carried out in the M47M upgrade in the late 1960s. Some 800 of these were produced in the United States and Iran. And though West Germany and France, another national user, have long since replaced their M47s with more modern AFVs, the M47 remains in service in the armies of Iran, Pakistan, South Korea, and Serbia.

As with the M47, its follow-on design, the M48 Patton II medium tank (also known as a main battle tank), was rushed into service as a consequence of the Korean War and of the Soviet pressures on West

Berlin. The difference was that whereas the M47 was an interim tank, the M48 was a brand-new design with new hull, turret, tracks, suspension, and transmission.

Initial problems were soon solved, and the M48 went through many modifications to become a highly effective fighting vehicle and one of the most important post–World War II tanks. Although it saw considerable service during the Vietnam War with both the U.S. Army and Marines beginning in 1965, this was rarely against communist armor. Fighting in the Middle East with the Israeli Army, however, the M48 achieved an enviable record against its Soviet counterparts.

Compared to the M47, the M48 had a more rounded cast turret and a wider, lower cast hull. It weighed approximately 114,000 pounds, had a 750-hp engine, and was capable of 30 mph. Design work began at the end of 1950 and the first prototype appeared for testing in December 1951. The tank entered service in July 1952.

The M48 was the first U.S. medium tank to do away with the hull-mounted machine gun. This change dispensed with the assistant driver/machine-gunner and reduced the crew size to four. The M48 was easily identified by a large infrared/white light, a 1 million candlepower searchlight for effective night operation, usually mounted atop the mantlet. The first variants of the M48 had the 90mm (3.54-inch) gun; the M48A5 version mounted the British-designed 105mm (4.1-inch) gun and substituted a diesel engine (also in the M48A3) for the earlier gasoline variants. It was thus virtually the follow-on M60 tank.

Many other nations received the M48, including West Germany, Greece, Iran, Israel, Jordan, Lebanon, Morocco, Pakistan, China, South Korea, South Vietnam, Spain, Thailand, Tunisia, and Turkey. The Israelis repeatedly modified and upgraded their M48s. During the 1982 Israeli invasion of Lebanon some Israeli M48s were the first tanks fitted with ERA. Many M48s remain in service, including more than 2,000 M48s with the Turkish Army (where it is designated the M45A5T1).

Concerns about the Soviet IS-3 heavy tank led the U.S. Army between 1946 and 1947 to test three prototype heavy tanks. The most promising of these was the T34, which entered service in 1952 as the M103 heavy tank. Longer than the M48, it had an extra wheel and return roller on each side. At nearly 125,000 pounds with an 810-hp engine that produced a top speed of 21 mph, the M103 was too heavy for its power train. It had a crew of five, two of whom were loaders, and was armed with one M58 120mm (4.71-inch) gun and two machine guns. The M103A2 for the Marine Corps had a diesel engine. Only about 200 M103s were built; they were not exported.

The M60 was essentially a refinement of the M48 begun in the late 1950s; later a number of M48s were rebuilt as M48A5s, essentially M60s, making the two tanks virtually indistinguishable. The first M60 prototypes appeared in 1958. The M60 entered production in 1959 and service in 1960.

A competition for the main gun of the M60 that included several weapons resulted in the selection of the new British L7A1 105mm (4.1-inch) gun (known in U.S. service as the M68). The M60 also had a new fire-control system. The new tank weighed nearly 116,000 pounds and had a four-man crew. Its 750-hp engine produced a maximum speed of 30 mph. Armament consisted of the 105mm gun and two machine guns. Variants included the M60A1, which had a new turret; the M60A2, which had a new turret with the 152mm gun/launcher developed for the M551 Sheridan; and the M60A3, which returned to the 105mm gun but with a thermal barrel jacket, a new fire-control computer with laser rangefinder, an infrared searchlight, and night-vision equipment. Most M60A1s were later modified to M60A3s. Other design improvements have been added, but with no change in model number.

The M60 was first supplied to U.S. Army units in Germany. As this theater was a priority and because there were no real armor-to-armor contests in Vietnam, the M60 did not serve in Indochina. Although no longer in U.S. active military service, a number of M60s remain in reserve and in the armed forces of other nations, including Austria, Bahrain, Bosnia, Brazil, Egypt, Greece, Iran, Israel, Jordan, Morocco, Oman, Portugal, Saudi Arabia, Spain, Sudan, Taiwan, Thailand, Tunisia, Turkey, and Yemen. Israel alone received some 1,350 M60s.

The M60 was the principal U.S. main battle tank for 20 years until the introduction of the M1 Abrams. The M60 saw combat in the Arab-Israeli Wars and in the Gulf War of 1991, when it served with the U.S. Marine Corps and the army of Saudi Arabia. It will undoubtedly continue in service for the indefinite future, in part because of an upgrade offered by the General Dynamics Land Systems Division that will convert the M60s of such nations as Egypt, Greece, and Turkey to the M60-2000. This upgrade incorporates many of the advantages of the M1 Abrams but at far less cost. Conversion kits include the M1 turret and 120mm (4.72-inch) smoothbore gun, a new diesel power plant, and the M1 transmission system.

The U.S. MBT-70. *Courtesy of the Patton Museum.*

The M60's replacement, the M1A1 and M1A2 Abrams, is today probably the top MBT in the world. It began as a joint project by West Germany and the United States for a new MBT that could engage and defeat the vast number of tanks the Soviet Union might field in an invasion of Central Europe. Designated the MBT-70, this new tank was to feature the Shillelagh gun/missile launcher and a 1,500-hp engine, neither of which was working out as planned.

Collapse of the MBT-70 project and cancellation of the follow-on XM803 program led to a brand-new program, which literally began from the ground up in 1972. That year, the army came up with a concept of what it wanted in the new MBT, and two companies—Chrysler Defense and the Detroit Diesel division of General Motors—built prototypes of what was then designated the XM1 MBT. Both were tested in early 1976, and that November the army declared Chrysler the winner. Following the manufacture of a number of test vehicles, the first production-model M1 tank came off the assembly line in February 1980. The new tank was named for General Creighton Abrams, armor tank battalion commander in World War II, Allied commander in Vietnam, and army chief of staff.

The M1 was a revolutionary design as well as a sharp departure from previous U.S. tanks, with their rounded surfaces and relatively high profiles. The M1 was more angular, with flat-plate composite Chobham-type armor, with armor boxes that can be opened and the

The U.S. M1 Abrams MBT. *Courtesy of Art-Tech/Aerospace/M.A.R.S/TRH/Navy Historical.*

armor changed according to the threat. At 8 feet tall, it is also considerably lower than the M60 (10 feet, 9 inches).

From the start, the army's intention was to arm the M1 with the 105mm gun. As a result of a program aimed at securing a common main armament for U.S., British, and West German tanks, the decision was taken, after initial M1 production had begun, to arm the M1 with a German-designed Rheinmetall 120mm smoothbore gun. But that gun was still under development when the tank was ready, and so the army decided to continue with the 105mm M68 gun utilized in the M60. The 120mm M256 gun, essentially the German-designed gun with a U.S. breech, was available in 1984, and the first M1A1 with this new armament came off the production line in August 1985. The M1A1HA introduced a new steel-encased depleted uranium armor, which is virtually impenetrable, but it also dramatically increased the tank's weight to nearly 146,000 pounds.

A total of 8,064 M1s were produced for the United States. The U.S. Army took the bulk of them, but the Marine Corps received 403 new vehicles to replace more than 700 M60A1s as well as other M1s transferred from the army. Kuwait also purchased 218 Abrams tanks, and Saudi Arabia bought 315. Egypt also arranged to produce

551 of them under a coproduction arrangement whereby they were built in Egypt by the Halwan Tank Plant.

MIDDLE EAST

Israel

Tanks were an essential weapon of war in the relatively flat and open terrain of the Middle East, and the Israelis were determined from the time of independence to build up their armored forces. The first Israeli armored vehicles were a hodge-podge of converted trucks and buses. In the 1948–1949 War for Independence, Israel had few tanks, apart from some left behind by the British and those captured from the invading Arabs.

The United States was quick to recognize the new Jewish state, and during the war the United States became a major source of arms for Israel, providing a number of World War II–vintage M4 Shermans. The Israelis also secured surplus Shermans from other armies. These saw long service with the Israeli Defense Forces (IDF); they underwent a succession of upgrades, including heavier guns, improved engines, and modified turrets. Once they had reached the limit of possible improvements, a number were turned into self-propelled guns.

Indeed, improvisation to gain maximum use of available resources became a hallmark of the IDF. The British Centurion, one of the world's most successful tank designs, underwent upgrades in Israeli service beginning in 1967 to improve its range as well as its protection. This latter included the installation of an ERA package and a new fire-control system. The Centurion also received a new diesel engine, in effect doubling its effective range.

France also became a major military source of arms for the Jewish state, including AMX-13 light tanks. France remained a principal arms supplier until an angry President Charles de Gaulle ended the relationship following the Israeli decision to launch a preemptive strike against its neighbors in 1967. Other tanks in the IDF included the U.S. M47 and M60 MBTs.

The Israelis also extensively remodeled the M60s they received from the United States. The IDF designated them the Magach 6, 7, and 8. Most were refitted with Blazer reactive armor, a new commander's cupola with an external 7.62mm machine gun, a 7.62mm machine gun for the loader, and a 12.7mm machine gun over the main gun and smoke grenade dischargers on either side of the main gun. The Magach 7 includes new passive armor, the Matador computerized fire-control system, and a 908-hp diesel engine. The Magach 7/8, fitted with a 120mm (4.72-inch) smoothbore gun, is known as the Sabra. It also features a redesigned turret, new add-on armor, thermal ranging, and the Knight fire-control system. Israel offered this tank to Turkey and has also converted a number of Turkish M60s to Sabras.

In their wars the Israelis also captured large numbers of Soviet T-54 and T-55 tanks supplied to the Arab states. These were modified and then added to the IDF inventory. Improvements included a new 105mm rifled gun, ERA, weapon stabilization system, fire-control system, passive night-vision equipment, and air-conditioning and fire-extinguishing systems.

The vagaries of overseas suppliers were a constant concern to the Israeli defense establishment and government, and in the 1970s Israel began development of its own tank. Known as the Merkava, it entered service in 1978. The Merkava built on lessons learned by the IDF in its many wars to that point, with the primary concerns being firepower and armor protection.

The Merkava underwent continued upgrades, with the Mark 2 appearing in 1983 and the Mark 3 in 1990. One of the world's most powerful tanks, the Merkava also affords perhaps the best crew protection. The Merkava's engine is mounted in front, and the turret is mounted slightly to the rear of the vehicle and has a distinctly pointed front. The turret also has a large bustle at the rear. The hull is of cast and welded armor and incorporates rear doors that allow access to the fighting compartment for resupply of ammunition or even transportation of a limited number of infantry if fewer main-gun ammunition rounds are carried.

The Merkava weighs some 132,000 pounds, has a crew of four, and has a 900-hp engine producing a maximum road speed of 34 mph. The Mark 1 mounts a 105mm gun, three machine guns, and a 60mm mortar in the turret roof; the Mark 2 has the same armament but improved armor and a new fire-control system. These two models were superceded by the Mark 3, introduced in 1990 (see Chapter 5).

Arab States

Tanks are very expensive and difficult to design and manufacture, and the Arab states lack such industrial capability. Egypt manufactures tanks under license and has produced an excellent APC. Saudi

Arabia has also produced light armored vehicles. But for the most part, the Arab states have chosen to rely on foreign-manufactured AFVs.

Iran

Because of its Islamic fundamentalist government's isolation from much of the world as well as its long war with neighboring Iraq, Iran was forced to manufacture its own tanks. Iran has several ongoing projects. One is to upgrade Soviet T-54 and T-55 tanks captured during the Iran-Iraq War. Known as the T-72Z Safir-74, this tank incorporates a 105mm rifled gun. The Zulfiqar MBT, however, combines components of the United States M48 and M60 and Russian T-72 tanks. The Iranians also produce their own APCs.

Pakistan and India

Aside from the Middle East, the largest postwar tank battles have occurred on the Indian subcontinent. The common border between India and Pakistan continues to be a flashpoint. Modern Pakistan and India were born from sectarian violence—the bloody partition of the subcontinent into Hindu India and Muslim Pakistan in the aftermath of World War II. Originally both armies were equipped with World War II–vintage U.S. M4 Shermans.

In order to upgrade its armored forces, nonaligned India initially turned to France and Britain. India secured from France the AMX-13 light tank, and from Britain it purchased the Centurion MBT. Pakistan, allied with the United States, equipped its forces with the U.S. M24 Chaffee light tank and the M48 MBT. These aforementioned AFVs were the principal tanks of the first war fought between India and Pakistan, in 1965. Another conflict occurred in 1971. Before that war, Pakistan secured Type 59 tanks from China, and India obtained T-55 tanks from the Soviet Union.

Following the 1971 war, India took steps to develop its own MBT, in part because of the limitations of its tanks in the inhospitable conditions of northwestern India, in Rajasthan bordering Pakistan, but also to free itself from dependence on foreign supplies and for national pride, however costly. Beginning in 1974 India began design work on the Arjun, named for a mythical Hindu warrior-prince. The Arjun was to mount an Indian-designed, rifled 120mm gun. Lacking an indigenous power plant, India used a German MTU-based diesel engine (by Motoren-Turbinen-Union GmbH). While the Arjun was undergoing development, India proceeded with local production of a Vickers MBT design, the Vijayanta (Victory), and also the Soviet T-72. As the arms race on the Indian subcontinent intensified, Pakistan developed the MBT-2000 Al Khalid beginning in 1988.

SOUTHEAST ASIA

The states of Southeast Asia acquired tanks from abroad. During the First Indochina War, the French employed tanks but chiefly along principal lines of communication (LOCs). In the Vietnam War (known by some as the Second Indochina War), the United States used AFVs itself and supplied the Army of the Republic of Vietnam (ARVN) with a number of AFVs, particularly M113 APCs modified as armored assault vehicles. At the same time, the People's Army of Vietnam (PAVN) of the Democratic Republic of Vietnam (i.e., North Vietnam) utilized armor supplied from the Soviet Union, chiefly the PT-76 and T-54 tanks.

CHINA

China produced no tanks of its own during World War II or the civil war that followed. In September 1949 the Communists triumphed over the Nationalists, and shortly thereafter China embarked on a program to build up an industrial base to enable it to produce modern tanks. The Soviets provided China with a number of T-54s, and China simply copied these for its first tank, the T-59 of 1959.

Developed by NORINCO (China North Industries Corporation) and virtually identical to the Soviet T-54, the T-59 incorporated over time slight modifications, such as a bore evacuator on the main-gun barrel, a gun-stabilization system, night-vision equipment, and laser rangefinding. The Type 59 weighed some 79,300 pounds, had a crew of four, and had a 520-hp engine producing a maximum speed of 31 mph. It mounted a 100mm smoothbore gun and two machine guns and had maximum armor thickness of 203mm. Dating from the early 1980s a Type II appeared with the substitution of a 105mm rifled main gun.

China exported the Type 59 widely. It remains in service today in China as well as Albania, Bangladesh, Cambodia, Democratic Republic of the Congo, Iran, Iraq, North Korea, Pakistan, Sudan, Tanzania, Vietnam, Zambia, and Zimbabwe. Western companies have since upgraded a number of these tanks by adding passive night-vision equipment and improved fire-control systems.

The first Chinese indigenous tank was the Type 62 light tank, introduced in 1962. In essence a reduced version of the T-59, it weighed only some 46,300 pounds and had a crew of four. Powered by a 430-hp diesel engine that provided a top speed of 37 mph, the Type 62 mounted an 85mm main gun and three machine guns. More suited than the T-59 to the rough and soft terrain prevailing in southern China, the T-62 was also exported to Albania, as well as to African and Asian states. Vietnam, with 200 T-62s, was the principal recipient of the tank abroad. Variants include an armored recovery vehicle and engineer vehicle. Most of the 800 T-62s built for the People's Liberation Army and its other armed forces remain in service.

Chinese armor doctrine copied that of the Soviet Union in placing reliance on large numbers of light amphibious tanks. The Soviets had their PT-76, but the Chinese Type 63 light tank actually improved on it. It combined the hull of the Type 77 APC with the Type 59 turret. This gave it the same 85mm main-gun armament and two machine guns. Weighing some 40,560 pounds, it had a crew of four, a 400-hp engine, and a maximum speed of 40 mph on land and 7 mph in water. The Type 63 was designed to provide support to the Type 77 and other APCs.

The next Chinese MBT design was the NORINCO Type 69. Believed to have appeared first in 1969 (hence the Western designation of Type 69), it was first seen in public in a parade in 1982. The Type 69 MBT employed the same basic hull and layout as the Type 59 but soon received the more accurate 100mm rifled main gun. The subsequent Type 79 (essentially the Type 69 but with a new gun) mounted the 105mm gun. A number of Type 69 tanks were exported to Iran and Iraq. Completely outclassed by the U.S. M1A1 Abrams and British Challenger MBTs, many Type 69s in the Iraqi forces were destroyed in the 1991 Gulf War. The Type 69 appeared in a wide variety of models, including antiaircraft tanks, bridge-layers, and engineer vehicles.

Whereas the Type 69 was simply an upgraded Type 59 tank, the NORINCO Type 80 introduced many improvements. Reportedly entering production in 1985, the Type 69 was introduced to the world when Chinese tanks crushed the prodemocracy student movement in Tiananmen Square in 1989.

The Type 80 had a new hull, a more powerful engine, a larger (105mm) gun that could fire both Chinese and Western ammunition, and an improved fire-control system. It weighed some 83,800 pounds, had a crew of four, was powered by a 730-hp engine capable of producing 37 mph, and had the 105mm main gun and two machine guns. The Type 80 also had a computerized fire-control system and a laser rangefinder. It was the basis for the subsequent Types 85-II and 90 MBTs (see Chapter 5).

FAR EAST

As with Southeast Asia, warring states in the Far East, chiefly the Democratic People's Republic of Korea (North Korea) and the Republic of Korea (South Korea), used Communist bloc and U.S. armor, respectively. South Korea had no tanks whatsoever in its army at the start of the conflict, but U.S. and British tanks were soon fighting in the conflict. North Korean armor came from the Communist bloc.

JAPAN

As with its Axis partner during World War II, Japan rearmed only as a consequence of the Cold War. Japan did not produce its first post–World War II tank until 1962, although development began in 1954. Its Type 61 MBT for the Japanese Ground Self-Defense Force was a conservative design that closely followed the U.S. M48 Patton. Weighing 77,140 pounds with a crew of four, it mounted a 90mm main gun and two machine guns. A small number continue in service.

No sooner had the Type 61 entered service than the Japanese began development of its successor. The Type 74 MBT appeared in prototype in 1974 and entered service in 1975. In all, 873 production models were manufactured, all by Mitsubishi Heavy Industries. Of conventional design, the Type 74 had a number of modern features, including complete gun stabilization, a laser rangefinder, a fire-control system, and a suspension system that allowed ground clearance to be adjusted depending on the nature of the terrain as well as to tilt the tank either left or right to aid with aiming the main armament. Weighing some 82,750 pounds and manned by a crew of four, the Type 74 had a 720-hp engine that provided a top speed of 38 mph. It mounted a British-built L7 105mm main gun and two machine guns. Armor characteristics remain classified. Thermal vision and side skirts were added later. Among the variants are a self-propelled antiaircraft gun and an armored recovery vehicle. The Type 74 remains the most numerous tank in the Japanese arsenal.

EMPLOYMENT OF TANKS IN THE COLD WAR

When World War II ended, the Soviet armies controlled much of Central Europe. Far from eradicating communism, Adolf Hitler's policies had in fact served to advance it. Soviet tanks helped secure Poland, the eastern portions of Germany and Austria, Hungary, Czechoslovakia, Romania, Bulgaria, Albania, and part of Yugoslavia. In 1919 following World War I, the Western powers had attempted to erect a barrier against the expansion of communism; given the favorable situation his armies enjoyed in 1945, Soviet dictator Joseph Stalin was no less determined to erect a similar cordon sanitaire in reverse, to protect his empire against the West.

By 1948 the Cold War was a reality. It came close to becoming a shooting war in several crises over Berlin. Fortunately for the world, the dreaded conflict in Central Europe between the North Atlantic Treaty Organization and the communist Warsaw Pact did not occur. Had there been armed conflict, it would have involved thousands of tanks on each side and seen some of the largest tank battles in history. Even without shooting, the Cold War had immense repercussions, and it led to the rearmament, only a decade after the end of World War II, of both West Germany and Japan.

Had war broken out in Europe between the two superpowers during the Cold War, its fault line would have been the border between the two German states; both sides maintained large armored forces there. But nuclear weapons soon became the chief U.S. deterrence to war, especially with the doctrine of *Massive Retaliation* under the Eisenhower administration. It touted nuclear weapons as less expensive (thus "more bang for a buck") and easier to maintain. Nuclear weapons, it was believed, could also make up for the inferiority of U.S. and allied NATO forces in West Germany in terms of both manpower and equipment vis-à-vis those of the Soviet Union and

Warsaw Pact. U.S. forces in Germany came to be seen more as a tripwire that would trigger use of nuclear weapons than as a shield capable of defending with conventional weapons against a Soviet invasion. In the 1950s the Soviet Union moved to a similar strategy of reliance on nuclear weapons.

The possibility of nuclear war, abetted by the use of chemical or biological weapons, helped ensure the continued presence of large numbers of tanks in Europe. It also impacted their design. The thick tank armor seemed to offer a degree of safety in the case of a nuclear blast, and the major armies took steps to provide AFVs with full NBC protection.

Generally speaking, the Soviets, who expected in the event of war to be utilizing their far larger numbers of AFVs in an offensive role, opted for fast, maneuverable tanks with excellent firepower. NBC protection was a low priority. The Western powers, assuming that they would be standing on the defensive against far larger Soviet formations, adopted defensive tactics. The British gave top priority to firepower, followed closely by protection for the tank crews, and then mobility. As a result, the British fielded some of the heaviest tanks of the Cold War era. The Americans adopted a middle position. Speed and maneuverability held top priority, followed by firepower, and then protection.

Having followed the United States in embracing nuclear warfare in the late 1950s, the Soviet Union gradually returned to maneuver warfare. By the 1970s the doctrine of the *deep battle* held sway in Soviet military thinking. This was shown in the 1981 maneuvers in Poland. The largest Warsaw Pact exercises in a decade, they involved more than 100,000 troops, in part the result of events in their increasingly restive satellite. Soviet doctrine evolved into something akin to that of World War II. Other forces would open gaps in an enemy front, which would then be exploited by massed armor formations, up to that point held in reserve. The armor columns would drive deep into the enemy's rear areas.

Meanwhile, the U.S. administration of John F. Kennedy moved away from massive retaliation in favor of the doctrine of *Flexible Response*. This called for greater reliance on conventional weapons and warfare. NATO's strategy by the late 1960s reflected this change, substituting a wide range of graduated options in the event of a general war in Europe. In the event of war the United States and its NATO allies expected to rely on firepower and slow withdrawal, yielding as little West German territory as possible while at the same time inflicting maximum punishment on the attackers.

Critics contended that this strategy played into Soviet hands, and in the early 1980s the United States shifted from a strategy of attrition warfare to maneuver warfare and adopted the *AirLand Battle.* This built on elements of German and Soviet World War II warfare, Israeli Defense Forces doctrine, and the Vietnam experience to produce a doctrine centered on airpower, air mobility, and armor in a united offensive strategy, by which NATO forces would outmaneuver and outfight those of the Warsaw Pact. Although fortunately never tested, AirLand Battle became NATO doctrine until the end of the Cold War.

In Central Europe there was fighting nonetheless as the restive Warsaw Pact satellites rebelled against rule from Moscow. Tanks played key roles in quelling the uprisings, first in East Germany in 1953 and then on a far larger scale in Hungary, when they put down the 1956 revolution there. In contrast to events in Hungary, the 1968 Warsaw Pact occupation of Czechoslovakia during the Prague Spring was almost completely bloodless. This was in large part because the Warsaw Pact states deployed 2,000 tanks in the operation, in what was in fact the largest display of armed might in Europe since World War II. Such a powerful armored presence actually led the reformist Czechoslovak government to urge its citizenry to give up a hopeless cause without armed struggle, in the process minimizing the human cost and the military reaction. Tanks also took part in fighting at the end of the Cold War in the Balkans as Yugoslavia broke up into its component states. And in southeastern Europe there was a protracted regional conflict between Armenia and Azerbaijan over Nagorno-Karabakh. Regional proxy wars also occurred elsewhere, with each side in the Cold War participating at least indirectly. Most of these wars were the result of decolonization in the Middle East and Asia. In the Middle East, Israel fought four wars with its Arab neighbors. There was also a protracted and exceedingly costly war between Iraq and Iran during 1980–1988, and the Soviet Union fought a war in Afghanistan during 1979–1989 trying to secure that nation for communism.

In Asia civil war broke out in China almost immediately following the end of World War II when the Nationalists sought to regain Manchuria. Much of this saw the use of U.S. hardware, including tanks, employed by both sides. The Communists triumphed in 1949. A bloody sectarian contest occurred in 1947 between the new states of India and Pakistan over the partition of the former empire in India. The two states fought substantial wars in 1947–1949, 1965, and 1971. China and India also fought a border war in 1962 when China challenged the 1913–1914 British demarcation line between the two states.

In Latin America there were border wars, and a wider conflict occurred when the military government of Argentina attempted to take the Falkland Islands from Britain in 1982. Fighting also occurred in Africa. Tanzania invaded Uganda in 1979 and many African states experienced protracted civil wars. In East Asia, Great Britain put down an insurgency in Malaya, but the Labor government's policy of giving up parts of its colonial empire also sparked wars, most notably in the cases of India and Palestine. Portugal and France, by contrast, fought wars to hold on to their overseas possessions. In the case of Portugal, the most notable instance was in Angola in Africa. For France it took place in Madagascar but most notably in Indochina during 1946–1954 and in Algeria in 1954–1962.

The First Indochina War ended with the 1954 Geneva Conference that led to an agreement that temporarily partitioned Vietnam into two states pending national reunification elections in 1956. When the anticommunist leader in the south, Ngo Dien Diem, refused to hold the promised 1956 elections, the war was renewed, this time as a civil war of North versus South. Each side found support from the opposing powers in the Cold War. China and the Soviet Union backed communist North Vietnam while the United States supported South Vietnam, eventually sending U.S. troops and making a major military commitment. The Vietnam War (known to some as the Second Indochina War) ended for the United States in 1973 and for the two Vietnams in 1975, when the communist North triumphed. In 1979 China and the new Socialist Republic of Vietnam fought a brief border war, sparked in large part because of Vietnam's invasion and occupation of Cambodia.

There was also a major war in Korea. The two Koreas—North and South—were similarly divided by the Cold War. What was intended to be a temporary dividing line for the surrender of Japanese troops at the end of World War II became permanent for the indefinite future. This situation led to the June 1950 invasion by North Korea of South Korea, North Korean leader Kim Il-sung's effort to unify the peninsula under communism. He believed he could accomplish this before the United States could intervene in any strength. The United Nations, led by the United States, condemned the invasion, and in the first war conducted under United Nations auspices, the coalition forces defeated the KPA. Communist China then entered the war. The only conflict of the Cold War between two major powers—the United States and China—the Korean War ended in June 1953 in stalemate and armistice.

Tanks participated in most of these wars, most notably in the fighting in the Middle East and in East Asia, but with the notable exception of the India-Pakistan wars, these conflicts did not see large-scale armored battles. In the 1965 war, principally around Chamb and Shakargarth, India and Pakistan each deployed more than 1,000 tanks. In the ensuing heavy fighting Pakistan lost perhaps 300 tanks, India about half that number. In the second war, fought in 1971 over the matter of Bangladeshi independence (East Pakistan declared its independence from West Pakistan as the new country of Bangladesh), India had the advantage, although losses were high on both sides.

It is a dictum of modern war that armor, infantry, and artillery work as a team in battle. Infantry and armor provide mutual support and protection. Tanks without accompanying infantry are vulnerable to enemy tank-killing weapons, and infantry is vulnerable to small arms, machine guns, and other direct-fire weapons. Infantrymen and artillery help to protect the tanks from tank-killers, and the tanks engage enemy direct-fire weapons and armor. Offensive tactics envision armor employed en masse, in large formations to overwhelm an enemy and make deep penetrations.

In the 1950–1953 Korean War armor was rarely used in this way, especially after the conflict became one of position and stalemate. The mountainous terrain and narrow valleys of Korea, as well as the flooded rice paddies of spring and summer, made it virtually impossible to employ tanks en masse. Attempts to deploy tanks in larger concentrations invariably led to a number of them becoming bogged down.

The Korean War is notable as the first war between U.S. and Soviet tanks. At the beginning of the conflict the KPA had a tremendous advantage in military hardware. In June 1950 it fielded some 150 T-34/85 tanks, 120mm heavy artillery, and an air force that included 70 Ilyushin Il 18 twin-engine bombers; South Korean forces had no tanks, no heavy artillery, and no air force except liaison craft. No wonder that Kim Il-sung was confident of a quick victory for the Communists. Although the KPA came close to winning the war in a matter of weeks, sufficient U.S. and United Nations forces reached Korea in time.

At first the fighting did not go well for the United Nations Command. In a clash near Osan, the Americans discovered that their 2.36-inch antitank bazooka rocket bounced off the T-34. One U.S. soldier fired 22 rounds at the KPA tanks, failing to stop a single one. The first tank-on-tank battle pitted KPA T-34s against M24 Chaffee light tanks of the U.S. 24th Infantry Division, the M24s fighting a delaying action against the more powerful T-34s. Although two M24s were lost in the engagement, they did knock out one T-34.

The tide turned against KPA armor with the arrival of more powerful M4 Shermans and M26 Pershings and the 3.5-inch antitank rocket launcher. UNC domination of the air was another important factor. In the employment of its armor, the KPA failed to send along infantry with the tanks. As a result, the T-34s could be destroyed by U.S. infantrymen with 3.5-inch rockets. All these came together in a series of battles fought at Obang-ni Ridge and in a valley known to the Americans as the "Bowling Alley," located near Taegu. Here U.S. ground-attack aircraft, M26 cannon fire, and 3.5-inch rockets destroyed a large number of T-34s and ended the myth of their invincibility.

The first part of the war, against the North Koreans, had been marked by maneuver warfare. The second phase of the war that followed the Chinese military intervention came to be a stalemate of position warfare. The obstacle of terrain, complete UNC air superiority, and the deep defensive belts built by both sides ended the threat of armor penetration. Each side, however, employed tanks in long-range, pinpoint sniping fire against enemy positions. Worked to vantage points, these "mobile pillboxes" could be dug in, and they proved highly effective.

Tanks also took part in the long wars in Indochina. At the beginning of the Indochina War, the French employed armored columns to secure the LOCs and cities, but French armor was largely useless in the interior jungles. The French used tanks in some of the big set-piece battles of the war, especially toward the end, and 10 M24 Chaffees were flown into Dien Bien Phu and assembled there to take part in the most important battle of the war, although they could not prevent the French defeat.

Both sides also employed tanks during the long Vietnam War that followed. Initially the ARVN forces used the M24 Chaffee light tank and M113 APCs. The U.S. military believed initially that Vietnam was not an appropriate environment for armor, but ultimately it deployed some 600 tanks in that theater. Although some lighter tanks, such as the M551 Sheridan and M50A1 Ontos, proved ill-suited for the local combat environment, the perception was eventually dispelled by the M48A3 Patton. Employed in search-and-destroy missions, the Patton came to be known for its jungle-busting ability in clearing paths through dense vegetation. Its 90mm main gun proved an effective bunker-buster, and its tracks and great weight could survive mines and could grind down Vietcong bunkers. The dozer variant of this tank commonly had claymore mines directly attached to its working blade for added firepower. Tanks helped protect convoys and secure LOCs, were a powerful asset in the defense of bases, and served as a rapid-reaction force. In a counterinsurgency support role, they helped clear out communist strong points, patrol secure areas, and engaged in sweeps and ambushes.

Tanks were prime targets for communist forces, who attacked them indirectly with mines or directly with RPGs, Sagger antitank missiles, satchel charges, or mines. The latter were the principal cause of U.S. armor losses in Vietnam. Whereas crews of the heavy M48 had a good chance of surviving a mine detonation, crews of lighter vehicles did not.

In the guerrilla warfare environment that marked so much of the Vietnam War, attacks on tanks with RPGs, such as the Soviet RPG2 (Vietnamese B40) and RPG7V (Vietnamese B41), were common, especially when tanks were in static positions. M48 crews sand-bagged their tank turrets for crew protection. When armor was used on the defensive, night laagers (defensive perimeters) would be set up with fighting positions between each vehicle. Concertina wire and claymore mines supported the defensive perimeters, and listening posts were set up. Harassment and interdiction artillery missions were employed to keep communist forces off balance and away from the laagers. The tankers learned that they could protect against RPGs by putting cyclone fencing around their positions.

Beginning in 1972 the Americans also had to contend with the Sagger (9M14M Malyukta) antitank guided missile. The tankers attempted to counter this threat by firing at the gray plume of smoke at the launch site in hopes of causing the gunner, who controlled the flight of the wire-guided missile with a joystick, to flinch and miss the target. Crews of tanks under way might also maneuver their vehicles sharply in hopes of disrupting the missile's flight path or attempt to confuse its control system by the use of flares. Suicide bombers with satchel charges or antitank grenades might be countered by throwing an explosive charge out of the tank or by using a tactic known as "back-scratching," whereby one tank fired small-caliber weapons at a buttoned-up friendly tank under attack.

Communist tanks, chiefly the PT-76, were deployed mostly during the conflict's last few years and primarily in an offensive role. PAVN forces deployed some 100 tanks in their unsuccessful invasion of South Vietnam in the Spring (or Easter) Offensive of 1972. These fell prey to ARVN tank-hunter teams armed with M72 LAWs (Light Antitank Weapons) and Allied aircraft. TOW (Tube-fired, Optically tracked, Wire-guided) weapons mounted on UH-1B helicopters scored a number of kills. Overall, the PAVN lost 80 percent of its tanks in the offensive. PAVN tank crews tended to be under-trained, and their tanks were not well integrated with infantry and artillery units.

Communist tanks were also inferior to their U.S. counterparts. The optic systems in the T-54 and T-55 were not up to the standards of the M-48, and the side-mounted fuel tanks and ammunition storage of the T-54 and T-55 proved vulnerable to enemy fire. In the final 1975 communist offensive, PAVN armor units, now better-trained and integrated with infantry and artillery, proved an important element in their swift conquest of South Vietnam.

Perhaps no other conflicts of the period captured the world's imagination as did the numerous wars in the Middle East. With the notable exception of the 1948–1949 War for Independence, the wars saw the employment of considerable numbers of AFVs and some of the largest tank battles in history. They also proved to be useful laboratories for the Western allies and the Soviet Union concerning the design and employment of AFVs (for the most part, the Soviet Union was the chief supporter and arms supplier to the Arab states; the Western powers, particularly the United States and France, at least until after the 1967 Six Day War, supported Israel). The fighting in the Middle East also saw the beginning of a new age, with the first use in warfare of antitank and antiship missiles.

In its war to gain independence, Israel initially had only a small armored force, the 8th Armored Brigade, equipped with a hodge-podge of pre–World War II French Hotchkiss light tanks, World War II–era British Cromwells, and U.S. Shermans, the latter purchased from Italy and the Philippines. These faced the far more numerous tanks of Lebanon, Syria, Jordan, Egypt, and Iraq. During the fighting, Israel managed to form a second armored brigade, the 7th.

In the war the Israelis utilized their advantages of interior lines, higher morale, better leadership, and more effective command and control to defeat the larger and better-equipped Arab armies. The major Arab problems were in logistics and organization. The Arab armies were spread out (it was 700 miles from Baghdad to Haifa, and Egyptian forces relied on a 250-mile-long supply line across the Sinai Desert), and there was no unity of command or common military strategy.

After 1949 the Israeli Defense Forces invested heavily in tanks, and the Jewish state became one of the most skillful practitioners of armored warfare in history. Working in collusion with France and Britain against Egypt in 1956, Israel Super Shermans and French tanks rolled across the Sinai Peninsula (covering more than 150 miles in only four days) to take that vast desert area from Egypt. In the process Israeli armor defeated a far larger Egyptian force of Shermans, British Centurions, and some JS-3s, in addition to 230 Soviet T-34/85s, as well as a number of armored personnel carriers and self-propelled guns.

As in the War for Independence, in 1956 it was not superior equipment but rather better training, leadership, and motivation, as well as tactical doctrine and domination of the air, that were vital in the subsequent crushing Israeli victory. Although international pressure, largely from the United States, forced Israel (and Britain and France) to quit Egypt, the war led Israel to go over to a wholly mechanized ground force centered on tanks. The war also brought improved tanks into the Israeli inventory as well as better training. In June 1967 Israel used its highly mechanized forces to launch a devastating preemptive strike against Egypt and Syria, and then engage Jordan, in the Six Day War. Israeli tactics were similar to those employed by the Germans in their blitzkrieg of World War II. Tanks would break through the enemy front and then push forward, closely followed by mechanized infantry that would engage enemy forces. This armored thrust was followed by motorized infantry to mop up enemy resistance in order to allow the vital supply column to proceed forward. Rapid Israeli envelopments allowed the numerically inferior Israeli armored forces to take the heavier Arab tanks from the rear and make short work of the Arab armies. Israel had some 264,000 troops, 800 tanks, and 300 combat aircraft; Egypt, Saudi Arabia, Jordan, Kuwait, Syria, Lebanon, and Iraq had a combined strength of some 541,000 men, 2,504 tanks, and 957 combat aircraft. Of 1,200 Egyptian tanks before the war, 820 were lost. Israeli armor losses amounted to 122 tanks, many of which were repaired and returned to battle. There was also heavy fighting involving Israeli and Syrian tanks in Israel's conquest of the Golan Heights, although the fighting there did not see the large-scale armor engagements that had marked combat on the Sinai front.

In the 1973 Yom Kippur War, the tables were almost turned, thanks to Israeli complacency and new Egyptian tactics. Israel had invested heavily in the Bar Lev Line, a static defensive front along the east bank of the Suez Canal, in effect rejecting maneuver tank warfare in which the bulk of armored forces are held back in mobile reserve. The Egyptians also subjected the canal defenses to nearly constant artillery fire, to which the Israelis grew accustomed. On 6 October 1973 (Yom Kippur, the Day of Atonement) Egyptian forces struck in force across the Suez Canal while Syrian forces simultaneously invaded the Golan Heights. These offensives caught the Israeli defenders completely off-guard.

On the Golan Heights, Syria deployed five divisions and three armored/mechanized brigades. Their 1,600 tanks included T-34s, T-54s, and the latest T-64 Soviet tanks. To break through the thick Israeli minefields and defenses, the Syrians also utilized specialized armor vehicles such as flail tanks, bridge-layers, and engineer tanks. Antiaircraft missiles protected the attackers against Israeli aerial intervention. The Israelis initially had only some 50 Israeli Centurion tanks of the 7th Armored Brigade to oppose the Syrian juggernaut. Following the British practice of using secondary armament for ranging purposes, the Centurions scored a high number of long-range, first-round kills. Ordered to prevent the Syrians from breaking through, the few Israeli defenders did just that. At the end of four days of savage fighting, an Israeli force totaling only 177 tanks supported by infantry and artillery defeated a far larger attacking Syrian force centered on 1,400 tanks.

With 1,700 tanks and another 2,500 armored vehicles, the Egyptian force on the Suez front was even larger. On the night of 5–6 October, by employing high-pressure water hoses and bulldozers and using bridging equipment, the Egyptians got across the canal and blasted through the sand embankment the Israelis had erected there. By 8 October, protected by a blanket of surface-to-air missiles (SAMs) and Soviet-supplied mobile antiaircraft artillery, the Egyptians had two armies of 100,000 men and more than 1,000 tanks east of the canal. After taking the Israeli positions, the Egyptians were content to set up their own defenses and put into effect their "sword and shield" tactics. The "shield" consisted of a belt of minefields, behind which infantry waited with Soviet-supplied Sagger and Snapper wire-guided antitank missiles. Beyond these, artillery, SAMs, and antiaircraft guns provided security for the defensive belt against the vaunted Israeli Air Force. The "sword" consisted of large tank formations ready to engage and destroy Israeli armored counterattacks.

On 8 October the Israelis unwisely committed two armored divisions in the Sinai to drive the Egyptians back across the canal. The Egyptian chief of staff, General Saad el Shazy, noted that the resulting confrontation saw "the first combat between the essentially World War II concept of armour and infantry weapons of the next generation."[1]

The Egyptians promptly inflicted heavy losses on the attacking Israeli forces. The Israelis at first did not understand why infantry would be standing out in the open—until they released a barrage of shoulder-fired missiles at the tanks. Although in time the Israelis were able to develop means to counter the antitank missiles and

SAMs, early in the fighting these new weapons gave the Arab forces the edge, and in two days the Israelis lost some 260 tanks.

The Egyptians won the first part of the war, but their success now emboldened President Anwar Sadat, who decided on a deeper penetration of the Sinai. In taking this step, Sadat overruled General Shazy's arguments that such a step would take his forces beyond the range of SAM cover. The Egyptian offensive began on 14 October and involved more than 2,000 tanks on both sides, making it second in history only to the World War II Battle of Kursk in numbers of tanks engaged. The Israelis brought up reinforcements but were still outnumbered 2:1 in numbers of tanks, a disadvantage that was offset by superior hardware and training and the involvement of the Israeli Air Force. The Israelis not only stopped the Egyptian advance but also destroyed some 500 tanks.

Israeli forces now moved toward the canal in an effort to cross over it and take the Egyptian forces from behind and to destroy the SAM sites. In the process, a large tank battle took place in the area known to the Israelis as the Chinese Farm. The Israelis managed to get some troops and a brigade of paratroopers across the canal, and once a bridge had been thrown across there numbers of tanks followed. The Israelis excelled at rapid maneuver warfare, and they now came up against second-echelon Egyptian troops. The advancing Israeli tanks cut off the Egyptian Third Army at Suez City and were moving north to cut off the Egyptian Second Army when Sadat managed to secure a cease-fire.

Israel won the Yom Kippur War but at a high cost, including the loss of 830 tanks. Sadat had, however, restored Arab pride and went on to visit Israel and conclude a peace settlement with the Jewish state. Many analysts concluded that the Yom Kippur War spelled the end of the tank era: small wire-guided missiles and RPGs had inflicted about a third of Israel's tank losses. Such a conclusion, however, proved to be premature.

The Israelis incorporated the lessons learned in 1973 in their new battle tank, the Merkava. As noted above, crew protection became the priority. Merkavas spearheaded the Israeli invasion of Lebanon in 1982 and destroyed the Syrian 1st Armored Division. Although Merkavas took numerous hits from enemy fire, they were not penetrated. Of 50 or so Israeli tankers wounded in the fighting in Lebanon, not one was the result of burns.

Although there have been no interstate wars involving Israel since 1982, tanks and other AFVs continue to play a key role in intrastate (i.e., occupation) operations. Tanks are perhaps the most visible component of Israeli security operations against the second Palestinian intifada (uprising). Despite the proliferation of new antitank weapons and predictions that the day of the tank was over, when the Cold War came to a close with the collapse of the Soviet Union, AFVs were still very much a part of the world's military establishments.

ENDNOTES

1. Christer Jorgensen and Chris Mann, *Strategy and Tactics: Tank Warfare: The Illustrated History of the Tank at War, 1914–2000.* Osceola, WI: MBI, 2001, p. 154.

CHAPTER 5

Contemporary Tanks, 1989 to the Present

TANKS OF THE POST–COLD WAR PERIOD registered considerable advances in armor, especially explosive reactive armor (ERA). Introduced first by the Israeli Defense Forces, ERA consisted of small panels of armor that could be bolted to the hull. Designed to be activated only by high-explosive antitank rounds and not small-arms ammunition, it exploded when hit, defeating the effect of the incoming warhead. Improvements also occurred in imaging and night-vision systems, as well as in computer-driven ballistics systems. Although many Cold War–era tanks continued in service, this chapter discusses the principal main battle tanks (MBTs) that are at the forefront of armored fighting vehicles today.

GREAT BRITAIN

Challenger II was the follow-on to Challenger I and remains the major British MBT. Vickers Defence Systems began work on Challenger II in 1986, presenting its work to the Ministry of Defence the next year. In 1991 the ministry ordered 127 Challenger II MBTs along with 13 driver training tanks. Production began two years later with the first tanks delivered in July 1994. That same month the ministry ordered an additional 259 Challenger II tanks and nine driver training tanks. The Challenger II is the first British tank to be produced since World War II that was entirely designed, developed, and produced by a private contractor. Oman has purchased 38 Challenger IIs.

Challenger II is similar to the Challenger I in that it utilizes the same hull and running system. However, the turret is completely re-designed and features an entirely new and sophisticated fire-control system that allows acquisition of a new target even as the old one is being engaged. The 120mm (4.72-inch) main gun also has a chromed bore for longer service life, and the turret and hull have new Chobham Series 2 composite armor for improved protection. Efforts have also been made to utilize stealth technology to reduce the Challenger's radar signature. It also takes advantage of a Russian innovation, allowing it to lay down its own smokescreen by injecting diesel fuel into the exhaust system. The tank weighs nearly 138,000 pounds and has a crew of four. Its 1,200-hp engine gives the tank a top speed of 37 mph. The Challenger II mounts a 120mm gun (the turret could handle a 140mm gun if required) and three 7.62mm machine guns. A variant, the Challenger IIE, introduced in 1997, has an improved fire-control system and a new, more powerful 1,500-hp engine that saves space and allows more fuel to be carried, increasing its range.

CHINA

The People's Republic of China introduced the NORINCO Type 85-II in 1989. An improved version of the Type 80, it has a new hull and turret and greatly improved armor protection. It is easily identified by its scallop-shaped side skirts. Utilizing a welded rather than cast turret as on the Type 80, the Type 85-II weighs approximately 90,400 pounds. It has an automatic loader and crew of three. Powered by a 730-hp engine, it is capable of reaching 35 mph. It mounts a powerful 125mm smoothbore gun and two machine guns. The Type 85-II and its follow-on Type 85-III (there does not seem to have been a Type 85-I) have a computerized fire-control system and a laser rangefinder. The Type 85-III has a more powerful 1,000-hp engine and a laser-jam device.

The Type 85-II is the first Chinese tank to be able to engage a moving target and fire while on the move. It also has full nuclear/biological/chemical (NBC) protection and night-vision equipment. The tank is coproduced in China and Pakistan and is in service with the armed forces of both nations.

In the early 1990s China introduced the Type 90-II, which is the follow-on to the Type 85 series. Developed in conjunction with Pakistan, the tank is known in that country as the Al Khalid or MBT-2000. It weighs some 105,800 pounds and has better mobility, firepower, and improved reactive armor. It has a 1,200-hp engine (the Khalid uses an even more powerful Ukrainian engine) that produces a top speed of 39 mph. Equipped with an automatic loader, it mounts a 125mm main gun and two machine guns. Although deliveries of the new tank were speeded up in order to ready 100 for the parade celebrating the fiftieth anniversary of the establishment of the People's Republic, reportedly few are in actual service.

The most advanced Chinese MBT is the Type 98, which first appeared in public at the 1999 anniversary parade for the People's Republic of China. Little is known about the new tank save that it has a new welded turret and a new hull. The hull mounts a dozer blade in front similar to the Russian T-72. The tank has a laser detector and a laser dazzler to help defeat enemy laser rangefinders. The T-98 is thought to have more sophisticated fire-control and battlefield communications systems and may well become the principal MBT for the People's Liberation Army.

In 2003 China maintained about 8,300 MBTs, more than any other nation. At least 6,000 are considered obsolete by Western standards, however. In the spring of 2003 *Jane's Defense Weekly* reported that China was developing a new MBT to mount a huge 152mm gun. The gun would have an automatic loader and an advanced aiming system that would allow the tank to fire either from a stationary position or while on the move with a high first-hit capability. Chinese interest in newer tank designs is hardly surprising given its military's interest in modernizing antiquated equipment and the fact that Taiwan is interested in purchasing the U.S. Abrams tank.

FRANCE

France, which lagged behind other major military powers in developing an effective Cold War MBT, came up with a truly advanced MBT in the Leclerc, one of the world's best tanks. Developed beginning in 1983 after the collapse of the joint Franco-German project to develop a common MBT, it entered production in 1991, with the French Army taking delivery of the first Leclercs the next year. Initially known as the *engin principal de combat* (EPC; literally, "main battle tank"), the Leclerc is the replacement for the AMX-30. The new tank was named for World War II French General Jacques Philippe Leclerc, whose 2nd Armored Division liberated Paris in August 1944. Agile, fast, and heavily gunned, the Leclerc is a low, wide, conventional design with a flat, multifaceted turret. The tank weighs nearly 125,000 pounds with a crew of three, is powered by a 1,500-hp engine, and has a road speed of 45 mph. The Leclerc is armed with a main 120mm gun and two machine guns. Armor is classified. The Leclerc has a computer-based fire-control system, laser rangefinder, thermal imaging system, and stabilized sights, all of which enable the gunner to fire the main gun accurately while under way.

The French Army claims that the tank's autoloader, holding 22 rounds, enables the gunner to bring under fire six different targets within 35 seconds. An additional 18 rounds are stowed next to the driver. All Leclercs dating from 2002 have a battlefield management system that identifies all known friendly and hostile forces on a colored map display. The Leclerc has been exported and is today the MBT of the United Arab Emirates. The lack of other sales of this excellent MBT means that the Leclerc's manufacturer, Giat Industries, will likely take a financial loss on the program.

WEST GERMANY

Following the collapse of the joint tank program, designated MBT-70 in 1970, Germany went ahead with a new MBT to replace its Leopard 1. The new tank incorporated some of the features of the abandoned MBT-70 program, including the drive train. Following the manufacture of a number of prototypes and their testing, full-scale production of the Leopard 2 commenced in 1977, divided between Krauss-Maffei (which became Krauss-Maffei-Wegmann in 1998) and MaK. Final deliveries of the 2,125 Leopard 2s ordered for the German Army were completed in 1992. The Netherlands purchased 445 Leopard 2s, some of which were later sold to Austria, and Denmark received 51. The tank is also manufactured under license in Spain, Sweden, and Switzerland.

The Leopard 2 weighs some 122,000 pounds, has a crew of four, and has a 1,500-hp multi-fuel engine, which, thanks to an improved torsion-bar suspension system, makes for a top speed of 45 mph.

The Leopard 2 mounts a 120mm smoothbore main gun and two machine guns and is protected by improved steel and ceramic sandwiched armor. The Leopard 2 utilizes the latest technological advances, including a ballistic computer, laser rangefinder, stabilized gunsights, and thermal ranging cameras for engaging targets in poor light conditions. Capable of engaging targets at a range of more than 3,000 meters, the Leopard 2 is one of the world's top MBTs.

The Leopard 2 has gone through a number of variants. The latest, the 2A5, is virtually a brand-new design. It includes a lengthened, 120mm main gun (55-caliber as opposed to the 44-caliber on the previous versions) with enhanced range and capabilities, as well as improved fire-control and gun-control systems and additional armor to the turret front.

ITALY

Italy's MBT is the Ariete, developed beginning in 1982. A half-dozen prototypes were produced by 1984, and the Ariete entered service in 1995. The Italian Army ordered 200. The Ariete weighs about 119,000 pounds, has a crew of four, is powered by a 1,300-hp engine, and has a maximum speed of 40 mph. It mounts a 120mm smoothbore main gun, which takes the same ammunition as the M1A1/M1A2 Abrams and Leopard 2, and two machine guns. The Ariete has NBC protection, a ballistic computer, day/night sight, and laser rangefinder. It also has an electric gun-control and stabilization system. The tank features blowout panels in the turret roof to release any internal explosion upward and away from the crew. A Mark 2 is currently under development.

ISRAEL

The Israeli Merkava is among the world's very best tanks, the result of a half-century of Israeli experience in Middle East desert warfare. It is not only among the world's most powerful tanks; it has perhaps the best crew protection. The current production model is the Mark 3, introduced beginning in 1990. A major improvement over its predecessors, it incorporates widespread upgrades in armament, armor, and other systems. The Mark 3 mounts a 120mm smoothbore gun in place of the 105mm gun on the Mark 1 and Mark 2. Its 900-hp engine has been upgraded to 1,200 hp. The tank weighs approximately 134,000 pounds, has a crew of four, and sports a new transmission, suspension system, and armor. It also has threat warning systems and an improved fire-control system. Its NBC package completely seals the tank and allows the crew to work in ordinary clothing. Merkava Marks 1–3 rely on some foreign-built components. A Mark 4, in development, is to be a greatly improved version, entirely of Israeli manufacture.

INDIA

India has also produced its own MBT. In 1990 Pakistan signed an agreement with the People's Republic of China for joint production of the MBT-2000 Al Khalid, essentially an improved T-90-IIM, which China had been working on for a number of years. A prototype was tested in 1991, and Pakistan completed a manufacturing plant at Taxila in 1992. Then in 1995 Pakistan announced it had signed an agreement with Ukraine to purchase T-80UD tanks. This led India to announce that its much-delayed Arjun MBT had entered production at Avadi, which also produced the Vijayanta and the T-72M1 (known as the Ajeya).

Costs were very high, with the Arjan running about $5.5 million per copy, whereas the T-72 could be secured for half that sum. In 2000 India signed an agreement to purchase 310 Russian T-90S MBTs, 190 of which were to be assembled in India.

India expected to produce about 125 Arjun MBTs in 2003. The tank weighs 127,600 pounds and has a crew of four. Its 1,400-hp engine yields a maximum speed of 45 mph. The tank utilizes steel/composite armor and mounts an Indian-designed, stabilized 120mm main gun and two machine guns. The Arjan has advanced fire-control systems with a combined day/night thermal imaging assembly and built-in laser rangefinder.

JAPAN

Although the Type 75 continues as Japan's most numerous MBT, in 1976 the Japanese began design of a new MBT, with the first prototype appearing in 1982. The Type 90 entered production in 1991. Somewhat resembling the German Leopard 2 and Abrams M1A1 in external appearance, the Type 90 is in fact an entirely indigenous design. It weighs some 110,200 pounds and is powered by a 1,500-hp engine that produces a maximum speed of 43 mph. At first the Type 90 mounted a Japanese-produced main gun, but the Japanese went over to the German Rheinmetall smoothbore 120mm (4.72-inch), built under license in Japan. The gun is equipped with an automatic loader that makes it possible to reduce the crew to only three. The loader is located in the turret bustle, and there is a 16-round ready rack. However, the gun must return to a loading angle of 10 degrees after each shot. Armor is classified but is believed to be of steel laminate with ceramic. The Type 90 is among the world's top tanks.

SOUTH KOREA

In 1983 tests began in the United States on a new MBT designed by the General Dynamics Land Systems Division to meet South Korean specifications. The Type 88 K1 entered production in 1986 and was officially introduced the next year. Strongly resembling the General Dynamics–designed U.S. M1 Abrams, the Type 88 has the same low-profile hull and faceted turret. However, it differs in having a diesel engine, ceramic-type armor, and a hybrid torsion-bar/hydro-pneumatic suspension system.

The Type 88 K1 weighs some 112,600 pounds, has a crew of four, a 1,200-hp engine, and a top speed of 49 mph. It mounts the same 105mm gun as the U.S. M1 Abrams along with three machine guns. The improved Type 88 K1A1 mounts a 120mm gun and entered production in 2000. The new gun has double the penetrating power of the 105mm. Range is also increased.

RUSSIA

With the demise of the Soviet Union, tank manufacturing facilities went to the successor states of Russia and Ukraine. While Ukraine built the T-84 (see Statistical Information), Russia produced the T-90 MBT. As the Soviet T-80 was a continuation of the T-64, so too the Russian T-90 built on the T-72. It is intended as an interim design, pending a new generation of Soviet MBTs. The T-90 continues the relatively low cost of the T-72 while at the same time upgrading it in a number of areas, including firepower, the fire-control system, armor, and speed. The T-80 weighs nearly 102,500 pounds, has a crew of three, and has an 840-hp engine that provides a top speed of 40 mph. It mounts the same 125mm smoothbore gun of the T-72 and T-80 and can fire the Refleks 9M119 (A-11 Sniper) laser-guided missile. It has excellent protection in the form of new-generation appliqué ERA; the turret is low and well-rounded, a desirable feature, especially because the bulk of the T-90s ammunition is stored in the turret.

UNITED STATES

The Abrams is the most powerful U.S. tank and is utilized by the U.S. Army and Marine Corps. The M1A1 mounts the 120mm main gun, and the next modification was the introduction of almost impenetrable steel-encased, depleted-uranium armor, designated HA (heavy armor). Prior to the 1991 Gulf War upgrades were carried out in Saudi Arabia on all in-theater M1A1 tanks to upgrade them to

The U.S. Abrams M1A2. *Courtesy of the Patton Museum.*

M1A1HA status. Of some 600 Abrams tanks that saw service during the war, not one was penetrated by enemy fire.

Most changes in the M1A2 over the M1A1 described earlier are internal. These include a thermal viewer for the tank commander, a new land navigation system, and the Inter-Vehicular Information System (IVIS). The IVIS is a datalink compatible with other advanced AFVs and helicopters. Only 77 M1A2s were delivered new, but a large number of M1A1s were upgraded to M1A2s. The M1A2 weighs some 139,000 pounds, mounts a 120mm gun and three machine guns: two 7.62mm (.30-caliber) and one 12.7mm (.50-caliber). Production was completed in 1996 but can be reopened if necessary. The M1A2 is also in service with Kuwait and Saudi Arabia.

CONTEMPORARY TANK WARFARE

Tanks have been employed in a variety of military roles in the post–Cold War period, including control and intimidation of populations. TV screens have been filled with images of Israeli Defense Forces armored units occupying West Bank towns in response to terrorist incidents within Israel. And though wide-scale warfare threatened to erupt in East Asia between Pakistan and India, and Korea remained one of the world's flashpoints, fighting in the post–Cold War era was been largely limited to the Balkans (Bosnia and Kosovo), to separatists in Chechnya, to Afghanistan, and to the Middle East.

Once again, for armored warfare at least, the Middle East occupied center stage in two major conflicts, neither of which involved Israel. Both saw U.S.-led coalitions of nations fighting Iraq. The first war was in response to the Iraqi invasion of Kuwait in August 1990. This came because Iraq had long claimed Kuwait as a province, but it was triggered by Kuwaiti slant drilling into Iraqi oilfields and to punish Kuwait for overproduction of oil that had driven down world prices. Having fought a long war with Iran and being deeply in debt to international creditors, Iraq, with the world's second largest oil reserves, wanted the price of oil to be as high as possible. The administration of U.S. President George H. W. Bush had evidently sent mixed signals to Iraqi leader Saddam Hussein. In any case, Saddam believed that Washington would take no military action, and the United States assumed that Iraq would not annex Kuwait.

When Saddam Hussein refused to remove his forces from Kuwait, the United States acted. It did so primarily because of fears that Iraq if unchecked would be able to pressure Saudi Arabia, with the world's largest oil reserves, and control the price and flow of oil to Western Europe. But President Bush also saw Saddam as a modern-day Hitler and was determined that there would be no appeasement.

On paper Iraq appeared formidable. Its army numbered in excess of 950,000 men and had some 5,500 MBTs, including a mix of T-55s and T-64s, as well as 1,000 T-72s. Saddam Hussein ultimately deployed 43 divisions to Kuwait, positioning most of them along the border with Saudi Arabia.

In Operation DESERT SHIELD, designed to protect Saudi Arabia and prepare for the liberation of Kuwait, the United States put together a formidable coalition that included Syria, Egypt, and Saudi Arabia, as well as Britain, France, and many other states. Altogether, Coalition assets grew to 650,000 men and 3,600 tanks, as well as substantial air and naval assets.

Saddam remained intransigent but also quiescent (he allowed the buildup of Coalition forces in Saudi Arabia to proceed unimpeded), and on 16 January 1991 the Coalition commander, General H. Norman Schwarzkopf, unleashed Operation DESERT STORM. It began with a massive air offensive, striking targets in Kuwait and throughout Iraq, including Baghdad. The supremacy of Coalition airpower over the battlefield became clear in the first few days. Iraq possessed nearly 800 combat aircraft and an integrated air-defense system controlling 3,000 antiaircraft missiles, but it proved unable to win a single air-to-air engagement, and Coalition aircraft soon destroyed the bulk of Iraq's air force. Coalition air superiority assured success on the ground.

The air campaign easily destroyed the lucrative Iraqi targets along the Saudi border. Night after night B-52s dropped massive bomb loads in classic attrition warfare; many Iraqi defenders were simply buried alive. Schwarzkopf also mounted an elaborate deception to convince the Iraqis that the Coalition would mount an amphibious assault against Kuwait. This feint pinned down a number of Iraqi divisions. In reality Schwarzkopf planned a return to large-scale maneuver warfare and the AirLand Battle concept. Schwarzkopf's plan involved three thrusts. On the far left, 200 miles from the coast, XVIII Airborne Corps, which consisted of the 82d Airborne Division and the 101st Airborne Division (Airmobile), supplemented by the French 6th Light Armored Division, would swing wide and cut off the Iraqis on the Euphrates from resupply or retreat. The center assault, the "mailed fist" of VII Corps, was mounted some 100 miles inland from the coast. It was made up of the heavily armored coalition divisions: the U.S. 1st and 3d Armored Divisions, 1st Cavalry Division, 1st Infantry (Mechanized) Division, and the British 1st Armored Division. VII Corps's mission was to thrust deep, engage, and destroy the elite Iraqi Republican Guards divisions. The third thrust occurred on the Kuwaiti border along the coast. It consisted of the U.S. 1st Marine Expeditionary Force of two divisions, a brigade from the U.S. 2d Armored Division, and Arab units. It would drive on Kuwait City.

On 24 February Coalition forces executed simultaneous drives along the coast, while the 101st Airborne Division established a position 50 miles behind the border. As the Marines moved up the coast toward Kuwait City they were hit in the flank by Iraqi armor. In the largest tank battle in Marine Corps history, the Marines, supported by Coalition airpower, easily defeated this force in a battle that was fought in a surrealist day-into-night atmosphere caused by the smoke of burning oil wells set afire by the retreating Iraqis. As the Marines, reinforced by the Tiger Brigade from the 2d Armored Division, prepared to enter Kuwait City, preceded by a light Arab force, Iraqi forces laden with booty fled north in whatever they could steal. Thousands of vehicles and personnel were caught in the open on the highway from Kuwait City and there pummeled by air and artillery along what became known as the "highway of death." In the major opening engagement, these divisions came up against an Iraqi rear guard of 300 tanks, covering for the withdrawal north toward Basra of four divisions of the Republican Guards. U.S. tanks were able to take the Iraqi armor under fire at nearly twice the effective range of the enemy. The M1's high muzzle velocity of 1,805–1,860 yards per second could destroy the Iraqi tanks well beyond the range at which they could engage the enemy. In perhaps the most lopsided massed tank battle in history, the Iraqi force was wiped out at a cost of only one U.S. fatality.

One British participant recalled the night action early on 26 February involving Challenger tanks of the British 7th Armoured Brigade (the famed "Desert Rats" of World War II; attached to the Marines):

> We had the bulk of a tank company to our front and soon there were several T55s burning. The ammunition on board them continued to explode as fires took hold inside. . . . Several enemy tanks returned fire but fortunately no Challengers were hit. . . .

At first light, we had a clearer view of our night's work. Burning tank hulks and the debris of battle littered the desert; disconsolate groups of Iraqis wandered about in a daze looking for someone to accept their surrender.[1]

Lieutenant General Frederick Franks Jr., commander of VII Corps to the west, enraged General Schwarzkopf by insisting on halting on the night of 24 February and concentrating his forces, rather than risk an advance through a battlefield littered with debris and unexploded ordnance and the possibility of casualties from friendly fire. When VII Corps resumed the advance early on 25 February, its problem was not the Iraqis but the supply of fuel; the M1s needed to be refueled every 8–9 hours.

The afternoon of 27 February saw VII Corps engaged in some of its most intense combat. Hoping to delay the Coalition advance, an armored brigade of the Medina Republican Guards Division established a 6-mile-long skirmish line on the reverse slope of a low hill, digging in their T-55 and T-72 tanks there. The advancing 2d Brigade of the 1st Armored Division came over a ridge, spotted the Iraqis, and took them under fire from 2,500 yards. The American tankers used sabot rounds to blow the turrets off the dug-in Iraqi tanks. The battle was the largest armor engagement of the war. In only 45 minutes U.S. tanks and aircraft destroyed 60 T-72 and nine T-55 tanks, in addition to 38 Iraqi armored personnel carriers. As VII Corps closed to the sea, XVIII Corps to its left, which had a much larger distance to travel, raced to reach the fleeing Republican Guards divisions before they could escape the trap to Baghdad.

At this point, only 100 hours into the war and after Coalition forces had liberated Kuwait, President Bush stopped the war. He feared the cost of an assault on Baghdad and that Iraq might then break up into a Kurdish north, Sunni Muslim center, and Shiite Muslim south. Bush wanted to keep Iraq intact against a resurgent Iran. Despite having been stopped early, the war was among the most lopsided in history. Iraq lost 3,700 tanks, more than 1,000 other armored vehicles, and 3,000 artillery pieces. In contrast, the Coalition lost four tanks, nine other combat vehicles, and an artillery piece. In human terms, the Coalition sustained 500 casualties (150 dead), many of them from accidents and so-called friendly fire. Iraqi casualties totaled 25,000–100,000 dead, with the best estimates being around 60,000. The Coalition also took 80,000 Iraqis prisoner.

During the fighting the Coalition's tanks, especially the M1A1 Abrams and British Challenger, had proved their great superiority over their Soviet counterparts, especially in night fighting. Of 600 M1A1 Abrams that saw combat, not one was penetrated by an enemy round; three were struck by depleted uranium shells fired from other M1s, but none of the three were permanently disabled, and there was only one crew fatality. This reflected the survivability features built into the tank, including armored bulkheads to deflect blasts outward. Conversely, the M1A1's 120mm gun proved lethal to Iraqi MBTs. It could engage the Iraqi armor at 3,000 meters (1.86 miles), twice the Iraqi effective range; its superior fire-control system could deliver a first-round hit while on the move; and the depleted uranium penetrators could almost guarantee a kill. Overall, the Coalition maneuver strategy bound up in the AirLand Battle had worked to perfection.

Following the cease-fire, Saddam Hussein reestablished his authority, put down revolts by the Shiites and Kurds, and defied United Nations (UN) inspection teams.

The administration of President George W. Bush adopted a tough stance toward Iraq. This increased in the wake of the terrorist attacks against New York and Washington, D.C., on 11 September 2001, and the war against the Taliban regime in Afghanistan when it refused to hand over members of the Al-Qaida terrorist organization. Bush asserted his intention to root out international terrorism and punish those states that supported it. Increasingly the Bush administration, supported among major international leaders only by Prime Minister Tony Blair of Great Britain, demanded the use of force against Iraq. The Security Council balked, and the United States and Britain proceeded almost alone. Increasingly Bush referred to a U.S. goal of not only disarming Saddam Hussein but of removing him from power and democratizing the country.

A buildup of allied forces had been under way for some time in Kuwait, with more than 300,000 personnel deployed in the theater (130,000 in Kuwait) under the U.S. commander of Central Command, U.S. Army General Tommy Franks. This time Saudi Arabia refused the use of its bases for air strikes against Iraq, and there was no broad coalition of forces arrayed with the United States or countries prepared to help pay the cost of the war. Support came from a number of states, including Britain, Spain, Italy, South Korea, some Central and Eastern European states, notably Poland and Australia. Some of the Gulf states, primarily Kuwait and Qatar, which was home to the coalition's military headquarters, cooperated, hosting troops from the United States (255,000), Britain (45,000), and Australia (2,000), plus Czechs and Slovaks (400) and Poles (200).

Washington experienced a major setback when the Turkish parliament refused to allow the United States to use Turkish territory to open a northern front, a key component of the U.S. military plan. This action prevented the 30,000-man U.S. 4th Infantry Division from taking part in the war. Its supplies, contained in ships off Turkish ports, had to be redirected through the Suez Canal and around the Arabian Peninsula to Kuwait.

The war, dubbed Operation IRAQI FREEDOM, began on the night of 19 March, a day earlier than planned, just hours after the expiration of President Bush's ultimatum. The first attack was a precision strike using cruise missiles against a reported meeting of the Iraqi leadership in Baghdad with Saddam Hussein in attendance. Over succeeding nights, Baghdad was repeatedly hit from the air with cruise missiles and air strikes by U.S. bombers against key headquarters and command and control targets. "Shock and Awe," as the air campaign was called, never seemed to be on the scale that Central Command had suggested; still, 41,850 sorties were flown, versus only 29,393 during the longer 1991 Gulf War. Part of this was the nature of the munitions involved: 67 percent smart (precision-guided) versus 33 percent dumb (unguided) aerial munitions in 2003, as opposed to only 9 percent smart weapons during the 1991 Gulf War. The munitions were also infinitely more accurate than their predecessors. The war also saw the use of unmanned aircraft for reconnaissance purposes and even as weapons platforms.

In contrast to the Gulf War, there was no long air offensive preceding the ground campaign. Rather, the ground war began almost immediately on 20 March. Although there were no great massed tank battles such as in the Gulf War, the 2003 Iraq War represented the culmination of armored warfare, with flying columns of tanks and armored vehicles playing the key role. The allies' airpower was vital, with Iraqi aircraft and helicopters never getting off the ground. Air support for the advancing ground forces included attack helicopters and the highly resilient A-10 Thunderbolt ("Warthog"), an effective tank-buster that had proven itself in 1991. The rapidity of the armor advance and ability to fight at night were also key factors to military success.

The 100,000-man ground force of the U.S.-led coalition drove into Iraq from the south in three thrusts. U.S. Army V Corps, centered on the 21,000-man 3d Infantry Division (Mechanized), was to the west; the 1st Marine Expeditionary Force occupied the center; and some 25,000 British troops, including the 1st Armored Division, were to the east along the coast. The ground force objective was Baghdad, the capital city of 5 million people 300 miles to the north. The 3d Infantry Division, with the 3rd Squadron leading, made the most rapid progress, largely because it swung west and moved through more scarcely populated areas.

In the center part of the front, the 1st Marine Expeditionary Force skirted to the west of the Euphrates River, through the cities of Nasiriya and on to Najaf and Karbala. On the eastern part of the front the British had the difficult task of taking the port of Umm Qasr and Iraq's second largest city, Basra, with its 500,000, largely Shiite, population. Meanwhile, in northwestern Iraq on the night of 22–23 March allied aircraft ferried men and supplies into the Kurdish-controlled zone. This opened a northern front, not only against the Iraqi Army but also against Ansar al-Islam, a militant Islamic group with a base camp and training facilities at Kalak on the Iranian border.

The rapidity of the advance enabled the Marines and Special Operations Forces to seize by *coup de main* the oil fields north of Basra, representing some 60 percent of the nation's total and the key refineries, which would be vital to Iraq's postwar reconstruction. A few wellheads were set afire and some equipment was sabotaged, but overall damage was slight. Clearing the port channel of mines to get relief supplies to Basra proved more time-consuming. Wishing to spare the civilian population and hopeful of an internal uprising, the British were not actually encamped in the city until the night of 2 April. In the meantime they imposed a loose blockade and, employing armor columns, carried out a series of raids into the city, destroying symbols of the regime, such as Baath Party headquarters and images of Saddam. This tactic demoralized the defenders and convinced them that the British could move at will. At the same time the British distributed food and water in an effort to convince the inhabitants that they came as liberators.

On 23 March U.S. troops got bogged down in Nasiriya. The Iraqis ambushed a supply convoy, and fierce sandstorms soon slowed the advance to a crawl. Meanwhile, U.S., British, and Australian special forces had secured the H2 and H3 air bases in western Iraq to prevent missile attacks against Israel, and on the night of 26 March 1,000 members of 173d Airborne Brigade dropped into Kurdish-held territory in northern Iraq to work in conjunction with several hundred U.S. special forces already there and lightly armed Kurdish forces to open a northern front and threaten the key oil production center of Mosul. A small number of Abrams tanks and other AFVs were also air-landed.

Meanwhile, Baath Party terrorist cells carried out attacks on the civilian population, including in Basra, while the so-called Saddam Fedayeen, also known as "technicals"—irregulars often wearing civilian clothes—carried out attacks from civilian vehicles mounting machine guns and rocket-propelled grenades on supply convoys along the LOCs from Kuwait north, which came to be dubbed by U.S. troops as "Ambush Alley." Near Najaf two M1A1 Abrams tanks were damaged by Iraqi missiles, the first time this had ever been accomplished. Another M1A1 was actually destroyed later, but all crews escaped injury.

Attacks by irregulars and Iraqi troops dressed in civilian clothing seemed more a threat than was actually the case, and the allies' advance north appeared to have stalled about 100 miles south of Baghdad. This was in part because of the fierce sandstorm extending over 25–26 March. The biggest mistake of the war on the part of the Iraqi leadership was the decision on 25 March to send military units south from Baghdad to engage U.S. forces near Najaf, thus exposing them to devastatingly effective U.S. air attacks. On 26 March 3rd Squadron, 7th Cavalry Regiment, and other 3d Division elements defeated the remaining Iraqi force near Najaf in the largest ground action of the war, killing some 450 Iraqis and destroying three dozen vehicles of all types.

With some units short of ammunition and food, a week into the campaign with an advance of 200 miles there was an "operational pause." At the time there were questions about the U.S. battle plan and whether sufficient forces had been allocated to the invading force. Friendly fire also remained a nagging problem, with two aircraft—one British and one U.S.—shot down by Patriot missiles, and a Patriot battery was engaged by a U.S. aircraft.

As the coalition forces moved north, the Iraqi leadership repositioned the six Republican Guards divisions around the city of Baghdad for a final defense of the capital. As some of the Republican Guards divisions moved to take up new positions south of Baghdad, they were subjected to heavy air attacks that cost them much of their equipment. The advance, which seemed to have stalled, quickened again during 1–2 April following the serious degrading of the Baghdad and Medina Divisions of the Republican Guards.

On 3 April U.S. forces reached the outskirts of Baghdad and over the next two days secured Saddam International Airport, a dozen miles from the city center. The speed of the armor advance gave the coalition control of the airport with minimal damage to its facilities and allowed it to serve as a staging area once the surrounding territory was secure. By that date the general Iraqi population seemed to sense the shift of momentum and an imminent coalition victory. By 5 April the 3d Infantry Division (Mechanized) was closing on Baghdad from the southwest, the Marines from the southeast, and a brigade of 101st Airborne Division from the north. Baghdad was in effect under a loose blockade. On that day 2d Brigade of 3rd Infantry Division (Mechanized) pushed through downtown Baghdad in a three-hour operation, inflicting an estimated 1,000 Iraqi casualties. This was a powerful psychological blow to the regime, which had claimed U.S. forces were nowhere near the city. The speed of the advance completely caught the defenders by surprise. Operating on the belief that war is often more a test of wills than of hardware, the strike into the city was designed to test Iraqi strength but also to show the flag and demonstrate that U.S. forces could move at will.

This process was repeated on 6 and 7 April, and in a fierce firefight on 6 April, U.S. forces killed an estimated 2,000–3,000 Iraqi soldiers at a cost of one U.S. dead. On 7 April the coalition claimed that of some 850 Iraqi tanks before the war began, only 19 remained; Iraqi artillery pieces had been reduced from 500 to only 40. There were more than 7,000 Iraqi prisoners. On 7 April three battalions of 3d Infantry Division (Mechanized) remained in Baghdad. Tanks and Bradley Fighting Vehicles led the way into Baghdad, destroying Iraqi strongpoints and barricades and clearing the way for the infantry. The ability of these vehicles to withstand rocket-propelled grenade and small-arms attacks was a key factor in ending Iraqi resistance within the city.

On 8 April U.S. forces closed the ring around the capital, and by that date there was at least one U.S. brigade inside the city. The next day, 9 April, resistance collapsed in Baghdad as a large statue of Saddam Hussein was toppled by Iraqi civilians and U.S. Marines. Although sniping continued for several more days, the battle for Baghdad was in effect over.

On 10 April a small number of Kurdish fighters, U.S. special forces, and 173d Airborne Brigade took Kurkuk. On 11 April Iraq's third largest city, Mosul, fell. The one remaining center of resistance was Saddam Hussein's ancestral home of Tikrit, which fell on 14 April. That same day the Pentagon announced that major military operations in Iraq had ended; all that remained was mopping up.

The speed of the land advance, the longest in U.S. Marine Corps history, coupled with coalition air supremacy, had enabled the armored forces to reach the outskirts of Baghdad before the Iraqis could mount an adequate defense. Superior equipment and training and better discipline had been decisive. The 26-day war claimed 109 U.S. and 31 British dead (12 reporters also died). Seven U.S. personnel were taken prisoner and 10 were missing. At least 2,500 Iraqi troops were killed, along with some 6,400 Iraqi civilians killed or wounded. Victory would have been even swifter had U.S. forces been able to operate from Turkey.

In summing up the war General Franks said that the war plan was different in two vital aspects: first, it was joint—a closely integrated effort involving not only branches of the U.S. military but also coalition forces working closely together; and second, it was flexible and adaptable—capable of rapid change to different circumstances.

In many ways the 2003 Iraq War marked the beginning of a new technological revolution in warfare, with more covert operations, more agile forces, more sophisticated hardware (including standoff weapons of unprecedented lethality), and a willingness to strike preemptively. Although the long-term effects of the war are uncertain and winning the "peace" has proven more difficult and costly in human terms for the occupying forces than the actual war itself, perhaps the war's most striking strategic consequence was the extension of U.S. military power in the region. Coupled with the U.S. military presence in Afghanistan, U.S. bases in Iraq would be felt chiefly in Syria and in Iran, countries that are now flanked by U.S. power on two sides.

Tanks had proven decisive in the war, and we can indeed expect that the world's principal MBTs—the Abrams, Challenger II, Leclerc, Leopard II, Merkava, and T-90—will all continue in service for decades to come. Although the contest between armor and armament will no doubt continue, for the foreseeable future tanks that combine effective firepower with mobility and protection will continue to play key roles in modern warfare.

ENDNOTES

1. Bryan Perrett, *Iron Fist: Classic Armored Warfare Case Studies*. London: Arms and Armour, 1995, p. 206.

Individual Tank Models

WORLD WAR I

PRE–WORLD WAR II

WORLD WAR II

COLD WAR

CONTEMPORARY

Armament: Main-gun armament is given first, followed by machine guns; major types and changes are included.

Weight: Weights vary widely, depending on the particular tank but also on the source. Weights given are for the tank when combat loaded and are expressed in U.S. pounds and kilograms (2.2046 U.S. pounds = 1 kilogram).

Length, Width, and Height: Dimensions are to the nearest inch. Unless otherwise specified, length is of hull only; height refers to the dimension from the ground to the top of a permanent structure on the tank, such as a cupola.

Maximum Speed: This is presumed to be on roads; cross-country speed is approximately two-thirds that for a paved surface.

Range: This is presumed to be on roads; cross-country range is about two-thirds to three-quarters of that for roads.

WORLD WAR I

FRANCE: CA1 (CHAR D'ASSAULT) SCHNEIDER
Courtesy of Art-Tech/Aerospace/M.A.R.S/TRH/Navy Historical.

SUMMARY: The first French tank. Based on the Holt Tractor design, the first were ordered beginning in February 1916. The Schneider Char d'Assaut 1 (CA1) went into action on the Chemin des Dames on 16 April 1917, during the Nivelle Offensive. Later the Japanese purchased a few.

PRODUCTION DATES: February 1916–May 1917

NUMBER PRODUCED: 400

MANUFACTURER: Schneider Company

CREW: 6

ARMAMENT: 1 x 75mm (2.95-inch) M1897 main gun; 2 x 8mm (.315-caliber) Hotchkiss machine guns

WEIGHT: 14,600 kg (32,178 lbs.)

LENGTH: 19'8"

WIDTH: 6'7"

HEIGHT: 7'10"

ARMOR: maximum 11.5mm

AMMUNITION STORAGE AND TYPE: 90 rounds of 75mm; 3,840 rounds of .30-caliber

POWER PLANT: Schneider four-cylinder 70-hp gasoline engine

MAXIMUM SPEED: 3.7 mph

RANGE: 30 miles

FORDING DEPTH: –

VERTICAL OBSTACLE: –

TRENCH CROSSING: 5'10"

SPECIAL CHARACTERISTICS (POS/NEG): Designed primarily for infantry support, the CA1 had poor cross-country mobility and trench-spanning ability; gasoline tanks were vulnerable to enemy fire.

SPECIAL MODELS: –

FRANCE: CHAR D'ASSAULT ST. CHAMOND
Courtesy of Art-Tech/Aerospace/M.A.R.S/TRH/Navy Historical.

SUMMARY: Ordered slightly after the CA1, the St. Chamond first saw action in the April 1917 Nivelle Offensive. At end of the war 72 of 400 were still in service. Later Lithuania and Spain secured some examples.

PRODUCTION DATES: 1916–?

NUMBER PRODUCED: 400

MANUFACTURER: Compagnie des Forges d'Honecort at Saint Chamond

CREW: 9

ARMAMENT: 1 x 75mm (2.95-inch) main gun and 4 x 8mm (.315-caliber) Hotchkiss machine guns

WEIGHT: 23,000 kg (50,692 lbs.)

LENGTH: 25'12" (with gun, 28'12")

WIDTH: 8'9"

HEIGHT: 7'6"

ARMOR: maximum 17mm

AMMUNITION STORAGE AND TYPE: 106 rounds of 75mm; 7,500 x .30-caliber

POWER PLANT: Panhard four-cylinder 90-hp water-cooled engine supplemented by a dynamo, two electric motors, and storage batteries

MAXIMUM SPEED: 5.3 mph

RANGE: 37 miles

FORDING DEPTH: –

VERTICAL OBSTACLE: –

TRENCH CROSSING: 8'

SPECIAL CHARACTERISTICS (POS/NEG): Dual controls allowed the St. Chamond to be driven from either end, but like the Schneider it suffered from poor cross-country performance.

SPECIAL MODELS: A number were converted into *char de ravitaillement* (supply tanks).

FRANCE: RENAULT FT-17

Courtesy of Art-Tech/Aerospace/M.A.R.S/TRH/Navy Historical.

SUMMARY: The first true light tank. Produced in large number by the Renault automobile company, it was employed en masse. The American Expeditionary Forces Tank Corps used the Renault. A profoundly influential design. Some were still in service during World War II.

PRODUCTION DATES: First entered service in May 1918

NUMBER PRODUCED: 4,000?

MANUFACTURER: Renault and other manufacturers

CREW: 2

ARMAMENT: 1 x 37mm (1.46-inch) or 1 x 8mm Hotchkiss machine gun

WEIGHT: 7,000 kg (15,428 lbs.)

LENGTH: 16'5" with tail

WIDTH: 5'7"

HEIGHT: 7'

ARMOR: maximum 22mm

AMMUNITION STORAGE AND TYPE: –

POWER PLANT: Renault four-cylinder 39-hp gasoline engine

MAXIMUM SPEED: 5 mph

RANGE: 24 miles

FORDING DEPTH: –

VERTICAL OBSTACLE: –

TRENCH CROSSING: 6'5"

SPECIAL CHARACTERISTICS (POS/NEG): full 360-degree revolving turret, the first tank to be so equipped

SPECIAL MODELS: self-propelled gun; radio-equipped

GERMANY: STURMPANZERWAGEN A7V
Courtesy of Art-Tech/Aerospace/M.A.R.S/TRH/Navy Historical.

SUMMARY: First and only German tank produced during World War I. The A7V *Sturmpanzerwagen,* which first saw action in March 1917, was a huge vehicle. Poorly made, it was also unstable and had very poor cross-country performance. Some saw service with the Polish Army after the war.

PRODUCTION DATES: Spring 1917–1918

NUMBER PRODUCED: 20 (of 100 ordered)

MANUFACTURER: Daimler

CREW: 18

ARMAMENT: 1 x 57mm and six machine guns

WEIGHT: 29,900 kg (65,900 lbs.)

LENGTH: 26'3"

WIDTH: 10'1"

HEIGHT: 10'10"

ARMOR: maximum 30mm; minimum 10mm

AMMUNITION STORAGE AND TYPE: –

POWER PLANT: 2 x Daimler 100-hp gasoline engines

MAXIMUM SPEED: 8 mph

RANGE: 25 miles

FORDING DEPTH: –

VERTICAL OBSTACLE: 18"

TRENCH CROSSING: 6'

SPECIAL CHARACTERISTICS (POS/NEG): An enormous vehicle; each track could be powered separately, allowing the very short turn radius of modern tanks. It suffered from extremely poor cross-country performance and short trench-spanning capability because of only 1.57-inch ground clearance and short length of track.

SPECIAL MODELS: *Uberlandwagen*: open, unarmored supply version and A7V/U with all-around tracks

UNITED KINGDOM: "LITTLE WILLIE"

Courtesy of Art-Tech/Aerospace/M.A.R.S/TRH/Navy Historical.

SUMMARY: Colonel Ernest Swinton of the British Army came up with the idea to build an armored fighting machine capable of spanning trenches. First Lord of the Admiralty Winston Churchill approved the concept, and the first prototype was produced by the firm of Foster & Co. of Lincoln. It first ran in September 1915. Although not armored, it was the first tracked, potentially armored vehicle for which specifications had been laid down. It also introduced the track system used by all wartime tanks.

PRODUCTION DATES: 1915

NUMBER PRODUCED: 1

MANUFACTURER: Foster & Co., Lincoln

CREW: 4–6

ARMAMENT: None

WEIGHT: 18,289 kg (40,320 lbs.)

LENGTH: 18'2"

WIDTH: 9'4"

HEIGHT: 10'2"

ARMOR: none; 6mm steel plate

AMMUNITION STORAGE AND TYPE: –

POWER PLANT: Foster-Daimler six-cylinder 105-hp gasoline engine

MAXIMUM SPEED: 1.8 mph

RANGE: –

FORDING DEPTH: –

VERTICAL OBSTACLE: 4'6"

TRENCH CROSSING: 5'

SPECIAL CHARACTERISTICS (POS/NEG):

SPECIAL MODELS: –

UNITED KINGDOM: "MOTHER" ("CENTIPEDE," THEN "BIG WILLIE")
Courtesy of Art-Tech/Aerospace/M.A.R.S/TRH/Navy Historical.

SUMMARY: Prototype of all British tanks of World War I. Ordered from the firm of Foster & Co. of Lincoln and designed by William Tritton of that firm, assisted by Major William Wilson; it was first demonstrated in January 1916 and proved sufficiently successful to be placed into production.

PRODUCTION DATES: January 1916

NUMBER PRODUCED: 1

MANUFACTURER: Foster & Co., Lincoln

CREW: 8

ARMAMENT: 2 x 7-pounders (57mm/2.25-inch) mounted in sponsons on sides and 2 x .303-caliber (7.7mm) Hotchkiss machine guns

WEIGHT: 31,500 kg (69,445 lbs.)

LENGTH (EXCLUDING GUN): 32'6" (including tail)

WIDTH: 13'9"

HEIGHT: 8'2"

ARMOR: Maximum 10mm

AMMUNITION STORAGE AND TYPE: –

POWER PLANT: Foster-Daimler six-cylinder 105-hp gasoline engine

MAXIMUM SPEED: 3.7 mph

RANGE: 23 miles

FORDING DEPTH: –

VERTICAL OBSTACLE: –

TRENCH CROSSING: 10'

SPECIAL CHARACTERISTICS (POS/NEG):

SPECIAL MODELS: –

UNITED KINGDOM: MARK I HEAVY

Courtesy of Art-Tech/Aerospace/M.A.R.S/TRH/Navy Historical.

SUMMARY: The first production model tank, essentially a copy of "Mother," designed by William Tritton of Foster & Co. of Lincoln. The Mark I first saw action in the Battle of the Somme on 15 September 1916.

PRODUCTION DATES: January 1916–

NUMBER PRODUCED: initial order was 150

MANUFACTURER: Foster & Co., Lincoln

CREW: 8

ARMAMENT: Male version, 2 x 57mm (6-pounders) mounted in sponsons on sides and four machine guns; female, no main gun but six machine guns

WEIGHT: 28,450 kg (62,721 lbs.)

LENGTH (EXCLUDING GUN): 32'6" (including tail)

WIDTH: 13'9"

HEIGHT: 8'2"

ARMOR: maximum 12mm; minimum 6mm

AMMUNITION STORAGE AND TYPE: –

POWER PLANT: Foster-Daimler 105-hp gasoline engine

MAXIMUM SPEED: 3.7 mph

RANGE: 23 miles

FORDING DEPTH: –

VERTICAL OBSTACLE: 4'6"

TRENCH CROSSING: 11'6"

SPECIAL CHARACTERISTICS (POS/NEG): steering assisted by means of a two-wheeled trailing unit, which was soon discarded as ineffective over rough ground and being vulnerable to enemy fire

SPECIAL MODELS: –

UNITED KINGDOM: MARK V HEAVY

Courtesy of Art-Tech/Aerospace/M.A.R.S/TRH/Navy Historical.

SUMMARY: Designed for the anticipated great tank offensive of 1919, the Mark V was the last of the lozenge-shaped British tanks to see service in any significant number.

PRODUCTION DATES: 1918

NUMBER PRODUCED: –
Mark V: 400 (200 males, 200 females)
Mark V*: 642

MANUFACTURER: Metropolitan Carriage Wagon and Finance Co.

CREW: 8

ARMAMENT: 2 x 57mm (6-pounders) mounted in sponsons on either side and 4 x .303-caliber (7.7mm) Hotchkiss machine guns in male; no main gun and 6 x .303-caliber (7.7mm) Hotchkiss machine guns in female

WEIGHT: 30,000 kg (66,120 lbs.)

LENGTH (EXCLUDING GUN): 26'5"

WIDTH (OVER SPONSONS): 13'6"

HEIGHT: 8'8"

ARMOR: maximum 14mm; minimum 6mm

AMMUNITION STORAGE AND TYPE: –

POWER PLANT: Ricardo six-cylinder 150-hp gasoline engine

MAXIMUM SPEED: 4.6 mph

RANGE: 25 miles

FORDING DEPTH: 2'

VERTICAL OBSTACLE: 4'6"

TRENCH CROSSING: 10'

SPECIAL CHARACTERISTICS (POS/NEG): The Mark V had a new transmission in its Wilson epicyclic gearbox. A considerable technological advance, this did away with the gearmen. For the first time, a tank could be driven by one man. The Mark V had improved visibility but was poorly ventilated.

SPECIAL MODELS: The Mark V* was the largest tank of the war. It had an additional 6-foot section on the hull to improve trench-spanning ability and increase internal space. It also had an additional machine gun: five for the male and seven for the female.

UNITED KINGDOM: MARK A WHIPPET

Courtesy of Art-Tech/Aerospace/M.A.R.S/TRH/Navy Historical.

SUMMARY: The first British medium tank, it was developed to replace horse cavalry for exploiting any battlefield breakthrough. Entered service in March 1918 on the Western Front and fought the remainder of the war.

PRODUCTION DATES: Beginning in 1917

NUMBER PRODUCED: Unknown, but 200 survived the war, when they were scrapped

MANUFACTURER: Foster & Co., Lincoln (200)

CREW: 3

ARMAMENT: 4 x .303-caliber (7.7mm) Hotchkiss machine guns

WEIGHT: 31,352 lbs.

LENGTH: 20'

WIDTH: 8'7"

HEIGHT: 9'

ARMOR: maximum 14mm; minimum 5mm

AMMUNITION STORAGE AND TYPE: −

POWER PLANT: 2 x Tylor four-cylinder 45-hp gasoline engines

MAXIMUM SPEED: 8.3 mph

RANGE: n/a (160 miles approx.)

FORDING DEPTH: −

VERTICAL OBSTACLE: −

TRENCH CROSSING: −

SPECIAL CHARACTERISTICS (POS/NEG): difficult to control; the driver had to combine the speeds of two separate engines in order to maneuver

SPECIAL MODELS: −

PRE–WORLD WAR II

FRANCE: RENAULT R-35 LIGHT

Courtesy of Art-Tech/Aerospace/M.A.R.S/TRH/Navy Historical.

SUMMARY: Mid-1930s successor to the Renault FT-17 light tank designed for infantry support. Widely exported before the war to Poland, Yugoslavia, Romania, and Turkey.

PRODUCTION DATES: 1935–

NUMBER PRODUCED: Approx. 2,000; 945 available in the Battle for France (the largest number of any French tank of the campaign)

MANUFACTURER: Renault

CREW: 2

ARMAMENT: 1 x 37mm (.46-inch) main gun in turret mount; 1 x 7.5mm (.295-caliber) machine gun (coaxial)

WEIGHT: 22,046 lbs.

LENGTH: 13'9"

WIDTH: 6'1"

HEIGHT: 7'9"

ARMOR: maximum 40mm

AMMUNITION STORAGE AND TYPE: –

POWER PLANT: Renault four-cylinder 82-hp gasoline engine

MAXIMUM SPEED: 12 mph

RANGE: 88 miles

FORDING DEPTH: 2'7"

VERTICAL OBSTACLE: 1'7.7"

TRENCH CROSSING: 5'3"

SPECIAL CHARACTERISTICS (POS/NEG): A high-quality fighting vehicle with well-designed cast turrets and hulls and Cletrac steering; its principal drawbacks were its insufficient main gun and unsatisfactory internal arrangement of the one-man turret. The R-35 never achieved its potential because it was deployed piecemeal against massed German armor formations.

SPECIAL MODELS: After the defeat of France in 1940, the Germans gave some R-35s to Italy and utilized others as garrison and training tanks or modified them for use as ammunition carriers and artillery tractors. Some also had their turrets removed and were employed as self-propelled gun carriers in coastal defense works.

FRANCE: HOTCHKISS H-39 LIGHT
Courtesy of Art-Tech/Aerospace/M.A.R.S/TRH/Navy Historical.

SUMMARY: Introduced just before the war, the H-39 was an outgrowth of the H-35, with a new gun and improved engine. It gave effective service in the Battle for France, although it was outgunned by heavier German tanks. The Germans used it in occupation duties. It was also employed by the Vichy French and Free French forces during fighting in the Middle East, where a number were taken over by the Israelis after the war and remained in service with them until 1956.

PRODUCTION DATES: 1939–1940

NUMBER PRODUCED: Approx. 1,000

MANUFACTURER: Hotchkiss

CREW: 2

ARMAMENT: 1 x 37mm (1.46-inch) main gun; 1 x 7.5mm (.295-caliber) machine gun

WEIGHT: 26,620 lbs.

LENGTH: 13'10"

WIDTH: 6'5"

HEIGHT: 7'1"

ARMOR: maximum 40mm

AMMUNITION STORAGE AND TYPE: –

POWER PLANT: Hotchkiss six-cylinder 120-hp gasoline engine

MAXIMUM SPEED: 22 mph

RANGE: 93 miles

FORDING DEPTH: 2'10"

VERTICAL OBSTACLE: 1'8"

TRENCH CROSSING: 5'11"

SPECIAL CHARACTERISTICS (POS/NEG):

SPECIAL MODELS: –

FRANCE: SOMUA S-35 MEDIUM

Courtesy of Art-Tech/Aerospace/M.A.R.S/TRH/Navy Historical.

SUMMARY: Principal French medium tank developed in the mid-1930s. An excellent design, it was perhaps the best Allied tank in service in 1940. Well-armed, mobile, and heavily armored, it was also the first tank with both a cast hull and a cast turret. France had too few of them; only about half of those produced actually were with front-line units in May 1940 at the time of the German invasion.

PRODUCTION DATES: 1935–1940

NUMBER PRODUCED: Approx. 430

MANUFACTURER: Société d'Outillage de Méchanique et d'Usinage d'Artillerie (SOMUA)

CREW: 3

ARMAMENT: 1 x 47mm (1.85-inch) main gun in turret mount; 1 x 7.5mm (.295-caliber) machine gun (coaxial)

WEIGHT: 44,198 lbs.

LENGTH (EXCLUDING GUN): 17'8"

WIDTH: 6'12"

HEIGHT: 8'7"

ARMOR: maximum 55mm; minimum 20mm

AMMUNITION STORAGE AND TYPE: –

POWER PLANT: Souma V-8 190-hp gasoline engine

MAXIMUM SPEED: 25 mph

RANGE: 143 miles

FORDING DEPTH: 3'3"

VERTICAL OBSTACLE: 2'6"

TRENCH CROSSING: 7'

SPECIAL CHARACTERISTICS (POS/NEG): Employed cast rather than riveted armor; radio standard; electric power traverse in turret. Its principal drawback was its unsatisfactory internal arrangement of a one-man turret in which the tank commander was also obliged to operate the main gun.

SPECIAL MODELS: various, utilized by the Germans and Italians

FRANCE: CHAR B-1 BIS HEAVY

Courtesy of Art-Tech/Aerospace/M.A.R.S/TRH/Navy Historical.

SUMMARY: Standard French heavy tank of the Battle for France, heavily gunned and armored. Developed from the Char B-1 of 1935–1937, the *bis* stood for "improved." About three-quarters of the 400 Char B-1s manufactured before the end of the 1940 Battle for France were Char B-1 bis models. The Char B-1 bis was probably the best tank in the war in 1940.

PRODUCTION DATES: 1937–1940

NUMBER PRODUCED: 365

MANUFACTURER: AMX, FAMH, FCM, Renault, Schneider

CREW: 4

ARMAMENT: 1 x 75mm (2.95-inch, hull mount); 1 x 47mm (1.85-inch, turret mount); 2 x 7.5mm (.295-caliber) machine guns

WEIGHT: 71,650 lbs.

LENGTH: 20'8"

WIDTH: 8'2"

HEIGHT: 9'2"

ARMOR: maximum 60mm

AMMUNITION STORAGE AND TYPE: –

POWER PLANT: Renault six-cylinder 307-hp water-cooled gasoline engine

MAXIMUM SPEED: 17 mph

RANGE: 112 miles

FORDING DEPTH: –

VERTICAL OBSTACLE: 3'1"

TRENCH CROSSING: 9'

SPECIAL CHARACTERISTICS (POS/NEG): Heavily gunned, exceptional armor, and excellent cross-country ability. Also included self-sealing gasoline tanks. The chief negatives were its mechanical unreliability, an unsatisfactory internal arrangement that widely separated the crew, and the need to rotate the entire tank to traverse the main 75mm gun.

SPECIAL MODELS: later used by the Germans, with turrets removed, for training purposes and as artillery carriages

GERMANY: PZKPFW 35(T) AUSF. A LIGHT
Courtesy of Art-Tech/Aerospace/M.A.R.S/TRH/Navy Historical.

SUMMARY: Originally the Czechoslovakian Army's main battle tank and designated the LT-35. The Germans later modified 219 of them following their absorption of Czechoslovakia in March 1939 and used them in the September 1939 Polish campaign. Most were destroyed in the Soviet Union by the end of 1941.

PRODUCTION DATES: 1935–1938

NUMBER PRODUCED: 424

MANUFACTURER: Skoda

CREW: 4

ARMAMENT: 37mm main gun and 2 x 7.92mm machine guns

WEIGHT: 23,523 lbs.

LENGTH: 16'

WIDTH: 6'10"

HEIGHT: 7'8"

ARMOR: maximum 25mm; minimum 8mm

AMMUNITION STORAGE AND TYPE: 72 x 37mm; 1,800 x 7.82mm.

POWER PLANT: Skoda T11

MAXIMUM SPEED: 21 mph

RANGE: 115 miles

FORDING DEPTH: –

VERTICAL OBSTACLE: –

TRENCH CROSSING: –

SPECIAL CHARACTERISTICS (POS/NEG): A fine tank for its day, it had adequate armor and firepower. It also was generally unreliable mechanically. The Germans gradually rebuilt them, and the tank remained in service for three years until the bulk of them were destroyed in the German invasion of the Soviet Union in late 1941.

SPECIAL MODELS: artillery tractor

GERMANY: PzKpfw 38(T)

Courtesy of Art-Tech/Aerospace/M.A.R.S/TRH/Navy Historical.

SUMMARY: This Czechoslovakian tank, designated LT vz 38, had not entered service prior to the German absorption of Bohemia and Moravia in March 1939. Produced for the Germans in Ausf. A through S models, it was soon obsolescent as a light tank and was relegated to reconnaissance duties.

PRODUCTION DATES: 1939–1942

NUMBER PRODUCED: 1,411

MANUFACTURER: CKD/Praga TNHP

CREW: 4

ARMAMENT: 37mm Skoda A7 main gun; also 2 x 7.92mm machine guns

WEIGHT: 20,723 lbs.

LENGTH: 14'11"

WIDTH: 7'

HEIGHT: 7'7"

ARMOR: maximum 25mm; minimum 10mm

AMMUNITION STORAGE AND TYPE: –

POWER PLANT: Praga EPA inline-6 water-cooled gasoline engine

MAXIMUM SPEED: 26 mph

RANGE: 125 miles

FORDING DEPTH: 3'

VERTICAL OBSTACLE: 2'7"

TRENCH CROSSING: 6'2"

SPECIAL CHARACTERISTICS (POS/NEG):

SPECIAL MODELS: chassis used for a number of variants, including the Marder tank destroyer; self-propelled antiaircraft gun platform; weapons carrier; and Hetzer tank destroyer, which remained in Swiss Army service until the 1960s.

GERMANY: PzKpfw I Ausf. A LIGHT

Courtesy of Art-Tech/Aerospace/M.A.R.S/TRH/Navy Historical.

SUMMARY: First German mass-production tank (*Panzerkampfwagen*), originally designated as an "agricultural tractor" in order to avoid the prohibition of tanks under the Treaty of Versailles.

PRODUCTION DATES: July 1934–June 1936

NUMBER PRODUCED: 818

MANUFACTURER: Krupp, Henschel, MAN, Krupp-Gruson, Daimler-Benz

CREW: 2

ARMAMENT: 2 x 7.92mm MG34 machine guns

WEIGHT: 12,100 lbs.

LENGTH (EXCLUDING GUN): 13'2"

WIDTH: 6'7"

HEIGHT: 5'7"

ARMOR: maximum 13mm; minimum 6mm

AMMUNITION STORAGE AND TYPE: 2,250 x 7.92mm

POWER PLANT: Krupp M305 57-hp gasoline engine

MAXIMUM SPEED: 21 mph

RANGE: 81 miles

FORDING DEPTH: 2'10"

VERTICAL OBSTACLE: 1'5"

TRENCH CROSSING: 5'9"

SPECIAL CHARACTERISTICS (POS/NEG): Used extensively in the invasions of Poland (1939) and France and the Low Countries (1940), the PzKpfw I Ausf. A was found to be too lightly armored and gunned and was withdrawn from frontline service in 1941.

SPECIAL MODELS: –

GERMANY: PzKpfw II Ausf. A LIGHT
Courtesy of Art-Tech/Aerospace/M.A.R.S/TRH/Navy Historical.

SUMMARY: First produced by MAN and Daimler-Benz in 1935, it was intended as a light reconnaissance AFV, but it formed the brunt of the panzer divisions that overran Poland in 1939 and France and the Low Countries in 1940. The PzKpfw II went through a series of upgrades—Ausf. B, C, D, E, and F—with the chief improvements being in armor. Rendered obsolete by the heavier-armored and -armed Soviet tanks, it became the basis of the Luchs reconnaissance tank.

PRODUCTION DATES: 1935–1942

NUMBER PRODUCED: 1,113

MANUFACTURER: MAN, Daimler-Benz, Henschel, Wegmann, Alkett, MIAG, FAMO

CREW: 3

ARMAMENT: 20mm KwK (0.79-inch) 38 L/55 main gun; also 1 x 7.92 MG34 (coaxial) machine gun

WEIGHT: 22,046 lbs.

LENGTH: 15'3"

WIDTH: 7'6.5"

HEIGHT: 6'7.5"

ARMOR: maximum 15mm, upgraded to maximum 35mm; minimum 20mm in Ausf. F version

AMMUNITION STORAGE AND TYPE: 180 x 20mm; 2,250 x 7.92mm

POWER PLANT: Maybach HL62TR six-cylinder 140-hp gasoline engine

MAXIMUM SPEED: 34 mph

RANGE: 125 miles

FORDING DEPTH: 2'10"

VERTICAL OBSTACLE: 1'5"

TRENCH CROSSING: 5'9"

SPECIAL CHARACTERISTICS (POS/NEG): Its armor was insufficient to keep out anything but small-arms fire, and its main gun not powerful enough to destroy opposing tanks, even at close range.

SPECIAL MODELS: amphibious tank, designed for Operation SEA LION, the invasion of Britain; flamethrower tank, the *Flammpanzer II*

GERMANY: PzKpfw III MEDIUM

Courtesy of Art-Tech/Aerospace/M.A.R.S/TRH/Navy Historical.

SUMMARY: First German medium tank design. Ausf. B, C, D, and E models saw service in Poland. Armament doubled in the course of the PzKpfw III's existence; the final version, Ausf. N, mounted a 75mm gun. The PzKpfw III formed the main firepower for the panzer divisions against France in 1940.

PRODUCTION DATES: 1937–1943

NUMBER PRODUCED: 5,691

MANUFACTURER: Daimler-Benz, Henschel, Wegmann, Alkett, MNH, MIAG, MAN

CREW: 5 (commander, gunner, loader, driver, and radio operator/hull machine-gunner)

ARMAMENT: 1 x 37mm main gun in Ausf. A; 1 x 50mm main gun in Ausf. H; 1 x 75mm main gun in Ausf. N; each model also mounted 2 x 7.92mm MG34 (coaxial, bow)

WEIGHT: 30,800–49,060 lbs.

LENGTH: 21'

WIDTH: 9'8"

HEIGHT: 8'3"

ARMOR: maximum 30mm

AMMUNITION STORAGE AND TYPE: 92 x 50mm; 4,950 x 7.92mm

POWER PLANT: Maybach HL 108 TR 12-cylinder 250-hp gasoline engine

MAXIMUM SPEED: 25 mph

RANGE: 110 miles

FORDING DEPTH: 2'8"

VERTICAL OBSTACLE: 2'

TRENCH CROSSING: 8'6"

SPECIAL CHARACTERISTICS (POS/NEG):

SPECIAL MODELS: *Tauchpanzer* (submersible) tank; command vehicle; armored recovery vehicle; chassis also utilized in a number of self-propelled gun models to the end of the war.

GERMANY: PzKpfw IV MEDIUM
Courtesy of Art-Tech/Aerospace/M.A.R.S/TRH/Navy Historical.

SUMMARY: Produced in response to a 1934 call for a medium infantry support tank, the PzKpfw IV formed the backbone of the German panzer divisions in the Soviet Union and was produced throughout the war. First produced by Krupp-Cruson, it appeared in 10 different models, Ausf. A–J.

PRODUCTION DATES: October 1937–March 1945

NUMBER PRODUCED: 8,519 + variants
Ausf. A, 35; Ausf. B, 42; Ausf. C, 134; Ausf. D, 229; Ausf. E, 223; Ausf. F, 462; Ausf. F, 175; Ausf. G, 1,687; Ausf. H, 3,774; Ausf. J, 1,758

MANUFACTURER: Krupp-Gruson, Vomag, Nibelungenwerke

CREW: 5

ARMAMENT: 75mm KwK37 L/24 main gun (Ausf. A); increased to 75mm KwK40 L/48 (Ausf. H and J); also 2 x 7.92mm MG34 machine guns (coaxial, bow)

WEIGHT: 40,565 lbs. (Ausf. A); 55,100 lbs. (Ausf. H, J)

LENGTH: 23'

WIDTH: 10'10"

HEIGHT: 8'10"

ARMOR: maximum 15mm, minimum 5mm (Ausf. A); maximum 80mm, minimum 10mm (Ausf. H, J)

AMMUNITION STORAGE AND TYPE: 87 x 75mm; 3,150 x 7.92mm (Ausf. H and J)

POWER PLANT: Mayback HL108TR 12-cylinder, 250-hp gasoline engine (Ausf. A); Mayback HL120TRM112 12-cylinder 300-hp gasoline engine (Ausf. B and later)

MAXIMUM SPEED: 24 mph

RANGE: 126 miles

FORDING DEPTH: 3'3"

VERTICAL OBSTACLE: 2'

TRENCH CROSSING: 7'3"

SPECIAL CHARACTERISTICS (POS/NEG): Despite its considerable increase in weight the PzKpfw IV had an effective power-to-weight ratio and thus good maneuverability.

SPECIAL MODELS: A wide variety, including submersible; assault gun; self-propelled guns; tank destroyers; self-propelled howitzers; self-propelled antiaircraft gun platforms; armored recovery vehicles; bridge-layers

ITALY: FIAT 3000 LIGHT

Courtesy of Art-Tech/Aerospace/M.A.R.S/TRH/Navy Historical.

SUMMARY: Italy's first post–World War I light tank.

PRODUCTION DATES: 1923–1930(?)

NUMBER PRODUCED: 105 Model 21s and 47 Model 30s

MANUFACTURER: Fiat

CREW: 2

ARMAMENT: 2 x 6.5mm machine guns (Model 21); 1 x 37mm main gun and 2 x 6.5mm machine guns (Model 30)

WEIGHT: 12,122 lbs.

LENGTH: 11'9" (dimensions are for Model 21; Model 30 varies slightly)

WIDTH: 5'4"

HEIGHT: 7'2"

ARMOR: maximum 16mm

AMMUNITION STORAGE AND TYPE: 68 x 37mm; 2,000 x 6.5mm

POWER PLANT: Fiat four-cylinder 64-hp gasoline engine

MAXIMUM SPEED: 15 mph

RANGE: 90 miles

FORDING DEPTH: 3'6"

VERTICAL OBSTACLE: 1'11"

TRENCH CROSSING: 4'9"

SPECIAL CHARACTERISTICS (POS/NEG): Based on the light Renault World War I tank, it was a considerable improvement, with greater speed and firepower. It formed the backbone of the Italian tank force in the 1930s and some saw service until 1943.

SPECIAL MODELS: –

ITALY: FIAT-ANSALDO LIGHT

Courtesy of Art-Tech/Aerospace/M.A.R.S/TRH/Navy Historical.

SUMMARY: Designed as the successor to the Fiat 3000; many sold abroad.

PRODUCTION DATES: 1930–1937

NUMBER PRODUCED: 2,530

MANUFACTURER: Ansaldo

CREW: 2

ARMAMENT: 2 x 8mm machine guns

WEIGHT: 10,645 lbs.

LENGTH: 11'6"

WIDTH: 5'7"

HEIGHT: 6'6"

ARMOR: maximum 12mm

AMMUNITION STORAGE AND TYPE: 3,200 x 8mm machine gun

POWER PLANT: Fiat four-cylinder 42-hp gasoline engine

MAXIMUM SPEED: 20 mph

RANGE: 75 miles

FORDING DEPTH: 2'4"

VERTICAL OBSTACLE: 2'2"

TRENCH CROSSING: 4'9"

SPECIAL CHARACTERISTICS (POS/NEG): –

SPECIAL MODELS: flamethrower; bridge-layer

JAPAN: TYPE 89B CHI-RO MEDIUM
Courtesy of Art-Tech/Aerospace/M.A.R.S/TRH/Navy Historical.

SUMMARY: Design work began in 1929, although production did not begin until 1934. It featured a small turret mounted well forward. Slow and not very maneuverable, it nonetheless remained in service, chiefly in the Philippines and Manchuria, until 1943.

PRODUCTION DATES: 1934–?

NUMBER PRODUCED: –

MANUFACTURER: Mitsubishi J, Osaka RZ, Nanman RZ, Kobe S, Nihon S

CREW: 4

ARMAMENT: 1 x 57mm Gun Type 90 main gun; also 2 x 6.5mm Type 91 machine guns (hull, turret rear)

WEIGHT: 25,346 lbs.

LENGTH: 14'1"

WIDTH: 7'

HEIGHT: 7'2"

ARMOR: maximum 17mm; minimum 6mm

AMMUNITION STORAGE AND TYPE: 100 x 57mm; 2,750 x 6.5mm

POWER PLANT: Mitsubishi six-cylinder 120-hp diesel engine

MAXIMUM SPEED: 15 mph

RANGE: 105 miles

FORDING DEPTH: 3'3"

VERTICAL OBSTACLE: 2'8.5"

TRENCH CROSSING: 8'2.3"

SPECIAL CHARACTERISTICS (POS/NEG): The first production-model diesel tank, slow and thus employed principally in infantry support; suspension by leaf springs

SPECIAL MODELS: –

JAPAN: TYPE 94 TANKETTE

Courtesy of Art-Tech/Aerospace/M.A.R.S/TRH/Navy Historical.

SUMMARY: Tankette, developed as armored tractor to pull tracked trailer for ammunition resupply in forward battle area; also to be employed as defensive weapon; modified version introduced beginning in 1936 employed a trailing idler, lowered drive sprocket, and increased track ground length, as well as asbestos lining to protect crew against heat.

PRODUCTION DATES: 1934–?

NUMBER PRODUCED: –

MANUFACTURER: Tokyo Gasu Denki Kokyo, Mitsubishi, Jukogyo, Kobe Seikosho

CREW: 2

ARMAMENT: 1 x 6.5mm Type 91 machine gun

WEIGHT: 7,500 lbs.

LENGTH (EXCLUDING GUN): 10'1"

WIDTH: 5'4"

HEIGHT: 5'4"

ARMOR: maximum 12mm; minimum 4mm

AMMUNITION STORAGE AND TYPE: 1,620 x 6.5mm

POWER PLANT: Type 94 inline-4 32-hp gasoline engine (diesel prototype also introduced)

MAXIMUM SPEED: 24 mph

RANGE: 124 miles

FORDING DEPTH: 2'

VERTICAL OBSTACLE: 1'7"

TRENCH CROSSING: 4'3"

SPECIAL CHARACTERISTICS (POS/NEG): welded and riveted construction

SPECIAL MODELS: –

JAPAN: TYPE 95 HA-GO LIGHT
Courtesy of Art-Tech/Aerospace/M.A.R.S/TRH/Navy Historical.

SUMMARY: One of the better Japanese tank designs, built to replace the Type 89B, which was too light to meet army requirements. Nonetheless, the Ha-Go, also known as the Kyo-Go and Ke-Go, was completely outclassed by comparable Allied designs.

PRODUCTION DATES: 1935–1942

NUMBER PRODUCED: 1,161

MANUFACTURER: Mitsubishi Heavy Industries, Niigata, Tekkosho, Kobe Seikosho, Kokura Rikugun Zoheisho

CREW: 3

ARMAMENT: 1 x 37mm (1.46-inch) main gun (later models had an upgunned 45mm/1.77-inch); 2 x 7.7mm (.30-caliber) machine guns (front hull, rear turret)

WEIGHT: 16,310 lbs.

LENGTH: 14'4"

WIDTH: 6'9"

HEIGHT: 7'2"

ARMOR: maximum 12mm; minimum 6mm

AMMUNITION STORAGE AND TYPE: –

POWER PLANT: Mitsubishi NVD 6120 six-cylinder 120-hp air-cooled diesel engine

MAXIMUM SPEED: 28 mph

RANGE: 152 miles

FORDING DEPTH: 3'3"

VERTICAL OBSTACLE: 2'8"

TRENCH CROSSING: 6'7"

SPECIAL CHARACTERISTICS (POS/NEG): Commander forced to operate the main gun in addition to other duties. The Type 95 also lacked firepower and had insufficient armor protection.

SPECIAL MODELS: The Type 95 Ha-Go became the basis of the Type 2 Ka-Mi amphibious tank employed in Pacific Theater operations.

JAPAN: TYPE 97 CHI-HA MEDIUM
Courtesy of Art-Tech/Aerospace/M.A.R.S/TRH/Navy Historical.

SUMMARY: Standard Japanese medium tank for most of World War II. Some of them saw service after World War II with the army of the People's Republic of China. The Type 97 later appeared as the Type 97 Shinhoto (new turret) Chi-Ha Medium with a high-velocity 47mm main gun.

PRODUCTION DATES: 1937–1940

NUMBER PRODUCED: 3,000?

MANUFACTURER: Mitsubishi, Hitachi, Nihon, Sagami

CREW: 4

ARMAMENT: 1 x 57mm Gun Type 97 (modified version mounted 12 x 47mm high-velocity long-barreled gun); 2 x 7.7mm Type 97 machine guns (bow, turret rear)

WEIGHT: 33,060 lbs.

LENGTH: 18'

WIDTH: 7'8"

HEIGHT: 7'4"

ARMOR: maximum 25mm; minimum 8mm

AMMUNITION STORAGE AND TYPE: 50 x 57mm; 2,000 x 7.7mm

POWER PLANT: Mitsubishi Type 97 V-12 170-hp diesel engine

MAXIMUM SPEED: 25 mph

RANGE: 130 miles

FORDING DEPTH: 3'3"

VERTICAL OBSTACLE: 2'11"

TRENCH CROSSING: 8'2"

SPECIAL CHARACTERISTICS (POS/NEG): The Type 97 Chi-Ha had a monocoque construction, diesel engine, and sloped armor but was too thin-skinned and small to deal with the U.S. tanks it encountered.

SPECIAL MODELS: command tank; engineer tank

POLAND: TK.3 TANKETTE

Courtesy of Art-Tech/Aerospace/M.A.R.S/TRH/Navy Historical.

SUMMARY: Improved version of the Polish TK.1 and TK.2 and the first Polish-produced tank of any quantity.

PRODUCTION DATES: 1930–1931

NUMBER PRODUCED: 300

MANUFACTURER: –

CREW: 2

ARMAMENT: 1 x 7.92mm machine gun

WEIGHT: 5,510 lbs.

LENGTH: 8'6"

WIDTH: 5'10"

HEIGHT: 4'4"

ARMOR: maximum 8mm; minimum 3mm

AMMUNITION STORAGE AND TYPE: –

POWER PLANT: Ford Model A four-cylinder 40-hp air-cooled engine

MAXIMUM SPEED: 29 mph

RANGE: 125 miles

FORDING DEPTH: –

VERTICAL OBSTACLE: –

TRENCH CROSSING: –

SPECIAL CHARACTERISTICS (POS/NEG): tankette, totally inadequate for combat

SPECIAL MODELS: In 1931 a four-wheeled trailer was developed that could be towed behind the tank so that when it was necessary to travel on a road the tankette could be driven on it; the tracks were then removed and the chain drive was connected to the trailer.

POLAND: 7 TP LIGHT

Courtesy of Art-Tech/Aerospace/M.A.R.S/TRH/Navy Historical.

SUMMARY: First production diesel tank; based on the Vickers 6-Ton; most numerous (169) Polish tank at the time of German invasion in September 1939; initial version had two side-by-side small turrets, each with a single machine gun; from 1937 it appeared as a single turret mounting a 37mm gun and a coaxial machine gun. The third version had an improved suspension and wider track.

PRODUCTION DATES: 1934–1939

NUMBER PRODUCED: 169+

MANUFACTURER: PZI

CREW: 3

ARMAMENT: 2 x 7.92mm (.312-caliber) machine guns in first twin-turret model; second model from 1937 had a single turret with 1 x 37mm Bofors antitank gun and 1 x 7.92mm machine gun (coaxial) in the single-turret

WEIGHT: 20,718 lbs.

LENGTH: 15'1"

WIDTH: 7'1"

HEIGHT: 7'1"

ARMOR: 17mm maximum in twin-turret model; 15mm maximum in single-turret; 40mm maximum in third, final version

AMMUNITION STORAGE AND TYPE: –

POWER PLANT: Swiss-patented, Polish-licensed Saurer six-cylinder diesel 110-hp diesel engine (the first production diesel-engine tank)

MAXIMUM SPEED: 20 mph

RANGE: 100 miles

FORDING DEPTH: –

VERTICAL OBSTACLE: –

TRENCH CROSSING: –

SPECIAL CHARACTERISTICS (POS/NEG): Twin-turret light tank in first version; single turret in second; single turret overhanging to the rear in third version. Most had totally inadequate armor and in any case were available in too small numbers.

SPECIAL MODELS: –

SOVIET UNION: T-26 LIGHT MODEL 1933
Courtesy of Art-Tech/Aerospace/M.A.R.S/TRH/Navy Historical.

SUMMARY: At first the T-26 was the Vickers 6-Ton tank built under license in the Soviet Union; later versions of the T-26 were wholly Russian developments. T-26s, although hopelessly obsolete by that time, fought in the early battles on the Eastern Front during World War II. Although there were many types within each, the T-26 appeared in two basic models: the twin-turreted infantry support A model and the single-turreted mechanized cavalry B model. The final T-26S (also known as the T-26C) series was a considerable redesign with welded armor and a new, more rounded superstructure

PRODUCTION DATES: 1931–1936

NUMBER PRODUCED: 5,500

MANUFACTURER: Bolshevik Factory No. 232 (Leningrad), Factory No. 174 K. E. Voroshilov (Omsk), Red Putilov Factory (Leningrad)

CREW: 3

ARMAMENT: T-26A: 2 x 7.62mm machine guns, or 1 x 27mm gun in right turret and 1 x 7.62mm machine gun, or 1 x 37mm gun in right turret and 1 x 7.62mm machine gun; T-26B: 1 x 37mm or 45mm main gun; some also had a machine gun in the turret rear; also close-support version had a short 76.2mm howitzer in place of the 45mm main gun; T-26S (T-26C): 1 x 45mm main gun and 2 x 7.62mm machine guns

WEIGHT: 19,020 lbs. (23,065 lbs. for T-26S [T-26C])

LENGTH: 15'9"

WIDTH: 7'10"

HEIGHT: 6'9" (7'8" on T-26S)

ARMOR: maximum 15mm; minimum 6mm (maximum 25mm, minimum 10mm on the T-26S)

AMMUNITION STORAGE AND TYPE: –

POWER PLANT: GAZ T-26 HO8 88-hp engine

MAXIMUM SPEED: 22 mph

RANGE: 120 miles

FORDING DEPTH: 2'7"

VERTICAL OBSTACLE: 2'4"

TRENCH CROSSING: 5'10.5"

SPECIAL CHARACTERISTICS (POS/NEG):

SPECIAL MODELS: commander's tank; flamethrower

SOVIET UNION: T-40 LIGHT

Courtesy of Art-Tech/Aerospace/M.A.R.S/TRH/Navy Historical.

SUMMARY: Light amphibious reconnaissance tank intended as a replacement for the T-27, T-37A, and T-38 series of tanks, all of which were essentially adopted from the British Vickers/Carden-Loyd tankette. The T-40S version was basically the same tank but without the propeller and folding trim vane. Flotation tanks were built into the tank hull.

PRODUCTION DATES: 1941–1942

NUMBER PRODUCED: –

MANUFACTURER: State factories

CREW: 2

ARMAMENT: 1 x 12.7mm DShK machine gun and 1 x 7.62mm machine gun coaxially mounted in turret

WEIGHT: 12,320 lbs.

LENGTH: 14'

WIDTH: 7'7"

HEIGHT: 6'6"

ARMOR: maximum 14mm; minimum 10mm

AMMUNITION STORAGE AND TYPE: 550 x 12.7mm; 2,016 x 7.62mm

POWER PLANT: GAZ-202 V-6 85-hp gasoline engine

MAXIMUM SPEED: 26 mph on road, 3 mph in water

RANGE: 215 miles

FORDING DEPTH: floats

VERTICAL OBSTACLE: 2'

TRENCH CROSSING: 5'7"

SPECIAL CHARACTERISTICS (POS/NEG): torsion-bar suspension; amphibian

SPECIAL MODELS: –

SOVIET UNION: BT-2 MEDIUM
Courtesy of the Patton Museum.

SUMMARY: Second in a long series of *Bystrochodny Tankovy* (BT; literally, "fast tank") tanks. The BT-1 was a direct copy of the U.S. Christie M1931 tank. The BT-2 was basically the same but with a new turret mounting a 37mm gun and one machine gun in place of the two machine guns of the BT-1. The BT was the key Soviet tank design of the 1930s. The BT-2 was still in service at the time of the German invasion in June 1941. The BT series gave way to the T-34.

PRODUCTION DATES: 1932

NUMBER PRODUCED: Approx. 300

MANUFACTURER: Factory No. 183, Kharkov Locomotive Works (KhPZ)

CREW: 3

ARMAMENT: 37mm Gun M1930; 1 x 7.92mm machine gun DT (turret)

WEIGHT: 24,244 lbs.

LENGTH: 18'

WIDTH: 7'4"

HEIGHT: 6'4"

ARMOR: maximum 13mm

AMMUNITION STORAGE AND TYPE: 96 x 37mm; 2,709 x 7.62mm

POWER PLANT: Liberty Aero/M-5 V-12 400-hp gasoline engine

MAXIMUM SPEED: 65 mph (wheels); 40 mph (tracks)

RANGE: 93 miles

FORDING DEPTH: 3'11"

VERTICAL OBSTACLE: 2'6"

TRENCH CROSSING: 6'10"

SPECIAL CHARACTERISTICS (POS/NEG): Excellent cross-country mobility

SPECIAL MODELS: –

SOVIET UNION: BT-5 MEDIUM

Courtesy of Art-Tech/Aerospace/M.A.R.S/TRH/Navy Historical.

SUMMARY: Follow-on to the BT-3, which was basically the BT-2 with solid road wheels instead of spoked and a 45mm gun instead of 37mm. The BT-5 formed the backbone of Soviet armor in the late 1930s. Some captured BT-5s were utilized by the Finns and the Germans.

PRODUCTION DATES: 1933–1935

NUMBER PRODUCED: Approx. 1,800

MANUFACTURER: Factory No. 183, Kharkov Locomotive Works (KhPZ)

CREW: 3

ARMAMENT: 1 x 45mm gun M1932; 1 x 7.62mm DT machine gun; BT-5A close-support tank mounted a 76.2mm howitzer in place of the 45mm gun

WEIGHT: 25,346 lbs.

LENGTH: 18'

WIDTH: 7'4"

HEIGHT: 7'3"

ARMOR: maximum 13mm; minimum 6mm

AMMUNITION STORAGE AND TYPE: 72 x 45mm without radio installed; 115 x 45mm with radio equipment; also 2,709 x 7.62mm

POWER PLANT: M-5 V-12 350-hp gasoline engine

MAXIMUM SPEED: 70 mph (wheels); 40 mph (tracks)

RANGE: 90 miles

FORDING DEPTH: 3'11"

VERTICAL OBSTACLE: 2'6"

TRENCH CROSSING: 6'6"

SPECIAL CHARACTERISTICS (POS/NEG):

SPECIAL MODELS: BT-6 commander's version with frame antenna around turret and a radio in the rear turret overhang

SOVIET UNION: BT-7 MEDIUM
Courtesy of Art-Tech/Aerospace/M.A.R.S/TRH/Navy Historical.

SUMMARY: Follow-on to BT-5; the main improvements were in the conical turret, heavier armor, more fuel and ammunition capacity, and a machine gun mounted in the turret rear (in some). The BT-7 was the major Soviet fighting tank at the beginning of World War II. Some captured BT-7s were utilized by the Finns and Germans. The BT-7 was the basis for the T-34.

PRODUCTION DATES: 1937–1939

NUMBER PRODUCED: Approx. 1,200

MANUFACTURER: Factory No. 183, Kharkov Locomotive Works (KhPZ)

CREW: 3

ARMAMENT: 1 x 45mm main gun M1934; 2 x 7.62mm DT machine guns

WEIGHT: 30,636 lbs.

LENGTH: 18'7"

WIDTH: 7'6"

HEIGHT: 7'11"

ARMOR: maximum 22mm; minimum 13mm

AMMUNITION STORAGE AND TYPE: 172 x 45mm; 2,394 x 7.62mm

POWER PLANT: M-17 V-12 450-hp gasoline engine

MAXIMUM SPEED: 45 mph

RANGE: 265

FORDING DEPTH: 3'11"

VERTICAL OBSTACLE: 2'6"

TRENCH CROSSING: 6'6"

SPECIAL CHARACTERISTICS (POS/NEG):

SPECIAL MODELS: commander's tank BT-7V, fitted with radio antenna around turret

SOVIET UNION: T-28 MEDIUM

Courtesy of Art-Tech/Aerospace/M.A.R.S/TRH/Navy Historical.

SUMMARY: First indigenous Soviet medium tank, but clearly influenced by both the Vickers A6 and German *Grosstraktor* designs. Intended for an attack role, it had a central main-gun turret and two machine-gun turrets in front to either side. Its suspension was copied from the Vickers tank. It served in the 1939–1940 Winter War with Finland and in the opening weeks of the German invasion of the Soviet Union in June 1941 but performed poorly in combat. Subsequent variants included the T-28C with increased hull front and turret armor.

PRODUCTION DATES: 1933–?

NUMBER PRODUCED: –

MANUFACTURER: Leningrad Korov Plant

CREW: 6

ARMAMENT: 1 x 76.2mm (3-inch) low-velocity main gun M1927; 3 x 7.62mm DT machine guns (some T-28s mounted a low-velocity 45mm gun in the right auxiliary turret in place of the machine gun)

WEIGHT: 62,720 lbs.

LENGTH: 24'5"

WIDTH: 9'5"

HEIGHT: 9'3"

ARMOR: maximum 30mm; minimum 10mm (maximum 80mm on T-28C)

AMMUNITION STORAGE AND TYPE: –

POWER PLANT: M-17 V-12 500-hp gasoline engine

MAXIMUM SPEED: 23 mph

RANGE: 137 miles

FORDING DEPTH: –

VERTICAL OBSTACLE: 3'5"

TRENCH CROSSING: 9'6"

SPECIAL CHARACTERISTICS (POS/NEG):

SPECIAL MODELS: commander's tank T-28 (V) with radio antenna frame around turret; small number of flamethrower tanks

SOVIET UNION: T-35 HEAVY

Courtesy of Art-Tech/Aerospace/M.A.R.S/TRH/Navy Historical.

SUMMARY: Soviet heavy tank, influenced by the Vickers Independent and mounting five turrets in an effort to secure all-around protection. All T-35s were in a single Soviet tank brigade near Moscow. The T-35 was not a successful design, proving all but worthless in combat.

PRODUCTION DATES: 1932–1939

NUMBER PRODUCED: 61

MANUFACTURER: Factory No. 183, Kharkov Locomotive Works (KhPZ)

CREW: 11

ARMAMENT: 1 x 76.2mm (3-inch) gun PS-3 (main turret); 2 x 45mm guns; 6 x 7.62mm DT machine guns (3 x coaxial, 2 x machine-gun turrets, 1 x rear main turret)

WEIGHT: 110,166 lbs.

LENGTH: 31'11"

WIDTH: 10'6"

HEIGHT: 11'3"

ARMOR: maximum 30mm; minimum 10mm

AMMUNITION STORAGE AND TYPE: 96 x 76.2mm; 220 x 45mm; 10,080 x 7.62mm

POWER PLANT: M-17T V-12 500-hp gasoline engine

MAXIMUM SPEED: 18.6 mph

RANGE: 93 miles

FORDING DEPTH: 3'11"

VERTICAL OBSTACLE: 3'11"

TRENCH CROSSING: 13'

SPECIAL CHARACTERISTICS (POS/NEG): five turrets

SPECIAL MODELS: –

UNITED KINGDOM: LIGHT TANK, MARKS II–VI
Courtesy of Art-Tech/Aerospace/M.A.R.S/TRH/Navy Historical.

SUMMARY: Light tank, based on Carden-Loyd 1920s tankette. Widely used in the 1930s throughout the British Empire and early in World War II, when it was, however, hopelessly obsolete. Mark VIs comprised the bulk of British armored strength in France in 1940.

PRODUCTION DATES: early 1933–1940

NUMBER PRODUCED: – (more Mark VIBs were produced than any other model in this series of light tanks)

MANUFACTURER: Vickers, Woolwich Arsenal

CREW: 2 (Mk II, III, IV, V) or 3 (Mk VI)

ARMAMENT: 1 x .303-caliber Vickers machine gun (1 x .50-caliber machine gun in some Mk IIIs); also coaxial 1 x 7.92mm and 1 x 15mm Besa machine guns in the Mk VI

WEIGHT: 9,250 lbs. (Mk II, IIA, IIB); 10,080 lbs. (MK III); 9,520 lbs. (Mks IV and V); 10,800 (Mk VI); 11,740 lbs. (Mks VIA, VIB, VIC)

LENGTH: 11'9" (Mk II); 12' (Mk III); 11'2" (Mks IV and V); 12'12" (Mk VI)

WIDTH: 6'4" (Mks II, III); 6'12" (Mks IV and V); 6'9" (Mk VI)

HEIGHT: 6'8" (Mk II); 6'11" (Mk III); 6'9" (Mks IV and V); 7'4" (Mk V)

ARMOR: maximum 14mm; minimum 4mm (Mk VI)

AMMUNITION STORAGE AND TYPE: –

POWER PLANT: Mk II: Rolls-Royce 49.2kW six-cylinder 66-hp engine; Mks IV-VI: Meadows ESTL six-cylinder 88-hp engine

MAXIMUM SPEED: 30 mph (Mk II); 35 mph (Mk VI)

RANGE: 130 miles (Mk VI)

FORDING DEPTH: 2'

VERTICAL OBSTACLE: –

TRENCH CROSSING: –

SPECIAL CHARACTERISTICS (POS/NEG): fast, with a long range but of light, riveted construction with very thin armor and inadequate armament

SPECIAL MODELS: Efforts to convert some of these light tanks into antiaircraft tanks mounting twin 15mm Besa guns were a failure, although the Germans did utilize some captured models as antitank gun carriers.

UNITED KINGDOM: LIGHT TANK, MARK VII, TETRARCH (A17)
Courtesy of Art-Tech/Aerospace/M.A.R.S/TRH/Navy Historical.

SUMMARY: Developed as a follow-on to the Marks II–VI light tanks to mount a main-gun armament instead of mere machine guns. Later replaced by the U.S. M22 Locust. Some Tetrarchs remained in service until 1949, when Britain abandoned gliders.

PRODUCTION DATES: November 1940–1941

NUMBER PRODUCED: 177

MANUFACTURER: Vickers

CREW: 3 (commander, gunner, driver)

ARMAMENT: 1 x 2-pounder (40mm/1.57-inch) gun; also 1 x 7.92mm Besa (coaxial) machine gun

WEIGHT: 16,800 lbs.

LENGTH: 13'6"

WIDTH: 7'7"

HEIGHT: 6'11.5"

ARMOR: maximum 14mm; minimum 4mm

AMMUNITION STORAGE AND TYPE: 50 x 2-pounder; 2,025 x 7.92mm

POWER PLANT: Meadows 12-cylinder 165-hp engine

MAXIMUM SPEED: 40 mph

RANGE: 140 miles

FORDING DEPTH: 3'

VERTICAL OBSTACLE: –

TRENCH CROSSING: 5'

SPECIAL CHARACTERISTICS (POS/NEG): The Hamilcar glider was especially designed to carry one Mark VII Tetrarch tank and carried an airborne reconnaissance regiment into battle during the Normandy invasion.

SPECIAL MODELS: A few Tetrarchs were converted for a close-support role, armed with 3-inch howitzers in place of the 2-pounder gun; some were also equipped with a duplex drive, giving them a swimming capability.

UNITED KINGDOM: MEDIUM TANK, MARKS II, IIA, AND II
Courtesy of Art-Tech/Aerospace/M.A.R.S/TRH/Navy Historical.

SUMMARY: Basic British Army medium tank during the period 1923–1938; used during World War II as a training vehicle, although some training Mark II training tanks were pressed into service in the early fighting in the Western Desert during 1940–1941

PRODUCTION DATES: 1923–1928

NUMBER PRODUCED: Approx. 200

MANUFACTURER: Vickers Armstrong

CREW: 5 (commander, driver, radio operator, two gunners)

ARMAMENT: 1 x 3-pounder QSFA main gun; also 3 x .303-caliber Vickers machine guns

WEIGHT: 29,560 lbs. (Mk II); 31,360 lbs. (Mk IIA)

LENGTH: 17'6"

WIDTH: 9'2"

HEIGHT: 9'11"

ARMOR: maximum 10mm; minimum 4mm

AMMUNITION STORAGE AND TYPE: –

POWER PLANT: Armstrong Siddeley 90-hp air-cooled engine

MAXIMUM SPEED: 18 mph

RANGE: 120 miles

FORDING DEPTH: –

VERTICAL OBSTACLE: –

TRENCH CROSSING: 6'6"

SPECIAL CHARACTERISTICS (POS/NEG): An influential design, the Mark II was nonetheless completely obsolete by the beginning of World War II. It was thinly armored and of riveted construction.

SPECIAL MODELS: –

UNITED KINGDOM: CRUISER TANK, MARK I AND MARK ICS (A9)
Courtesy of Art-Tech/Aerospace/M.A.R.S/TRH/Navy Historical.

SUMMARY: Medium tank developed by Sir John Carden of Vickers Armstrong

PRODUCTION DATES: 1937–1938

NUMBER PRODUCED: 125

MANUFACTURER: Vickers Armstrong (50), Harland and Wolff of Belfast (75)

CREW: 6 (commander, gunner, loader, driver, two machine gunners)

ARMAMENT: 1 x 2-pounder (40mm/1.57-inch) main gun; also 3 x .303-caliber (7.7mm) machine guns

WEIGHT: 26,867 lbs.

LENGTH: 19'

WIDTH: 8'3"

HEIGHT: 8'9"

ARMOR: maximum 14mm; minimum 6mm

AMMUNITION STORAGE AND TYPE: 100 x 2-pounder, 3,000 x .303-caliber

POWER PLANT: AEC Type A179 six-cylinder 150-hp gasoline engine

MAXIMUM SPEED: 25 mph

RANGE: 150 miles

FORDING DEPTH: –

VERTICAL OBSTACLE: 3'

TRENCH CROSSING: 8'

SPECIAL CHARACTERISTICS (POS/NEG): First British tank with hydraulic power traverse; no external vertical hull facing; riveted construction; poor suspension, tended to throw tracks.

SPECIAL MODELS: –

UNITED KINGDOM: CRUISER TANK, MARK II AND MARK IIA (A10)

Courtesy of the Patton Museum.

SUMMARY: Follow-on to the Cruiser Tank, Mark I and Mark ICS (A9)

PRODUCTION DATES: 1938–1940

NUMBER PRODUCED: 175

MANUFACTURER: Vickers (10), Birmingham Railway Carriage Co. (120), Metropolitan-Cammell (45)

CREW: 5 (commander, loader, gunner, driver, hull machine gunner)

ARMAMENT: 1 x 2-pounder (40mm/1.57mm) main gun (1 x 3.7-inch howitzer in CS model); also 2 x 7.92mm Besa machine guns

WEIGHT: 31,696 lbs.

LENGTH: 18'4"

WIDTH: 8'4"

HEIGHT: 8'9"

ARMOR: maximum 30mm; minimum 6mm

AMMUNITION STORAGE AND TYPE: 100 x 2-pounder; 4,050 x .303-caliber/7.92mm

POWER PLANT: AEC Type A179 six-cylinder 150-hp gasoline engine

MAXIMUM SPEED: 16 mph

RANGE: 100 miles

FORDING DEPTH: 3'

VERTICAL OBSTACLE: 2'

TRENCH CROSSING: 6'

SPECIAL CHARACTERISTICS (POS/NEG): first British tank with composite armor construction; also the first armed with the Besa machine gun

SPECIAL MODELS: –

UNITED KINGDOM: CRUISER TANK, MARK III (A13)

Courtesy of Art-Tech/Aerospace/M.A.R.S/TRH/Navy Historical.

SUMMARY: The first of a long line of World War II British tanks to incorporate the Christie suspension. Built under license and modified from the original design, it utilized the same lightweight Liberty aircraft engine of Christie's tanks.

PRODUCTION DATES: 1939–1940

NUMBER PRODUCED: 65

MANUFACTURER: Nuffield Mechanisations and Aero Ltd.

CREW: 4 (commander, gunner, loader, driver)

ARMAMENT: 1 x 40mm QFSA (2-pounder) main gun; also 1 x .303-caliber (7.7mm) Vickers machine gun (coaxial)

WEIGHT: 31,360 lbs.

LENGTH: 19'9"

WIDTH: 8'4"

HEIGHT: 8'6"

ARMOR: maximum 14mm; minimum 6mm

AMMUNITION STORAGE AND TYPE: 87 x 2-pounder; 3,750 x .303-caliber machine gun

POWER PLANT: Nuffield Liberty Mk I and Mk II 340-hp gasoline engine

MAXIMUM SPEED: 38 mph

RANGE: 90 miles

FORDING DEPTH: 3'

VERTICAL OBSTACLE: —

TRENCH CROSSING: 7'6"

SPECIAL CHARACTERISTICS (POS/NEG): similar turret to the A9

SPECIAL MODELS: —

UNITED KINGDOM: CRUISER TANK, MARK IV AND MARK IVA (A13 MK II)
Courtesy of the Patton Museum.

SUMMARY: Uparmored version of the Cruiser Tank, Mark III

PRODUCTION DATES: 1939–1940

NUMBER PRODUCED: 655

MANUFACTURER: Nuffield, LMS, Leyland, English Electric

CREW: 4 (commander, gunner, loader, driver)

ARMAMENT: 1 x 2-pounder (40mm, 1.57-inch) OQF main gun; 1 x .303-caliber Vickers (Mk IV) machine gun (1 x 7.92mm Besa in Mk IVA)

WEIGHT: 33,040 lbs.

LENGTH: 19'9"

WIDTH: 8'4"

HEIGHT: 8'6"

ARMOR: maximum 30mm; minimum 6mm

AMMUNITION STORAGE AND TYPE: 87 x 2-pounder; 3,750 x .303-caliber or 7.92mm machine gun

POWER PLANT: Nuffield Liberty Mk I and Mk II 340-hp gasoline engine

MAXIMUM SPEED: 30 mph

RANGE: 90 miles

FORDING DEPTH: 3'

VERTICAL OBSTACLE: 2'6"

TRENCH CROSSING: 7'6"

SPECIAL CHARACTERISTICS (POS/NEG): extra armor over the Mark III on the nose, glacis, and turret front, but most evident in the form of V-section plating on the turret that produced a faceted turret side

SPECIAL MODELS: A few Mark IV CS tanks substituted a 3.7-inch mortar for the 2-pounder main gun. Some had additional armor on the mantlet.

UNITED KINGDOM: INFANTRY TANK, MARK I, MATILDA I (A11)
Courtesy of Art-Tech/Aerospace/M.A.R.S/TRH/Navy Historical.

SUMMARY: Infantry tank (tank designed to support infantry) but armed only with a machine gun.

PRODUCTION DATES: April 1937–August 1940

NUMBER PRODUCED: 140 (including the pilot model)

MANUFACTURER: Vickers Armstrong

CREW: 2 (commander-gunner, driver)

ARMAMENT: 1 x .50-caliber or 1 x .303-caliber Vickers machine gun; 2 x 4-inch smoke discharger

WEIGHT: 24,640 lbs.

LENGTH: 15'11"

WIDTH: 7'6"

HEIGHT: 6'2"

ARMOR: maximum 60mm; minimum 10mm

AMMUNITION STORAGE AND TYPE: 4,000 x .303-caliber machine gun ammunition

POWER PLANT: Ford V-8 commercial 70-hp gasoline engine

MAXIMUM SPEED: 8 mph

RANGE: 80 miles

FORDING DEPTH: 3' (short distance only)

VERTICAL OBSTACLE: 2'1"

TRENCH CROSSING: 7'

SPECIAL CHARACTERISTICS (POS/NEG): all-riveted construction with cast turret

SPECIAL MODELS: Coulter Plough device for mine-clearing

UNITED KINGDOM: INFANTRY TANK, MARK II, MATILDA II (A12)
Courtesy of Art-Tech/Aerospace/M.A.R.S/TRH/Navy Historical.

SUMMARY: Successor to the interim Matilda I, the Matilda II rectified the limitations of a single machine gun on the Matilda I. Design of the new tank was authorized in November 1936.

PRODUCTION DATES: December 1937–August 1943

NUMBER PRODUCED: 2,987

MANUFACTURER: Vulcan Foundry of Warrington produced the prototypes. Production models also manufactured by Fowler, Ruston & Horsnby; and later with LMS, Harland and Wolff, and North British Locomotive Company

CREW: 4 (commander, gunner, loader, driver)

ARMAMENT: 1 x 2-pounder (40mm/1.57-inch) (3-inch howitzer in Mk IV CS version); 1 x 7.92mm Besa machine gun

WEIGHT: 59,360 lbs.

LENGTH: 18'5"

WIDTH: 8'6"

HEIGHT: 8'3"

ARMOR: maximum 78mm; minimum 13mm

AMMUNITION STORAGE AND TYPE: 93 2-pounder rounds; 2,925 Besa machine gun rounds

POWER PLANT: 2 x Leyland E 148 six-cylinder 95-hp gasoline engines

MAXIMUM SPEED: 15 mph

RANGE: 160 miles

FORDING DEPTH: 3'

VERTICAL OBSTACLE: 2'

TRENCH CROSSING: 7'

SPECIAL CHARACTERISTICS (POS/NEG): Heavy side skirts helped protect the suspension system. The Matilda II was the most heavily armored British tank in service in 1940. It played an important role in the early battles in North Africa; the Italians had no tank or antitank gun capable of penetrating its armor. Only in April 1941 did this situation change, when the Germans employed their 88mm antiaircraft guns in an antitank role.

SPECIAL MODELS: Frog and Murray flamethrower tanks; dozer tanks, mine-clearing, also with Inglis bridge-laying and trench-crossing devices; CDL (Canal Defense Light) equipped with powerful searchlight in place of the turret to illuminate the battlefield at night

UNITED KINGDOM: INFANTRY TANK, MARK III, VALENTINE
Fitted with sand shields and auxiliary fuel tanks for Middle East service
Courtesy of Art-Tech/Aerospace/M.A.R.S/TRH/Navy Historical.

SUMMARY: Designed as a heavy infantry support tank (it lacked the "A" because it was not designed to meet a specific General Staff specification), the Valentine was pressed into service as a cruiser tank in Eighth Army in North Africa, beginning in June 1941. A stable gun platform with good mechanical reliability, it was nonetheless obsolete by 1942 because of low speed and small turret, which prevented it from mounting a larger-caliber gun. The Valentine continued in service for the remainder of the war.

PRODUCTION DATES: May 1940–1944

NUMBER PRODUCED: 8,275

MANUFACTURER: Vickers Armstrong; Canadian Pacific (Montreal) produced 1,420, beginning with Valentine VI (all but 30 of these, retained for training, were delivered to the Soviet Union)

CREW: 3–4 (commander, gunner, driver; loader on Mks III and V)

ARMAMENT: 1 x 2-pounder (40mm) ROQF Mk. IX or X; 1 x 7.92mm Besa machine gun (coaxial) (Valentine VIII, IX, X mounted a 6-pounder/57mm in place of the 2-pounder; Valentine XI mounted a 75mm gun)

WEIGHT: 39,000 lbs. (41,000 lbs. in Mks VIII–XI)

LENGTH: 17'9"

WIDTH: 8'8"

HEIGHT: 7'6"

ARMOR: maximum 65mm; minimum 8mm

AMMUNITION STORAGE AND TYPE: 79 x 2-pounder; 3,150 x 7.92mm (53 rounds in 6-pounder Valentine VIII, IX, and X; with 1,575 x 7.92mm)

POWER PLANT: AEC six-cylinder 135-hp engine; Valentine II, AEC 131-hp diesel engine; Valentine IV, GMC 135-hp diesel engine; Valentine X, GMC 165-hp diesel engine

MAXIMUM SPEED: 15 mph

RANGE: 90 mph

FORDING DEPTH: 3'

VERTICAL OBSTACLE: 2'9"

TRENCH CROSSING: 7'6"

SPECIAL CHARACTERISTICS (POS/NEG): Excellent mechanical reliability and stable gun platform. Rendered obsolete by 1942 as a consequence of its low speed and small turret, which prevented mounting a larger main gun.

SPECIAL MODELS: observation platform and command tank; antimine tank; bridge-layer; DD (Duplex Drive); flamethrower

UNITED STATES: M1 AND M2 SERIES COMBAT CAR (LIGHT TANK)
Courtesy of Art-Tech/Aerospace/M.A.R.S/TRH/Navy Historical.

SUMMARY: Developed for infantry support, the M1 and M2 were the forerunners of subsequent U.S. light tanks up to 1944.

PRODUCTION DATES: 1938–1940

NUMBER PRODUCED: 24 (M1A1, 17; M2, 7)

MANUFACTURER: Rock Island

CREW: 4 (commander, turret gunner, driver, hull gunner)

ARMAMENT: 3 machine guns: 1 x .50-caliber and 1 x 30-caliber in turret; 1 x .30-caliber in hull

WEIGHT: 19,644 lbs.

LENGTH: 13'7"

WIDTH: 7'10"

HEIGHT: 7'9"

ARMOR: maximum 16mm; minimum 6mm

AMMUNITION STORAGE AND TYPE: 1,100 x .50-caliber; 6,000 x .30-caliber

POWER PLANT: Continental W-670 7-cylinder 250-hp gasoline engine (M1A1); Guiberson T1020 diesel engine (M2)

MAXIMUM SPEED: 45 mph

RANGE: 135 miles

FORDING DEPTH: 4'4"

VERTICAL OBSTACLE: ?

TRENCH CROSSING: ?

SPECIAL CHARACTERISTICS (POS/NEG): riveted construction

SPECIAL MODELS: —

UNITED STATES: M2 SERIES LIGHT

Courtesy of Art-Tech/Aerospace/M.A.R.S/TRH/Navy Historical.

SUMMARY: Light infantry support tank. Originally the T2E1, it was the follow-on to M1 and M2 combat cars. None of the M2A1, M2A2, or M2A3 models saw combat, being used as training tanks. A small number of M2A4 models were sent to the British, and a few of these may have been employed in Burma.

PRODUCTION DATES: 1935–1941

NUMBER PRODUCED: Approx. 380 (M2A1, 19; M2A2, n/a; M2A3, n/a; M2A4, 365)

MANUFACTURER: Rock Island

CREW: 4 (commander, driver, codriver, gunner)

ARMAMENT: 37mm main gun on M2A4 only; also 1 x .50-caliber and 1 x .30-caliber machine guns in turret and 1 x .30-caliber in hull in M2A1 (one machine gun each in two side-by-side turrets in M2A2 and M2A3; three hull machine guns in M2A4)

WEIGHT: 18,790 lbs. (M2A1); 19,100 lbs. (M2A2); 20,000 lbs. (M2A3); 23,000 lbs. (M2A4)

LENGTH: 13'7" (M2A1, M2A2); 14'6" (M2A3, M2A4)

WIDTH: 8'1.25"

HEIGHT: 7'4" (M2A1, M2A2, M2A3); 8'2" (M2A4)

ARMOR: maximum 16mm (24mm on M2A4); minimum 6mm

AMMUNITION STORAGE AND TYPE: 102 x 37mm (M2A4); 2,137 x .50-caliber; 7,185 x .30-caliber

POWER PLANT: Continental W-670 7-cylinder gasoline 250-hp engine; Guiberson T 1020 diesel engine in some models; GM diesel engine in M2A2

MAXIMUM SPEED: 25–30 mph

RANGE: 130 miles

FORDING DEPTH: 3'8"

VERTICAL OBSTACLE: 2'

TRENCH CROSSING: 6'

SPECIAL CHARACTERISTICS (POS/NEG): riveted construction

SPECIAL MODELS: –

WORLD WAR II

AUSTRALIA: CRUISER TANK, SENTINEL AC I
Courtesy of Art-Tech/Aerospace/M.A.R.S/TRH/Navy Historical.

SUMMARY: The result of an effort to produce a tank entirely in Australia, the Sentinel was an excellent medium tank design. Production of the AC I (Australian Cruiser) was halted when the United States was able to supply all of Australia's tank requirements. The AC I never saw combat, being used thereafter as a training vehicle. Nonetheless, it was a considerable technological accomplishment.

PRODUCTION DATES: August 1942–July 1943

NUMBER PRODUCED: 66

MANUFACTURER: Chullona Tank Assembly Shops, New South Wales

CREW: 5 (commander, driver, hull gunner, gunner, loader)

ARMAMENT: 1 x 2-pounder (40mm) QQF main gun; 2 x .303-caliber Vickers machine guns

WEIGHT: 62,720 lbs.

LENGTH: 20'9"

WIDTH: 9'6"

HEIGHT: 8'9"

ARMOR: maximum 89mm; minimum 25mm

AMMUNITION STORAGE AND TYPE: 130 x 2-pounder; 4,250 x .303-caliber

POWER PLANT: 3 x Cadillac V-8 117-hp gasoline engines

MAXIMUM SPEED: 25 mph

RANGE: 200 miles

FORDING DEPTH: 4'

VERTICAL OBSTACLE: 2'

TRENCH CROSSING: 9'6"

SPECIAL CHARACTERISTICS (POS/NEG):

SPECIAL MODELS: AC III was an upgunned version, mounting a 25-pounder in place of the 2-pounder in a larger turret; few, if any, AC IIIs were completed. An AC IV prototype was tested for the 17-pounder high-velocity gun.

CANADA: CRUISER TANK, RAM MARK I

Courtesy of Art-Tech/Aerospace/M.A.R.S/TRH/Navy Historical.

SUMMARY: Cut off from a supply of British tanks during World War II, Canada undertook to build its own. The Ram was the basic U.S. M3 tank with the sponson-mounted 75mm main gun removed in favor of a turret mounting a 2-pounder (40mm) gun.

PRODUCTION DATES: 1941–1942

NUMBER PRODUCED: 50

MANUFACTURER: Montreal Locomotive Works Tank Arsenal

CREW: 5

ARMAMENT: 1 x 2-pounder (40mm) main gun; two coaxial 7.62mm machine guns

WEIGHT: 64,000 lbs.

LENGTH: 19'

WIDTH: 9'6"

HEIGHT: 8'9"

ARMOR: maximum 89mm; minimum 25mm

AMMUNITION STORAGE AND TYPE: –

POWER PLANT: Continental R-975 9-cylinder radial 400-hp gasoline engine

MAXIMUM SPEED: 25 mph

RANGE: 125 miles

FORDING DEPTH: 3'

VERTICAL OBSTACLE: 2'

TRENCH CROSSING: 7'5"

SPECIAL CHARACTERISTICS (POS/NEG):

SPECIAL MODELS: A number had their turrets removed and were used as armored personnel carriers; the Ram also served as the basis for the Sexton self-propelled gun.

CANADA: CRUISER TANK, RAM MARK II
Courtesy of Art-Tech/Aerospace/M.A.R.S/TRH/Navy Historical.

SUMMARY: Follow-on to the Ram Mk I. Production ceased when Canada decided to adopt the U.S. M4 Sherman as its main battle tank. The changeover to the Sherman was accomplished by D-Day in June 1944.

PRODUCTION DATES: 1942–September 1943

NUMBER PRODUCED: 1,094

MANUFACTURER: Montreal Locomotive Works Tank Arsenal

CREW: 5

ARMAMENT: 1 x 6-pounder (57mm) main gun; 3 x 7.62mm machine guns

WEIGHT: 65,000 lbs.

LENGTH: 19'

WIDTH: 9'6"

HEIGHT: 8'9"

ARMOR: maximum 89mm; minimum 25mm

AMMUNITION STORAGE AND TYPE: 92 x 6-pounder (57mm); 2,500 x 7.62mm

POWER PLANT: Continental R-975 9-cylinder radial 400-hp gasoline engine

MAXIMUM SPEED: 25 mph

RANGE: 125 miles

FORDING DEPTH: 3'

VERTICAL OBSTACLE: 2'

TRENCH CROSSING: 7'5"

SPECIAL CHARACTERISTICS (POS/NEG):

SPECIAL MODELS: Final 84 Ram IIs were made into command/observation post tanks, with dummy main-gun barrels. This enabled more space inside the turret for additional communications equipment and other gear. A number had their turrets removed and were used as armored personnel carriers; the Ram also served as the basis for the Sexton SP gun.

GERMANY: PzKpfw V PANTHER
Courtesy of Art-Tech/Aerospace/M.A.R.S/TRH/Navy Historical.

SUMMARY: Heavy medium tank developed to combat the Soviet T-34 tanks, which were more than a match for the PzKpfw IVs on the Eastern Front. Some consider it to be the best all-around tank of World War II. A number of Panthers remained in service after the war with the French Army.

PRODUCTION DATES: January 1943–April 1945

NUMBER PRODUCED: 5,976
Ausf. D, 850 (January–September 1943); Ausf. A, 2,000 (August 1943–May 1944); Ausf. G, 3,126 (March 1944–April 1945)

MANUFACTURER: MAN, Daimler-Benz, Demag, MNH

CREW: 5

ARMAMENT: 75mm KwK42 L/70 main gun; 3 x 7.92mm MG34 machine guns (coaxial, bow, antiaircraft)

WEIGHT: 94,770 lbs., Ausf. D; 100,282 lbs., Ausf. G

LENGTH: 29'1"

WIDTH: 11'3"

HEIGHT: 10'2"

ARMOR: maximum 100mm, minimum 16mm (Ausf. D); maximum 110, minimum 16mm (Ausf. G)

AMMUNITION STORAGE AND TYPE: 79 x 75mm; 5,100 x 7.92mm; 81 x 75mm; 4,800 x 7.92mm (Ausf. G)

POWER PLANT: Maybach HL230P30 12-cylinder 700-hp diesel engine

MAXIMUM SPEED: 28 mph

RANGE: 120 miles

FORDING DEPTH: 5'7"

VERTICAL OBSTACLE: 3'

TRENCH CROSSING: 6'3"

SPECIAL CHARACTERISTICS (POS/NEG): Regarded as one of the best tanks of World War II, the PzKpfw V mounted a powerful gun and had excellent mobility and armor protection.

SPECIAL MODELS: command tank/heavy tank destroyer/ armored recovery vehicle (347); antiaircraft tank

GERMANY: PzKpfw VI TIGER I HEAVY

Courtesy of Art-Tech/Aerospace/M.A.R.S/TRH/Navy Historical.

SUMMARY: Germany's first true heavy MBT of the war. It first saw service in the Leningrad sector of the Eastern Front in August 1942 and then in Tunisia. It served until the end of the war, taking a heavy toll on enemy tanks in the process.

PRODUCTION DATES: July 1942–August 1944

NUMBER PRODUCED: 1,354

MANUFACTURER: Henschel, Wegmann

CREW: 5

ARMAMENT: 88mm (3.46-inch) KwK36 main gun; 2 x 7.92mm MG34 machine guns (coaxial, bow)

WEIGHT: 125,662 lbs.

LENGTH (EXCLUDING GUN): 27'7"

WIDTH: 12'3"

HEIGHT: 9'7"

ARMOR: maximum 100mm on the hull front (120mm on the gun mantlet), minimum 25mm

AMMUNITION STORAGE AND TYPE: 92 x 88mm 4,800 x 7.92mm

POWER PLANT: Maybach HL210P45 12-cylinder 700-hp gasoline engine

MAXIMUM SPEED: 24 mph

RANGE: 85 miles

FORDING DEPTH: 3'11"

VERTICAL OBSTACLE: 2'7"

TRENCH CROSSING: 5'11"

SPECIAL CHARACTERISTICS (POS/NEG): Excellent tank with a superb long-range gun capable of killing any other tank. The Tiger was, however, complicated and thus difficult to maintain. It had an overlapping wheel suspension that tended to clog in muddy conditions or freeze up in cold weather, immobilizing the tank.

SPECIAL MODELS: command tank; armored recovery vehicle; assault rocket launcher; heavy assault gun; heavy tank destroyer

GERMANY: PzKPFW VI AUSF. B (TIGER II; KÖNIGSTIGER/KING TIGER)

Courtesy of Art-Tech/Aerospace/M.A.R.S/TRH/Navy Historical.

SUMMARY: The last German heavy tank of the war. Similar to the Panther in design, it carried much heavier armor. It first arrived in German units in July 1944, five months after production began.

PRODUCTION DATES: January 1944–March 1945

NUMBER PRODUCED: 489

MANUFACTURER: Henschel

CREW: 5

ARMAMENT: 88mm KwK43 L/71; also 2 x 7.92mm MG34 machine guns (coaxial, bow)

WEIGHT: 149,870 lbs.

LENGTH: 33'8"

WIDTH: 12'4"

HEIGHT: 10'2"

ARMOR: maximum 180mm, minimum 40mm

AMMUNITION STORAGE AND TYPE: 72 x 88mm; 5,850 x 7.92mm

POWER PLANT: Maybach HL230P30 12-cylinder 700-hp gasoline engine

MAXIMUM SPEED: 21 mph

RANGE: 102 miles

FORDING DEPTH: 5'3"

VERTICAL OBSTACLE: 2'10"

TRENCH CROSSING: 8'2"

SPECIAL CHARACTERISTICS (POS/NEG): The first 50 Tiger II tanks had a Porsche-designed turret with a curved front plate. This was then replaced with one designed by Henschel, which then produced the remaining tanks in their entirety. The heavily armored Tiger II could stop most Allied antitank weapons, but it was mechanically unreliable and, with the same engine as the Panther, suffered from slow speed and poor maneuverability.

SPECIAL MODELS: heavy tank destroyer; heavy self-propelled gun

HUNGARY: 40M TURAN I MEDIUM

Courtesy of Art-Tech/Aerospace/M.A.R.S/TRH/Navy Historical.

SUMMARY: Medium tank based on the Czech Skoda S-2r medium design of 1937, produced under license with the Germans after their takeover of Czechoslovakia. The Turan utilized a modified Vickers bogie suspension with eight road wheels in four pairs per side. The turret was enlarged to hold three, a Hungarian-manufactured 40mm main gun, and a more powerful engine. The Turan I formed the chief equipment of the Hungarian 1st Tank Division from 1943. The Turan II was essentially an upgunned Turan I with a short 75mm gun. Manufacture ended in 1944 when the Hungarian Army adopted the PzKpfw III and IV tanks.

PRODUCTION DATES: October 1941–1944

NUMBER PRODUCED: 285

MANUFACTURER: Weiss

CREW: 5

ARMAMENT: 40mm 41M 40/51 main gun; also 2 x 8mm 34/40AM machine guns (coaxial, bow)

WEIGHT: 35,800 lbs.

LENGTH: 18'8"

WIDTH: 8'4"

HEIGHT: 7'8"

ARMOR: maximum 50mm; minimum 14mm

AMMUNITION STORAGE AND TYPE: 101 x 40mm; 3,000 x 8mm

POWER PLANT: Manfred Weiss V-8 260-hp gasoline engine

MAXIMUM SPEED: 29 mph

RANGE: 103 miles

FORDING DEPTH: 2'11"

VERTICAL OBSTACLE: 2'7.5"

TRENCH CROSSING: 7'2.3"

SPECIAL CHARACTERISTICS (POS/NEG): too lightly armed and armored to face Soviet tanks on equal terms

SPECIAL MODELS: 105mm self-propelled gun, from 1942

ITALY: FIAT L6/40 LIGHT

Courtesy of Art-Tech/Aerospace/M.A.R.S/TRH/Navy Historical.

SUMMARY: Light tank developed as successor to the Fiat-Ansaldo 5-Ton.

PRODUCTION DATES: 1941–February 1943

NUMBER PRODUCED: 287

MANUFACTURER: Ansaldo

CREW: 2

ARMAMENT: 1 x 20mm Breda M35 main gun; 1 x 8mm (.315-caliber) Breda M38 machine gun (coaxial)

WEIGHT: 14,987 lbs.

LENGTH: 12'5"

WIDTH: 6'4"

HEIGHT: 6'8"

ARMOR: maximum 40mm; minimum 6mm

AMMUNITION STORAGE AND TYPE: 296 x 20mm and 1,560 x 8mm

POWER PLANT: SPD 18D four-cylinder 70-hp gasoline engine

MAXIMUM SPEED: 25 mph

RANGE: 125 miles

FORDING DEPTH: 2'8"

VERTICAL OBSTACLE: 2'4"

TRENCH CROSSING: 5'7"

SPECIAL CHARACTERISTICS (POS/NEG): Far outclassed by Allied AFVs in a front-line role, it nonetheless saw considerable action in cavalry and reconnaissance roles in North Africa, Italy, and the Soviet Union.

SPECIAL MODELS: command tank; flamethrower; converted into *Semovente* self-propelled antitank guns

ITALY: FIAT M 13/40 MEDIUM

Courtesy of Art-Tech/Aerospace/M.A.R.S/TRH/Navy Historical.

SUMMARY: Italy's principal medium tank of World War II, based on the earlier M11/39. The Model 21 version had machine-gun armament only.

PRODUCTION DATES: mid-1940–1941

NUMBER PRODUCED: 1,960

MANUFACTURER: Fiat, Ansaldo

CREW: 4 (commander-gunner, loader, driver, front machine-gunner/radio operator)

ARMAMENT: 1 x 47mm L/32 main gun; 4 x 8mm Breda M38 machine guns (coaxial, 2 x bow, one antiaircraft on the turret)

WEIGHT: 30,856 lbs.

LENGTH: 16'2"

WIDTH: 7'3"

HEIGHT: 7'10"

ARMOR: maximum 42mm; minimum 6mm

AMMUNITION STORAGE AND TYPE: 104 x 47mm; 3,048 x 8mm

POWER PLANT: SPA TM40 eight-cylinder 125-hp diesel engine

MAXIMUM SPEED: 20 mph

RANGE: 125 miles

FORDING DEPTH: 3'3"

VERTICAL OBSTACLE: 2'8"

TRENCH CROSSING: 6'11"

SPECIAL CHARACTERISTICS (POS/NEG): mechanically unreliable and inadequately armored for 1940 with cramped crew arrangement; the M 13/40 also easily caught fire

SPECIAL MODELS: flamethrower and command tanks; also *Semovente* self-propelled 75mm gun on same chassis

SOVIET UNION: T-60 LIGHT
Courtesy of Art-Tech/Aerospace/M.A.R.S/TRH/Navy Historical.

SUMMARY: Light tank, replacing all previous Soviet light tanks, especially the T-40. In contrast to its predecessors, the T-60 was nonamphibious, but it retained the unusual offset turret alongside engine in the center of the hull.

PRODUCTION DATES: July 1941–1943

NUMBER PRODUCED: 6,292

MANUFACTURER: Factory No. 37, Factory No. 38 GAZ

CREW: 2

ARMAMENT: 1 x 20mm TNSh aircraft cannon; 1 x 7.62mm DT coaxial machine gun

WEIGHT: 11,350 lbs.

LENGTH: 13'1"

WIDTH: 5'6"

HEIGHT: 6'7"

ARMOR: maximum 25mm (35mm frontal armor on the T-60A); minimum 7mm

AMMUNITION STORAGE AND TYPE: 780 x 20mm; 945 x 7.62mm

POWER PLANT: GAZ-202 inline-6 70-hp gasoline engine

MAXIMUM SPEED: 27 mph

RANGE: 380 miles

FORDING DEPTH: 2'11"

VERTICAL OBSTACLE: 1'11.5"

TRENCH CROSSING: 5'6.6"

SPECIAL CHARACTERISTICS (POS/NEG): Very light armament and armor meant limited survivability on the battlefield. The T-60A had solid-disk road wheels instead of earlier spoked wheels and also thicker frontal armor.

SPECIAL MODELS: On retirement, many T-60s were converted to gun tractors and rocket carriers.

SOVIET UNION: T-70 LIGHT

Courtesy of Art-Tech/Aerospace/M.A.R.S/TRH/Navy Historical.

SUMMARY: Follow-on to the T-60 and the last Soviet light tank to be built in quantity. It was designed to rectify the problems of light armament and armor and to be mass-produced by the automotive industry. The T-70 also had greater power, with two 70-hp engines. Still, it was usually outgunned by the German tanks of the period.

PRODUCTION DATES: March 1942–August 1943

NUMBER PRODUCED: 8,226

MANUFACTURER: Factory No. 37, Gorki Automobile Factory No. 1 (GAZ), Factory No. 38.

CREW: 2

ARMAMENT: 1 x 45mm Gun Model 38; 1 x 7.62mm machine gun Model 38

WEIGHT: 21,930 lbs.

LENGTH: 15'2"

WIDTH: 7'8"

HEIGHT: 6'9"

ARMOR: maximum 60mm; minimum 10mm

AMMUNITION STORAGE AND TYPE: 94 x 45mm; 945 x 7.62mm gun

POWER PLANT: 2 x GAZ-202 inline-6 70-hp gasoline engines

MAXIMUM SPEED: 31 mph

RANGE: 280 miles

FORDING DEPTH: 2'11"

VERTICAL OBSTACLE: 2'3"

TRENCH CROSSING: 5'10"

SPECIAL CHARACTERISTICS (POS/NEG): new welded turret

SPECIAL MODELS: –

SOVIET UNION: T-34/76 MEDIUM
Courtesy of Art-Tech/Aerospace/M.A.R.S/TRH/Navy Historical.

SUMMARY: One of the best all-around tanks of the entire war, the T-34 was based on the last BT-series medium tank, the prototype BT-IS, as well as the T-32 medium. The T-34 was produced in models A through F. The B introduced a longer main gun and rolled plate turret; later production models introduced a cast instead of welded turret, then an entirely new turret design, cooling improvements, and commander's cupola.

PRODUCTION DATES: June 1940–1944

NUMBER PRODUCED: Approx. 53,000 (all T-34 models)

MANUFACTURER: Komintern Tank Plant (Kharkov)

CREW: 4

ARMAMENT: 1 x 76.2mm gun (A Model had a short .30-caliber gun; the B Model a .40-caliber); 2 or 3 x 7.62mm machine guns (one coaxial and one hull-mounted)

WEIGHT: 58,900 lbs. (A Model); 66,120 (C Model),

LENGTH: 20' (21'7" with gun forward)

WIDTH: 9'9"

HEIGHT: 8'5"

ARMOR: 45mm maximum, 14mm minimum (A Model); 70mm maximum, 18mm minimum (C Model)

AMMUNITION STORAGE AND TYPE: 56–60 x 76.2mm; 1,890 x 7.62mm

POWER PLANT: V-2-34M V-12 500-hp diesel engine

MAXIMUM SPEED: 33 mph

RANGE: 190 miles

FORDING DEPTH: 4'6"

VERTICAL OBSTACLE: 2'4"

TRENCH CROSSING: 9'8"

SPECIAL CHARACTERISTICS (POS/NEG): Simple design, easily manufactured and with excellent maneuverability and reliability, save for its transmission, which remained a problem throughout the war (where possible, many T-34s carried spares). Wide 18.7-inch tracks provided excellent traction in poor conditions.

SPECIAL MODELS: in addition, 5,000 T-34 chassis were produced for SP guns; flamethrower tank (T-34/76D ATO-42); commander's tank had radio

SOVIET UNION: T-34/85 MEDIUM

Courtesy of Art-Tech/Aerospace/M.A.R.S/TRH/Navy Historical.

SUMMARY: The answer to larger German tanks. The T-34/85 was the basic T-34/76 above, with the same chassis, track, and engine but new five-speed gearbox and thicker frontal armor and a larger cast steel turret, thickened glacis plate, and commander's cupola; up-gunned to 85mm. The T-34/85 was perhaps the best all-around tank of the war. It continued in service well after the war. An improved version, the T-34/85 II, appeared in 1947 and was produced in the Soviet Union, then in Czechoslovakia and Poland (until 1964). Exported widely, it saw extensive combat during the Korean War and in the Middle East.

PRODUCTION DATES: January 1944–1964 (Poland)

NUMBER PRODUCED: 17,680

MANUFACTURER: Factory No. 183 UVZ, Factory No. 112, Factory No. 174

CREW: 5

ARMAMENT: 1 x 85mm gun ZiS-S-53; 2 x 7.62mm DTM machine guns

WEIGHT: 70,530 lbs.

LENGTH: 20'3"

WIDTH: 9'7"

HEIGHT: 9'

ARMOR: maximum 90mm; minimum 45mm

AMMUNITION STORAGE AND TYPE: 56–60 x 85mm; 1,890 x 7.62mm

POWER PLANT: V-2-34M V-12 500-hp diesel engine

MAXIMUM SPEED: 31 mph

RANGE: 190 miles

FORDING DEPTH: 4'3"

VERTICAL OBSTACLE: 2'7"

TRENCH CROSSING: 8'2"

SPECIAL CHARACTERISTICS (POS/NEG):

SPECIAL MODELS: hull used for antiaircraft tanks, as well as flamethrower tanks, engineer vehicles, and bridge-layers

SOVIET UNION: T-44 MEDIUM

Courtesy of Art-Tech/Aerospace/M.A.R.S/TRH/Navy Historical.

SUMMARY: Redesign of T-34/85, but with more streamlined appearance, thicker hull and turret armor, and torsion-bar rather than Christie suspension system. It was the first tank to mount its engine transversely. Unreliable mechanically but perhaps the most advanced tank design of World War II, it was the basis of the subsequent T-54, T-55, and T-62 Soviet tanks.

PRODUCTION DATES: 1944–1945

NUMBER PRODUCED: –

MANUFACTURER: State factories

CREW: 4 (eliminated hull gunner on T-34, providing additional ammunition storage)

ARMAMENT: 1 x 85mm D-57 gun, 2 x 7.62mm machine guns

WEIGHT: 76,137 lbs.

LENGTH: 21'4"

WIDTH: 10'9"

HEIGHT: 8'2"

ARMOR: maximum 120mm

AMMUNITION STORAGE AND TYPE: –

POWER PLANT: V-12 512-hp diesel engine

MAXIMUM SPEED: 32 mph

RANGE: 155 miles

FORDING DEPTH: –

VERTICAL OBSTACLE: –

TRENCH CROSSING: –

SPECIAL CHARACTERISTICS (POS/NEG):

SPECIAL MODELS: –

SOVIET UNION: KV-1 HEAVY
Courtesy of Art-Tech/Aerospace/M.A.R.S/TRH/Navy Historical.

SUMMARY: KV designation was for Klimenti Voroshilov, the Soviet defense commissar. Intended as the replacement for the T-35 heavy; design work began on the KV-1 in 1938. It incorporated many of the features of the T-34. Subsequent models of the KV-1 incorporated extra armor, new cast turret, and upgraded engine. The KV-85 version, produced beginning in 1943, mounted the 85mm gun. The KV-1 was an important step forward toward the next generation of Soviet tanks, including the Joseph Stalin.

PRODUCTION DATES: 1940–1943

NUMBER PRODUCED: –

MANUFACTURER: Kirov, Chelyabinsk

CREW: 5

ARMAMENT: 1 x 76.2mm (3-inch) gun L-11 (early versions had the short .30-caliber length; later models had the 40-caliber; the KV-85, produced beginning in 1943, mounted 1 x 85mm/3.34-inch gun); 3 x 7.62mm DT machine guns

WEIGHT: 95,874 lbs. (increased weight in subsequent upgraded armor models; KV-85 version weighed 101,400 lbs.)

LENGTH: 22'7"

WIDTH: 10'8"

HEIGHT: 8'9"

ARMOR: maximum 77mm; minimum 25mm (B and C Models had additional armor totaling 130mm)

AMMUNITION STORAGE AND TYPE: 111 x 76.2mm; 3,024 x 7.62mm

POWER PLANT: V-2K V-12 550-hp diesel engine (600-hp in the C Model)

MAXIMUM SPEED: 22 mph

RANGE: 93 miles

FORDING DEPTH: 4'11"

VERTICAL OBSTACLE: 3'3"

TRENCH CROSSING: 8'10"

SPECIAL CHARACTERISTICS (POS/NEG): excellent design with balance of armor, armament, and speed; chief problems were maneuverability and mechanical reliability.

SPECIAL MODELS: KV-2 close-support version, also produced beginning in 1940, mounted either a 122mm or 152mm howitzer in a large, high turret

SOVIET UNION: IS-1 HEAVY
Courtesy of Art-Tech/Aerospace/M.A.R.S/TRH/Navy Historical.

SUMMARY: The IS or JS (Iosef [Joseph] Stalin) heavy tank developed from the KV-1. In its three models it was the most powerful tank of World War II and for a decade thereafter.

PRODUCTION DATES: early 1944

NUMBER PRODUCED: 107

MANUFACTURER: Factory No. 100

CREW: 4

ARMAMENT: 85mm Gun D-5T85 (later upgraded to 100mm; some of these had the 100mm replaced with a 122mm gun in a new, larger turret); 4 x 7.62mm DT machine guns

WEIGHT: 98,540 lbs.

LENGTH: 27'4"

WIDTH: 10'3"

HEIGHT: 8'11"

ARMOR: maximum 120mm; minimum 19mm

AMMUNITION STORAGE AND TYPE: 59 x 85mm; 2,520 x 7.62mm

POWER PLANT: V-2-IS (V2-K) V-12 600-hp diesel engine

MAXIMUM SPEED: 23 mph

RANGE: 100 miles

FORDING DEPTH: 4'3"

VERTICAL OBSTACLE: 3'2"

TRENCH CROSSING: 8'2"

SPECIAL CHARACTERISTICS (POS/NEG): Well-armed and well-armored, its chief shortcoming was the slow rate of fire, the consequence of separate shells and cartridges.

SPECIAL MODELS: ISU-122 (JSU-122) SP gun, mounting a 122mm gun; ISU-152 (JSU-152) SP gun, mounting a 152mm gun. Both were exported to the postwar Soviet bloc and remained in service into the late 1970s, as did the IS-2 and IS-3.

SOVIET UNION: IS-2 HEAVY
Courtesy of the Patton Museum.

SUMMARY: Redesign of the IS-1 in order to work out problems but also to reduce the weight, improve the armor, provide an improved shape, and simplify production.

PRODUCTION DATES: April 1944–June 1945

NUMBER PRODUCED: 2,250

MANUFACTURER: Factory No. 100, Kirovskiy Works (Chelyabinsk)

CREW: 4

ARMAMENT: 122mm gun D-25T; 1 x 12.7mm DShK machine gun; 2 x 7.62mm DT machine guns

WEIGHT: 101,184 lbs.

LENGTH: 32'

WIDTH: 10'2"

HEIGHT: 8'10"

ARMOR: maximum 129mm; minimum 60mm

AMMUNITION STORAGE AND TYPE: 28 x 122mm; 945 x 12.7mm; 2,330 x 7.62mm

POWER PLANT: V-2-IS (V2-K) V-12 600-hp diesel engine

MAXIMUM SPEED: 23 mph

RANGE: 100 miles

FORDING DEPTH: 4'3"

VERTICAL OBSTACLE: 3'2"

TRENCH CROSSING: 8'2"

SPECIAL CHARACTERISTICS (POS/NEG): Well-armed and well-armored, its chief shortcoming was the slow rate of fire of the main gun, the consequence of separate projectiles and cartridges.

SPECIAL MODELS: see IS-1

SOVIET UNION: IS-3 HEAVY

Courtesy of Art-Tech/Aerospace/M.A.R.S/TRH/Navy Historical.

SUMMARY: Last of the IS series of heavy tanks; completely redesigned from the IS-1 and IS-2 to eliminate shell traps. It featured the "inverted frying pan" turret of smooth, curved shape. The IS-3 entered service in early 1945 and participated in the Battle for Berlin. The most powerful tank in the world for a decade and a major influence on subsequent tank design worldwide. It was supplied to the Soviet bloc countries of Czechoslovakia, East Germany, and Poland as well as to Egypt, Libya, and Syria.

PRODUCTION DATES: 1945–

NUMBER PRODUCED: –

MANUFACTURER: Kirov, Chelyabinsk

CREW: 4

ARMAMENT: 122mm Gun D-25; 1 x 12.7mm DShK machine gun; 2 x 7.62mm DT machine guns

WEIGHT: 102,486 lbs.

LENGTH: 22'4"

WIDTH: 10'6"

HEIGHT: 8'11"

ARMOR: maximum 132mm; minimum 60mm

AMMUNITION STORAGE AND TYPE: 28 x 122mm; 945 x 12.7mm; 1,000 x 7.62mm

POWER PLANT: V-2-IS (V2-K) V-12 600-hp diesel engine

MAXIMUM SPEED: 23 mph

RANGE: 100 miles

FORDING DEPTH: 4'3"

VERTICAL OBSTACLE: 3'2"

TRENCH CROSSING: 8'2"

SPECIAL CHARACTERISTICS (POS/NEG): separate ammunition problem of IS-1 and IS-2 remedied in the IS-3

SPECIAL MODELS: see IS-1

UNITED KINGDOM: CRUISER TANK, MARK V, COVENANTER (A13 MK III)
Courtesy of Art-Tech/Aerospace/M.A.R.S/TRH/Navy Historical.

SUMMARY: Essentially a more heavily armored cruiser Mark IV designed for independent action, but many problems meant it was not employed operationally; it was utilized for training purposes until 1943. The first British tank to be officially named.

PRODUCTION DATES: 1940–?

NUMBER PRODUCED: 1,771

MANUFACTURER: LMS

CREW: 4 (commander, gunner, loader, driver)

ARMAMENT: 1 2-pounder (40mm/1.57-inch) OQF (1 x 3-inch howitzer on CS models); also 1 x 7.92mm Besa machine gun

WEIGHT: 40,320 lbs.

LENGTH: 19'1"

WIDTH: 8'7"

HEIGHT: 7'4"

ARMOR: maximum 40mm; minimum 7mm

AMMUNITION STORAGE AND TYPE: –

POWER PLANT: Meadows Fiat-12 D.A.V. 280-hp engine

MAXIMUM SPEED: 31 mph

RANGE: 100 miles

FORDING DEPTH: 3'2"

VERTICAL OBSTACLE: 2'6"

TRENCH CROSSING: 7'

SPECIAL CHARACTERISTICS (POS/NEG): Similar appearance to the Cruiser Mark IV with the V-shaped turret side, but with a foot less height. Frequent breakdowns from overheating caused by a faulty cooling system were never completely solved.

SPECIAL MODELS: –

UNITED KINGDOM: CRUISER TANK, MARK VI, CRUSADER (A15)
Courtesy of Art-Tech/Aerospace/M.A.R.S/TRH/Navy Historical.

SUMMARY: Developed at the same time as the Covenanter, the Crusader was intended to fulfill the role of a "medium" cruiser tank for independent operations. Produced in Mark I–III and CS versions, it was the principal British tank from 1941 onward.

PRODUCTION DATES: 1940–1943

NUMBER PRODUCED: 5,300

MANUFACTURER: Nuffields, acting as "parent" to nine companies engaged in production

CREW: 3–5 (commander, gunner, driver in Mk III; plus loader and hull gunner in Mks I and II)

ARMAMENT: 1 x 2-pounder (40mm) on Mks I and II; 1 x 6-pounder (57mm) on Mk III; 1 x 3-inch howitzer on CS version; also 1 or 2 x 7.92mm Besa machine guns

WEIGHT: 42,560 lbs. (Mks I and II); 44,240 (Mk III)

LENGTH: 19'8"

WIDTH: 8'8"

HEIGHT: 7'4"

ARMOR: maximum 40mm (Mk I), 49mm (Mk II), 51mm (Mk III); minimum 7mm

AMMUNITION STORAGE AND TYPE: 110 x 2-pounder (65 x 4-pounder [Mk III]; maximum 5,000 x 7.92mm machine gun

POWER PLANT: Nuffield Liberty V-12 340-hp gasoline engine

MAXIMUM SPEED: 27 mph

RANGE: 100 miles (127 miles with extra fuel tank)

FORDING DEPTH: 3'3"

VERTICAL OBSTACLE: 2'3"

TRENCH CROSSING: 8'6"

SPECIAL CHARACTERISTICS (POS/NEG): Riveted hull; welded turret of composite construction with extra bolted-on armor. Fast and mobile, it was nonetheless insufficiently armored and gunned and was replaced by the U.S. M4 Sherman. It was then adapted for a variety of other roles later in the war.

SPECIAL MODELS: antiaircraft tank (turret removed in favor of 40mm Bofors mount); command tank; armored recovery vehicle; dozer; antimine roller; gun tractor for the 17-pounder (76.2mm) antitank gun

UNITED KINGDOM: CRUISER TANK, MARK VII, CAVALIER (A24)
Courtesy of Art-Tech/Aerospace/M.A.R.S/TRH/Navy Historical.

SUMMARY: Heavy cruiser interim design developed as a consequence of fighting in North Africa in order to overcome the deficiencies of the Covenanter and Crusader tanks.

PRODUCTION DATES: 1942

NUMBER PRODUCED: 500

MANUFACTURER: Nuffield Mechanisations and Aero

CREW: 5 (commander, gunner, loader, driver, codriver)

ARMAMENT: 1 x 6-pounder (57mm) OQF main gun; also 1 x or 2 x 7.92mm Besa machine guns

WEIGHT: 59,360 lbs.

LENGTH: 20'10"

WIDTH: 9'6"

HEIGHT: 8'

ARMOR: maximum 76mm; minimum 20mm

AMMUNITION STORAGE AND TYPE: 64 x 6-pounder (57mm); 4,950 x 7.92mm

POWER PLANT: Nuffield V-12 410-hp gasoline engine

MAXIMUM SPEED: 24 mph

RANGE: 165 miles

FORDING DEPTH: 3'

VERTICAL OBSTACLE: 3'

TRENCH CROSSING: 7'6"

SPECIAL CHARACTERISTICS (POS/NEG): With the same engine as the Crusader and much heavier weight, the Cavalier suffered in performance and short engine life. It was also prone to mechanical breakdowns.

SPECIAL MODELS: Initially used only for training purposes as a gun tank, about half of the Cavaliers in 1943 were converted for use as observation posts for artillery and were supplied to the artillery regiments of British armored divisions, seeing service in Europe during 1944–1945. Others were also converted to armored recovery vehicles.

UNITED KINGDOM: CRUISER TANK, MARK VIII, CENTAUR (A27L)
Courtesy of the Patton Museum.

SUMMARY: Heavy cruiser follow-on to Cavalier design utilizing the Liberty engine (L model).

PRODUCTION DATES: 1942–?

NUMBER PRODUCED: about 950 (80 of which were Mk IV)

MANUFACTURER: Leyland

CREW: 5 (commander, gunner, loader, driver, codriver)

ARMAMENT: 1 x 6-pounder (57mm) OQF (Mk I) main gun (1 x 95mm howitzer in Mk IV); also 1 or 2 x 7.92mm Besa machine guns

WEIGHT: 63,600 lbs.

LENGTH: 20'10"

WIDTH: 9'6"

HEIGHT: 8'2"

ARMOR: maximum 76mm; minimum 20mm

AMMUNITION STORAGE AND TYPE: 64 x 6-pounder (Mk I); 51 x 95mm (Mk IV); 4,950 x 7.92mm

POWER PLANT: Liberty V-12 395-hp gasoline engine

MAXIMUM SPEED: 27 mph

RANGE: 165 miles

FORDING DEPTH: 3'

VERTICAL OBSTACLE: 3'

TRENCH CROSSING: 7'6"

SPECIAL CHARACTERISTICS (POS/NEG):

SPECIAL MODELS: close support (95mm gun, Mk IV); artillery observation post (with dummy gun); antiaircraft tank; dozer tank; armored recovery vehicle; armored personnel carrier, the Centaur Kangaroo

UNITED KINGDOM: CRUISER TANK, MARK VIII, CROMWELL (A27M)
Courtesy of Art-Tech/Aerospace/M.A.R.S/TRH/Navy Historical.

SUMMARY: Heavy cruiser follow-on to Cavalier design, utilizing the Rolls-Royce Merlin aero engine, designated the Meteor (M) in its tank version. Numerically the most important British heavy cruiser tank of World War II, with extensive service during the fighting in northern Europe (1944–1945). The Cromwell continued in service after World War II; after 1950 a number received new turrets and 20-pounder guns, designated the Charioteer.

PRODUCTION DATES: January 1943–1945

NUMBER PRODUCED: –

MANUFACTURER: Leyland

CREW: 5 (commander, gunner, loader, driver, codriver)

ARMAMENT: 1 x 6-pounder (57mm) OQF in Mks I–III (1 x 95mm howitzer in Mks VI and VIII and 1 x 75mm in Mks IV, V, VII); also 2 x 7.92mm Besa machine guns (1 x 7.92mm on Mk II)

WEIGHT: 61,600 lbs.

LENGTH: 20'10"

WIDTH: 9'6.5"

HEIGHT: 8'2"

ARMOR: maximum 76mm (100mm with appliqué armor); minimum 8mm

AMMUNITION STORAGE AND TYPE: 64 x 6-pounder (Mks I–III); 51 x 95mm (Mks VI and VII); 4,950 x 7.92mm

POWER PLANT: Rolls-Royce Meteor V-12 600-hp gasoline engine

MAXIMUM SPEED: 40 mph

RANGE: 173 miles

FORDING DEPTH: 3' (4' prepared)

VERTICAL OBSTACLE: 3'

TRENCH CROSSING: 7'6"

SPECIAL CHARACTERISTICS (POS/NEG):

SPECIAL MODELS: training tank; artillery observation post (with dummy gun); antiaircraft tank; "prong" fitted with Hedgerow cutting device utilized in the Normandy countryside in 1944; armored recovery vehicle

UNITED KINGDOM: CRUISER TANK, CHALLENGER (A30)
Courtesy of Art-Tech/Aerospace/M.A.R.S/TRH/Navy Historical.

SUMMARY: British effort to produce a tank utilizing a modified Cromwell chassis but mounting a 17-pounder gun capable of knocking out the heaviest German tanks. Rushed into service to deal with the PzKpfw IV with its long 75mm gun, it was employed chiefly as a tank destroyer but proved inferior in this role to the Sherman Firefly.

PRODUCTION DATES: 1943–1945

NUMBER PRODUCED: 200

MANUFACTURER: Birmingham Carriage & Wagon Company

CREW: 5 (commander, driver, gunner, two loaders)

ARMAMENT: 17-pounder (76mm) Mk II main gun; also 1 x .30-caliber (coaxial) (hull machine gun eliminated to provide additional room for main-gun ammunition)

WEIGHT: 72,800 lbs.

LENGTH: 16'9"

WIDTH: 9'7"

HEIGHT: 9'1"

ARMOR: maximum 110mm; minimum 10mm

AMMUNITION STORAGE AND TYPE: 42 x 17-pounder

POWER PLANT: Rolls-Royce Meteor V-12 600-hp gasoline engine

MAXIMUM SPEED: 31 mph

RANGE: 135 miles

FORDING DEPTH: 4'6" (prepared)

VERTICAL OBSTACLE: 3'

TRENCH CROSSING: 8'6"

SPECIAL CHARACTERISTICS (POS/NEG): height, which made it a vulnerable target

SPECIAL MODELS: some mounted 25mm appliqué armor on turret

UNITED KINGDOM: CRUISER TANK, COMET (A34)

Courtesy of Art-Tech/Aerospace/M.A.R.S/TRH/Navy Historical.

SUMMARY: Excellent British medium tank, approximating the German Panther in capabilities and main gun. Based on the A27, it nonetheless was about 60 percent new. It appeared too late in the war to have any major impact but remained in service until the early 1960s.

PRODUCTION DATES: September 1944–Postwar

NUMBER PRODUCED: 1,200

MANUFACTURER: Leyland

CREW: 5 (commander, gunner, loader, driver, codriver)

ARMAMENT: 77mm OQF Mk II main gun; also 2 x 7.92mm Besa machine guns (coaxial, bow)

WEIGHT: 78,800 lbs.

LENGTH: 21'6" (25'1.5" with gun forward)

WIDTH: 10'

HEIGHT: 8'10"

ARMOR: maximum 101mm; minimum 14mm

AMMUNITION STORAGE AND TYPE: 58 x 77mm; 5,175 x 7.92mm; 12 smoke rounds

POWER PLANT: Rolls-Royce Meteor V-12 600-hp gasoline engine

MAXIMUM SPEED: 29 mph

RANGE: 123 miles

FORDING DEPTH: 3' (4' prepared)

VERTICAL OBSTACLE: 3'

TRENCH CROSSING: 7'6"

SPECIAL CHARACTERISTICS (POS/NEG): Of all-welded construction. Distinguishable from Cromwell by track return rollers above road wheels. Also had all-around vision cupola and mounted 2 x 6-barrel smoke dischargers.

SPECIAL MODELS: later production types with fishtail exhausts and improved "breathing" system

UNITED KINGDOM: INFANTRY TANK, MARK IV, CHURCHILL (A22)

Courtesy of Art-Tech/Aerospace/M.A.R.S/TRH/Navy Historical.

SUMMARY: Heavy infantry tank; it first saw combat in the 19 August 1942 raid on Dieppe. The Churchill remained in service with the British Army well into the 1950s and participated in the Korean War.

PRODUCTION DATES: June 1941–1945(?)

NUMBER PRODUCED: 5,640 (Mks I through XI)

MANUFACTURER: Dennis Bros., GRCW, Newton Chambers, Metro-Cammell, Charles Roberts, Leyland, Beyer Peacock

CREW: 5 (commander, gunner, loader, driver, codriver/hull gunner)

ARMAMENT: 2-pounder (40mm) gun and 7.92mm Besa machine gun in turret; 3-inch howitzer in the front of the hull. Mk II mounted a Besa machine gun (in the hull) in place of the 3-inch howitzer; Mk III was the first to mount a 6-pounder in the turret in place of the 1-pounder, necessitating a new, welded turret; Mk V-VII mounted a 75mm in the turret; Mks V and VIII mounted a 95mm howitzer

WEIGHT: 87,360 lbs. (Mks III–VI); 89,600 lbs. (Mks VII–VIII)

LENGTH: 24'5"

WIDTH: 9' (8'2", Mks I–II)

HEIGHT: 10'8" (11'4", Mks VII–VIII)

ARMOR: maximum 102mm; minimum 16mm (maximum 152mm; minimum 25mm on Mks VII–VIII)

AMMUNITION STORAGE AND TYPE: Mk I: 150 x 2-pounder; 58 x 3-inch, 6,925 x 7.92mm

POWER PLANT: Bedford twin-six 350-hp engine

MAXIMUM SPEED: 15.5 mph (12.5 mph Mks VII–VIII)

RANGE: 90 miles

FORDING DEPTH: 3'4" (unprepared)

VERTICAL OBSTACLE: 2'6"

TRENCH CROSSING: 10'

SPECIAL CHARACTERISTICS (POS/NEG): Once initial problems had been worked out, the Churchill proved a reliable, effective cruiser tank.

SPECIAL MODELS: flamethrower (Churchill Okie and Crocodile, capable of engaging a target at ranges to nearly 400 feet); engineer tank; armored recovery vehicle; bridging vehicles; antimine tanks; mat-layers

UNITED STATES: M3 SERIES LIGHT

Courtesy of Art-Tech/Aerospace/M.A.R.S/TRH/Navy Historical.

SUMMARY: The most widely used light U.S. tank of the war, developed following the defeat of France in 1940 to replace the obsolete M2. Manufactured in large quantities, it served in a variety of armies, including those of the Soviet Union and Great Britain (where it was known as the General Stuart). Some served during the postwar period.

PRODUCTION DATES: March 1941–October 1943

NUMBER PRODUCED: 13,859 (M3, 5,811; M3A1, 4,621; M3A3, 3,427)

MANUFACTURER: American Car & Foundry

CREW: 4

ARMAMENT: 37mm Gun M5 main gun; also 3 x .30-caliber M1919A4 machine guns (1 x .30-caliber in M3A1; two in sponsons on M3; discarded on M3A1)

WEIGHT: 27,400 lbs. (M3); 28,500 lbs. (M3A1); 31,752 (M3A3)

LENGTH: 14'10"

WIDTH: 7'4"

HEIGHT: 8'3"

ARMOR: maximum 51mm; minimum 10mm

AMMUNITION STORAGE AND TYPE: 103 37mm (M3); 116 (M3A1); 174 (M3A3); 6,400–8,270 x .30-caliber

POWER PLANT: Continental W-670 7-cylinder gasoline or Guilberson T1020 9-cylinder radial diesel

MAXIMUM SPEED: 36 mph

RANGE: 70 miles

FORDING DEPTH: 2'7"

VERTICAL OBSTACLE: 2'

TRENCH CROSSING: 7'6"

SPECIAL CHARACTERISTICS (POS/NEG): The most widely used U.S. light tank of the war, the M3 went through a number of modifications that improved its capabilities in its basic reconnaissance role. Declared obsolete by the U.S. Army in July 1943, the M3 continued in service with other countries, including the Soviet

Union and Great Britain, until the end of the war and beyond.

SPECIAL MODELS: Flamethrower version removed the 37mm gun in favor of flame projector with range of 40–60 yards for use against Japanese bunkers in the Pacific Theater. It was also used as a command tank and appeared in antiaircraft and mine-clearing versions. Experimentations were also conducted to convert the M3 into a close-support vehicle as a 75mm howitzer motor carriage, but these proved unsuccessful.

UNITED STATES: M5 SERIES GENERAL STUART LIGHT
(STUART VI IN BRITISH SERVICE)
Courtesy of Art-Tech/Aerospace/M.A.R.S/TRH/Navy Historical.

SUMMARY: Light tank; successor to the M3 of the same name.

PRODUCTION DATES: February 1942–October 1944

NUMBER PRODUCED: 6,810

MANUFACTURER: Various Cadillac facilities, Massey-Harris, American Car & Foundry

CREW: 4

ARMAMENT: 37mm Gun M6 main gun; also 2 x .30 M1919A4 machine guns, plus 1 x antiaircraft machine gun on most vehicles

WEIGHT: 33,000 lbs. (M5); 33,907 lbs. (M5A1)

LENGTH: 14'3"

WIDTH: 7'4"

HEIGHT: 7'7"

ARMOR: maximum 67mm; minimum 12mm

AMMUNITION STORAGE AND TYPE: 133 x 37mm (M5); 147 x 37mm (M5A1); 6,250 (M5) and 6,750 (M5A1) x .30-caliber

POWER PLANT: 2 x Cadillac Twin V-8 220-hp gasoline engines

MAXIMUM SPEED: 36 mph

RANGE: 100 miles

FORDING DEPTH: 3'

VERTICAL OBSTACLE: 1'6"

TRENCH CROSSING: 5'4"

SPECIAL CHARACTERISTICS (POS/NEG): This follow-on to the M3 light tank utilized the same body design as its predecessor but is distinguishable by the stepped-up rear deck to accommodate the twin Cadillac engines. It was produced until the appearance of the M24 series. In July 1944 the U.S. Army reclassified the M5 as "substitute standard."

SPECIAL MODELS: command vehicle; psychological warfare vehicle (with loudspeaker and public address equipment); flamethrowers; rocket launchers; mortar carriers; and howitzer carriers. M5s and M5A1s were also fitted with welded-on prongs in front to remove hedgerows in Normandy.

UNITED STATES: M22 LOCUST LIGHT/AIRBORNE
Courtesy of National Archives.

SUMMARY: Light/airborne (or air-transportable) tank. The firm of Marmon-Herrington won a design competition with J. Walter Christie and General Motors Corporation for an air-transportable tank, delivering a prototype in the autumn of 1941. Following modifications, the tank was standardized in August 1944 as the Light Tank M22, nicknamed the "Locust" by the British. It resembles a smaller-version M4. The British took several hundred of the production run, and the 6th Airborne Division lifted them in General Aircraft Hamilcar gliders during the Rhine crossing operations of March 1945.

PRODUCTION DATES: April 1943–February 1944

NUMBER PRODUCED: 830

MANUFACTURER: –

CREW: 3 (commander, gunner, driver)

ARMAMENT: 1 x 37mm M6 main gun; 1 x .30-caliber M1919A4 machine gun

WEIGHT: 16,400 lbs.

LENGTH: 12'11"

WIDTH: 7'1"

HEIGHT: 6'1"

ARMOR: maximum 25mm; minimum 13mm

AMMUNITION STORAGE AND TYPE: 50 x 37mm; 2,500 x .30-caliber

POWER PLANT: Lycoming 0-435T six-cylinder 162-hp gasoline engine

MAXIMUM SPEED: 40 mph

RANGE: 135 miles

FORDING DEPTH: 3'2"

VERTICAL OBSTACLE: 1'.5"

TRENCH CROSSING: 5'5"

SPECIAL CHARACTERISTICS (POS/NEG): Developed as an airborne tank to be transportable inside or underneath a cargo aircraft, such as the C-54, to which it was attached by means of four brackets on the upper hull. The T22 could also be carried in the hold of a British Hamilcar glider. Of conventional, although compact, design, the T22 was too thinly armored to have widespread tactical application.

SPECIAL MODELS: –

UNITED STATES: M24 CHAFFEE LIGHT
Courtesy of Art-Tech/Aerospace/M.A.R.S/TRH/Navy Historical.

SUMMARY: Light tank successor to the M5 series, satisfying the need for a heavier main gun. Main U.S. light tank until 1953. Exported extensively abroad and upgunned, the Chaffee remained in service into the 1990s.

PRODUCTION DATES: March 1944–August 1945

NUMBER PRODUCED: 4,415

MANUFACTURER: Cadillac, Massey-Harris

CREW: 5 (commander, gunner, loader, driver, codriver/radio operator)

ARMAMENT: 75mm Gun M6 main gun with a concentric recoil system to save space; 1 x .50-caliber machine gun HB (heavy-barrel) M2 antiaircraft gun; 2 x .30-caliber M1919A4 machine guns (one coaxial)

WEIGHT: 40,500 lbs.

LENGTH: 16'5" (18'2" with gun forward)

WIDTH: 9'8"

HEIGHT: 8'2"

ARMOR: maximum 25mm; minimum 9mm

AMMUNITION STORAGE AND TYPE: 48 x 75mm; 440 x .50-caliber; 3,750 x .30-caliber

POWER PLANT: 2 x Cadillac 44T24 110-hp gasoline engines

MAXIMUM SPEED: 35 mph

RANGE: 100 miles

FORDING DEPTH: 3'4"

VERTICAL OBSTACLE: 3'

TRENCH CROSSING: 8'

SPECIAL CHARACTERISTICS (POS/NEG): Follow-on to the M5 series of light tanks, the M24 proved to be an excellent combination of simple design, reliability, speed, and armament. It served as the main U.S. light tank until 1953.

SPECIAL MODELS: The M24 was designed so that it might be used in a variety of configurations, all of which employed the same engine, power train, and suspension. It also appeared as gun, howitzer, and mortar motor carriages.

UNITED STATES: M2 AND M2A1 MEDIUM

Courtesy of Art-Tech/Aerospace/M.A.R.S/TRH/Navy Historical.

SUMMARY: U.S. medium tank entering service early in World War II in Europe. The improved M2A1 model, of which more than 1,000 were ordered, was rendered obsolete by the demonstrated superiority of the German PzKpfw III and PzKpfw IV, the latter with a 75mm gun, in the 1940 Battle for France. Work on the M2A1 was then halted, and it was superceded by the M3 series with a 75mm gun. The M2A1 was nonetheless an important development vehicle leading to the M4 Sherman medium tank.

PRODUCTION DATES: August 1939–August 1941

NUMBER PRODUCED: Approx. 16 (M2); 94 (M2A1)

MANUFACTURER: Rock Island Arsenal

CREW: 6 (commander, driver, four gunners)

ARMAMENT: 37mm M6 main gun; also 8 x .30-caliber M1919A4 machine guns

WEIGHT: 38,000 lbs. (M2); 47,040 lbs. (M2A1)

LENGTH: 17'6"

WIDTH: 8'6"

HEIGHT: 9'3"

ARMOR: maximum 25mm (M2); maximum 32mm (M2A1)

AMMUNITION STORAGE AND TYPE: 200 x 37mm; 12,250 x .30-caliber machine gun

POWER PLANT: Continental 350-hp (M2); Wright radial 9 cylinder 400-hp (M2A1)

MAXIMUM SPEED: 26 mph

RANGE: 130 miles

FORDING DEPTH: –

VERTICAL OBSTACLE: 2'

TRENCH CROSSING: 7'6"

SPECIAL CHARACTERISTICS (POS/NEG): The M2's hull was partly riveted and partly welded; its turret was welded.

SPECIAL MODELS: Test vehicle M2 with flamethrower mounted in place of the 37mm gun

UNITED STATES: M3 SERIES LEE AND GRANT MEDIUM
Courtesy of Art-Tech/Aerospace/M.A.R.S/TRH/Navy Historical.

SUMMARY: Medium Tank, hurriedly rushed from design into production because of the obsolescence of the M2. The British contracted for 1,000 of this tank, known as the Lee in their service.

PRODUCTION DATES: April 1941–December 1942

NUMBER PRODUCED: 6,258

MANUFACTURER: M3 (April 1941–August 1942; 4,924 total): Detroit Arsenal (3,243); American Locomotive (385); Baldwin (295); Pressed Steel (501, British contract); Pullman (500, British contract); M3A1 (February–August 1942): American Locomotive (300); M3A2 (from March 1942): Baldwin (12); M3A3 (March–December 1942): Baldwin (322); M3A4 (June–August 1942): Detroit Arsenal (109); M3A5 (January–November 1942): Baldwin (591)

CREW: 6 (commander, driver, two loaders, two gunners)

ARMAMENT: 75mm Gun M2 (later M3) main gun, hull mounted in right sponson; 37mm Gun M5 or M6 in turret; also 3 x .30-caliber M1919A4 machine guns (turret, coaxial with 37mm bow)

WEIGHT: 60,000 lbs. (M3A3, 63,000 lbs.; M3A4, 64,000 lbs.)

LENGTH: 18'6"

WIDTH: 8'11"

HEIGHT: 10'3"

ARMOR: maximum 37mm

AMMUNITION STORAGE AND TYPE: 46 x 75mm; 178 x 37mm; 9,200 x .30-caliber

POWER PLANT: Wright radial Continental R-975 340-hp (M3); 2 x General Motors 6-71 375-hp diesels (M3A3); Chrysler A57 Multibank 370-hp (M3A4)

MAXIMUM SPEED: 26 mph; 29 mph (M3A3)

RANGE: 120 miles (M3A3); 160 miles (M3A5)

FORDING DEPTH: 3'4" (3', M3A31)

VERTICAL OBSTACLE: 2'

TRENCH CROSSING: 6'3"

SPECIAL CHARACTERISTICS (POS/NEG): This interim design was rushed into service to secure a 75mm gun medium tank armament. Its riveted hull armor, corrected beginning in the M3A2, experienced "rivet popping" during battle.

SPECIAL MODELS: A wide variety of different models and types were produced. These included mine exploders, flamethrower tanks, tractors, armored recovery vehicles, and gun motor carriages.

UNITED STATES: M4 SERIES SHERMAN MEDIUM
Courtesy of Art-Tech/Aerospace/M.A.R.S/TRH/Navy Historical.

SUMMARY: The M4 medium was the most important and widely used Allied tank of the war. More than 40,000 M4s of all types (including the 76mm-gun version and 4,680 close infantry support M4 models with a 105mm howitzer) were produced, and they saw action on virtually all fighting fronts.

PRODUCTION DATES: July 1942–1946

NUMBER PRODUCED: 32,528; M4: 6,748; M4A1: 6,281; M4A2: 8,053; M4A3: 3,071; M4A4: 7,499; M4A5: 1; M4A6: 75

MANUFACTURER: Alco, Baldwin, Detroit Arsenal, Federal Machine, Fisher Body, Ford, Lima, Pacific Car, Pressed Steel Car, Pullman-Standard

CREW: 5 (commander, driver, gunner, loader, codriver/hull gunner)

ARMAMENT: 75mm M3 main gun; also 2 x .30-caliber M1919A4 machine guns; 1 x .50-caliber HB (heavy-barrel) M2 anti-aircraft machine gun

WEIGHT: 66,500 lbs. (M4A1); 69,000 lbs. (M4A2); 68,500 lbs. (M4A3)

LENGTH: 19'4" (average)

WIDTH: 8'7"

HEIGHT: 9'

ARMOR: maximum 75mm (turret); maximum 50mm (hull)

AMMUNITION STORAGE AND TYPE: 97 x 75mm; 300 x .50-caliber; 4,750 x .30-caliber

POWER PLANT: Continental R-975 air-cooled radial (M4); General Motors 6-71 diesel engines (M4A2); Caterpillar RD-1820 radial diesel (M4A6); Chrysler WC multibank (M4A4)

Maximum speed: 24–29 mph

Range: 100–150 miles, depending on type of engine

Fording depth: 3'

Vertical obstacle: 2'

Trench crossing: 7'5"

Special characteristics (pos/neg): Rugged, simple in design, easy to maintain and repair, and fast. The Sherman was an excellent tank with an incredibly long life; a number remained in service in some parts of the world for five decades after the end of World War II.

Special models: a wide range of special variants, including 105mm howitzer for close infantry support (1,641 manufactured); mine-clearing; engineer tank; mobile assault bridge; dozer; armored recovery vehicle; flamethrower tank; gun motor carriage; and rocket launcher

UNITED STATES: M4 SHERMAN (76MM GUN) MEDIUM
Courtesy of Art-Tech/Aerospace/M.A.R.S/TRH/Navy Historical.

SUMMARY: The most advanced M4 variant, it was upgraded with the far more powerful 76mm gun and was the last produced in World War II. It was widely exported after the war and continued in service with the Israeli Army at least into the 1990s.

PRODUCTION DATES: January 1944–June 1945

NUMBER PRODUCED: 8,380

M4A1: 3,396 (Pressed Steel, January 1944–June 1945)

M4A2: 1,614 (1,593, Grand Blanc, June–December 1944; 21, Pressed Steel, May–June 1945)

M4A3: 1,925 (1,400, Detroit Arsenal, February–July 1944; 525, Grand Blanc, September–December 1944)

M4A3 HVSS (horizontal volute spring suspension): 1,445 (Detroit Arsenal, August–December 1944)

MANUFACTURER: Pressed Steel, Grand Blanc, Detroit Arsenal

CREW: 5

ARMAMENT: 1 x 76mm gun M1, M1A1, M1A1C, or M1A2; also 2 x .30-caliber M1919A4 machine guns; 1 x .50-caliber HB M2 antiaircraft machine gun

WEIGHT: 71,100 lbs

LENGTH: 20'7" (24'8" with gun forward)

WIDTH: 8'10"

HEIGHT: 9'9"

ARMOR: maximum 100mm; minimum 15mm

AMMUNITION STORAGE AND TYPE: 71 x 76mm; 600 x .50-caliber; 6,250 x .30-caliber

POWER PLANT: Continental R-975 engine; Ford GAA V-8 400-hp or 500-hp gasoline engine

MAXIMUM SPEED: 26–29 mph, depending on engine

RANGE: 85–100 miles, depending on engine

FORDING DEPTH: 3'

VERTICAL OBSTACLE: 2'

TRENCH CROSSING: 7'6"

SPECIAL CHARACTERISTICS (POS/NEG): M4A3 model with the addition of horizontal volute spring suspension for easier and faster field maintenance and repair; also addition of a wider (23-inch) track for improved cross-country performance

SPECIAL MODELS: Israeli Sherman tanks, kept in operation from a wide variety of sources, were armed with a number of different weapons, including antiradiation missiles. The French upgraded a number of these with 75mm and 105mm main guns. Known as the M50 and M51 Super Shermans, these fought modified M4 Shermans of the Egyptian Army in 1973.

UNITED STATES: M26 (T26E3) PERSHING HEAVY

Courtesy of Art-Tech/Aerospace/M.A.R.S/TRH/Navy Historical.

SUMMARY: Long-delayed U.S. heavy tank; not shipped to Europe until January 1945.

PRODUCTION DATES: November 1944–June 1945

NUMBER PRODUCED: 1,436

MANUFACTURER: Grand Blanc Tank Arsenal (1,190), Detroit Tank Arsenal (246)

CREW: 5 (commander, driver, codriver, gunner, loader)

ARMAMENT: 90mm Gun M3 (T7) main gun; also 2 x .30-caliber M1919A4 machine guns and 1 x .50-caliber HB M2 antiaircraft machine gun

WEIGHT: 92,000 lbs.

LENGTH: 21'2" (28'10" with gun forward)

WIDTH: 11'6"

HEIGHT: 9'1"

ARMOR: maximum 102mm; minimum 13mm

AMMUNITION STORAGE AND TYPE: 70 x 90mm; 550 x .50-caliber; 5,000 x .30-caliber

POWER PLANT: Ford GAF V-8 500-hp gasoline engine

MAXIMUM SPEED: 20 mph

RANGE: 92 miles

FORDING DEPTH: 4'

VERTICAL OBSTACLE: 3'10"

TRENCH CROSSING: 8'6"

SPECIAL CHARACTERISTICS (POS/NEG): turret included commander's vision cupola and hatch for loader; two escape doors in hull floor

SPECIAL MODELS: heavy assault version; howitzer motor carriage

COLD WAR

CHINA: TYPE 59 MBT

Courtesy of Art-Tech/Aerospace/M.A.R.S/TRH/Navy Historical.

SUMMARY: Developed by NORINCO (China North Industries Corporation), this is the first Chinese-produced tank. A virtual copy of the Soviet T-54, it nonetheless introduced modifications over time, including a barrel fume extractor, night-vision equipment, and laser rangefinding. China exported the Type 59 to a number of countries. It remains in service today in China as well as Albania, Bangladesh, Cambodia, Democratic Republic of the Congo, North Korea, Iran, Iraq, Pakistan, Sudan, Tanzania, Vietnam, Zambia, and Zimbabwe.

PRODUCTION DATES: 1959–? (production complete)

NUMBER PRODUCED: –

MANUFACTURER: State factories

CREW: 4

ARMAMENT: 1 x 100mm (3.94-inch) smoothbore gun (the Type 59-II, from the early 1980s, mounts a 105mm rifled gun); 1 x 12.7mm machine gun (antiaircraft); 2 x 7.62mm machine gun (one coaxial)

WEIGHT: 79,344 lbs.

LENGTH: 29'6"

WIDTH: 10'8"

HEIGHT: 8'6"

ARMOR: maximum 203mm

AMMUNITION STORAGE AND TYPE: 34 x 100mm; 3,700 x machine-gun rounds

POWER PLANT: Type 12150L V-12 520-hp diesel engine

MAXIMUM SPEED: 40 mph

RANGE: 260 miles

FORDING DEPTH: 4'7"

VERTICAL OBSTACLE: 2'7"

TRENCH CROSSING: 8'10"

SPECIAL CHARACTERISTICS (POS/NEG): Upgrades by Western companies to some include passive night-vision equipment and improved fire-control systems. The T-59 can lay its own smokescreen by the injection of diesel fuel into the exhaust. To extend the range, the T-59 can mount additional fuel drums. No NBC equipment.

SPECIAL MODELS: armored recovery vehicle

CHINA: TYPE 69 MBT
Courtesy of Art-Tech/Aerospace/M.A.R.S/TRH/Navy Historical.

SUMMARY: Basically an improved Type 59 rather than a new design. Believed to have been developed in 1969 (hence the Western designation of Type 69), but its first public appearance was in 1982. The Type 69 initially utilized the same 100mm smoothbore gun of the Type 59, but the more accurate 100mm rifled gun replaced it in the Type 69 II. In addition there is a Type 79, which mounts a 105mm gun. The Type 69 had improved fire-control equipment and slightly more power than its predecessor Type 59.

PRODUCTION DATES: 1980

NUMBER PRODUCED: –

MANUFACTURER: State factories

CREW: 4

ARMAMENT: 1 x 100mm (4.72-inch) gun; 1 x 12.7mm machine gun (antiaircraft); 2 x 7.62mm machine guns (coaxial, bow)

WEIGHT: 80,887 lbs.

LENGTH: 20'6"

WIDTH: 10'9"

HEIGHT: 9'2"

ARMOR: not disclosed

AMMUNITION STORAGE AND TYPE: 44 x 100mm; 3,900 x machine-gun rounds

POWER PLANT: V-12 580-hp diesel engine

MAXIMUM SPEED: 31 mph

RANGE: 260 miles

FORDING DEPTH: 4'7"

VERTICAL OBSTACLE: 2'7"

TRENCH CROSSING: 8'10"

SPECIAL CHARACTERISTICS (POS/NEG): NBC; night-vision equipment; the T-69 can lay its own smoke by injecting diesel fuel into the exhaust pipe

SPECIAL MODELS: antiaircraft tanks; bridge-layers; engineer vehicle

CHINA: TYPE 80 MBT
Courtesy of Art-Tech/Aerospace/M.A.R.S/TRH/Navy Historical.

SUMMARY: The Type 80, which built on the Type 69, was a vastly improved tank. It introduced a brand-new hull, a more powerful engine, a computerized fire-control system, and a 105mm gun able to fire either Chinese or Western ammunition. It remains in service with China and Myanmar.

PRODUCTION DATES: 1985–

NUMBER PRODUCED: –

MANUFACTURER: State factories

CREW: 4

ARMAMENT: 1 x 105mm gun; 1 x 12.7mm machine gun (antiaircraft); 1 x 7.62mm machine gun (coaxial); 2 x 4 smoke grenade launchers

WEIGHT: 83,752 lbs.

LENGTH: 20'9"

WIDTH: 11'0"

HEIGHT: 7'5"

ARMOR: not disclosed, but steel/composite

AMMUNITION STORAGE AND TYPE: 44 x 105mm; 500 x 12.7mm; 2,750 x 7.62mm

POWER PLANT: Model VR36 V-12 730-hp diesel engine

MAXIMUM SPEED: 40 mph

RANGE: 267 miles

FORDING DEPTH: 4'7"

VERTICAL OBSTACLE: 2'7"

TRENCH CROSSING: 8'10"

SPECIAL CHARACTERISTICS (POS/NEG): NBC capability; standardized fire-control system; day/night sighting systems; may be fitted with a snorkel to allow deep fording

SPECIAL MODELS: –

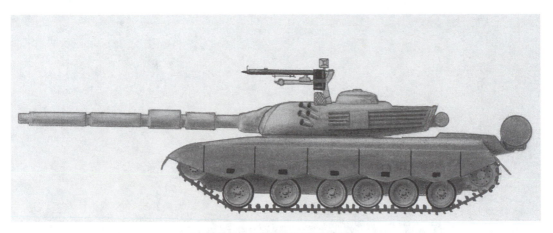

CHINA: TYPE 85-II MBT
Courtesy of Art-Tech/Aerospace/M.A.R.S/TRH/Navy Historical.

SUMMARY: The NORINCO Type 85-II is an improved version of the Type 80, with a new hull again but also a new turret and greatly enhanced armor protection. The turret is welded, rather than cast, and is lower in profile than the Type 80. The Type 85-II also introduced an automatic loader, resulting in the reduction of the crew size to only three. The Type 85-II is the first Chinese tank to be able to take under fire a moving target while it is itself under way. The tank is also coproduced in Pakistan as the Type 85-IIAP.

PRODUCTION DATES: 1989–

NUMBER PRODUCED: 600(?) for the People's Liberation Army

MANUFACTURER: Chinese state factories; Pakistan

CREW: 3

ARMAMENT: 1 x 125mm smoothbore (4.92-inch) gun; 1 x 12.7mm machine gun (antiaircraft); 1 x 7.62mm machine gun (coaxial); 2 x 6 smoke grenade launchers

WEIGHT: 99,364 lbs.

LENGTH: 20'9"

WIDTH: 11'4"

HEIGHT: 7'6"

ARMOR: not disclosed, but steel/laminate type

AMMUNITION STORAGE AND TYPE: 40 x 125mm; 300 (estimate) x 12.7mm; 2,000 x 7.62mm

POWER PLANT: V-12 supercharged 730-hp diesel engine

MAXIMUM SPEED: 35 mph

RANGE: 310 miles (estimate)

FORDING DEPTH: 4'7"

VERTICAL OBSTACLE: 2'7"

TRENCH CROSSING: 8'10"

SPECIAL CHARACTERISTICS (POS/NEG): NBC capability; night-vision equipment; computerized fire-control system with laser rangefinder

SPECIAL MODELS: –

FRANCE: CHAR AMX-13 LIGHT

Courtesy of Art-Tech/Aerospace/M.A.R.S/TRH/Navy Historical.

SUMMARY: Excellent, light, air-transportable tank with a reasonably powerful gun, developed by Atelier de Construction d'Issy-les-Moulineaux. The tank features an automatic loader with two six-round magazines, allowing the gunner to get off a dozen quick shots. A total of 3,400 AMX-13 tanks were purchased by two dozen nations, including Chile, Djibouti, Israel, Nepal, the Netherlands, Singapore, Switzerland, and Venezuela. A number of nations now offer upgrades for this tank, some of which remain in service.

PRODUCTION DATES: 1952–1980s

NUMBER PRODUCED: 7,700

MANUFACTURER: Initially Atelier de Construction Roanne, then transferred in the 1960s to Méchanique Creusot-Loire

CREW: 3 (commander, gunner, driver)

ARMAMENT: initially 1 x 75mm main gun (upgraded to 1 x 90mm with thermal sleeve; a model with 1 x 105mm main gun was developed for export purposes); 1 x 7.62mm machine gun (coaxial); 1 x 7.62mm machine gun (antiaircraft); 2 x 2 smoke grenade dischargers

WEIGHT: 33,000 lbs.

LENGTH: 16' excluding gun

WIDTH: 8'3"

HEIGHT: 7'7"

ARMOR: maximum 40mm; minimum 10mm

AMMUNITION STORAGE AND TYPE: 32 x 90mm; 3,600 x 7.62mm

POWER PLANT: SOFAM Model 8Gxb eight-cylinder 250-hp water-cooled gasoline engine

MAXIMUM SPEED: 37 mph

RANGE: 250 miles

FORDING DEPTH: 2'

VERTICAL OBSTACLE: 22'2"

TRENCH CROSSING: 5'3"

SPECIAL CHARACTERISTICS (POS/NEG): no NBC, no night-vision

SPECIAL MODELS: self-propelled gun; armored recovery vehicle; engineer vehicle; armor bridge-laying vehicle

FRANCE: CHAR AMX-30 MBT

Courtesy of Art-Tech/Aerospace/M.A.R.S/TRH/Navy Historical.

SUMMARY: Developed by the Atelier de Construction d'Issy-les-Moulineaux. Excellent design, with half of production going into export, including to Iraq, Saudi Arabia, and Spain. Consistently upgraded; the major change occurred in 1979 in the B2 Model with an advanced fire-control system, including laser rangefinder and thermal imaging. Armor is relatively thin for an MBT, the designers preferring speed and agility. The AMX-30 was superceded in French service by the Leclerc, but it remains in service with Cyprus, Greece, Saudi Arabia, Spain (where it has been produced under license), and Venezuela.

PRODUCTION DATES: 1966–

NUMBER PRODUCED: 3,500+ (1,250 for the French Army)

MANUFACTURER: GIAT Industries, Roanne, France

CREW: 4

ARMAMENT: 1 x 105mm CN-105-F1 main gun; 1 x 20mm cannon or 12.7mm machine gun (coaxial); 1 x 7.62 machine gun (antiaircraft); 2 x 2 smoke grenade dischargers

WEIGHT: 79,072 lbs.

LENGTH: 21'7" (31'1" with gun forward)

WIDTH: 10'2"

HEIGHT: 9'4"

ARMOR: 80mm maximum; 15mm minimum

AMMUNITION STORAGE AND TYPE: 47 x 105mm; 1,050 x 20mm; 2,050 x 7.62mm

POWER PLANT: Hispano-Suiza HS 110 12-cylinder 720-hp water-cooled supercharged multifuel engine

MAXIMUM SPEED: 40 mph

Range: 373 miles

Fording depth: 4'3"

Vertical obstacle: 3'1"

Trench crossing: 9'6"

Special characteristics (pos/neg): improved to include NBC and night-vision

Special models: numerous, including Pluton tactical nuclear missile launcher; self-propelled antiaircraft gun; armored recovery vehicle; engineer vehicle; bridge-layer; antimine flail tanks; chassis was used for a 155mm self-propelled gun

ISRAEL: MERKAVA MBT
Courtesy of Art-Tech/Aerospace/M.A.R.S/TRH/Navy Historical.

SUMMARY: First tank manufactured in Israel for the Israeli Defense Forces (previous weapons were modifications of British, French, or U.S. tanks). The Merkava series of tanks does, however, utilize some specialized foreign-manufactured parts. The Mark 1 appeared in 1978, the Mark 2 in 1983, and the current-production model Mark 3 in 1990. The Merkava is recognizable by the location of the turret slightly to the rear, its pointed front, and a large turret bustle to the rear.

PRODUCTION DATES: 1978–

NUMBER PRODUCED: –

MANUFACTURER: Israeli Ordnance Corps at Tel a Shomer

VARIANTS:

Mark 1: mounts 105mm gun

Mark 2: same armament but improved armor and fire-control system

Mark 3: mounts new 120mm smoothbore gun; more powerful 1,200-hp engine; new transmission, suspension, armor (both composite and explosive reactive all over the tank), and NBC system; threat warning systems; and improved fire-control system

CREW: 4

ARMAMENT: 1 x 105mm main gun (Mks 1 and 2) or 120mm smoothbore main gun (Mk 3); 3 x 7.62mm machine guns (one coaxial, two antiaircraft); 1 x 60mm mortar in turret roof

WEIGHT: 132,240 lbs. (Mk 1); 136,648 lbs. (Mk 3)

LENGTH: 24'4" (28'2" over gun); 24'11" (Mk 3)

WIDTH: 12'2"

HEIGHT: 8'8"

ARMOR: not disclosed

AMMUNITION STORAGE AND TYPE: 62 x 105mm (can be increased to 85 rounds); 10,000 x 7.62mm

POWER PLANT: General Dynamics Land Systems AVDS-1790-6A V-12 900-hp diesel engine (Mks 1 and 2); Teledyne ADVS 1790-9Ar V-12 turbo-charged 1,200-hp diesel engine (Mk 3).

MAXIMUM SPEED: 34 mph (Mks 1 and 2); 46 mph (Mk 3)

RANGE: 310 miles

FORDING DEPTH: 4'6" (6'6" with preparation)

VERTICAL OBSTACLE: 3'1"

TRENCH CROSSING: 9'10"

SPECIAL CHARACTERISTICS (POS/NEG): upper part of suspension protected by skirts with wavy bottom shape

SPECIAL MODELS: –

SOVIET UNION: PT-76 LIGHT
Courtesy of Art-Tech/Aerospace/M.A.R.S/TRH/Navy Historical.

SUMMARY: Easily identifiable by its pointed hull front and round turret with sloping sides and flat roof, the PT-76 was developed after World War II to lead amphibious assaults and for reconnaissance. It entered Soviet service in 1955 and was replaced by either MBTs or specialized versions of the BMP-1/BMP-2. The People's Republic of China produced an improved version with a new turret and 85mm gun. The PT-76 is probably the longest-lived AFV still in regular service. Obtained by the armies of Afghanistan, Benin, Cambodia, Congo, Croatia, Cuba, Guinea, Guinea-Bissau, Indonesia, Iraq, Madagascar, Nicaragua, North Korea, Laos, Uganda, Democratic Republic of Vietnam (North Vietnam), Yugoslavia, and Zambia, it continues in service in most of those countries today.

PRODUCTION DATES: 1952–1967

NUMBER PRODUCED: Approximately 7,000

MANUFACTURER: Soviet state factories

CREW: 3

ARMAMENT: 1 x 76.2mm main gun; 1 x 7.62mm machine gun (coaxial)

WEIGHT: 32,178 lbs.

LENGTH: 22'8"

WIDTH: 10'4"

HEIGHT: 7'3"

ARMOR: 17mm maximum; 5mm minimum

AMMUNITION STORAGE AND TYPE: 40 x 76.2mm; 1,000 x 7.62mm

POWER PLANT: Model V-6B inline-6 240-hp water-cooled diesel engine

MAXIMUM SPEED: 28 mph

RANGE: 174 miles (40 miles in water)

FORDING DEPTH: amphibious

VERTICAL OBSTACLE: 3'1"

TRENCH CROSSING: 9'2"

SPECIAL CHARACTERISTICS (POS/NEG): infrared for driver, but no NBC

SPECIAL MODELS: The PT-76 has been the platform for many variants.

SOVIET UNION: T-54/T-55 MBT
Courtesy of Art-Tech/Aerospace/M.A.R.S/TRH/Navy Historical.

SUMMARY: A further development of the mechanically unreliable T-44, itself derived from the T-34. The chief difference between the T-54 and T-55 is a more powerful diesel engine. With the largest production run of any tank in history, the T-54/T-55, even at the end of the Cold War, constituted 38 percent of the Soviet tank inventory and about 85 percent of the non-Soviet Warsaw Pact inventory. The T-54/T-55 has been exported to more than 35 different nations, and although obsolescent today, it remains in widespread use.

PRODUCTION DATES: 1948–1981

NUMBER PRODUCED: Approx. 95,000

MANUFACTURER: Soviet state factories

CREW: 4 (the bow gun reappeared but not the bow gunner; handling it is the responsibility of the driver)

ARMAMENT: 1 x 100mm main gun; 1 x 12.7mm DShK machine gun (antiaircraft); 2 x 7.62mm machine guns (bow, coaxial)

WEIGHT: 79,344 lbs.

LENGTH (EXCLUDING GUN): 21'2"

WIDTH: 10'9"

HEIGHT: 7'10"

ARMOR: maximum 203mm (steel)

AMMUNITION STORAGE AND TYPE: 34 x 100mm; 500 x 12.7mm; 3,000 x 7.62mm

POWER PLANT: V-2-5412-cylinder 520-hp diesel engine (T-54); V-55 580-hp diesel engine (T-55)

MAXIMUM SPEED: 30 mph (T-54); 31 mph (T-55)

RANGE: 250 miles

FORDING DEPTH: 4'7"

VERTICAL OBSTACLE: 2'7"

TRENCH CROSSING: 8'10"

SPECIAL CHARACTERISTICS (POS/NEG): Can be equipped with snorkel device to allow submerged fording. Long-range fuel tanks extend mileage to 450 miles. T-55A added infrared NBC system. In the late 1980s T-55s received new supercharged V-55U engines, improved fire-control system, laser rangefinders, and appliqué and explosive armor.

SPECIAL MODELS: many, including recovery vehicles; engineer vehicles; bridge-layers; mine-clearers

SOVIET UNION: T-62 MBT
Courtesy of Art-Tech/Aerospace/M.A.R.S/TRH/Navy Historical.

SUMMARY: Further development of the T-54/T-55 and the Soviet MBT of the 1960s and much of the 1970s. It still constituted about 24 percent of Soviet tanks at the end of the Cold War. Somewhat wider and longer than its predecessor, with more powerful gun and engine. Its new 115mm gun was the first smoothbore tank gun to enter service in the world.

PRODUCTION DATES: 1961–1975

NUMBER PRODUCED: Approx. 20,000, plus those produced abroad under license

MANUFACTURER: Soviet state factories; also produced in the People's Republic of China, Czechoslovakia, and North Korea

CREW: 4

ARMAMENT: 1 x 115mm (4.53-inch) U-5TS (2A20 Rapira 1) smoothbore main gun; 1 x 12.7mm machine gun (antiaircraft); 1 x 7.62mm machine gun (coaxial)

WEIGHT: 88,160 lbs.

LENGTH: 21'9"

WIDTH: 10'10"

HEIGHT: 7'10"

ARMOR: maximum 242mm (steel)

AMMUNITION STORAGE AND TYPE: 40 x 115mm; 300 x 12.7mm; 2,500 x 7.62mm

POWER PLANT: Model V-55-5 V-12 580-hp water-cooled diesel engine

MAXIMUM SPEED: 31 mph

RANGE: 280 miles

FORDING DEPTH: –

VERTICAL OBSTACLE: 2'7"

TRENCH CROSSING: 9'4"

SPECIAL CHARACTERISTICS (POS/NEG): NBC; night-vision, snorkel equipment. It lays its own smoke screen by injecting diesel fuel into the exhaust. An unditching beam is usually carried rear.

SPECIAL MODELS: command tank; armored recovery vehicle; flamethrower (OT-62, with flame gun fitted coaxially with the main gun)

SOVIET UNION: T-64 MBT

Courtesy of Art-Tech/Aerospace/M.A.R.S/TRH/Navy Historical.

SUMMARY: Soviet MBT introduced as the replacement to both the T-54/T-55 and T-62 series of tanks. A completely new design, although somewhat resembling the T-62 in its turret, it initially mounted a 115mm main gun; the T-62 was upgraded in its definitive T-62A version to the formidable 125mm smoothbore gun. The T-64B fires the AT-8 Songster anti-tank guided-missile with a range of 4,000 meters. Not exported because of its complexity, the T-64 was issued only to Soviet tank units.

PRODUCTION DATES: 1966–

NUMBER PRODUCED: Approx. 14,000

MANUFACTURER: Soviet state factories

CREW: 3 (commander, driver, gunner; the elimination of the loader was possible by the addition of an autoloader for the main gun)

ARMAMENT: 1 x 125mm (4,92-inch) D-81TM (2A46 Rapira) smoothbore main gun; 1 x 12.7mm NSVT machine gun (antiaircraft); 1 x 7.62 PKT machine gun (coaxial)

WEIGHT: 92,568 lbs.

LENGTH (EXCLUDING GUN): 24'3"

WIDTH: 11'11"

HEIGHT: 7'3"

ARMOR: maximum 200mm (laminate/steel/reactive)

AMMUNITION STORAGE AND TYPE: 36 x 125mm; 300 x 12.7mm; 1,250 x 7.62mm

POWER PLANT: 5DTF 5-cylinder opposed 750-hp diesel engine

MAXIMUM SPEED: 47 mph

RANGE: 250 miles

FORDING DEPTH: 5'11"

VERTICAL OBSTACLE: 2'7"

TRENCH CROSSING: 7'6"

SPECIAL CHARACTERISTICS (POS/NEG): numerous automotive and suspension problems

SPECIAL MODELS: T-64BV: explosive reactive armor; T-62: NBC, radiation detection system, night-vision, infrared

SOVIET UNION: T-72 MBT

Courtesy of Art-Tech/Aerospace/M.A.R.S/TRH/Navy Historical.

SUMMARY: Actually the second design for a tank to replace the T-62, the T-72 was somewhat less capable than the T-64 but far more reliable. The main gun has an automatic loader. Sold extensively abroad, the T-72 remains today the world's most widely deployed MBT. Despite this, the T-72 has had a less than impressive combat record.

PRODUCTION DATES: 1971

NUMBER PRODUCED: –

MANUFACTURER: Chelyabinsk, Nizhni-Tagil, Kirov; also produced under license in Czechoslovakia, India, Iran, Iraq, Poland, and the former Yugoslavia; Romania attempted to copy it

CREW: 3

ARMAMENT: 1 x 125mm D-81TM (4.92-inch) smoothbore gun with thermal sleeve and fume extractor; 1 x 12.7mm machine gun (antiaircraft); 1 x 7.62mm machine gun (coaxial); 2 x 6 turret-mounted smoke grenade launchers

WEIGHT: 100,282 lbs.

LENGTH: 22'10" excluding gun

WIDTH: 12'9"

HEIGHT: 7'3"

ARMOR: 280mm (composite/steel)

AMMUNITION STORAGE AND TYPE: 45 x 125mm; 300 x 12.7mm; 2,000 x 7.62mm

POWER PLANT: V-46 V-12 transverse-mount 840-hp diesel engine

MAXIMUM SPEED: 40 mph

RANGE: 250 miles (additional fuel tanks may be mounted)

FORDING DEPTH: 5'11" (16'4" with preparation)

VERTICAL OBSTACLE: 2'9"

TRENCH CROSSING: 9'2"

SPECIAL CHARACTERISTICS (POS/NEG): dozer blade mounted on tank nose; night-vision; infrared searchlight; laser rangefinder. During the 1991 Gulf War T-72s ignited easily when hit because of the lack of ammunition compartmentalization.

SPECIAL MODELS: command tank (T-72AK); armored recovery vehicle; bridge-layer; engineer vehicle

SOVIET UNION: T-80 MBT

Courtesy of Art-Tech/Aerospace/M.A.R.S/TRH/Navy Historical.

SUMMARY: Designed as an improved T-64, eliminating its chief operating problems, the T-80 has a gas turbine engine and the ability to fire AT-8 Songster antitank guided missile from its 125mm main gun. The most recent version, the T-80U, has a new and more efficient engine and can also fire the A-11 Sniper (9K120 Svir) laser-guided antitank missile. The tank is fitted with the same autoloader as the main gun on the T-72 and is rated at 6–8 rph. Issued to Soviet forces in the mid-1980s, it continues to be produced by both Russia and Ukraine and remains in their armed forces. It has been sold abroad to the People's Republic of China, Cyprus, Pakistan, and South Korea.

PRODUCTION DATES: 1980–

NUMBER PRODUCED: –

MANUFACTURER: Omsk, Russia; Kharkov, Ukraine

CREW: 3

ARMAMENT: 1 x DT-81M (2A46 Rapira) 125mm smoothbore main gun/missile launcher; 1 x 12.7mm machine gun (antiaircraft); 1 x 7.62mm machine gun (coaxial); smoke grenade dischargers (number depends on model)

WEIGHT: 93,670 lbs.

LENGTH: 24'3"

WIDTH: 11'2"

HEIGHT: 7'3"

ARMOR: Not disclosed but steel/composite/explosive reactive

AMMUNITION STORAGE AND TYPE: 36 x 125mm; 5 AT-8 Songster ATGW; 500 x 12.7mm; 1,250 x 7.62mm

POWER PLANT: GTD 1000 12-cylinder 1,100-hp gasoline turbine engine (T-80U has a more powerful and fuel-efficient GTD-1250 1,250-hp gasoline turbine engine)

MAXIMUM SPEED: 43.5 mph

RANGE: 208 miles

FORDING DEPTH: 5'11"

VERTICAL OBSTACLE: 3'3"

TRENCH CROSSING: 9'4"

SPECIAL CHARACTERISTICS (POS/NEG): NBC package included, along with infrared and thermal sights; first production model Soviet tank fitted with a ballistic computer and laser rangefinder

SPECIAL MODELS: command tank

SWEDEN: S-TANK (STRIDSVAGEN 103)
Courtesy of Art-Tech/Aerospace/M.A.R.S/TRH/Navy Historical.

SUMMARY: Sweden produced the Strv 103 S-Tank to replace its 300 Centurion tanks and other armored vehicles with a heavy tank of its own manufacture. One of the most interesting of modern tank designs, it incorporates a variety of technical innovations, perhaps the most dramatic of which is that it has no turret. This is in order to achieve the lowest possible silhouette for defensive purposes, to simplify manufacture, and to reduce the required crew to three men. The S-Tank mounts a dozer blade in front that enables it to dig itself in to reduce further its visible profile. The engine and transmission are also located in the front of the vehicle with the magazine and automatic loader at the rear. The tank also has two engines, a primary multifuel and a secondary gasoline turbine, the second assisting the first when extra power is required. Sweden replaced the S-Tank with the Leopard 2.

PRODUCTION DATES: 1966–1971

NUMBER PRODUCED: 300

MANUFACTURER: Borfors Weapons Systems

CREW: 3

ARMAMENT: 1 x 105mm (4.13-inch) gun; 2 x 7.62mm machine guns (coaxial), 1 x 7.62mm machine gun (antiaircraft)

WEIGHT: 87,500 lbs.

LENGTH: 27'7"

WIDTH: 11'10"

HEIGHT: 8'3"

ARMOR: Classified

AMMUNITION STORAGE AND TYPE: –

POWER PLANT: Rolls-Royce K60 multifuel 240-hp and Boeing 553 490-hp gasoline turbine

MAXIMUM SPEED: 31 mph

RANGE: 242 miles

FORDING DEPTH: 4'11"

VERTICAL OBSTACLE: 2'11"

TRENCH CROSSING: 7'6"

SPECIAL CHARACTERISTICS (POS/NEG): Very low silhouette, but entire tank must be turned to aim the main gun, which is impossible when the tank is dug in. Must be put in neutral steer to track moving targets. Automatic loader capable of 15 rounds per minute. No night-vision equipment. Notably, the S-Tank was not that much cheaper to build than other tanks, and no other country bought it or developed its concept further.

SPECIAL MODELS: Amphibious skirt on later models; Strv 103C may be fitted with mine-clearing rollers at the front of the hull

UNITED KINGDOM: CRUISER TANK, CENTURION (A41)
Courtesy of Art-Tech/Aerospace/M.A.R.S/TRH/Navy Historical.

SUMMARY: Last British cruiser tank of World War II, developed in an attempt to produce a universal all-purpose heavy cruiser tank. Although a half-dozen Centurions were sent to Europe for battle tests, they arrived too late (May 1945) to see combat. The Centurion I never entered production. The uparmored Centurion II was the production model. Ultimately it appeared in 13 basic models and many other variants and was still in service in 1969. It saw combat in Korea, the Middle East, Pakistan, southern Africa, and Vietnam. Some of the Royal Engineers variants served in the 1991 Gulf War. In all, some 2,500 Centurions were exported. It is in service in Austria (turrets only in static role), Israel, Jordan (where it is known as the Tariq), Singapore, South Africa (where it is known as the Olifant or Elephant), and Sweden. Most of those in service today are the 105mm gun varieties.

PRODUCTION DATES: 1945–1962

NUMBER PRODUCED: 4,423

MANUFACTURER: AEC, Leyland Motors, Royal Ordnance Factory Leeds, Vickers, Royal Ordnance Factory Woolwich

CREW: 4 (commander, driver, gunner, loader)

ARMAMENT: Mk I: 1 x 17-pounder (76.2mm) OQF main gun; 1 x 20mm Polsten cannon in turret front; Mk II (1945) substituted 1 x 7.92mm Besa machine gun in turret front; Mk III (1948) substituted a 20-pounder (84mm) gun for the 17-pounder main gun; Mark IV (never approved for service) was to mount a 95mm gun for close support; Marks V–XIII had a 105mm main gun.

WEIGHT: 107,520 lbs. (Mk II); 114,211 lbs. (Mk VII)

LENGTH: 25'2"

WIDTH: 11'

HEIGHT: 9'8"

ARMOR: maximum 152mm (Mk II); minimum 17mm

AMMUNITION STORAGE AND TYPE: 70 x 17-pounder or 64 x 105mm and 4,250 x 7.62mm (in Mk VII)

POWER PLANT: Rolls-Royce Meteor V-12 650-hp gasoline engine

MAXIMUM SPEED: 21.4 mph

RANGE: 60 miles

FORDING DEPTH: 4'9"

VERTICAL OBSTACLE: 3'

TRENCH CROSSING: 11'

SPECIAL CHARACTERISTICS (POS/NEG): armored side skirts and Horstmann suspension; partly cast turret and sloping glacis plate; first British tank with stabilizer for main gun; all-welded construction

SPECIAL MODELS: Centurion Armoured Fighting Vehicle Royal Engineers (AVRE), based on the Mk V, remained in service. Armed with a 165mm (6.5-inch) demolition gun, it served in the 1991 Gulf War. Israel also uses the Centurion chassis with turret removed as an APC, known as the Nakpadon.

UNITED KINGDOM: CHIEFTAIN MARK 5 MBT

Courtesy of Art-Tech/Aerospace/M.A.R.S/TRH/Navy Historical.

SUMMARY: Developed in the late 1950s, the Chieftain had a computerized fire-control system and stabilized main armament. It was phased out of British Army service in 1996. Some 450 Chieftains were exported to Iran, Kuwait, Jordan, and Oman.

PRODUCTION DATES: 1963–1970

NUMBER PRODUCED: Approx. 900

MANUFACTURER: Royal Ordnance Factory Leeds, Vickers

CREW: 4

ARMAMENT: 1 x 120mm (4.72-inch) L11A5 main gun; 1 x 12.7mm machine gun on commander's cupola that can be aimed and fired from inside the tank; 2 x 7.62mm machine guns (1 coaxial); 2 x 6 smoke grenade dischargers

WEIGHT: 121,200 lbs.

LENGTH: 24'7" (35'3" over gun)

WIDTH: 11'6"

HEIGHT: 9'6"

ARMOR: not disclosed

AMMUNITION STORAGE AND TYPE: 64 x 120mm; 300 x 12.7mm; 6,000 x 7.62mm

POWER PLANT: Leyland L60 vertically opposed 12-cylinder two-stroke 750-hp multifuel engine

MAXIMUM SPEED: 30 mph

RANGE: 310 miles

FORDING DEPTH: 3'6"

VERTICAL OBSTACLE: 3'

TRENCH CROSSING: 10'3"

SPECIAL CHARACTERISTICS (POS/NEG): NBC and night-vision systems

SPECIAL MODELS: armored engineer vehicle; armored recovery vehicle; armored vehicle–launched bridge; Chieftain can also be fitted with a dozer blade

UNITED KINGDOM: CHALLENGER I MBT
Courtesy of Art-Tech/Aerospace/M.A.R.S/TRH/Navy Historical.

SUMMARY: Further development of *Shir* tank ordered by Iran; the principal British MBT of the late 1980s and 1990s. Phased out of British service; some transferred to Jordan.

PRODUCTION DATES: 1983–1990

NUMBER PRODUCED: 420

MANUFACTURER: Vickers Defence Systems, Leeds

CREW: 4

ARMAMENT: 1 x 120mm (4.72-inch) L11A5 rifled main gun with thermal sleeve, fume extractor, and muzzle reference system; 3 x 7.62mm machine guns (1 coaxial, 1 antiaircraft); 2 x 5 smoke grenade dischargers (66mm)

WEIGHT: 136,648 lbs.

LENGTH: 26'3"

WIDTH: 11'7"

HEIGHT: 8'3"

ARMOR: Chobham; exact specifications not disclosed

AMMUNITION STORAGE AND TYPE: 64 x 120mm; 5,000 x 7.62mm

POWER PLANT: Perkins Condor V-12 1,200-hp diesel engine

MAXIMUM SPEED: 35 mph

RANGE: 240 miles

FORDING DEPTH: 3'6"

VERTICAL OBSTACLE: 3'

TRENCH CROSSING: 9'2"

SPECIAL CHARACTERISTICS (POS/NEG): NBC and night-vision systems; fire-control system with laser, thermal imaging equipment, and a ballistic computer (the Bar and Stroud Thermal Observation and Gunnery System)

SPECIAL MODELS: Challenger may be fitted with a dozer blade or mine-clearing system. As it is being phased out of British service some chassis are being modified for engineer and armored vehicle–launched bridge service roles fulfilled by similarly modified Chieftains.

UNITED STATES: M41 WALKER BULLDOG LIGHT

Courtesy of Art-Tech/Aerospace/M.A.R.S/TRH/Navy Historical.

SUMMARY: Developed to replace the M24 Chaffee light tank. The M41 was widely exported abroad, seeing service in the armies of Brazil, Chile, Denmark, the Dominican Republic, Guatemala, Taiwan, Thailand, and Uruguay. Bernardini of Brazil rebuilt more than 400 M41s for its armed services. Among modifications are improved engines and better armor, as well as bored-out 90mm guns.

PRODUCTION DATES: mid-1951–late 1950s

NUMBER PRODUCED: 5,500

MANUFACTURER: Cleveland

CREW: 4 (commander, driver, gunner, loader)

ARMAMENT: 1 x 76mm M32 main gun; also 1 x .30-caliber coaxial machine gun and 1 x .50-caliber antiaircraft machine gun

WEIGHT: 51,783 lbs.

LENGTH: 19'1" (26'11" with gun forward)

WIDTH: 10'6"

HEIGHT: 10'1"

ARMOR: maximum 32mm

AMMUNITION STORAGE AND TYPE: 57 x 76mm; 2,175 x .50-caliber; 5,000 x .30-caliber

POWER PLANT: Continental AOS-895-3 six-cylinder air-cooled 500-hp supercharged gasoline engine

MAXIMUM SPEED: 45 mph

RANGE: 100 miles

FORDING DEPTH: 3'4"

VERTICAL OBSTACLE: 2'4"

TRENCH CROSSING: 6'

SPECIAL CHARACTERISTICS (POS/NEG): optional night-vision

SPECIAL MODELS: –

UNITED STATES: M551 SHERIDAN LIGHT

Courtesy of Art-Tech/Aerospace/M.A.R.S/TRH/Navy Historical.

SUMMARY: The M551 was designed to counter the growing weight and armament of tanks with a heavily gunned, lighter weight vehicle capable of being airlifted and airdropped. It was designed primarily for fire support for airborne units and as a reconnaissance vehicle for armored cavalry units. The M551 experienced a wide variety of teething problems, including with its main gun and transmission. It served with U.S. units in the Vietnam War, where there were also other problems. Sheridans remained in service into the 1990s as a tank for airborne forces.

PRODUCTION DATES: 1966–

NUMBER PRODUCED: 1,562

MANUFACTURER: –

CREW: 4 (commander, driver, gunner, loader)

ARMAMENT: 1 x 152mm (5.98-inch) Shillelagh main gun/launcher; 1 x .50-caliber antiaircraft gun on the commander's cupola; 1 x 7.62mm coaxial machine gun; 8 smoke grenades

WEIGHT: 34,889 lbs.

LENGTH: 20'8"

WIDTH: 9'3"

HEIGHT: 7'5"

ARMOR: not disclosed; aluminum

AMMUNITION STORAGE AND TYPE: 10 x 152mm (5.98-inch) conventional rounds or Shillelagh missiles; 4,080 machine-gun rounds

POWER PLANT: Detroit diesel 6-V 53t turbocharged 300-hp engine

MAXIMUM SPEED: 43 mph

RANGE: 370 miles

FORDING DEPTH: –

VERTICAL OBSTACLE: 2'8"

TRENCH CROSSING: –

SPECIAL CHARACTERISTICS (POS/NEG): Combustible cartridge cases for the conventional 153mm HEAT round ignited when hit by spall during a penetration by an RPG

SPECIAL MODELS: M551s used as surrogate Soviet vehicles at the National Training Center

UNITED STATES: CADILLAC GAGE STINGRAY LIGHT
Courtesy of Art-Tech/Aerospace/M.A.R.S/TRH/Navy Historical.

SUMMARY: Designed by Textron Marine & Land Systems (previously Cadillac Gage Textron) as a private venture and candidate for the U.S. Army's aborted Mobile Gun System program. Prototype unveiled in 1984. Purchased by Thailand and currently in service with that country.

PRODUCTION DATES: 1988–1990

NUMBER PRODUCED: 106

MANUFACTURER: Textron Marine & Land Systems, New Orleans, Louisiana

CREW: 4

ARMAMENT: 1 x 105mm Royal Ordnance Nottingham Low Recoil Force rifled gun with stabilizer; 1 x .50-caliber machine gun (antiaircraft); 1 x 7.62mm coaxial machine gun; 2 x 4 smoke grenade dischargers

WEIGHT: 46,736 lbs.

LENGTH: 21'1" (30'5" over gun)

WIDTH: 8'19"

HEIGHT: 8'4"

ARMOR: not disclosed

AMMUNITION STORAGE AND TYPE: 32 x 105mm; 1,100 x .50-caliber; 2,400 x 7.62mm

POWER PLANT: Detroit Diesel Model 8V-92TA 535-hp engine

MAXIMUM SPEED: 43 mph

RANGE: 300 miles

FORDING DEPTH: 4'

VERTICAL OBSTACLE: 2'6"

TRENCH CROSSING: 5'7"

SPECIAL CHARACTERISTICS (POS/NEG): NBC; night-vision; fitted with a Marconi Digital Fire Control System for improved first-round hit probability

SPECIAL MODELS: –

UNITED STATES: M46 PATTON MEDIUM
Courtesy of Art-Tech/Aerospace/M.A.R.S/TRH/Navy Historical.

SUMMARY: The M46 medium, known both as the Pershing and unofficially as the Patton, was simply an overhauled version of the M26 Pershing. As the tanks came in for service they received the Continental V-12 engine and Allison cross-drive transmission.

PRODUCTION DATES: 1947

NUMBER PRODUCED: 360

MANUFACTURER: Detroit Arsenal

CREW: 5

ARMAMENT: 1 x 90mm M3A1 main gun; 1 x .50-caliber antiaircraft machine gun; 2 x .30-caliber machine gun (coaxial, bow)

WEIGHT: 96,976 lbs.

LENGTH: 23'

WIDTH: 11'5"

HEIGHT: 9'3"

ARMOR: maximum 102mm; minimum 13mm

AMMUNITION STORAGE AND TYPE: 70 x 90mm; 550 x .50-caliber; 5,000 x .30-caliber

POWER PLANT: Continental AV-1190-5 series V-12 air-cooled 704-hp gasoline engine

MAXIMUM SPEED: 30 mph

RANGE: 80 mph

FORDING DEPTH: 4'

VERTICAL OBSTACLE: 3'

TRENCH CROSSING: 8'6"

SPECIAL CHARACTERISTICS (POS/NEG): M46A1 version had new wiring, better brakes, and fire extinguishers, as well as upgraded engine

SPECIAL MODELS: small-turret flamethrower tank

UNITED STATES: M47 PATTON II MEDIUM

Courtesy of Art-Tech/Aerospace/M.A.R.S/TRH/Navy Historical.

SUMMARY: The Korean War caught the United States in the midst of developing a new medium tank, the T42. The M47, officially designated the Patton, was essentially the T42 turret and gun fitted to an M46 chassis. A surprisingly successful hybrid, it saw extensive service with the U.S. Army and still serves abroad in the armies of Iran, Pakistan, South Korea, and Serbia.

PRODUCTION DATES: 1952–

NUMBER PRODUCED: 8,676

MANUFACTURER: Alco, Detroit Arsenal

CREW: 5 (commander, driver, gunner, bow machine gunner, loader)

ARMAMENT: 1 x 90mm main gun; 1 x .50-caliber antiaircraft machine gun; 2 x 7.62mm machine guns (bow, coaxial)

WEIGHT: 101,759 lbs.

LENGTH: 23'3" (28' with gun forward)

WIDTH: 11'6"

HEIGHT: 10'11"

ARMOR: maximum 100mm (cast homogeneous steel)

AMMUNITION STORAGE AND TYPE: 71 x 90mm; 440 x .50-caliber; 4,125 x 7.62mm

POWER PLANT: Continental AV-1790-5B V-12 air-cooled 810-hp gasoline engine

MAXIMUM SPEED: 37 mph

RANGE: 100 miles

FORDING DEPTH: 1.219m

VERTICAL OBSTACLE: .914m

TRENCH CROSSING: 2.59m

SPECIAL CHARACTERISTICS (POS/NEG): Among the first tanks to have its gun equipped with a blast deflector and bore evacuator. It also had an optical rangefinder in the turret roof; some had an early ballistic computer.

SPECIAL MODELS: –

UNITED STATES: M48 PATTON MEDIUM MBT
Courtesy of Art-Tech/Aerospace/M.A.R.S/TRH/Navy Historical.

SUMMARY: Developed beginning in late 1950 with first prototype completed in December 1951. The tank entered service in 1953. Production ended with the introduction of the M60. Among nations receiving the M48 were West Germany, Greece, Iran, Israel, Jordan, Lebanon, Morocco, Norway, Pakistan, South Korea, Republic of Vietnam (South Vietnam), Taiwan, Thailand, Tunisia, and Turkey (where more than 2,000 remain in service).

PRODUCTION DATES: July 1952–1959

NUMBER PRODUCED: 11,703

MANUFACTURER: Alco Products, Chrysler Corporation, Ford Motor Company, Fisher Body Division of General Motors

VARIANTS:

M48: 90mm gun, commander's .50-caliber machine gun. M48A1: mild steel hull and turret, commander's gun mounted within the cupola

M48A2: incorporated fuel-injection engine, larger fuel tanks, and modified suspension

M48A3: rebuilt previous models with diesel engine

M48A4: fitted with M60 turret and Shillelagh gun/missile system

M48A5: more than 2,000 earlier M48s were rebuilt and fitted with the M68 105mm main gun developed from the British L7A1, also diesel engine

CREW: 4 (commander, driver, gunner, loader)

ARMAMENT: 1 x 90mm main gun (1 x 105mm gun on M48A5); 3 x 7.62mm (.30-caliber) machine guns (commander at cupola, loader, coaxial); 2 x 6 smoke grenade dischargers

WEIGHT: 103,969 lbs.

LENGTH: 22'7" (30'5" with gun forward)

WIDTH: 11'11"

HEIGHT: 10'2"

Armor: maximum 120mm

Ammunition storage and type: 54 x 105mm; 10,000 x 7.62mm

Power plant: General Dynamics Land Systems AVDS-1790-2D750-hp diesel engine

Maximum speed: 30 mph

Range: 300 miles

Fording depth: 4'

Vertical obstacle: 3'

Trench crossing: 8'6"

Special characteristics (pos/neg): No NBC equipment; does have night-vision equipment; may be fitted with dozer blade

Special models: mine-clearing tank; bridge-layer; M67A1 flamethrower tank (74)

UNITED STATES: M60 PATTON MBT
M60 Patton preparing to ford a water body. Note the raised exhaust aft.
Courtesy of Art-Tech/Aerospace/M.A.R.S/TRH/Navy Historical.

SUMMARY: Further development of M48 series. Welded hull with less of a boat shape than the M48. The M60 entered services in 1960. It was widely supplied to other nations, including Austria, Bahrain, Bosnia, Brazil, Egypt, Greece, Iran, Israel, Jordan, Morocco, Oman, Portugal, Saudi Arabia, Spain, Sudan, Taiwan, Thailand, Tunisia, Turkey, and Yemen. Israel received some 1,350 M60s, and Turkey retains some 1,000 in service.

PRODUCTION DATES: 1959–1987

NUMBER PRODUCED: 15,000+

MANUFACTURER: Chrysler Corporation (first production), Delaware Defense Plant; from 1960 at Detroit Tank Plant, operated by Chrysler, later by General Dynamics Land Systems

VARIANTS:

M60: Original model, same turret as M48 and similar to it, with searchlight over main gun

M60A1: new turret more pointed toward front with improved ballistic properties (production began in 1962); explosive reactive armor package installed on Marine Corps M60A1s used for the 1991 Persian Gulf War.

M60A2: new turret with the 152mm Shillelagh gun/launcher developed for M551 Sheridan but difficulties with this delayed its introduction into service until 1972. Only 200 M60A2s were built and they were then withdrawn from service, converted into bridge-layers and combat engineer vehicles

M60A3: principal production version, entering production in 1978. It mounted the 105mm gun but with thermal barrel jacket, new fire-control computer with laser rangefinder, infrared searchlight, and night-vision equipment. A number of M60A1s were brought up to M60A3 standard

CREW: 4

ARMAMENT: 1 x 105mm M68 main gun (developed from the British L7A1); 1 x 7.62mm machine gun (coaxial); 1 x 12.7mm machine gun (antiaircraft) in commander's cupola; 2 x 6 smoke grenade dischargers

WEIGHT: 115,868 lbs.

LENGTH: 22'10" (30'10" over gun)

WIDTH: 11'11"

HEIGHT: 10'9"

ARMOR: maximum 120mm (estimate)

AMMUNITION STORAGE AND TYPE: 63 x 105mm; 900 x 12.7mm; 5,950 x 7.62mm

POWER PLANT: General Dynamics Land Systems AVDS-1790-2C 12-cylinder 750-hp air-cooled diesel engine

MAXIMUM SPEED: 30 mph

RANGE: 300 miles

FORDING DEPTH: 4'

VERTICAL OBSTACLE: 3'

TRENCH CROSSING: 8'6"

SPECIAL CHARACTERISTICS (POS/NEG):

SPECIAL MODELS: combat engineer vehicle; bridge-layer; roller type mine-clearing devices and dozer blades may be fitted to hull front

UNITED STATES: M1 ABRAMS MBT

Courtesy of Art-Tech/Aerospace/M.A.R.S/TRH/Navy Historical.

SUMMARY: Current U.S. MBT. Also in service with Kuwait and Saudi Arabia.

PRODUCTION DATES: 1983–1995

NUMBER PRODUCED: 8,064

MANUFACTURER: General Dynamics Land Systems, Lima, Ohio, Tank Factory

VARIANTS:

M1: mounts 105mm gun

M1A1: (from August 1985) mounts 120mm gun, heavier armor, and an integrated NBC system and improved crew compartment; nearly 5,000 produced

M1A1HA: (1988) had heavy armor (HA), in which the composite armor incorporates almost impenetrable steel-encased depleted uranium, although this increased the weight dramatically

M1A2: most changes are internal, including a thermal viewer for the tank commander; a new navigation system; and the Inter-Vehicular Information System (IVIS), a datalink compatible with other advanced AFVs and helicopters; 77 delivered new, and 600 M1A1s upgraded to M1A2

CREW: 4

ARMAMENT: 1 x 105mm main gun or 1 x 120mm M256 main gun; 1 x 7.62mm machine gun (coaxial); 1 x 7.62mm machine gun (antiaircraft)

WEIGHT: 120,218 lbs. (M1A1); 145,552 lbs. (M1A1HA); 130,042 lbs. (M1A2)

LENGTH: 21'9" (32'3" over gun)

WIDTH: 12'

HEIGHT: 8'

ARMOR: not disclosed, but flat-plate composite Chobham-type composite armor on M1, improved protection armor on M1A1, and steel-encased depleted uranium armor on M1A1HA (heavy armor)

AMMUNITION STORAGE AND TYPE: 55 x 105mm; 1,000 x 12.7mm; 11,400 x 7.62mm

POWER PLANT: Textron Lycoming AGT1500
   1,500-hp gasoline turbine engine
MAXIMUM SPEED: 45 mph
RANGE: 311 miles
FORDING DEPTH: 4' (6'6" with preparation)
VERTICAL OBSTACLE: 4'1"
TRENCH CROSSING: 9'
SPECIAL CHARACTERISTICS (POS/NEG):
SPECIAL MODELS: mine-roller and plow can be attached to the front of the hull, widely used during the 1991 Gulf War

WEST GERMANY: LEOPARD 1 MBT
Courtesy of the Patton Museum.

SUMMARY: First tank produced by the Federal Republic of Germany. It flowed from a plan by France, Italy, and Germany to develop a common MBT, but each nation then went its own way. A reliable, effective tank, the Leopard was also built under license in Italy, and it was exported to a number of other countries, including Australia, Brazil, Canada, Chile, Greece, and Norway. Although withdrawn from German service in 1999, the Leopard 1 remains in service in the armies of a half-dozen states.

PRODUCTION DATES: 1965–1984

NUMBER PRODUCED: 2,437 for West Germany

MANUFACTURER: Krauss-Maffei

VARIANTS:
  1: initial production model
  1A1: improvements include additional turret armor
  1A2: improved turret and passive night-vision equipment for commander and driver
  1A3: new all-welded turret and enhanced armor protection
  1A4: all-welded turret and integrated fire-control system
  1A5: A4 with computerized fire-control system and thermal night-vision equipment

CREW: 4 (commander, driver, gunner, loader)

ARMAMENT: 1 x 105mm (4.13-inch) gun; 2 x 7.62mm machine gun (one coaxial and one antiaircraft); 2 x 4 smoke grenade launchers

WEIGHT: 89,041 lbs.

LENGTH: 23'2" (31'4" over gun)

WIDTH: 11'2"

HEIGHT: 9'1"

ARMOR: maximum 70mm

AMMUNITION STORAGE AND TYPE: 60 x 105mm; 5,000 x 7.62mm

POWER PLANT: MTU MB 828 Ca M-500 10-cylinder 830-hp multifuel engine

MAXIMUM SPEED: 40 mph

RANGE: 373 miles

FORDING DEPTH: 3'4" (7'4" with preparation; 13'1" with snorkel)

VERTICAL OBSTACLE: 3'9"

TRENCH CROSSING: 9'11"

SPECIAL CHARACTERISTICS (POS/NEG): NBC system

SPECIAL MODELS: armored recovery vehicle; armored vehicle–launched bridge; armor engineer vehicle; artillery observation vehicle; air-defense tank (with twin 35mm guns)

YUGOSLAVIA: M-84 MBT

Courtesy of Art-Tech/Aerospace/M.A.R.S/TRH/Navy Historical.

SUMMARY: The M-84 is essentially the Russian T-72 built under license in Yugoslavia with modifications, including laser rangefinder and ballistic computer, and night-vision equipment manufactured in Yugoslavia. Its V-12 diesel engine is also locally manufactured and an improvement over the Russian model.

PRODUCTION DATES: 1983–1992?

NUMBER PRODUCED: 600+

MANUFACTURER: Former Yugoslav state factories

CREW: 3

ARMAMENT: 1 x 125mm main gun; 1 x 7.62mm machine gun (coaxial), 1 x 12.7mm machine gun (antiaircraft)

WEIGHT: 92,568 lbs.

LENGTH: 22'6"

WIDTH: 11'9"

HEIGHT: 7'2"

ARMOR: not disclosed

AMMUNITION STORAGE AND TYPE: 45 x 125mm; 300 x 12.7mm; 2,000 x 7.62mm

POWER PLANT: V-12 turbocharged 840-hp diesel engine

MAXIMUM SPEED: 40 mph

RANGE: 435 miles

FORDING DEPTH: 5'11" (16'4" with preparation)

VERTICAL OBSTACLE: 2'9"

TRENCH CROSSING: 9'2"

SPECIAL CHARACTERISTICS (POS/NEG): night-vision; infrared

SPECIAL MODELS: laser rangefinder (T-72A)

CONTEMPORARY

CHINA: TYPE 90-II MBT

Courtesy of Art-Tech/Aerospace/M.A.R.S/TRH/Navy Historical.

SUMMARY: China's most modern tank in service; the follow-on design to the Type 85-II. Developed in conjunction with Pakistan, the tank is manufactured there as well and is known as the Khalid or MBT-2000. It may not be produced in large numbers, however, in favor of the newer Type 98 tank now reaching Chinese units.

PRODUCTION DATES: 1995(?)–

NUMBER PRODUCED: –

MANUFACTURER: Chinese state factories

CREW: 3

ARMAMENT: 1 x 125mm (4.92-inch) gun; 1 x 12.7mm machine gun (antiaircraft); 1 x 7.62mm machine gun (coaxial); 2 x 6 smoke grenade launchers

WEIGHT: 105,792 lbs.

LENGTH: 33'2"

WIDTH: 11'6"

HEIGHT: 7'9"

ARMOR: not disclosed, but steel/composite/reactive

AMMUNITION STORAGE AND TYPE: –

POWER PLANT: Perkins V-12 1,200-hp diesel engine

MAXIMUM SPEED: 39 mph

RANGE: 280 miles

FORDING DEPTH: –

VERTICAL OBSTACLE: –

TRENCH CROSSING: –

SPECIAL CHARACTERISTICS (POS/NEG): NBC; computerized fire-control system, night-vision equipment; laser rangefinder

SPECIAL MODELS: –

FRANCE: LECLERC MBT

Courtesy of Art-Tech/Aerospace/M.A.R.S/TRH/Navy Historical.

SUMMARY: Current MBT of the French Army and United Arab Emirates.

PRODUCTION DATES: 1991–

NUMBER PRODUCED: Approx. 400 for the French Army; 436 for the UAE

MANUFACTURER: Giat Industries

CREW: 3

ARMAMENT: 1 x 120mm main gun; 1 x 12.7mm machine gun (coaxial); 1 x 7.62 machine gun (antiaircraft); 2 x 9 smoke grenade launchers

WEIGHT: 124,526 lbs.

LENGTH: 22'5" (32'5" with gun forward)

WIDTH: 12'2"

HEIGHT: 8'4"

ARMOR: 80mm maximum; 15mm minimum

AMMUNITION STORAGE AND TYPE: 40 x 105mm (22 in autoloader; 18 in drum next to driver)

POWER PLANT: SACM V8X 1500 eight-cylinder 1,500-hp diesel engine

MAXIMUM SPEED: 45 mph

RANGE: 280 miles

FORDING DEPTH: 4'3"

VERTICAL OBSTACLE: 3'1"

TRENCH CROSSING: 9'6"

SPECIAL CHARACTERISTICS (POS/NEG): Has computer-based fire-control system, laser rangefinder, thermal imaging, stabilized sights, and battle-management system. An autoloader with 22 rounds, it is claimed, enables the gunner to engage six targets within 35 seconds. All French Leclercs from 2002 have the FINDERS battlefield management system providing a display of the battlefield with the identification of known friendly and hostile forces.

SPECIAL MODELS: armored recovery vehicle; engineer vehicle; bridge-layer; training vehicle

INDIA: ARJUN MBT

Courtesy of the Patton Museum.

SUMMARY: First indigenous Indian MBT, although utilizing some components from abroad.

PRODUCTION DATES: 1995–

NUMBER PRODUCED: –

MANUFACTURER: Avadi

CREW: 4

ARMAMENT: 1 x 120mm (4.72-inch) gun; 1 x 7.62mm machine gun (coaxial); 1 x 12.7mm machine gun (antiaircraft); 2 x 9 smoke grenade launchers

WEIGHT: 127,600 lbs.

LENGTH: 32'2" (with gun forward)

WIDTH: 10'5"

HEIGHT: 8'

ARMOR: not disclosed, but steel/composite type

AMMUNITION STORAGE AND TYPE: 39 x 120mm; 1,000 x 12.7mm; 3,000 x 7.62mm

POWER PLANT: MTU 838 Ka-501 12-cylinder 1,400-hp liquid-cooled diesel engine

MAXIMUM SPEED: 45 mph

RANGE: 250 miles

FORDING DEPTH: 3'3"

VERTICAL OBSTACLE: 3'7"

TRENCH CROSSING: 9'10"

SPECIAL CHARACTERISTICS (POS/NEG): NBC capability; standardized fire-control system; day/night sighting systems

SPECIAL MODELS: armored recovery vehicle; engineer vehicle; armor vehicle–launched bridge

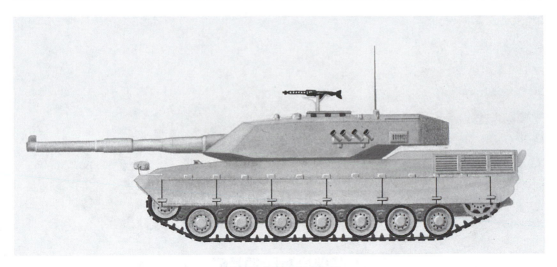

ITALY: ARIETE MBT

Courtesy of Art-Tech/Aerospace/M.A.R.S/TRH/Navy Historical.

SUMMARY: Italy's current MBT. The Ariete features a ballistic computer, day/night sight, and laser rangefinder. It also has an electric gun-control and stabilization system, along with blowout panels in the turret roof to release any internal explosion upward and away from the crew. A Mark 2 is now under development.

PRODUCTION DATES: 1995–

NUMBER PRODUCED: 200

MANUFACTURER: OTOBREDA, La Spezia, Italy

CREW: 4 (commander, gunner, loader, driver)

ARMAMENT: 1 x 120mm (4.72-inch) OTO-BREDA smoothbore gun; 1 x 12.7mm machine gun (antiaircraft); 2 x 7.62mm machine guns (coaxial); 4 smoke grenade launchers

WEIGHT: 119,016 lbs.

LENGTH: 24'11" (31'7" with gun forward)

WIDTH: 11'10"

HEIGHT: 8'2"

ARMOR: not disclosed

AMMUNITION STORAGE AND TYPE: 40 x 120mm; 2,400 x 7.62mm

POWER PLANT: IVECO V-12 MTCA turbocharged 12-cylinder 1,300-hp diesel engine.

MAXIMUM SPEED: 40 mph

RANGE: 342 miles

FORDING DEPTH: 3'11" (6'10" with preparation)

VERTICAL OBSTACLE: 3'3"

TRENCH CROSSING: 9'10"

SPECIAL CHARACTERISTICS (POS/NEG): Galileo computerized fire-control system, including daylight sights, laser rangefinder

SPECIAL MODELS: –

JAPAN: TYPE 90 MBT

Courtesy of Art-Tech/Aerospace/M.A.R.S/TRH/Navy Historical.

SUMMARY: Latest Japanese MBT; a completely new design and one of the world's finest tanks. Somewhat resembling the German Leopard 2 and U.S. M1 Abrams, the Type 90's surfaces are almost all vertical or horizontal. It utilizes the German-designed 120mm main gun. It also has an automatic loader, allowing a crew of only three.

PRODUCTION DATES: 1991–

NUMBER PRODUCED: Approx. 200 to date

MANUFACTURER: Mitsubishi Heavy Industries

CREW: 3

ARMAMENT: 1 x 120mm (4.72-inch) German Rheinmetall smoothbore gun; 1 x 12.7mm machine gun (antiaircraft); 1 x 7.62mm machine gun (coaxial); 2 x 3 smoke grenade launchers

WEIGHT: 110,200 lbs.

LENGTH: 24'7"

WIDTH: 11'3"

HEIGHT: 7'8"

ARMOR: not disclosed, but composite

AMMUNITION STORAGE AND TYPE: Information not available, although the automatic loader operates from a ready rack in the turret bustle containing 16 rounds.

POWER PLANT: Mitsubishi 10ZG 10-cylinder 1,500-hp water-cooled diesel engine

MAXIMUM SPEED: 43 mph

RANGE: 250 miles

FORDING DEPTH: 6'6"

VERTICAL OBSTACLE: 3'3"

TRENCH CROSSING: 8'10"

SPECIAL CHARACTERISTICS (POS/NEG): computerized fire-control system; laser rangefinder; day/night sighting systems, including thermal imaging; full NBC protection; laser detector mounted on turret roof

SPECIAL MODELS: dozer blade

RUSSIA: T-90 MBT

Courtesy of Art-Tech/Aerospace/M.A.R.S/TRH/Navy Historical.

SUMMARY: Further development of the T-72, although it incorporates some subsystems of the T-80. Basically it is the T-72 with greater mobility, better fire-control systems, and improved armor protection.

PRODUCTION DATES: 1994–

NUMBER PRODUCED: –

MANUFACTURER: Nizhnyi, Tagli, Russia

CREW: 3

ARMAMENT: 1 x 125mm D-81TM (2A46 Rapira 3) smoothbore gun/missile launcher; 1 x 12.7mm machine gun (antiaircraft); 1 x 7.62mm machine gun (coaxial); 2 x 6 smoke grenade launchers.

WEIGHT: 102,486 lbs.

LENGTH: 22'6"

WIDTH: 11'1"

HEIGHT: 7'4"

ARMOR: not disclosed, but steel/composite/appliqué explosive-reactive

AMMUNITION STORAGE AND TYPE: 43 x 125mm; 300 x 12.7mm; 2,000 x 7.62mm

POWER PLANT: Model V-84MS 12-cylinder 840-hp multifuel diesel engine

MAXIMUM SPEED: 40 mph

RANGE: 400 miles

FORDING DEPTH: 5'11" (16'4" with preparation)

VERTICAL OBSTACLE: 2'9"

TRENCH CROSSING: 9'2"

SPECIAL CHARACTERISTICS (POS/NEG): NBC; night-vision; Shotra TShU-1-7 optronic countermeasures system to disrupt laser targeting antitank missile guidance

SPECIAL MODELS: command tank; export models (T-90E/T-90S)

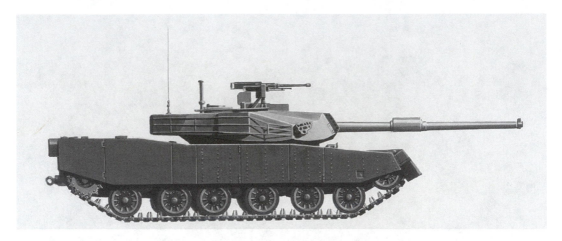

SOUTH KOREA: TYPE 88 K1 MBT

Courtesy of Art-Tech/Aerospace/M.A.R.S/TRH/Navy Historical.

SUMMARY: Developed by General Dynamics Land Systems Division to South Korean requirements, the Type 88 first underwent testing in the United States in 1983, entered production in 1986, and was formally introduced in 1987. Strongly resembling the General Dynamics–designed M1 Abrams in external appearance and mounting its same 105mm gun, the Type 88 has a diesel engine and ceramic-type armor on the front surfaces as well as a hybrid torsion-bar/hydropneumatic suspension system. The improved K1A1, which entered production in 2000, has a 120mm main gun.

PRODUCTION DATES: 1986–

NUMBER PRODUCED: 1,000(?)

MANUFACTURER: Hyundai

CREW: 4

ARMAMENT: 1 x 105mm (4.13-inch) gun (1 x 120mm/4.72-inch on K1A1); 1 x 12.7mm machine gun (antiaircraft); 2 x 7.62mm machine guns (coaxial, antiaircraft); 2 x 6 smoke grenade launchers

WEIGHT: 112,624 lbs.

LENGTH: 31'8"

WIDTH: 11'8"

HEIGHT: 7'5"

ARMOR: unknown but of laminate/steel

AMMUNITION STORAGE AND TYPE: 47 x 105mm; 2,000 x 12.7mm; and 8,800 x 7.62mm

POWER PLANT: MTU MB 871 Ka-5011, 200-hp diesel engine

MAXIMUM SPEED: 40 mph

RANGE: 272 miles

FORDING DEPTH: 3'11" (7'2" with preparation)

VERTICAL OBSTACLE: 3'3"

TRENCH CROSSING: 8'11"

SPECIAL CHARACTERISTICS (POS/NEG): computerized fire-control system with stabilized sight for tank commander; digital computer; day/night sights; laser rangefinder

SPECIAL MODELS: armored recovery vehicle; bridge-layer (developed by Vickers Defence Systems of the UK), which will span nearly 72 feet

UKRAINE: T-84 MBT

Courtesy of Art-Tech/Aerospace/M.A.R.S/TRH/Navy Historical.

SUMMARY: Following the demise of the Soviet Union, Ukraine inherited a significant portion of Soviet tank production facilities. In 1993 the Malyshev facility that had previously built the T-64 and T-80 began development of a new MBT. Based on the T-80 and designated the T-84, it used Ukrainian components. The Ukrainians replaced the Russian cast steel turret with a Ukrainian-designed welded turret. In service with the Ukraine Army, the T-84 has also been exported to Pakistan. A variant, the T-84-120 Oplot, fitted with the NATO standard 120mm gun, has been developed in cooperation with Turkey.

PRODUCTION DATES: 1995–

NUMBER PRODUCED: –

MANUFACTURER: Malyshev, Kiev, Ukraine

CREW: 3

ARMAMENT: 1 x 125mm (4.92-inch) Ukrainian-built smoothbore gun with automatic loader; 1 x 12.7mm machine gun (antiaircraft); 1 x 7.62mm machine gun (coaxial); 2 x 6 smoke grenade launchers

WEIGHT: 101,384 lbs.

LENGTH: 23'3"

WIDTH: 10'3"

HEIGHT: 7'3"

ARMOR: Unknown, but explosive reactive type fitted to hull front and turret front and sides

AMMUNITION STORAGE AND TYPE: 43 x 125mm; 450 x 12.7mm; 1,250 x 7.62mm

POWER PLANT: 6TD-2 six-cylinder 1,200-hp diesel engine

MAXIMUM SPEED: 40 mph

RANGE: 335 miles

FORDING DEPTH: 5'11" (16'4" with preparation)

VERTICAL OBSTACLE: 3'3"

TRENCH CROSSING: 9'4"

SPECIAL CHARACTERISTICS (POS/NEG): computerized fire-control system; day/night sighting systems

SPECIAL MODELS: armored recovery vehicle

UNITED KINGDOM: CHALLENGER II MBT

Courtesy of Art-Tech/Aerospace/M.A.R.S/TRH/Navy Historical.

SUMMARY: Similar to Challenger I, but with entirely different turret to take advantage of stealth technology for smaller radar signature. Developed by Vickers entirely as a private venture beginning in 1986 and ordered by the British Ministry of Defence in 1991. Challenger IIE was introduced in 1997, employing a new engine and improved fire-control system.

PRODUCTION DATES: 1992–

NUMBER PRODUCED: 386, plus 22 driver training tanks

MANUFACTURER: Vickers Defence Systems, Leeds

CREW: 4

ARMAMENT: 1 x 120mm (4.72-inch) L30A1 rifled main gun, chromed for longer service life; 2 x 7.62mm machine guns (1 coaxial, 1 antiaircraft); 2 x 5 smoke grenade dischargers (66mm)

WEIGHT: 137,750 lbs.

LENGTH: 27'4"

WIDTH: 11'6"

HEIGHT: 8'2"

ARMOR: exact specifications not disclosed; Chobham/steel

AMMUNITION STORAGE AND TYPE: 50 x 120mm; 4,000 x 7.62mm

POWER PLANT: Perkins Condor CV-12 TCA diesel V-12 1,200-hp diesel engine (IIE: MTU MT883 Ka501 1,500-hp diesel engine)

MAXIMUM SPEED: 37 mph (IIE, 45 mph)

RANGE: 280 miles (IIE, 340 miles)

FORDING DEPTH: 3'6"

VERTICAL OBSTACLE: 3'

TRENCH CROSSING: 9'2"

SPECIAL CHARACTERISTICS (POS/NEG): fire-control computers and thermal imaging system

SPECIAL MODELS: dozer blade or mine-clearing system

WEST GERMANY: LEOPARD 2 MBT
Courtesy of Art-Tech/Aerospace/M.A.R.S/TRH/Navy Historical.

SUMMARY: Developed beginning in 1970 with the collapse of the international MBT-70 tank program, the Leopard 2 replaced the Leopard 1 as West Germany's MBT. It incorporates ballistic computer, laser rangefinder, stabilized gunsights, and thermal ranging cameras for engaging targets in poor light conditions. A number of other nations, including those purchasing the Leopard 1, adopted the Leopard 2. The Netherlands has purchased 445, while Switzerland, Sweden, and Spain all have produced models of the Leopard 2 under license.

PRODUCTION DATES: 1977–Present

NUMBER PRODUCED: 2,125 for the German Army (delivered by 1992), 445 for the Netherlands (114 of which were later sold to Austria), 35 for Switzerland (with an additional 345 built under license in that country), and 21 for Denmark, along with those produced under license by Spain and Sweden

MANUFACTURER: Krauss-Mauffei Wegmann and MaK in Germany; Federal Construction Works, Switzerland

VARIANTS : Among upgrades is additional armor over frontal arc (Leopard 2s of Germany and the Netherlands have been upgraded to this standard; those being built in Spain, Switzerland, and Sweden are being built to this standard). Leopards produced by Sweden have additional exterior armor protection as well as a spall liner to provide protection for the crew from "scabs" of armor produced when the tank is hit with a nonpenetrating projectile.

CREW: 4 (commander, gunner, loader, driver)

ARMAMENT: 1 x 120mm (4.72-inch) Rheinmetall smooth-bore gun; 2 x 7.62mm machine gun (coaxial, antiaircraft); 2 x 8 smoke grenade launchers

WEIGHT: 121,551 lbs. (Swedish variant, 136,648 lbs.)

LENGTH: 25'5" (31'7" over gun)

WIDTH: 12'1"

HEIGHT: 8'1"

ARMOR: not disclosed, but Chobham-type

AMMUNITION STORAGE AND TYPE: 42 x 120mm; 4,750 x 7.62mm

POWER PLANT: MTU MB 873 Ka-501 four-stroke 12-cylinder 1,500-hp multifuel exhaust turbocharged liquid-cooled diesel engine

MAXIMUM SPEED: 45 mph

RANGE: 310 miles

FORDING DEPTH: 3'4" (7'4" with preparation; 13'1" with snorkel)

VERTICAL OBSTACLE: 3'7"

TRENCH CROSSING: 9'10"

SPECIAL CHARACTERISTICS (POS/NEG):

SPECIAL MODELS: armored recovery vehicle; driver training vehicle

GLOSSARY OF TERMS FOR TANKS
AND THEIR ORDNANCE

"A" vehicle: UK descriptor for all armored vehicles, including tanks, self-propelled guns, and armored-personnel carriers

AA: antiaircraft

AAMG: antiaircraft machine gun

AAV: amphibious assault vehicle [tracked]

ack-ack: British term for antiaircraft fire

ACP: armored command post

active armor: A type of armor designed to defeat dynamically incoming warheads; embedded sensors in explosive cassettes detect an incoming shell and explode outwards to defeat the effects of the incoming warhead. Also known as explosive reactive armor (ERA).

ACV: armored combat vehicle

AEV: armored engineer vehicle

AFD (automatic feeding device): mechanism designed to feed ammunition into the breech of the gun automatically

aft: rear of tank

AFV (armored fighting vehicle): term used for military vehicles with both armor protection and armament

AGLS: automatic gun-laying system

AIFV: armored infantry fighting vehicle

AMC (*Automitrailleuse de découverte*): French, mobile machine gun, scouting; the French term for armored car

AML (*Automitrailleuse léger*): French, light mobile machine gun; the French term for light armored car

ammunition: complete unit of fire, including primer, case, propellant, and projectile

AMR (*Automitrailleuse de reconnaissance*): French, mobile reconnaissance machine gun; the French term for scout car

antenna: radio communications aerial, usually mounted on the top of the vehicle

AP (armor-piercing): A type of ammunition that is specifically designed to penetrate and destroy armored targets. Usually this refers to AP shot, or solid shot fired at high velocity relying solely on kinetic energy to penetrate. An AP shell is hollow with a charge and a delayed-action fuse; it relies on kinetic energy to penetrate, when the shell then explodes and causes damage within the tank.

APAM (antipersonnel, antimateriel): ammunition designed to be used against "soft" targets

APC: armored personnel carrier

APC (armor-piercing capped): ammunition consisting of solid AP shot with penetrative cap on nose for effectiveness against sloping armor

APCBC (armor-piercing capped, ballistic capped): ammunition consisting of solid AP shot with a thin metal ballistic cap placed over the penetrative cap to enhance flight characteristics

APCNR (armor-piercing composite, nonrigid; also known as "squeeze-bore"): ammunition that resembles APCR but is compressed when fired down a gun tube with a tapering bore, and the ratio of weight to diameter is more favorable to flight after the shot leaves the bore

APCR (armor-piercing composite, rigid): round originally consisting of tungsten carbide core, later replaced by depleted uranium, with a light alloy casing, resulting in a light projectile capable of high velocity

APDS (armor-piercing discarding sabot): type of AP ammunition with a subprojectile containing a heavy penetrative core smaller than the bore and surrounded by a sabot (French for "shoe"). When an APDS round is fired, the sabot breaks up in the bore but drops away once the projectile clears the muzzle. APDS subprojectiles maintain their velocity better than standard full-bore projectiles and are designed for use with rifled guns.

APDS-T (armor-piercing discarding sabot tracer): same as the APDS but with a tracer compound in the base of the round so that the gunner can follow the flight of the shot

APFSDS (armor-piercing fin-stabilized discarding sabot): similar to APDS, but the projectile is stabilized by fins rather than by spinning and is designed for use in smoothbore guns

APHE (armor-piercing high-explosive): armor-piercing projectile with small high-explosive charge designed to detonate once the round has penetrated an enemy tank

API (armor-piercing incendiary): AP projectile with an incendiary compound designed to start a fire once target has been penetrated

armor: generic term for armored fighting vehicles; also refers to protection on a vehicle against enemy fire: first iron, then hardened steel, now a series of layers of metals, composites, and organic fibers

armored car: wheeled vehicle protected by armor, usually employed for reconnaissance purposes

ARV (armored recovery vehicle): a vehicle, usually with a tank chassis, used to recover crippled tanks from the battlefield

AT (antitank): the term applied to guns and other weapons used to destroy enemy AFVs

ATGM/ATGW: antitank guided missile/guided weapon

ATM: antitank mine, designed for specific use against tanks

Ausf (German *Ausführung,* or "batch"): the term referring to a production run of a particular type of tank

autoloader: mechanical system that automatically feeds ammunition into the breech of the main gun, doing away with the need for a separate crewman (loader) in some tanks

automatic: term applied to a weapon that continues to fire as long as the triggering device is activated

AVLB (armored vehicle-launched bridge): device for crossing obstacles, laid by a special vehicle, usually a tank chassis

AVRE (Armoured Vehicle, Royal Engineers): UK specialized assault engineer tank

"B" Vehicle: UK descriptor for all unarmored ("soft") vehicles, including trucks, cars, and tractors

B-40: The Soviet/Russian term for a shaped charge projectile fired from RPG2 and RPG7 antitank weapons; used by the People's Army of Vietnam (North Vietnam) forces against U.S. and South Vietnamese forces during the Vietnam War

ballistic shaping: referring to the shaping of a tank hull/turret with the aim of deflecting shot that is fired at it.

ballistics: the science of projectiles and their course ("interior" refers to inside the gun; "exterior" is the path to the target; "terminal" is point of impact)

barbette: open gun mounting, although usually providing both front and side crew protection; most often employed for SP guns and antiaircraft guns on tank chassis

basket: framework suspended below the turret, which rotates with the turret so that the crew does not have to change positions

BB (base-bleed): long-range shell in which air passes through slots at the base to reduce drag

beam-riding: system in which missile fires a laser or radar beam to the target

beehive round: antipersonnel rounds developed for the U.S. 105mm tank gun and the 152mm gun-launcher on the Sheridan. The Beehive was also available for the 105mm howitzer, its original purpose. Used extensively in the Vietnam War, it contained 8,500 flechettes (darts).

Beutepanzerkampfwagen: German term used during World War I and World War II for "booty tanks," those captured from the enemy and then used by the Germans themselves

Blindé: French term for "armored" (as in *Divisions blindés,* or "armored divisions")

blitzkrieg (literally, "lightning war"): The German way of war in World War II, consisting of rapid offensive action by combined arms teams centered on tanks

BMP (*Boevaia mashina Pekhoti*): the Soviet/Russian term for "combat vehicle infantry" and the world's first infantry fighting vehicle, introduced by the Soviet Union and in service around the world

bore: interior of any firearm, forward of the chamber

bore evacuator: U.S. term for a device around the barrel designed to evacuate all gases left behind in the bore of the gun after firing and before the breech is opened for a new round. It consists of a hollow sleeve around the barrel one-half to two-thirds of the way along its length and connected to the bore by holes sloping backward into the sleeve from the direction of the muzzle. When the round is fired the gases behind the projectile move through these holes and fill the sleeve. After the projectile leaves the muzzle and the pressure in the bore drops, the gasses in the extractor seep back into the bore; because the holes are sloped forward, this sets up a current toward the muzzle, expelling the remaining fumes. The British term is "fume extractor."

bore sighting: method of sighting along the axis of the bore; see "muzzle reference"

BT (*Bystrochodny tankovy*): the Soviet/Russian term for "fast tank"

BTR (Bronirovanniy Transportnaya Rozposnania): the Soviet/Russian term for an eight-wheeled armored personnel carrier

bullet: projectile fired by small arms and machine guns; usually solid; can also be filled with incendiary or tracer or both

bustle: overhang at the rear of the turret

CA (*Carro armato*): literally, "armored chariot"; the Italian term for "armored vehicle/tank"

cal.: caliber (diameter of bore), expressed in both inches and millimeters

caliber: The internal diameter of a gun, or diameter of a bullet, or shell, expressed in inches (.50-caliber = 1/2 inch), centimeters (usually for larger guns), or millimeters (smaller guns, such as a 7.62mm machine gun). "Caliber" also refers to the length of a gun barrel, be it artillery piece or a tank or ship gun. Thus a 3-inch/.50-caliber naval gun is 50 x 3 inches or 150 inches in length.

canister: see case shot

carrier: wheeled or tracked armored vehicle for transporting supplies or men on the battlefield

cartridge: unit of ammunition, consisting of projectile, charge, and primer, all in a metal case

case shot (or canister): antipersonnel round employed by tank guns or artillery at short range, consisting of small projectiles, usually round metal balls, inside a thin case that bursts apart when the round is fired, much like a shotgun

CBSS (closed breech scavenging system): the use of compressed air to force any remaining burning pieces of ammunition from the gun-launcher of the M551 Sheridan and M60A2 tanks

CCC: combustible cartridge case

CET: combat engineer tractor (United Kingdom)

CEV (combat engineer vehicle): specialist vehicle, usually on a tank chassis, and employed by combat engineers in a variety of tasks, including mine-clearing and demolishing obstacles

CFV (cavalry fighting vehicle): the M3 reconnaissance variant of the M2 Bradley fighting vehicle.

Char: "chariot," the French term for "tank"

chassis: lower part of tank hull with engine, transmission, and suspension system onto which tracks are attached

Chobham armor: improved armor on latest MBTs that incorporates spaced, multiple layers of steel interspersed with metallic or nonmetallic layers of thinner material, first developed at the Fighting Vehicle Research Establishment, Chobham, England

Christie suspension: A system designed by American J. Walter Christie in the 1920s, it consisted of independently sprung road wheels on vertical helical springs; the wheels were attached to swing arms connected to the springs; many vehicles with this suspension system could run with or without tracks (see discussion in Chapter 2).

CITV (commander's independent thermal viewer): night/all-weather vision device on the turret roof, operated independently from gunner's sighting system

CKD (completely knocked down): term used in the United Kingdom and United States to describe vehicles transported in a dismantled state to save space.

CLGP (cannon-launched guided projectile): artillery round with flip-out fins that deploy when the projectile leaves the gun; it can be guided by laser to the target.

cm: centimeter (unit of measurement; 3.92cm = 1 inch)

coaxial: two guns mounted together in the same turret and firing on the same axis—usually a main gun and a machine gun

combustible cartridge case: cartridge case made of combustible material that burns up when fired, obviating the need for extraction gear for a metal cartridge case

composite armor: armor made from layers of different materials that provides increased protection against kinetic and shaped charges

CP: concrete-piercing (artillery shell)

cradle: mount for main gun and mantlet, pivoted on trunnions to allow elevation and depression of gun

cruiser: British term for fast medium tanks before and during World War II designed specifically for independent action in rapid exploitation of a breakthrough

CS: close support

cupola: armor-plated revolving dome on top of turret to provide observation by the AFV commander

CV (*Carro veloce*): the Italian term for "fast vehicle"

DCA (*Défense contre avions*): literally, "aircraft defense," the French term for antiaircraft defense

depression: angle at which a tank's main gun can point below the horizontal, limited by the length of the gun inside the turret and the height of the turret itself

direct fire: line-of-sight fire on target, the opposite of indirect fire; most tanks employ direct fire in battle

ditched: term used to describe a tank that has been disabled by being unable to move

DIVADS: Divisional Air Defense [Gun] System

DP: dual-purpose (having more than one use)

drive sprocket: the wheel that transmits power from the transmission to the track

DU (depleted uranium): A dense, almost nonradioactive uranium isotope of heavy weight used as the penetrating core in AP projectiles. It usually breaks into fragments that spontaneously ignite and set on fire any inflammable objects. Also used in Abrams tank composite armor.

EBG (*Engin blindé du génie*): French term for engineer armored vehicle

EBR (*Engin blindé de reconnaissance*): French term for armored reconnaissance vehicle

EFP (explosively formed penetrator): French term for mass of melted metal projected by the detonation of a shaped charge

EGS (external gun system): automatically loaded tank gun carried externally above the hull that does away with the need for a turret

elevation: angle at which a tank's main gun can point above the horizontal; greater angle yields greater range

EO (electro-optical): generic term for visual, laser, and thermal infrared sights

EPC (*Engin principal de combat*: French term for main battle tank

episcope: periscope in a fixed mounting

ER (extended range): any one of a number of techniques extending the range of a projectile

ERA: explosive reactive armor (see active armor)

ERFB (extended range, full bore): projectile with tapering head shape and stubby wings providing additional aerodynamic lift during flight.

ERFB-BB (extended-range, full bore, base bleed): similar to ERFB but with smokeless powder in its base that burns to fill the void behind the shell base and reduce drag

ESRA (electro-slag refined steel): purified steel that is more resistant to heat and pressure and used in manufacturing modern tank guns

FAAD (forward area air defense): air defense systems protecting front-line troops

FAASVL (forward area ammunition support vehicle): tracked, armored vehicle used to bring ammunition forward

faceted: refers to the shaping of the tank turret or hull into a series of small angular flat planes so as to present surfaces likely to deflect shot; comparable to stealth technology in deflecting radar signals

fascine: A large bundle of wood longer than the width of the tank and bound tightly into a round shape by chains or wire. Carried by the tank, the fascine would then be dropped into a trench or gap to allow the tank to cross.

FAV (fast attack vehicle): light vehicle used by special forces in raids behind enemy lines.

FCS (fire-control system): devices used to control and maintain accurate fire.

FEBA (forward edge of the battle area): term used to describe the front line.

female: British term for World War I Mark I–Mark V tanks that mounted machine guns only (cf. male)

fire height: height to centerline of main gun of AFV when that gun tube is at 0 degrees elevation

flak: From the German *Flugzeugabewehrkanonen* or *Fliegerabewehrkanonen* ("antiaircraft gun"); the term was used by both sides to describe antiaircraft fire during World War II.

flank: either side of a military formation

FLIR (forward-looking infrared): an imaging system that uses the heat of a target to generate an image at day or night

FO (forward observer): artillery spotter identifying targets and calling in artillery fire on them. *Also:* fiber optic, cables utilizing light instead of electricity to transmit information

FOO (forward observation officer): the artillery spotter identifying targets and calling in artillery fire on them

fording: depth of water through which a military vehicle can wade without flooding engine, usually quoted either as without or with preparation

fps (feet per second): the measurement of speed in a projectile

fragmentation: explosive antipersonnel technique for projectiles, mines, and hand grenades, usually accomplished by scoring the explosive device so that it will shatter along those lines in as many different projectiles as possible

fume extractor: British term for bore evacuator (see entry)

FV (fighting vehicle): accompanied by a number, it forms the nomenclature of any British "A" (armored) vehicle

glacis plate: the plate, usually sloped, forming the upper surface of the front of a tank; slope provides better driver visibility and also serves to deflect shot

GMC (gun motor carriage): U.S. Army's World War II term for self-propelled gun; also applied to tank destroyers, or lightly armored tank hunters armed with powerful guns in open-topped turrets

GP: general purpose

GPMG (general-purpose machine gun): the machine gun adopted both for infantry and AFV use

GPS (Global Positioning System): the navigation system using satellites to fix one's location precisely

gradient: degree of slope off horizontal that a vehicle can travel

grenades: originally the hand-held high-explosive and fragmentation devices but also applied to weapons delivered by rifles (rifle grenades) or other launchers; most contemporary tanks have launchers enabling them to fire smoke grenades

ground contact length: distance between the center of a tracked vehicle's first and last road wheels

Guerro di rapido corso: The Italian concept of mechanized warfare conceived in the maneuvers of 1937 and formally expressed in 1938. Italy's inability to produce more than 1,800 tanks a year was a leading factor in the failure of this doctrine.

gun: high-velocity weapon used for direct, low, flat-trajectory fire as opposed to howitzer (intermediary-angle fire) and mortar (high-angle fire)

gunship: armed helicopter and sometimes a fixed-wing aircraft capable of loitering on target and providing support to ground troops with guns, rockets, and guided missiles

hard target: protected target with some degree of immunity to light weapons fire; requires armor-piercing or HEAT shells to penetrate

HB (heavy barrel): the heavy-barreled, air-cooled machine guns that do not require a water jacket around the barrel to cool them during firing

HE (high explosive): standard artillery projectile, most effective against troops in the open

HE/Frag (high explosive, fragmentation): high-explosive shell designed to produce on bursting the maximum number of fragments

HEAP (high explosive, antipersonnel): dual-purpose HE round providing both blast and antipersonnel effects

HEAT (high explosive, antitank): armor-defeating projectile that utilizes explosive energy in a shaped charge

HECP (high explosive, concrete-piercing): similar to HE but designed for use against concrete structures

HE-I (high explosive, incendiary): projectile often utilized in antiaircraft weapons

HE-I-T (high explosive, incendiary, tracer): projectile designed to provide a trail, utilized especially at night and in antiaircraft weapons

HEP (high explosive, plastic): HE shell with a thin wall, filled with plastic explosive. When the projectile strikes a tank target, the shell's wall collapses and the explosive sticks to the surface, blowing shards of metal from the tank's inner surface.

HEPF (high explosive, prefragmented): Shell in which fragments are positioned, usually in a plastic matrix, around the inside of the shell wall. On the explosion of the filler, the fragments add to those of the shell itself for optimum effect.

HERA (high-explosive, rocket-assisted): a type of artillery shell

hermaphrodite: World War I British tank, part "male" and part "female," armed with a 6-pounder in one sponson and machine guns in the other (see male and female)

herringbone formation:: This is an armor formation whereby the vehicles involved turn alternately to the sides of the direction of march. Their heaviest guns and armor are thus placed obliquely toward the flanks. This maneuver leaves the center of the column free for movement and provides maximum protection to it.

HESH (high-explosive, squash-head): British term for HEP

HE-T (high explosive, tracer): shell with a tracer element to enable the gunner to direct fire

HMC (howitzer motor carriage): a self-propelled howitzer

hollow charge/shaped charge: warhead that utilized the Munro effect; detonation of a shaped explosive charge around an open-ended cavity concentrates the blast in that direction

howitzer: short-barreled artillery piece capable of high-angle fire popularized by Frederick the Great of Prussia in the mid-eighteenth century; particularly valued for indirect fire behind hills and originally a low-velocity, short-range weapon, howitzers today have much longer-range fire

HRV (heavy recovery vehicle): vehicle designed to recover disabled tanks

hull: main part of an armored vehicle; the hull consists of the chassis and superstructure on which the tracks/wheels and turret are mounted

HVAP (high-velocity armor-piercing): armor-piercing shell with a core of heavy tungsten or depleted uranium inside a lightweight, full-caliber round; entire round stays together during flight

HVSS (horizontal volute spring suspension): A type of suspension whereby a pair of dual road wheels on each bogie are sprung against each other with a volute spring. Replacing the previous suspension on the M4 Sherman, it allowed utilization of a wider track while increasing wheel travel and facilitating easier maintenance.

ICV: infantry combat vehicle (equivalent to an IFV)

idler: the end wheel of a tracked vehicle at opposite end of the drive sprocket; not driven, the idler takes up track tension

IFV (infantry fighting vehicle): vehicle providing fire support as well as transportation to infantry

illuminating: term used to describe a shell providing battlefield illumination at night; usually consists of a bright flare attached to a parachute, fired at high elevation to provide maximum illumination time

indirect fire: A weapon capable of firing at something that cannot be seen by direct line of sight. Most artillery weapons, especially mortars and howitzers, are capable of indirect fire (see direct fire).

infantry: applied to tanks, refers to vehicles specifically designated for infantry support and assault; usually applied by the British to the slow, heavily armed armored vehicles before and during World War II

internal security: term utilized to describe the use of military or paramilitary formations to maintain order

IRA/infrared: electromagnetic radiation that is below light in the spectrum, identifiable as heat; IR sensors identify heat given off by humans or by vehicles and serve as an effective targeting means in the dark

Kampfgruppe: World War II German term for ad hoc brigade-level military formation, usually named for its commander

KE (kinetic energy): energy possessed by a particular body thanks to its motion; dense, heavy projectiles moving at high speed have high kinetic energy, essential to penetrating armor

KfPzBefWg (*Kleine Panzerbefehlswagen*): term for small armored command vehicle

Kfz (*Kraftfahrzeug,* or "motor vehicle"): term generally applied to a "soft-skinned" (unarmored) vehicle

Königstiger ("King Tiger"): German name for PzKpfw VI Tiger II

KPz (*Kampfpanzer*): German term for battle tank

Kwk (*Kampfwagen Kanone*): German term for fighting vehicle cannon; tank gun

L/: The caliber length of a gun. Length of guns is measured in bore diameters. Thus a 90mm L/50 gun would be 50 x 90mm or 4,500mm (9'6.79") long. Generally speaking, the longer the gun, the greater the velocity (and hence range and penetration).

LADS: light air defense system

laminated armor: see composite armor

LAPES (low-altitude parachute extraction): technique for landing heavy equipment, including AVs, from the rear door of a slow-flying transport aircraft at very low altitude

laser (light amplification by stimulated emission of radiation): intense beam of single wavelength light used primarily for rangefinding and target illumination

Laser Detection and Warning System: Electronic sensing device activated when struck by a laser beam, as in the case of a laser-guided missile or laser illuminator. The warning provided could enable the target, in the case of a tank, to take evasive maneuvering or the crew to prepare for attack.

LAV: light armored vehicle

LAW (light antiarmor weapon): handheld rocket launcher that provides some antitank protection to infantry

light tank: classification of tanks, designed primarily for reconnaissance purposes

LMG: light machine gun

LOS (line of sight): firing directly on a target that can be seen, rather than indirect fire; tanks employ direct fire

LRF (low recoil force): large-caliber gun with lower recoil, enabling its use in smaller turrets

LRV: light recovery vehicle

LST: landing ship, tank

LTD (laser target designator): laser generator producing a beam that may be directed on a target; laser-guided weapons fire on the reflected "splash" from the target

LVT (landing vehicle, tracked): amphibious assault vehicles, originally employed by the Allies in the Pacific and European Theaters of World War II; LVTs continued through LVTP-5 and LVTP-7 into the 1990s; now replaced with designation AAV, or amphibian assault vehicle

LVTA: landing vehicle, tracked, armored

LVTE: landing vehicle, tracked, engineer

LVTH: landing vehicle, tracked, howitzer

LVTP: landing vehicle, tracked, personnel

LVTR: landing vehicle, tracked, recovery

M: U.S. designation for model accepted for production

machine gun: A small-caliber weapon capable of automatic fire. The modern machine gun was invented by Hiram Maxim in the 1880s. Machine guns are the secondary armament on armored vehicles.

male: British term for World War I Mark I–Mark V tanks that mounted heavy guns in addition to machine guns (see female)

mantlet: The movable piece of armor surrounding the main gun of a tank. A large slot in the front of the turret is necessary in order that the main gun might be elevated and depressed. The mantlet, attached to the moving mass rather than to the gun, provides additional armor protection to the front of the turret and conceals the slot, preventing enemy shot from entering the turret.

MBA (main battle area): the area in which combat occurs

MBT (main battle tank): primary modern battlefield tanks, superceding the medium and heavy tanks of World War II

MG: machine gun

MGMC (multiple gun motor carriage): self-propelled artillery vehicle equipped with multiple rapid-fire guns, often for antiaircraft purposes

MICV: mechanized infantry combat vehicle

Mk (Mark): used to identify variations of a major design

MLRS (multiple-launch rocket system): M270 armored vehicle capable of firing 12 rockets to a range of 19 miles

mm: millimeter (unit of measurement: 39.2mm = 1 inch)

mph: miles per hour

MRL (multiple rocket launcher): launch platform for unguided artillery missiles

MRS (muzzle reference system): Means of ensuring that the tank gun muzzle and sights are aligned. A mirror permanently fitted to the gun muzzle operates in conjunction with a fixed light source in the gun mounting. At a particular setting, the gunner's sight should see the mirror and reflection of the pinpoint light source. If not, the gunner can adjust it until it does.

muzzle brake: device attached to the gun muzzle to reduce recoil

muzzle velocity: speed at which a projectile emerges from the muzzle of a gun

NATO (North Atlantic Treaty Organization): an alliance of Western nations formed after World War II to deter a Soviet invasion of Central Europe

NBC (nuclear, biological, chemical): NBC capability in a tank refers to its protection against such contamination

obstacle: one of the ways to measure an armored vehicle's performance; the maximum height of an obstacle it can surmount

Ontos ("thing" in classical Greece): name of the M50 U.S. Marine Corps light tank killer, consisting of six 106mm (4.2-inch) recoilless rifles mounted on a small tracked chassis

OP: observation post

OPTAR: optical tracking, acquisition, and ranging

OQF: ordnance, quick firing

ordnance: military term for tube artillery

PAK (*Panzer Abwehr Kanone*): German, antitank gun

panzer: German term for armor or tank

Panzerabwehrkanone ("tank defense cannon"): German, antitank gun

Panzerjäger ("tank hunter"): German; known in the U.S. Army as a tank destroyer

Panzerkampfwagen: see PzKpfw

pdr (pounder): refers to gun caliber, loosely determined by weight of the shell it fires

periscope: optical device allowing the viewer to see over obstacles and to look out without leaving the protection of the vehicle

POL: petroleum, oil, and lubricants

prime mover: vehicle used for towing heavy equipment; can be either wheeled or tracked

proximity fuse: Fuse supplied with a proximity sensor that enables a weapon to be detonated when within lethal range

PT (*Plavayushtshiy Tank*): Soviet/Russian term for amphibious tank

PzBfW (*Panzerbefehlswagen*): German, command tank

PzKpfw (*Panzerkampfwagen*, "armored fighting vehicle"): German, tank

QMC: Quartermaster Corps

quick-firing: fixed ammunition in which the cartridge case and projectile are already joined

RAP: rocket-assisted projectile

rate of fire: number or rounds that may be fired from a gun in a particular period of time, usually in a minute and usually expressed as rounds per minute (see rpm)

RCT (regimental combat team): World War II U.S. equivalent to the German *Kampfgruppe*; designation is usually more permanent

RDF: rapid deployment force

reconnaissance vehicle: mobile, lightly armored vehicle utilized to gather battlefield information

rifling: grooves twisting down the barrel of a gun that impart spin to the projectile, increasing its range and accuracy

RMG (ranging machine gun): a machine gun coaxial with the main gun of a tank, the bullets of which have the same ballistic performance as the main gun; used to establish range to target prior to firing main gun

road wheel: the wheels on a tank that run on the part of the track that comes into contact with the ground

RP: rocket-propelled

RPG (rocket-propelled grenade): ubiquitous shoulder-fired antitank and antimateriel weapon

rpm: revolutions per minute; also: rounds per gun per minute (describing the rate of fire)

RPV: remotely piloted vehicle

RTC (Royal Tank Corps): the world's first regular tank formation, established in the British Army in World War I

running gear: suspension, transmission, wheels, and track of a tank

SA (squad automatic weapon): U.S. Army term for light machine gun

sabot (Fr., "wooden shoe"): the clodding around an APDS round

SAM: surface-to-air missile

SAP/HE (semi–armor piercing, high explosive): an AP shell not capable of penetrating its own caliber in armor thickness

semiautomatic: a firearm that fires only once on each pull and release of the trigger

separate loading ammunition: ammunition in which the projectile and its propellant are loaded into the gun separately

shaped charge: see hollow charge

shell: a hollow projectile, now usually fired from a rifle gun; may have a variety of different fillers

shoe: individual section of track

shot: solid projectile, now usually armor-piercing

skirt/skirting plate: Vertical armor plates on the side of a tank hull that extend to conceal much of the suspension system. The skirts are designed to intercept incoming missiles before they strike the main tank structure, taking away much of the explosive charge and preventing them from penetrating the tank hull. Skirting plates are no longer much of a deterrent because of the dramatic increase in the energy of modern APFSDS projectiles.

sloped armor: armor that is angled in order to cause a projectile to ricochet or to penetrate at an angle

SMG (submachine gun): small fully automatic individual firearm, developed during World War I to spray down a trench line; later often carried as sidearm of tank crewmen

smoke: aid to conceal location on the battlefield; may be produced either with special shells, by means of grenade launchers usually found on either side of the turret of modern tanks, or by a tank spraying fuel into its engine exhaust smoke WP (Smoke White Phosphorous): a shell utilizing burning white phosphorous, known either as "WP" or "Willie Pete"

smoothbore: gun without rifling; on a tank it is used to fire fin-stabilized projectiles

snorkel: breathing tube that delivers air to the engine of a vehicle, enabling it to operate while submerged

SOG: speed over ground

SOMUA (Société d'Outillage de Mécanique et d'Usinage d'Artillerie): French tank manufacturer

SP: self-propelled

SPAA: self-propelled antiaircraft system

Spall, or splash: Interior fragments of armor broken loose by penetration of HEAT or AP (or APDS or APFSDS) projectiles, or the nonpenetrating explosion of HEP/HESH projectiles. In the case of HEAT, these fragments may be of molten metal. Such fragments act on objects, including personnel, inside the tank.

SPAT: self-propelled antitank system

SPG: self-propelled gun

sponson: half-turrets located on the side of early tanks for the guns to provide arc of fire

Sturmartillerie ("assault artillery"): German term for assault guns, which were part of the artillery. Better-trained than normal field artillery in direct-fire techniques, assault artillery gunners could more easily destroy enemy tanks and defensive works.

Sturmpanzer ("assault armored vehicle) name given to the first German (AV7) tanks

SU (Samokhodnya Ustanovka): Russian, self-propelled

superstructure: upper part of the hull of an armored vehicle

support rollers: small wheels that carry the track of a tank on its upper run between the idler and sprocket

t (Czech., "Tschechoslawakisch"): German designation of Czech origin for a vehicle in the German Army during World War II

T (Tahk, "tank"): designation for all Soviet/Russian tanks

T (Test): U.S. designation for prototype U.S. Army vehicles

tank: heavily armed and armored, fully tracked fighting vehicle; term originated in World War I (see Chapter 1)

tankette: small, unsophisticated, easily manufactured AFVs of the 1920s and 1930s

TC: tank or track (AFV) commander

TD (Tank Destroyer): U.S. Army World War II term for lightly armored tracked or wheeled tank hunters that were armed with a powerful gun in an open-topped turret

thermal imaging: sensing system that detects heat generated by a target and projects it as an image on a display screen

Thermal Sleeve (or blanket): Modern tank guns are long and of thin steel.

In order to prevent bending from differential expansion caused by temperature differences, they are provided with an insulated blanket wrapped around the barrel. This provides a constant temperature and eliminates differential expansion, which might otherwise cause a projectile to miss a target at long range. In conjunction with the muzzle reference system (see entry) it greatly improves a first-round hit probability.

time on target: artillery barrage in which all shells fired by a battery are timed to arrive on the target simultaneously

TOE: table of organization and equipment (i.e., of a particular military unit)

torsion-bar suspension: The predominant suspension system of most modern armored, tracked vehicles. In it independently sprung road wheels are attached by swing arms to torsion bars, steel tubes that run from the road wheel swing arm to an anchor on the side of the tank hull. The bars twist in response to wheel movement. Vehicles with torsion-bar suspensions have their road wheels slightly offset from each other, because each torsion bar runs the width of the tank hull.

TOW (tube-launched, optically tracked, wire-guided missile system): mounted on vehicles or helicopters, antitank missiles that can be rapidly repositioned on the battlefield

TP (target practice): practice shells

tracer: bullet or projectile with a phosphorescent insert that glows in flight, aiding in aiming

track: the endless belt that circles the sprocket, idler, road wheels, and return rollers of a tracked suspension, providing the surface on which the wheels run

trajectory: the path taken by a projectile in flight

transmission: system whereby the power of the engine is transmitted to the rotary movement of the wheels or tracks of a vehicle

traverse: the horizontal swing of the gun off center; a fully rotating turret has a traverse of 360 degrees

tread: the distance between the centerlines of a vehicle's tracks or wheels

trim vane (or trim plate): plate at the front of an amphibious vehicle that diverts water from the glacis plate, preventing the nose from diving under the water surface

TRV: tank recovery vehicle

TTS: tank thermal sight

turret: revolving armored box that mounts a gun

turret basket: Initially the tank turret was a structure that rotated on top of the hull. The turret occupants simply moved their positions as the turret rotated. The turret basket eliminated the need for the crew to change position as the turret rotated. Essentially a floor plate attached to the turret, it enables the crew to remain seated at their stations as the turret turns.

turret bustle: that part of the tank turret extending beyond the turret well at the rear of the turret

turret ring: The ring on the hull on which the turret rides supported by bearings. The size of the turret ring determines the size of the gun that can be mounted; the larger the ring, the larger the gun.

unditching beam: a heavy wooden beam carried on early tanks and mounted transversally; used to gain extra traction when the tank became bogged down

VAB (*Véhicle d'Avant Blindé*): French, armored car

VADS (Vulcan Air Defense System): designated M163; an M113 APC fitted with a six-barrel 20mm Gatling gun turret

VBC (*Véhicle blindé de combat*): French, armored fighting vehicle

VBL (*Véhicle blindé léger*): French, light armored vehicle

VCG (*Véhicle combat du génie*): French, armored engineer vehicle

VCI (*Véhicle combat d'infanterie*): French, infantry fighting vehicle

VCTP (*Véhicle de combat transport de personnel*): French, armored personnel carrier

velocity: the speed of a projectile in flight, usually calculated in feet or meters per second

volute spring: stiff coil spring used in tank suspension systems; may be arranged both vertically and horizontally, with the latter allowing a slightly lower tank profile

W (wet, i.e., ammunition storage): As a suffix on U.S. World War II tank designations, "W" indicated a tank in which the main gun ammunition was in double-walled boxes. In-between the walls was a mixture of water, antifreeze, and anticorrosive agent. If the boxes were penetrated, the water delayed or prevented an ammunition fire, giving the tank crew time to escape.

Warsaw Pact: Eastern bloc alliance established by the Soviet Union in response to NATO

Sources: Various, but see especially Christopher J. Foss, general editor, *The Encyclopedia of Tanks and Armored Fighting Vehicles*; and Ian V. Hogg, *Armored Fighting Vehicles: Data Book*.

REFERENCES

Baily, Charles M. *Faint Praise: American Tanks and Tank Destroyers During World War II*. Hamden, CT: Archon Books, 1983.

Barbier, M. K. *Kursk: The Greatest Tank Battle, 1943*. London: Brown Books, 2002.

Beale, Peter. *Death by Design: The Fate of British Tank Crews in the Second World War*. Stroud, UK: Sutton, 1998.

Bean, Tim, and William Fowler. *Russian Tanks of World War II: Stalin's Armored Might*. St. Paul, MN: MBI, 2002.

Browne, Douglas G. *The Tank in Action*. Edinburgh and London: William Blackwood and Sons, 1920.

Caidin, Martin. *The Tigers Are Burning: The Story of the Battle of Kursk: The Greatest Single Land-and-Air Combat Engagement in Military History*. New York: Hawthorn Books, 1974.

Carruthers, Bob. *German Tanks at War*. London: Cassell, 2000.

Chamberlain, Peter. *Tanks of World War I: British and German*. New York: Arco, 1969.

Chamberlain, Peter, and Chris Ellis. *British and American Tanks of World War Two: The Complete Illustrated History of British, American, and Commonwealth Tanks, 1933–1945*. London: Cassell, 2000.

———. *Pictorial History of Tanks of the World, 1915–1945*. London: Arms and Armour, 1972.

Chamberlain, Peter, H. L. Doyle, and Thomas L. Jentz. *Encyclopedia of German Tanks of World War Two: A Complete Illustrated Directory of German Battle Tanks, Armoured Cars, Self-propelled Guns, and Semi-tracked Vehicles, 1933–1945*. New York: Arco, 1978.

Chant, Christopher. *An Illustrated Data Guide to Battle Tanks of World War II*. London: Tiger Books International, 1997.

Childs, David J. *A Peripheral Weapon? The Production and Employment of British Tanks in the First World War*. Westport, CT: Greenwood, 1999.

Churchill, Winston S. *The World Crisis, 1914–1918*, vols. 2 and 3. New York: Charles Scribner's Sons, 1923, 1927.

Cooper, Belton Y. *Death Traps: The Survival of an American Armored Division in World War II*. Novato, CA: Presidio, 1998.

Cooper, Bryan. *The Ironclads of Cambrai: The First Great Tank Battle*. London: Cassell, 2002.

_____. *Tank Battles of World War I*. London: Allan, 1974.

Crawford, Steve. *Tanks of World War II*. Osceola, WI: MBI, 2000.

Crow, Duncan, ed. *AFV's of World War I*. Windsor, UK: Profile, 1970.

_____. *Armored Fighting Vehicles of Germany: World War II*. New York: Arco, 1999.

Cullen, Stephen M. "Armored Cars." In *The European Powers in the First World War: An Encyclopedia*. Edited by Spencer C. Tucker. New York: Garland, 1996, pp. 65–66.

Devey, Andrew. *Jagdtiger: The Most Powerful Armoured Fighting Vehicle of World War II: Operational History*. Atglen, PA: Schiffer, 1999.

Donnelly, Thomas, et al. *Clash of Chariots: The Great Tank Battles*. New York: Berkley Books, 1999.

Doughty, Robert Allan. *The Seeds of Disaster: The Development of French Army Doctrine, 1919–1939*. Hamden, CT: Archon Books, 1985.

Dunstan, Simon. *Challenger: Main Battle Tank, 1982–1997*. London: Osprey, 1998.

_____. *Vietnam Tracks: Armor in Battle, 1945–1975*. Novato, CA: Presidio, 1982.

Edwards, Roger. *Panzer: A Revolution in Warfare, 1939–1945*. London: Arms and Armour, 1989.

Ellis, Chris. *German Tanks and Fighting Vehicles of World War II*. Secaucus, NJ: Chartwell Books, 1976.

_____. *Tanks of World War II*. London: Chancellor, 1997.

Elson, Aaron C. *Tanks for the Memories: An Oral History of the 712th Tank Battalion from World War II*. Hackensack, NJ: Chi Chi, 1994.

Fitzsimons, Bernard, ed. *Tanks & Weapons of World War I*. London: Phoebus, 1973.

_____. *Tanks & Weapons of World War II*. New York: Beekman House, 1973.

Fletcher, David. *British Armour in the Second World War: The Great Tank Scandal*. London: H.M. Stationery Office, 1989.

_____. *British Armour in the Second World War: The Universal Tank*. London: H.M. Stationery Office, 1993.

Fletcher, David., ed. *Tanks and Trenches: First Hand Accounts of Tank Warfare in the First World War*. Stroud, UK: Sutton, 1994.

_____. *Tanks in Camera: The Western Desert, 1940–1943: Archive Photographs from the Tank Museum*. Stroud, UK: Buddings Book, 1998.

Fletcher, David, et al. *The British Tanks, 1915–19*. Marlborough, UK: Crowood, 2001.

_____. *Crusader Cruiser Tank, 1939–1945*. London: Reed Consumer. 1995.

Fleischer, Wolfgang, and Edward Force. *Panzerfaust: And Other German Infantry Anti-Tank Weapons*. Atglen, PA: Schiffer, 1994.

Folkestad, William B., et al. *The View from the Turret: The 743d Tank Battalion During World War II.* Shippensburg, PA: Burd Street Press, 1996.

Ford, Roger. *The Sherman Tank.* Osceola, WI: MBI, 1999.

Forty, George. *German Tanks of World War Two in Action.* London: Blandford, 1998.

————. *Tank Action: From the Great War to the Gulf.* Stroud, UK: Alan Sutton, 1996.

————. *United States Tanks of World War II in Action.* New York: Blandford, 1983.

Forty, George, and Jonathan Forty. *Panther Ausf A, D, G Panzer V.* Hersham, UK: Ian Allan, 2003.

Foss, Christopher F. *Armoured Fighting Vehicles of the World.* New York: Charles Scribner's Sons, 1971.

Foss, Christopher F., and Ray Bonds. *An Illustrated Guide to World War II Tanks and Fighting Vehicles.* New York: Arco, 1981.

Fuchs, Karl. *Sieg Heil! War Letters of Tank Gunner Karl Fuchs, 1937–41.* Ed. Horst Fuchs Richardson. Hamden, CT: Archon Books, 1987.

Fuller, J. F. C. *Tanks in the Great War, 1914–1918.* London: John Murray, 1920.

Gander, Terry J. *Anti-Tank Weapons.* Marlborough, UK: Crowood, 2000.

————. *Tanks of World War II.* London: HarperCollins, 1999.

Geibel, Adam. *Iron Coffins: Italian Medium Tanks M13 and M14.* Darlington, MD: Darlington Productions, 1994.

Gilbert, Oscar E. *Marine Tank Battles in the Pacific.* Conschocken, PA: Combined, 2001.

Glantz, David M., and Jonathan M. House. *The Battle of Kursk.* Lawrence: University Press of Kansas, 1999.

Greene, Jack, and Alessandro Massignani. *Rommel's North African Campaign, September 1940–November 1942.* Conshohocken, PA: Combined, 1999.

Grove, Eric. *World War II Tanks.* New York: Excalibur Books, 1976.

Guderian, Heinz. *Achtung—Panzer! The Development of Amoured Forces: Their Tactics and Operational Potential.* Trans. Christopher Duffy. London: Arms and Armour, 1992.

————. *Panzer Leader.* Translated by Constantine Fitzgibbon. London: Harborough, 1957.

Gudgin, Peter. *The Tiger Tanks.* London: Arms and Armour, 1991.

————. *With Churchills to War: 48th Battalion Royal Tank Regiment at War, 1939–45.* Stroud, UK: Sutton, 1996.

Habeck, Mary R. *Storm of Steel: The Development of Armour Doctrine in Germany and the Soviet Union, 1919–1939.* Ithaca, NY: Cornell University Press, 2003.

Harris, Harvey L. *The War as I Saw It: 1918 Letters of a Tank Corps Lieutenant.* St. Paul, MN: Pogo, 1998.

Harris, J. P., and F. H. Toase, eds. *Armoured Warfare.* New York: St. Martin's, 1990.

Hart, Stephen, and R. Hart. *German Tanks of World War II.* New York: Barnes & Noble, 1999.

Hartman, Ted J. *Tank Driver with the 11th Armored: A Memoir from the Battle of the Bulge to VE Day.* Bloomington: Indiana University Press, 2003.

Hay, John H. Jr. *Tactical and Materiel Innovations: Vietnam Studies.* Washington, DC: U.S. Government Printing Office, 1974.

Hills, Stuart. *By Tank into Normandy.* London: Cassell, 2002.

Hoffschmidt, Edward J., and W. H. Tantum. *German Tank and Antitank in World War II.* Boulder: Sycamore Island Books, 1979.

Hofmann, George F., and Donn A. Starry, eds. *Camp Colt to Desert Storm: The History of the U.S. Armored Forces.* Lexington: University Press of Kentucky, 1999.

Hughes, Matthew, et al. *The T-34 Russian Battle Tank.* Osceola, WI: MBI, 1999.

Hundleby, Maxwell, and Rainer Strasheim. *The German A7V Tank and the Captured British Mark IV Tanks of World War I.* Newbury Park, CA: Haynes, 1990.

Hunnicutt, Richard P. *Sheridan: A History of the American Light Tank.* Navato, CA: Presidio, 1992.

_____. *Sherman: A History of the American Medium Tank.* San Rafael, CA: Taurus Enterprises, 1978.

Jarymowycz, Roman Johann. *Tank Tactics: From Normandy to Lorraine.* Boulder: Lynne Rienner, 2001.

Jensen, Marvin. *Strike Swiftly: The 70th Tank Battalion: From North Africa to Normandy to Germany.* Navato, CA: Presidio, 1997.

Jentz, Thomas L. *Germany's Panther Tank: The Quest for Combat Supremacy: Development, Modifications, Rare Variants, Characteristics, Combat Accounts.* Atglen, PA: Schiffer, 1995.

_____. *Germany's Tiger Tanks: Tiger I and II: Combat Tactics.* Atglen, PA: Schiffer, 1996.

_____. *Germany's Tiger Tanks: Tigers at the Front.* Atglen PA: Schiffer, 2001.

_____. *Panzertruppen: The Complete Guide to the Creation & Combat Employment of Germany's Tank Force.* Atglen, PA: Schiffer, 1996.

_____. *Tank Combat in North Africa: The Opening Rounds: Operations Sonnenblume, Brevity, Skorpion, and Battleaxe, February 1941–June 1941.* Atglen, PA: Schiffer, 1998.

Jentz, Thomas L., and Tony Bryan. *Panzerkampfwagen IV, Ausf. G, H and J, 1942–45.* Oxford, UK: Osprey, 2001.

Jentz, Thomas L., and Hilary L. Doyle. *German Panzers in World War II: From Pz.Kpfw.I to Tiger II.* Atglen, PA: Schiffer, 2001.

_____. *Germany's Tiger Tanks D.W. to Tiger I: Design, Production & Modifications*. Atglen, PA: Schiffer, 2000.

_____. *Germany's Tiger Tanks: VK45.02 to Tiger II*. Atglen, PA: Shiffer, 1997.

_____. *Kingtiger Heavy Tank, 1942–1945*. Oxford, UK: Osprey, 1993.

_____. *Panzerkampfwagen VI P (Sd.Kfz.181): The History of the Porsche Type 100 and 101 Also Known as the Leopard and Tiger (P)*. Darlington, MD: Darlington Productions, 1997.

Johnson, David E. *Fast Tanks and Heavy Bombers: Innovation in the U.S. Army, 1917–1945*. Ithaca, NY: Cornell University Press, 1998.

Johnson, Hubert G. *Breakthrough! Tanks, Technology, and the Search for Victory on the Western Front in World War I*. Novato, CA: Presidio, 1994.

Jones, Ralph E., George H. Rarey, and Robert J. Icks. *The Fighting Tanks Since 1916*. Washington, DC: National Service Publishing, 1933.

Jorgensen, Christer, and Chris Mann. *Strategy and Tactics: Tank Warfare: The Illustrated History of the Tank at War, 1914–2000*. Osceola, WI: MBI, 2001.

Kershaw, Andrew. *Tanks at War*. London: Phoebus, 1975.

Kinnear, Jim, Peter Sarson, and Steven J. Zaloga. *KV-1 & 2: Heavy Tanks, 1939–1945*. Oxford, UK: Osprey, 1996.

Koch, Fred. *Russian Tanks and Armored Vehicles: 1946 to the Present: An Illustrated Reference*. Atglen, PA: Schiffer, 1998.

Liddell Hart, Basil. *The Tanks: The History of the Royal Tank Regiment and Its Predecessors: Heavy Branch, Machine-Gun Corps, Tank Corps, and Royal Tank Corps, 1914–1945*. New York: Praeger, 1959.

Loza, Dimitry, and James F. Gebhardt. *Commanding the Red Army's Sherman Tanks: The World War II Memoirs of Hero of the Soviet Union Dimitry Loza*. Lincoln: University of Nebraska Press, 1996.

Luck, Hans von. *Panzer Commander: The Memoirs of Colonel Hans von Luck*. New York: Praeger, 1984.

McCarthy, Peter, and Mike Syron. *Panzerkrieg: The Rise and Fall of Hitler's Tank Divisions*. London: Constable, 2002.

Macksey, Kenneth. "Guderian," in *Hitler's Generals*, edited by Correlli Barnett. New York: Grove Weidenfeld, 1989, pp. 244–245.

_____. *Guderian: Creator of the Blitzkrieg*, New York: Stein and Day, 1976.

_____. *The Tank Pioneers*. New York: Jane's Publishing, 1981.

_____. *Tank Versus Tank: The Illustrated Story of Armored Battlefield Conflict in the Twentieth Century*. New York: Barnes & Noble, 1999.

Macksey, Kenneth, and John H. Batchelor. *Tank: A History of the Armoured Fighting Vehicle*. New York: Charles Scribner's Sons, 1970.

Manstein, Erich von. *Lost Victories*. Ed. and trans. Anthony G. Powell. Chicago: Henry Regnery, 1958.

Mellenthin, F. W. von. *Panzer Battles: A Study of the Employment of Armor in the Second World War.* Trans. H. Betzler. Norman: University of Oklahoma Press, 1956.

Miller, David. *The Great Book of Tanks: The World's Most Important Tanks from World War I to the Present Day.* St. Paul, MN: MBI, 2002.

Mitcham, Samuel W. *The Panzer Legions: A Guide to the German Army Tank Divisions of World War II and Their Commanders.* Westport: CT: Greenwood, 2001.

Moore, William. *Panzer Bait: With the Third Royal Tank Regiment, 1939–1945.* London: Leo Cooper, 1991.

Ness, Leland. *Jane's World War II Tanks and Fighting Vehicles: The Complete Guide.* London: Collins, 2002.

Ogorkiewicz, Richard. *Armoured Forces: A History of Armoured Forces and Their Vehicles.* New York: Arco, 1970.

Perrett, Bryan. *Iron Fist: Classic Armoured Warfare Case Studies.* London: Arms and Armor, 1995.

———. *Panzerkampfwagen III Medium Tank.* London: Osprey, 1999.

———. *Tank Warfare (Combat Development in World War II).* London: Arms and Armour, 1990.

Perrett, Bryan, and Jim Laurier. *Panzerkampfwagen IV Medium Tank, 1936–1945.* Oxford: Osprey, 1999.

Piekalkiewicz, Janusz. *Operation Citadel: Kursk and Orel: The Greatest Tank Battle of the Second World War.* Navato, CA: Presidio, 1987.

———. *Tank War, 1939–1945.* New York: Blandford Press, 1986.

Quarrie, Bruce. *Hitler's Teutonic Knights: SS Panzers in Action.* New York: Patrick Stephens, 1986.

Regenberg, Werner. *Captured American & British Tanks Under the German Flag.* West Chester, PA: Schiffer, 1993.

Regenberg, Werner, and Horst Scheibert. *Captured Tanks Under the German Flag: Russian Battle Tanks.* West Chester, PA: Schiffer, 1990.

Restayn, Jean. *Tiger I on the Western Front.* Paris: Histoire & Collections, 2001.

Riccio, Ralph. *Italian Tanks and Fighting Vehicles of World War 2.* London: Pique, 1975.

Ripley, Tim. *Tank Warfare.* Oxford, UK: Compendium, 2003.

Scheibert, Horst. *Panzer: A Pictorial Documentation of World War II German Battle Tanks.* West Chester, PA: Schiffer, 1990.

———. *Russian T-34 Battle Tank.* Trans. Edward Force. Atglen, PA: Schiffer, 1992.

Schneider, Wolfgang, and Rainer Stasheim. *German Tanks in World War I: The A7V and Early Tank Development.* West Chester, PA: Schiffer, 1990.

Senger und Etterlin, F. M. von. *German Tanks of World War II: The Complete Illustrated History of German Armoured Fighting Vehicles, 1926–1945.* New York: Galahad Books, 1969.

Smithers, A. J. *Cambrai: The First Great Tank Battle, 1917.* London: Leo Cooper, 1992.

Spielberger, Walter K. *Panzer III and Its Variants*. Atglen, PA: Schiffer, 1993.

Starry, Donn A. *Armored Combat in Vietnam*. New York: Bobbs-Merrill, 1980.

Steiger, Rudolf. *Armour Tactics in the Second World War: Panzer Army Campaigns of 1939–41 in German War Diaries*. Trans. Martin Fry. New York: St. Martin's, 1991.

Surlémont, Raymond. *Japanese Armour: A Detailed Review of Japanese Armour Development, Production, Organization, and Tactics During the Period 1925–1945*. Milwaukee: Z & M Publishing Enterprises, 1976.

Swinton, Sir Ernest D. *Eyewitness: Being Personal Reminiscences of Certain Phases of the Great War, Including the Genesis of the Tank*. Garden City: Doubleday, Doran, 1933.

Tout, Ken. *Tank!* London: Robert Hale, 2001.

White, B. T. *Tanks and Other Armoured Fighting Vehicles of World War II*. London: Peerage, 1975.

Wilson, Dale E. *Treat 'Em Rough!: The Birth of American Armor, 1917–20*. Novato, CA: Presidio, 1989.

Winchester, Jim, and Ian V. Hogg. *The World War II Tank Guide*. Edison, NJ: Chartwell Books, 2000.

Wright, Patrick. *Tank: The Progress of a Monstrous War Machine*. New York: Viking, 2000.

Zaloga, Steven J. *U.S. Marine Tanks in World War Two*. New York: Arms and Armour, 1988.

Zaloga, Steven J., and Jim Laurier. *M3 and M5 Stuart Light Tank, 1940–1945*. Oxford, UK: Osprey, 1999.

Zaloga, Steven J., and Peter Sarson. *T-34/76 Medium Tank: 1941–45*. London: Osprey, 1994.

INDEX